BOWEN

BOWEN
The Years as Governor
By William J. Watt

BIERCE ASSOCIATES INC.
Indianapolis
1981

First edition, September, 1981

Printed in the United States of America
Library of Congress Catalog Card Number: 81-68753

To the memory of
ELIZABETH ANN STEINMANN BOWEN
First Lady of Indiana
January 8, 1973 — January 1, 1981

TABLE OF CONTENTS

PREFACE

Otis Bowen's popularity as a public official suggested almost from the onset that he might be an appropriate subject for a marketable volume concerning his administration. I say "marketable" from the very practical consideration that a book about a person of interest primarily within the confines of one state could have tough going in the commercial publishing marketplace unless one was fortunate enough to obtain a subsidy or was willing to provide it himself. In this case the former seemed an unlikely prospect, the latter an unappealing one.

In the belief that a forum might be found for a book on the Bowen administration, I had maintained at least a half-hearted attempt to preserve many of my own notes and records from Bowen's years as governor. In time — as the physician-governor attained near-legendary status while still sitting as chief executive — I became persuaded that a book about this unique public official might return a publisher's investment if it could be brought out within a reasonably short period after he left office. Even the lapse of a few years would dilute an already constrained market, for Hoosiers are not inclined to venerate their political leaders — active or retired.

When Harley Bierce, president of Bierce Associates, proposed that his firm publish the book, I began work in earnest. Much of the research was completed during the period May-October, 1980. Writing was compressed into the months of November, 1980, and January-April, 1981.

The foregoing information is both an explanation to readers who may question my haste in getting into print and a warning that this relatively brief time span imposes certain limitations. This is not a biography of Otis Bowen; time did not permit sufficient research into his years in the General

Assembly, a period about which I have only limited first-hand knowledge. Its themes are built upon his 1972 campaign for the governorship and the eight turbulent years that followed.

Understand, too, that it is a sympathetic account. While I have tried to preserve the objectivity in which I took pride both as a journalist and a public official, my affection for Otis Bowen runs very deep.

The result is one insider's version of what happened during an extraordinary period of Indiana political and governmental history. In presenting this account of Bowen's years as governor, I have tried to structure it to portray people, events, and institutions in a light that will help others understand the processes of government and the mental attitudes of its practitioners. A few subjects may seem to have received more attention than they might merit. The extensive treatment of issues such as energy, for example, is founded upon my belief that these issues provide particularly valuable illustrations about how the "system" operates. This is coupled with a recognition that my ability to make others aware of the nuances of the governmental process would result from a description of issues with which I am most familiar.

For all this mixed bag of objectives, *BOWEN: The Years as Governor* follows the common thread of how one man's personality and unique public acceptance so dominated the operations of Indiana's state government and political processes during this eight-year period.

A number of people have contributed to this venture. Otis and Beth Bowen opened both their records and their home to me as I sorted through his extensive personal files. Wendell Phillippi, managing editor of the Indianapolis *News*, was kind enough to provide access to his library's voluminous collection of clippings about legislative sessions and state government. His staff was more than considerate of an outsider's intrusions. Bruce Melchert, Alan Sutherlin, and Wesley Bucher of the Republican State Committee made available election results and the party-financed opinion polls conducted during Bowen's administration. Former colleagues at the governor's office — Susan Davis, James Smith, Judith Palmer, and Raymond Rizzo — reminded me of events, offered information, and in some cases critiqued sections of the manuscript. State Parks Director William Walters and Corrections Department Adult Authority Director Cloid Schuler submitted information relative to their agencies. Help in rounding up speeches and other documents was freely given by other former associates in the governor's office — Mary McIntyre, Mary Lundy, Mary Kay Davis, Sue Senff, and Viola Walker. Harley Bierce read the full manuscript, restoring a semblance of tautness to a writing style that had gone flabby in the public sector.

Great appreciation must also be expressed to Dan Carpenter who edited the manuscript, providing many useful suggestions which improved the flow of information and eliminated grammatical and structural flaws; to Peg Harrison who tirelessly kept track of the manuscript, shepherding it from rough form through typesetting; and to Laura Sandin and Kitty

Pierce for developing the design for the book and dustcover.

The brief biographical sketches which precede the narrative are intended as a ready reference to the names which appear most frequently. The roster is not a *Who's Who* of state government during the period, for the names of many senior officials are absent. It identifies those persons most central to this account. Detailed biographical sketches of Otis and Beth Bowen may be found in appendix.

Despite the brief lapse of time since the Bowen administration ended, this undertaking has taken on the trappings of a voyage to nostalgia. As I sorted through boxes of clippings and documents I was constantly reminded of events which seemed important at the time, but now are almost forgotten; the sheer volume of incidents and controversies was one of the most striking features of the Bowen era. It was an exciting time, and those privileged to be a part of this drama are not likely to forget an administration and a governor that now seem to occupy a very special place in the governmental and political heritage of the state of Indiana.

William J. Watt
Indianapolis
June, 1981

Biographical Briefs of Individuals Prominent In This Account

ALFRED F. AHNER. Teacher; World War II Army officer; full-time National Guard officer since 1953; assistant adjutant general; chief of staff, military Department of Indiana; adjutant general during closing months of the Handley administration; appointed adjutant general again by Governor Whitcomb in January, 1972; remained in that post throughout Bowen's administration. President, Adjutants General Association. Retained as adjutant general by Governor Orr.

PHILLIP E. BAINBRIDGE. Attorney; state representatve; House minority leader; speaker, 1975-76; member, State Budget Committee. Returned to law practice in 1977.

BIRCH E. BAYH. Attorney; farmer; four-term member of Indiana House of Representatives; minority leader; speaker, 1959; defeated Homer Capehart in the 1962 U.S. Senate race; twice re-elected. Chairman of Senate Judiciary Committee and Select Committee on Intelligence. Defeated for re-election in 1980 by Congressman Dan Quayle.

BRIAN W. BOSWORTH. Foreign service officer, Agency for International Development; director, "Title 20" program for Indiana Welfare Department. An executive assistant to the governor from November, 1978, to the end of Bowen's administration, he was responsible for welfare, education, and mental health agencies. Appointed deputy director, Indiana Department of Commerce, by Lieutenant Governor John Mutz.

KERMIT O. BURROUS. Farmer; nine-term state representative; majority caucus chairman; speaker of the House, 1973-74, 1977-80; minority leader, 1975-76. Unsuccessful candidate for lieutenant governor in the 1980 GOP primary.

DONALD H. CLARK. Field examiner, State Board of Accounts; deputy state auditor; state budget director; assistant vice-president and treasurer, Indiana University; vice-president and treasurer, Indiana Vocational Technical College. Appointed commissioner of the Department of Revenue and served throughout the Bowen administration.

JOSEPH D. CLOUD. Businessman; six-term member of Indiana House of Representatives; chairman of Public Policy and Education committees. Director of the Department of Natural Resources throughout the Bowen administration. Vice-chairman, Ohio River Basin Commission; ex-officio member of other natural resource-related boards. Retained in Orr administration as executive director of a gubernatorial task force on state government efficiency.

LARRY A. CONRAD. Attorney; legislative assistant to Senator Bayh; chief counsel, Senate Subcommittee on Constitutional Amendments; Indiana Secretary of State, January 1971, to January, 1979. Defeated by Bowen in 1976 general election for governor.

SUSAN J. DAVIS. Attorney; assistant attorney general. An executive assistant to the governor from May, 1978, to the end of Bowen's term, she supervised liaison with regulatory agencies, the Highway Department, Public Service Commission, and Republican State Committee. Retained by Governor Orr as an executive assistant and chairman of the Transportation Coordinating Board.

ROBERT L. DEBARD. State Police officer; director of criminal justice training, Indiana University; Air National Guard colonel; campaign aide to Bowen in 1972. Executive assistant to the governor from January to October, 1973, with responsibility for law enforcement and public safety agencies. Appointed State Police superintendent, October, 1973. Resigned, December, 1976; retained as State Police lieutenant colonel.

MARTIN K. EDWARDS. Attorney; Indiana securities commissioner; three-term state senator; majority caucus chairman, 1971-76; president pro-tempore, 1979-80. Resigned 1980.

GORDON W. FAULKNER. Corrections professional in Florida, Ohio, and West Virginia; director of corrections for West Virginia; appointed commissioner of the Indiana Department of Corrections in March, 1977, and served throughout Bowen's second term. Retained as corrections commissioner by Governor Orr.

LEE ELLEN FORD. Scientist; attorney; writer; educator; held faculty positions at several universities; executive director, Legislative Bureau, Notre Dame Law School; weekly newspaper publisher. Issues adviser during Bowen's 1972 campaign for governor. An executive assistant to the governor from January, 1973, her liaison duties included health and human services agencies, minority and women's affairs. Resigned, January, 1976.

PHILLIP E. GUTMAN. Attorney; state senator. President pro-tempore of the Senate, 1973-77. Unsuccessful candidate for the Republican gubernatorial nomination in 1972.

JOHN C. HART. Businessman; homebuilder; three-term state representative; chairman of the House Ways and Means Committee; unsuccessful candidate for lieutenant governor in the 1972 Republican convention; president of the National Association of Home Builders; Indiana Republican national committeeman.

R. VANCE HARTKE. Attorney; Vanderburgh County deputy prosecutor; mayor of Evansville; U.S. Senator, 1959-1977; chairman of the Senate Committee on Veterans' Affairs; defeated by Richard G. Lugar in 1976.

ROBERT P. HEYNE. Career corrections official. Appointed state corrections commissioner in July, 1969, by Governor Whitcomb. Remained in that position under Bowen until January, 1977, when he became administrator of the joint corrections-mental health facility at Beatty Hospital.

JOHN A. HILLENBRAND II. Industrialist; conservationist. Chairman, Indiana Natural Resources Commission and Governor's Water Resources Study Commission. Resigned state appointments in May, 1979, to pursue Democratic nomination for governor. Defeated by Lieutenant Governor Orr in the 1980 general election.

JOHN M. HUIE. Agricultural economist and finance specialist at Purdue University; adviser to the Legislative Council on school and welfare finance. Appointed State Budget Director in July, 1976, and served to the end of the Bowen administration. Appointed chairman of the State Tax Board by Governor Orr.

JOHN B. KING. Attorney; director of various corporations; member of State Election Board; held numerous tax policy advisory positions and was a principal architect of the 1973 tax restructuring program, chairman of Bowen's 1972 and 1976 campaigns for governor.

WILLIAM C. LLOYD. Attorney; Monroe County deputy prosecutor; Seventh District Bowen-for-Governor chairman in 1972; administrative assistant to Governor Whitcomb during transition period. Executive assistant to the governor from January, 1973, he was responsible for liaison with regulatory agencies, Public Service Commission, Highway Department, Alcoholic Beverage Commission, and Republican State Committee. Member of the Commission on Interstate Cooperation. Resigned, May, 1978.

RICHARD G. LUGAR. Businessman; mayor of Indianapolis, 1968-75; keynote speaker, 1972 Republican national convention; president, National League of Cities; unsuccessful candidate for the U.S. Senate in 1974; defeated Vance Hartke in 1976.

BRUCE B. MELCHERT. Former fraternity executive; manager of several political campaigns; administrative assistant to Congressman Hudnut; deputy mayor of Indianapolis; President Ford's 1976 Indiana campaign chairman; Republican state chairman since 1977.

THOMAS S. MILLIGAN. Attorney; Wayne County Republican chairman; state Republican chairman, 1973-77; member of the executive committee of the GOP national committee; member, State Election Board.

ROBERT D. ORR. Businessman; state senator; Vanderburgh County Republican chairman; lieutenant governor from January, 1973, to January, 1981, and director of the Department of Commerce and State Planning Services Agency; president of the Senate; commissioner of agriculture; ex-officio member of several state commissions. Defeated John A. Hillenbrand II in the 1980 general election for the governorship.

JUDITH G. PALMER. Attorney, analyst for State Budget Agency. An executive assistant from January, 1977, to the end of Bowen's administration, she was responsible for health and human services agencies. Staff assistant to the National Governor's Association during Bowen's term as its chairman. Appointed state budget director by Governor Orr.

J. DANFORTH QUAYLE. Attorney, newspaper publisher; assistant attorney general; administrative assistant to Governor Whitcomb; director, state inheritance tax division; served two terms in the U.S. House; defeated Birch Bayh in the 1980 U.S. Senate race.

WILLIAM T. RAY. Real estate and insurance dealer; active in Marion County Republican, civic, and civil rights organizations. An executive assistant to the governor throughout Bowen's administration, he was in charge of liaison with economic development, local government, labor, and several other agencies. Assumed additional duty as acting labor commissioner in May, 1980, upon the death of William Lanam. Appointed director of the Department of Financial Institutions by Governor Orr.

RAYMOND W. RIZZO. Teacher; research analyst, Indiana Legislative Council; supervisor of non-merit personnel, Department of Administration; administrative assistant to House Speaker Bowen. Executive assistant to the governor from January, 1973, he supervised administration legislative programs and liaison with mental health, welfare, and education agencies. Bowen's principal speechwriter and the governor's staff representative to the Education Commission of the States. Resigned, October, 1978.

RAYMOND E. SANDERS. Businessman; active in Marion County Republican politics; twice elected to the Indiana House of Representatives. Commissioner of Administration throughout Bowen's governorship, supervising state government's facilities management, supply, contracts, and personnel. Member of several commissions, including State Office Building Commission and State Personnel Board.

THEODORE L. SENDAK. Attorney; journalist; business executive; colonel in the Army Reserve; Lake County and First District Republican chairman; attorney general from January, 1969, to January, 1981. President, National Association of Attorneys General. Did not seek re-election in 1980.

JAMES D. SIMS. Businessman; deputy sheriff; two terms as DeKalb County sheriff; chairman of "Sheriffs for Bowen" during 1972 campaign; chairman of the Alcoholic Beverage commission throughout Bowen's administration.

JAMES T. SMITH. Utility executive; attorney; management consultant to governor's office, January-September, 1973. An executive assistant to the governor from September, 1973, to the end of the administration, he was responsible for criminal justice and public safety agencies, and, in 1979-80, liaison with the General Assembly. Chairman, Criminal Justice Planning Commission; staff representative to Midwestern Governor's Conference and to crime and public safety committee of National Governor's Association during Bowen's term as chairman of the committee.

WAYNE A. STANTON. Corrections official in Indiana and Michigan; Marion County Welfare Director for 14 years; appointed State Welfare Director in January, 1973, and served throughout Bowen's administration. Retained in that position by Governor Orr.

EDISON L. THUMA. University professor; research director, Indiana Department of Commerce; executive director, Indiana Legislative Council during Bowen's term as speaker of the House. Appointed State Budget Director in January, 1973. Resigned, July, 1976, to become fiscal and systems management director, State Board of Health.

LARRY J. WALLACE. Attorney; deputy prosecutor; Marion County criminal courts commissioner; one-term state representative; legislative counsel to Bowen in 1973 and 1974. Appointed chairman, Public Service Commission, in April, 1974. Retained in that position by Governor Orr.

WILLIAM J. WATT. Journalist; administrative assistant to Lieutenant Governor Folz. Executive assistant to the governor throughout Bowen's administration, he served as news secretary, liaison with energy, transportation, and environmental agencies. Chairman: State Transportation Coordinating Board, Governor's Water Resources Study Commission, Governor's Energy Committee, and Governor's Rail Reorganization Task Force; Vice-chairman, Great Lakes Basin Commission. Army National Guard Major.

EDGAR D. WHITCOMB. Attorney; assistant U.S. attorney; Air National Guard colonel; state senator; secretary of state, 1967-69; governor, 1969-73; unsuccessfully opposed Richard Lugar in 1976 Republican senatorial primary.

JAMES B. YOUNG. Attorney; state senator; legislative counsel to Bowen in 1973-74; U.S. attorney for Southern District of Indiana; judge, Indiana Court of Appeals.

I PORTRAIT OF A GOVERNOR

He is most of all a polite man, utterly without pretense, who charms you with an almost diffident air not often found among the peacocks of politics. His presence is quiet and restrained, except for a tendency to wear suits that are, perhaps, a touch too loud. In contrast to iron-jawed beauties who face the television cameras with a glib confidence that borders on arrogance, his soft, sometimes stumbling sentences, delivered in a monotone, reassure the listener that he is a person and not an actor. This is not to say that Otis Bowen is not a handsome man, for he is, but in a Spencer Tracy sort of way.

There are elements of the Bowen background which afford him automatic political appeal. Chief among them are his years as a family physician — a profession that made contributions to gubernatorial style far beyond the trust and confidence that political office would inspire.

A medical practice, inherently demanding, with its long hours and frequent interruptions of one's private life, forced him to come to terms with the need to balance profession and family. It was an accommodation that all too few men in public life are able to make, with occasionally disastrous results for their personal lives or political careers. While other politicians learned how to talk, Bowen learned how to listen. The duties of a family doctor require a patient ear to gather the outpouring of symptoms, or personal grief, or simply respond to a need to communicate in confidence with someone. He learned how to deal with people on their own terms and on their own turf. This is a man who came away from a house call with a bushel of vegetables as partial payment for his services and who quit wearing hats years ago because he frequently mislaid them at rural farmhouses.

Bowen is not viewed as a commanding intellectual by some people who know him, but their assessments have overlooked the mental ability required to complete medical training. More important, an education requiring the absorption of a vast amount of information and a profession demanding that this storehouse of knowledge be regularly replenished are valuable training for one called upon to manage state government's diversity.

He is a man of deeply-held religious beliefs of a fundamentalist sort, but they are private convictions seldom shared with even close associates. In eight years of almost daily contact in which our discussions ranged over broad landscapes, I cannot remember that the subject of religion ever was raised. Yet it was one of the factors that shaped his point of view on matters of public policy.

The underlying strength of the Bowen personality is that the public person and the private person are one and the same. When he attended a basketball game as governor it was in the role of an unabashed fan of the sport, not as a ceremonial obligation of high office. A composed man in public, he is not given to private rages either. Occasionally the irritation will show, but only for a flash of a moment. A stern jaw and a pronounced abruptness of speech are better clues to his anger. The infrequent chewing of a Gelusil is the only barometer of inner tension. He seldom uses profanity — only in private and usually only one word uttered quietly, almost furtively. A faint tapping of the right foot or the pulling from his pocket of a set of fingernail clippers were signs to his staff that a meeting had gone overlong. He might also turn his large, black chair away from his visitors on the office couch and discreetly face the desk. A glance at the paperwork piled thereon was a signal that the governor was restless to resume his chores.

Another element of this public and private oneness was Beth, his full partner for more than 40 years in everything that was important to him. The wife was a near mirror image of the husband and an additional assurance that he was what he seemed to be. It must also be said that he was a near mirror image of her.

Politics can be cruel to spouses. Too often, they barely are tolerated as ceremonial necessities, victims of endless gossip, and unwelcome intruders insofar as subordinates are concerned. The system is patently unfair to them and more than an occasional political marriage is under strain. Beth, however, fit in. The old-fashioned nature of their relationship gave it a special public charm. She achieved the right blend of visibility and unobtrusiveness, an unassuming yet engaging hostess at a reception, but a quiet observer seeming to focus only on her needlepoint as she sat above the balcony railing during his years as speaker of the House. While Beth has been described as the governor's closest adviser she filled that role in private and did not insert herself into affairs of state, except in her frequent support of charities and the auxiliary to the Indiana State Medical Association. The Rosalynn Carter degree of participation — and the criticism it generated —

never applied to her because a correct and cautious sense of propriety underlay a warm and outgoing personality.

Those of us who worked for the governor were aware of Beth's influence, especially when it came to his assessments of people. Yet she conveyed the impression of one whom you wanted to befriend for the sake of friendship and not as an insurance policy against potential criticism. No probing of the personality of Otis Bowen can ignore the pervasiveness of Beth; they were inseparable. They also were in private what they projected to the public. Her lingering illness and death all but destroyed his spirit during the closing months of the administration.

Bowen's public style of leadership has been scrutinized by many observers. Did his popularity stem from his being a non-politician? Or did it reflect the fact that he was the best politician Hoosiers have seen in recent times?

Of course he was a politician. The skills of a politician — securing the allegiance of others, crafting compromises, prevailing over contrary points of view, winning — simply were wielded by Bowen with an infinitely greater degree of patience than is customary in politics and a low-key approach that attracted less attention than conventional methods. His success as a political leader also was enhanced by a broader view of the Republican party than that shared by many of his contemporaries in the GOP. Ask most politicians for a definition of their party and the initial instinct would be to think in terms of the organization — the state committee and county chairmen. Bowen's view of the party covered all who voted Republican, including those independents who might be persuaded to do so. He reached out to the public and did so in a way that often skirted the formal apparatus, but handled himself so discreetly that it did not offend the regulars. This capacity, more than any other, explains his outmaneuvering of the organization in 1972.

Bowen considered himself a product of the political system, to the extent that he was careful to consult with the party hierarchy and was an active supporter of its candidates and fund-raising efforts, but kept himself apart from its factionalism except for a few critical occasions.

As speaker and governor, Bowen was a subdued, consensus-oriented leader. A number of journalists have accurately captured the flavor of his style. Bill Roberts of the Indianapolis *News*, writing at the end of Bowen's final session as speaker, reflected:

> There were times during this span (1967-72) that he almost became a fixture on the rostrum, a symbol of the chamber like the huge chandelier that hangs from the ceiling. Cool and unflappable, he wielded the gavel with great discretion. There was no yelling and shouting for order. When any commotion became a nuisance, he would say, "the noise level in here is far too high", or "this is a motion to amend and you'll be voting on this soon, so you'd better pay attention". And the members would quiet down.[1]

Writing on the eve of Bowen's inauguration as governor, Indianapolis *News* Political Editor Edward Ziegner described the new chief of state, a candidate about whom he had written frequently throughout the speaker's legislative career:

> He is a complex man. Often, in the House, it was deceptive. He appeared what he was in private life, a doctor of medicine practicing in a small town, easy to approach, seeming, perhaps, to be a little too friendly, a little naive, a little too trusting.
>
> But when some of the end-around artists who are always looking for an opening or a weakness in the speaker so they can zip by him with a triple reverse, double lateral, hidden ball play tried that, they found they had a very tough man on their hands who could smile even as he cracked down and busted up their little game just when it appeared they would score.
>
> It takes him a long time to become angry, but he can get there, and when that time arrives, it never lasts very long, and the anger is almost inevitably expressed in private. . . The anger is a cold anger, but those who know him well have seen it. He has said for many years he is not vindictive and he does not hold grudges, and that is true, but he also can remember who has been his friend and who has been his enemy over the years, and some of those who were enemies are learning that their influence with the Bowen administration will be, to put it politely, minimal.[2]

Bowen's patience was equalled by his stubbornness. It was not the stubbornness one usually sees in a face-to-face argument, but the determination to defend a deeply-felt position and to cling to what he believed to be a good idea — for years, if necessary. He pressed for tax reform, lost the initial battles, but pressed again — and harder. Without this stubbornness, Bowen would have failed again on taxes in the pivotal year, 1973, and his administration might have taken a radically different, less successful turn.

He coupled determination with a superb sense of timing. Budget Director Edison Thuma, a bright but impatient member of Bowen's inner circle during the first term, often observed that the governor always seemed to get better mileage out of a decision by holding it off long enough to milk the most out of it, but not delaying so long as to let a proposition go stale. Timing was corollary to patience. Longtime assistant Raymond Rizzo once said, "I have never known anyone who could outwait him, or could hold the cards longer, until he makes sure he plays the right card."[3]

He did not let himself become overwhelmed by detailed information, seldom aspiring to become an expert on an issue unless it had the importance of the property tax package or sparked a peculiar personal interest. As legislator, he monitored hundreds of hours of debate on issues of public policy and absorbed a vast amount of information over a period of fourteen years. A disciplined reader of documentation placed before him, he nonetheless preferred to learn from people. Issues requiring frequent responses were reduced to shirt pocket filing cards in order that he could recite the statistics recorded thereon. During the 1976 campaign, the Bowen for Governor staff compiled two thick books encompassing every issue considered to be a possible factor. Bowen read these in detail, then boiled down each issue section to a one-page handwritten summary. This was further telescoped to a brief outline on a three-by-five card. When assistants professed amazement that a chief executive would find time — or take time — to complete such an exercise, he shrugged it off by saying, "This helps me remember."

He was careful to develop various networks of advice and information which enabled him to test the quality of what he received and protected him against relying upon a handful of people for intellectual fodder. These networks were rewired from time to time as they became obsolete, or when a particular issue receded, or when the advisory capacity they were intended to provide was diluted by dissension, or when the bodies themselves threatened to become too visible and influential. Bowen's kitchen cabinet of personal friends was his main sounding board prior to settling in at the governor's office. When it was augmented by a few additional members of his staff and representatives of the party, it became clear to him that these interests were too diverse and might fragment the group. He let the organization wither.

Bowen's background provided few real clues as to how well he might function as the chief executive of a sprawling bureaucracy of nearly 25,000 employees. A one-man medical practice would hardly seem the environment for executive education. Beth kept the family books; the doctor typed his own reports during his term as coroner.

What the governor lacked in training was almost fully compensated for in the style with which he managed. Again, the medical experience came into play. He frequently described his role as governor in physicians' terms — listening to the problems, evaluating the symptoms to get at their true meaning, and then prescribing a remedy. Bowen was a good listener. He seemed to strain forward from a chair too big for him to catch every word, perhaps with his chin resting against one arm. Occasionally, he would take notes. In staff meetings he might only open the subject, then allow his less-restrained subordinates to toss it back and forth until a solution became obvious. The governor simply would ratify the conclusion. When strong disagreements developed he might begin to guide the discussion his way, but only asking questions as a means of doing so. Bowen often let others undertake his advocacy for him, injecting himself into the debate often enough to give them fuel to proceed forward. There is a standing joke about the governor's style: he let others have his way.

Bowen did not demand loyalty from his subordinates, but earned it by working harder than they did, by being considerate of them. He conducted himself in a way that made those closest to him want to perform at a level that would sustain his trust. In turn, he was loyal to them, almost to a fault. At times his staff thought him too loyal, overly protective of those inadequate to their jobs, but it was forgiven, for we knew that his unyielding defense of subordinates was our best insurance against an array of outsiders who had their knives out. However, if one failed him in what he considered to be an important way, the bond was quietly cut, severed for good. Once you fell from grace there was no coming back.

The governor was a strong delegator of responsibility; his decision to establish a cadre of executive assistants was an early example. They were given loose rein and, unless the issue was of overriding personal importance, he often was content just to be kept informed of developments. Bowen has described the energy crisis as one of the three major issues facing his administration during the first term, yet he seldom determined energy policy. I regularly informed him of the situation and of recommendations for dealing with the problem. If this was in written form, the memorandum would come back with a series of check marks to the left of each paragraph and, "O.K., ORB", scrawled on page one. Oral presentations amounted to little more than briefings. Although he was intensely concerned about energy and conversant about the subject, a typical Bowen reaction was, "Bill, you're the expert; you know what to do; just let me know what you're going to say so we tell the same story to the reporters."

This approach could work only if a great deal of trust and confidence existed between the governor and a subordinate. However, Bowen's other antennae provided a check whenever a subordinate began to go awry. At times the governor reasserted his authority when matters were not handled to his satisfaction.

Bowen was not without faults. At times he was inclined to overestimate the talents of public officials because he held them in high regard as people. In a number of personnel choices, his staff feared that he set his sights too low, accepting people with whom he was comfortable. Early in his governorship, Bowen sometimes placed an inflated value upon issues advice if it carried the imprimatur of academic credentials or was submitted in copious (and sometimes tedious) detail. Like many in politics he was a bit too much in awe of academia, although eight years of experience gradually lowered that esteem.

While his low-key manner was one of the foundation-stones of his success, it also was the basis for his most significant shortcoming. Bowen's style did not lend itself to giving ultimatums or clear marching orders. People, especially the political breed, hear what they want to hear. It was easy to come away from a meeting with the governor believing that he had assented to one's point of view. He might express a quiet preference that, in his manner of operation, represented clear direction. He sometimes failed to recognize that department heads, legislators, or party officials would take advantage of any loopholes provided them in order to proceed on a course of action that suited their preferences, not his. The governor sowed many loopholes and occasionally reaped their consequences. No matter how consensus-oriented he happens to be, at times a governor must be prepared to tell a subordinate, "This is the way it is going to be, and if you don't like it — move on." He toughened a bit on this point during the second term, in part because he recognized that a few episodes would not have occurred had he been more forthright, but also because the fatigue of the governorship and the trauma of Beth's illness took their toll. The governor slowly lost much of the stamina that sustained the patience with which he had guided negotiations and decision-making.

Otis Bowen is an image-maker's dream. The components of personality, profession, compassion, and honesty represent traits that people seek in their public officials. But it is an image that could not have kept alive for long if it had not been a faithful portrait. Having observed him closely for eight years, I conclude that his political popularity rests upon two characteristics. First, there is nothing transparent about the man; he is in fact what people perceive him to be. Second, the voters identify him as one of them.

If you were to ask Statehouse observers to name the politician who best exemplified the essence of Hoosiers, they might mention Governor Henry Schricker, whose quiet, quaint appeal is akin to that of Bowen. More likely, they would identify another governor, Roger Branigin, for he represented the macho image admired by political types — a bit rowdy with a frontier-era sort of roughness, hard-living, witty, and profane. Branigin was an engaging character, but he was essentially a journalistic caricature of a political stereotype. Bowen, by contrast, is the genuine article. He is the most Hoosier of Hoosiers.

II   STATE OF THE STATE

The state that Otis Bowen was called upon to govern was considerably more diverse than political mythology, journalistic nostalgia, or conventional wisdom would have tended to suggest. Mention Indiana to a New Yorker, or an Oregonian, or even many Hoosiers and you would evoke thoughts of a sleepy agricultural backwater of Indian summers, Rileyesque swimming holes, barn lot basketball games, and quiet August nights interrupted only by the scratching of crickets and the moan of far-off train whistles. A very charming notion — and, indeed, the actual experience of more than a few rural Hoosiers. But it is a picture far removed from the reality of the state's economy and social organization.

A few statistics supply the perspective. Although 38th in size and the smallest state west of Appalachia, Indiana at the beginning of the seventies ranked eleventh in population, eleventh in industry, seventh in agricultural production, and eighth in exports. On the main line of the nation's highway and rail systems, it had as extensive a system of surface transport arteries as any state outside the Northeast corridor. The compression of all this activity and population within a relatively small boundary placed intense pressure upon Indiana's land and natural resource base.

There remained more than a grain of validity in the "North-of-40, South-of-40" concept held by many people who viewed the federal highway across the state's midsection as a social and economic border between "two Indianas." A truer demarcation might have been the meandering line through south-central Indiana where the glaciers had dumped their rubble, separating hill country from flat land.

Southward, the traditional economy had been based upon natural resources — coal, timber, limestone, and aggregates. When mechanization replaced labor-intensive extraction of these resources after World War I, the region went into an economic decline from which it has not yet recovered.

Scores of small wood products manufacturing firms, the mainstay of the region's industry, stagnated and then expired.

The economy of central and northern Indiana, on the other hand, grew from tillage of some of the world's most fertile soil. It was combined with burgeoning industrial growth first spurred by a natural gas boom in the latter nineteenth century. These upstate regions shared in the industrial development surge of the 1950s and 1960s. American manufacturing went through a significant phase of decentralization, gradually abandoning its concentration in the larger urban areas of the northeast.

In terms of gross manufacturing, upstate Indiana's output was based upon heavy industry — steel and automotive. Knowledgeable observers wrestled with the advantages and disadvantages of having an industrial base so narrowly structured. Granted, when markets for durable goods flourished during prosperous times, Indiana's economy was healthier than the national average. On the other hand, the plagues of economic recession were especially virulent here because durable goods manufactures were early casualties when the economy turned sour. This cyclical pattern was the source of concern in the late 1960s. A few public officials began to ponder whether diversification was feasible and what direction a diversification strategy might take. At that point economists were only beginning to speculate about the implications of a population and economic shift from the cold-weather states to the sunbelt. Indiana for the most part escaped the early phases of this migration, except for the erosion of petroleum industry operations in the northwest part of the state. Later assessments would indicate that Indiana may have been a "halfway house" between the northeast and southern tier.

Indiana's already favorable reputation as a place to do business was enhanced by governmental policies adopted during the Bowen administration. Unfortunately, this would be offset by the abrupt decline of the automotive industry. Auto manufacturers were assailed by two bitter recessions, the oil embargo and its legacy of uncertainty about both fuel availability and the cost of private transportation. No less important was the automakers' own failure to keep abreast of consumer demand at home and stiff competition in world markets. What had been a growing population was a gradually stabilizing one, and raw data still concealed a growing trickle of out-migration.

When Bowen took office, it was fair to say that most people were contented with Indiana's economic climate, although there was growing dissatisfaction over the scale of property taxes and business inventory levies.

The Indiana of 1973 included a collection of medium-sized industrial cities, none of them economically or politically overpowering. No Chicago, Detroit, or Denver dominated the hinterlands; the state was better balanced than many of its industrial counterparts. However, the presence of three large urban areas on its borders tended to fragment Indiana politically and culturally — and in terms of the various preferences among Hoosiers as to how to set their clocks.

Indiana's historical prominence in national politics, made much of during the era in which it and New York as electoral swing states delivered a procession of national candidates, had diminished after the First World War. By the 1970s Indiana's influence probably placed it in the forefront of the second rank of states. Indiana barely missed being one of the "megastates", to use the term eventually coined by political geographers and whose category included its neighbors to the immediate east, north, and west.

Indiana's own political traditions were rather unique among the industrialized states. Its political parties had a reputation more for the intensity of their organization, the ferocity with which they battled for power, and the abandon with which they used the political rewards of victory, than for contributions to public policy. Organization, not issues, dominated their thinking.

Neither prairie populism nor the rise of organized labor to political prominence had made much of a dent here.

Indiana's Democratic party was substantially more conservative than counterparts in other northern manufacturing states. This had special significance for the conduct of state government. A conservative Republican party and a moderately conservative Democratic party found middle ground in legislative compromise. The result was decisions of a more conservative flavor than would have been made if Indiana Democrats had embraced the liberalism of their brethren in other northern states. Indiana's Democratic party included a liberal wing built around its labor unions, and from time to time this group prevailed in the selection of successful candidates for congressional and senatorial seats. However, the governorship, the only prize of real value to professional politicians, eluded this faction.

Republican voter ranks were thinning in line with national trends, but in recent years this development had not produced serious consequences, inasmuch as certain groups normally affiliated with the Democrats voted with the GOP out of dissatisfaction with some of the social philosophies of the national Democratic party.

Indiana's industrial cities had been among the first to accept racial integration, but it was of a superficial nature. The state escaped much of the violence that had raged through northern urban areas in the 1960s, but racial tension lingered throughout the 1970s. Indiana's black population, about eight percent of the total, was concentrated in the larger industrial cities; certain downstate regions remained for all practical purposes "sundown" communities. No black ever had been elected to statewide political office.

The conservatism of Indiana politics carried over into the conduct of its state government. Indiana's tradition was that of caretaker government — collecting taxes, stamping permits, pouring concrete, and maintaining human services programs of only modest proportions. State government had focused upon what it perceived to be the essentials and lacked a flair for activism. This atmosphere began to change in the post-war era. Good examples of a commitment to broader social concerns can be found in projects such as the modernization of the state's mental institutions completed during the administration of Governor George Craig in the early 1950s.

It might be proper to characterize Matthew E. Welsh (1961-1965) as the state's first "modern" governor. Coming to office on the boiling tide of enthusiasm surrounding Jack Kennedy and the New Frontier, Indiana's ruling Democrats were infected with the national mood and began striking out in more non-traditional directions. That spirit went into partial eclipse after the election of a staunchly conservative Roger Branigin (1965-1969). While Lyndon Johnson's Great Society was completely reworking American federalism and was setting the scene for vastly expanded state responsibilities in human services programs, Indiana government went into quiet retreat under the camouflage of a governor whose personality, rather than policies, beguiled lawmakers, lobbyists, and journalists. Branigin was followed by Edgar Whitcomb (1969-1973), also a strong conservative but whose administration undertook a number of management improvements in state agencies that made the road easier for his successor. That accomplishment generally has gone unrecognized. Whitcomb tended to come off rather badly in journalistic and political assessments. The achievements of his administration were overshadowed by commentators' dismay over the vehement political struggles within the Republican party during his term. Warring factions, hungry for power, left the impression that they considered state government little more than a sandbox for politicians to frolic in. They appeared to have little regard for the needs of the people or to the quiet revolution that already was under way. The Great Society began to pour billions of dollars into the federal aid system in a manner that eventually overwhelmed the administrative capacities of both federal and local governments. The states were left the duty of making these hastily conceived programs function.

By the time the physician from Bremen came to power, the federal system was in serious trouble. All its levels were choking on the vast volumes of dollars and dictates accompanying Great Society programs. Congress and the President had lost control of their own creations. The bureaucracy spawned recklessly and the *Federal Register* ballooned in size and in the complexity of new regulations it reported. The management tools designed to sort out this chaos — such as the regional offices of federal agencies established in ten major cities — failed to solve the problems. Often, they made them worse. Congressional "oversight" exercises only added to the confusion. More than with property taxes, energy shortages, or economic troubles, the Bowen administration would encounter its most nagging frustrations in coping with the collapse of the federal executive branch and in the maddening bureaucratic obstacles to the resolution of pressing issues. With the public still raising its expectations, but for the first time harboring serious doubts about the ability of government to meet them, state capitols and governors became lightning rods for public involvement and popular discontent. They were visible and accessible, unlike the faceless acronyms that now passed for federal agencies in a far-off Washington. The federal bureaucracy was made even more remote by the tremendous gap in communications and credibility between the citizens and their federal government. The breech soon would be widened by the Watergate scandal. Watergate did not, as some suggest, destroy the people's confidence in public officials and the governmental process, but only provided harsh confirmation of what many had long suspected.

These circumstances would present the Bowen administration with its greatest challenges. Yet, at the same time, they provided one source of its strength. The character of Otis Bowen and his style of leadership would come to represent a striking, pleasing contrast to what then was presumed to be the norm.

III   THE FIRST CAMPAIGN

Bowen's election as governor in 1972 reflected the triumph of a political outsider who was only reluctantly accepted by a party organization unable to build a coalition against him. It had drained too much of its blood in a series of bitter struggles during the administration of Governor Edgar Whitcomb. Presumably the second most powerful state official in his role as speaker of the House of Representatives, Bowen did not attract widespread enthusiasm on the part of the "pols" until it became apparent that it would be difficult to deny him the nomination. Many county and district chairmen considered Bowen to be a political amateur but could not find an acceptable candidate with whom to confront him. Meanwhile, he had built a solid base of rank-and-file delegate support from five years of intensive campaigning throughout the state. As late as the spring of 1972 Bowen still struggled to overcome a "nice-guys-finish-last" image that caused party professionals to discount him as unelectable in the fall.

Bowen had run well in the 1968 Republican state convention, losing the governor's nomination to then-Secretary of State Whitcomb but surprising many observers by finishing ahead of the popular dean of the Purdue University School of Agriculture, Dr. Earl Butz. The speaker was embittered by a convention process that he felt was manipulated by a handful of powerful county and district chairmen who stacked the rolls with ghost delegates elected only because their surnames began with the letters A and B. Their proxies then were cast by handpicked cronies of the chairmen. Bowen resumed the chase for the nomination the next year anyway.

The speaker probably was better off as a political outsider during the Whitcomb administration, which spent its vitality in recurring rounds of political infighting that may have been exceeded in modern times only by the bloodbaths of the Craig administration. The coalition of convenience that had vaulted Whitcomb to the governorship soon fell apart over issues of patronage and party preferment. Several of Whitcomb's strongest campaign supporters quickly became his most implacable enemies.

Within a short time three factions predominated. One was the governor's, which centered on a few key advisers and department heads in his administration. It was coupled with support from the party's conservative wing, led by former U.S. Attorney Donald Tabbert and M. Stanton Evans, editor of the Indianapolis *News*. The second grouping was that of several district chairmen, State Treasurer John Snyder, and Lieutenant Governor Richard Folz. This faction reflected an alliance between political professionals and a number of other conservatives (such as Folz) who had been associated with the organization once led by former U.S. Senator William Jenner. The third faction surrounded L. Keith Bulen, the Republican national committeeman and leader of the influential Marion County Republican organization. Bulen, admired by many as an exceptional political tactician, drew support from a number of other county chairmen, including Orvas Beers, who controlled the Allen County GOP.

At times it seemed difficult to keep track of these factions because their boundaries were obscured by temporary alliances forged to deal with individual political issues. For example, after the 1970 election, the Bulen and Whitcomb factions joined forces in an effort to oust Republican State Chairman Buena Chaney, who withstood their assault because he enjoyed the support of the Snyder forces, although only nominally aligned with them. A short time later Chaney stepped aside after Snyder had mustered enough votes to be elected. The governor then announced that state employees no longer would be obligated to contribute two per cent of their salaries to the party, a time-honored method of fueling the apparatus regardless which party was in power.

The various combatants overlooked growing discontent among party members throughout the state, who were weary of turmoil and attached equal blame to all who were involved in what seemed to be unending and purposeless feuds.

The speaker, meanwhile, stood apart from the governor largely over the issue of tax policy. Whitcomb's conservative advisers were unalterably opposed to any form of tax increase. They focused on reductions in government programs as the cornerstone of an economy program. Bowen was warning of taxpayer revolts in Indiana and other states if government did not act to reduce its over-reliance upon property taxes as a means of financing state and local operations. Reductions in government spending would not be sufficient to correct the property tax imbalance, he argued. Increases in either general income or sales taxes were required.

Bowen advanced a tax restructuring program in the 1971 legislative session. The administration remained hostile, although Governor Whitcomb stated that he was not irrevocably opposed to tax increases if they were accompanied by ironclad and foolproof measures to reduce property taxes. The House proposal, he contended, did not meet those conditions.[1] Bowen countered by saying his program would not involve spending more money than would have been spent otherwise, and that it would be raised on a fairer basis. The speaker agreed with the need for local option taxes but contended that they should be "in addition to" rather than "instead of" other taxes.[2]

When the effort to revise taxes collapsed late in the 1971 session, Bowen forecast that property tax relief would become a "growing, ballooning" issue during the next 18 months:

> The howl for relief heard last year will become a roar next year. The Democrats and the editorial policies of the Indianapolis newspapers defeated our best efforts this year. As a result, the governor has a budget within which he has told people it would be hard to live.[3]

The speaker's continued hammering on the issue of property tax relief was an important factor in the reluctance of some Republican leaders to attach themselves to his campaign. They tended to view tax issues solely within the context of the political fallout from Lieutenant Governor Richard Ristine's 1963 tie-breaking vote on a conference committee report which resulted in a state sales tax. Ristine's ticket-trailing defeat in the governor's race in 1964 was presumed to be the consequence of this vote. The fact that Ristine ran poorest in districts where Jenner forces were strongest, and may have been getting revenge upon him after an especially divisive state convention, was overlooked in the second-guessing after that campaign. In addition, Ristine appeared to be a poor contender by contrast to Senate nominee D. Russell Bontrager, who ran well, despite the Goldwater debacle, against Senator Vance Hartke. Hartke already had gathered some of the negative voter impressions that would dog him through his three terms.

Whatever the evidence, many Republicans accepted the Ristine episode as an item of political gospel — namely, that a vote for a tax increase means sure death at the polls. It was easily believed, too. The leadership of both parties looked upon a governor as the chieftain of a political organization, fully as much as a government executive expected to advance solutions to state problems. Throughout the 1972 campaign Bowen would press home the theme that the 1963 program — which also had been undertaken in the name of property tax relief — failed because it lacked controls on local spending, a feature that was the keystone of the speaker's tax programs during the early 1970s.

Bowen's active though unofficial drive for the governorship had gathered enough momentum by early 1971 that political writers such as Edward Ziegner of the Indianapolis *News* were describing him as the man beat.[4] At this point, however, there was considerable uncertainty as to who might emerge to beat him.

The logical opponent seemed to be Lieutenant Governor Folz, who by virtue of his position was the crown prince of a state administration in which a sitting governor constitutionally was denied a second term. Folz gave the appearance of active pursuit of the nomination, but in reality was disillusioned by the endless political strife. Unhappy in his first elective office (although he gave no outward sign of it), the Evansville businessman was unsure that he could accept either the rigors of a statewide campaign or the exhausting demands of service as the state's chief executive. Folz had been propelled to the lieutenant governorship as a result of a 1968 pre-convention bargain that included awarding that prize to Vanderburgh County. As lieutenant governor, Folz had played a modest role in thwarting Bowen's tax restructuring efforts. In doing so, he had earned the enmity of a cluster of Republican senators loosely allied with Bowen. Folz also ran afoul of the leadership aspirations of Senator Phillip Gutman, a Fort Wayne Republican. Gutman became president pro-tempore in 1971 and succeeded in removing most of the lieutenant governor's powers as presiding officer.

Meanwhile, Folz' relationship with Whitcomb had deteriorated due to the frequent collisions between the political ambitions of the Snyder group and the governor's faction. Despite this erosion of his authority, the lieutenant governor was considered by Bowen strategists as the opponent who could give them the most trouble. He could combine a southern Indiana political base with support from businessmen with whom he had strong rapport.

However, by September, 1971, the lieutenant governor had decided not to run, but he did not share this information with political associates. Folz concluded that his withdrawal would make Bowen the odds-on favorite and began discreetly to make overtures to the Bowen camp. He saw the speaker's nomination as almost inevitable and could not foresee circumstances under which he would back a candidate sponsored by either Bulen or Whitcomb, given the long-standing sourness of their relations. It was not until the spring of 1972 that Folz personally confirmed to Bowen that he had no intention of running. At this time a few Folz political associates, such as Eighth District Republican Chairman Seth Denbo, began to approach Bowen with offers of endorsement.

As the GOP edged toward its state convention the governor's race became little more than a stop-Bowen affair. Whitcomb's faction was unwilling to accept the speaker because his nomination would result in their eclipse, politically and philosophically. The governor and his lieutenants began to promote the candidacy of newly-robed Owen Circuit Judge William Sharp, a former Marion County municipal judge who was highly regarded by capital city conservatives.

Bulen was less than enchanted with a Bowen candidacy because it would diminish the national committeeman's influence and because Marion County interests assumed that the speaker would be hostile to them. They drew this conclusion primarily because of a rift during the passage of the Unigov bill, in which Indianapolis Mayor Richard Lugar irked Bowen by giving out his private telephone number and urging Marion County Unigov supporters to deluge him with calls. Initially, Bulen lacked a candidate, although Public Service Commission Chairman W.W. Hill had entered the race. To many observers it seemed a Hill entry only divided the Marion County delegate vote without presenting a candidate of sufficient stature to halt Bowen's momentum.

Gutman saw an opportunity to take advantage of the overall confusion and to emerge as the only acceptable alternative to the speaker. The potential for deal-making was further clouded by the fact that House Ways and Means Committee Chairman John Hart of Indianapolis had entered the contest for lieutenant governor and was considered by some to be the front-runner. Bulen might be required to take Hart's candidacy into account because it could be the only consolation available to the Indianapolis delegation.

Meanwhile, State Senator and Vanderburgh County GOP Chairman Robert Orr also jumped into the fray as a candidate for the number two position, adding a new dimension to the possibilities for deal-cutting. Vanderburgh County's votes could be crucial if added to a block-Bowen movement. Certain members of the Snyder-Folz group were opposed to Orr and wanted to forestall his nomination by throwing their support to Hart. Folz, however, was convinced that Orr would be an almost automatic nominee. Bowen's supporters could not afford to offend Vanderburgh County by formally aligning with someone else, yet any anti-Bowen coalition would have to have the backing of the Evansville contingent to be successful. The price for that backing would be Orr's nomination as lieutenant governor. Orr was a likely winner under anyone's strategy.

As the delegates converged upon Indianapolis the action became fast and furious. On the day before the balloting Whitcomb lashed out at the speaker's property tax program, describing it as "nothing more than a hoax" to get more money. He stated that he would find it very difficult to support Bowen.[5] Mayor Lugar also endorsed Sharp, again hoping to blunt the speaker's drive. Bowen's campaign manager, J.B. King, claimed 1,040 delegates, which put the speaker within short striking distance of the 1,118 needed to win. Bulen's "public" count gave Bowen 800 and Sharp 700, with Gutman running a good third, though he did not attach numbers to the senator's strength. Gutman, meanwhile, was dismissing a Bowen first-ballot victory as "purely a pipe dream".[6]

Although public pronouncements appeared calculated to consolidate the anti-Bowen effort around Sharp, Bulen quietly was engineering an

Allen-Marion-Vanderburgh combination that would result in a Gutman-Orr ticket. Such an amalgamation represented a classic strategy in GOP conventions, since these three urban counties anchor four congressional districts. Therefore, Bowen's managers were quick to read the ploy, as was Folz, who saw that the best way to thwart it was to keep his hometown delegation committed to the speaker. During an acrimonious late-night caucus Gutman's forces pressed ferociously for at least a split of the Evansville Republicans, but Folz held them for Bowen. He did not stand fast out of a deep-seated commitment to the speaker, but because he relished the idea of outmaneuvering Bulen, a foe of long standing.

When the Vanderburgh delegates pledged themselves to Bowen and Orr, the governor's race was over, although Bulen battled on the convention floor the next morning to frustrate the inevitable result. At one point he confronted the lieutenant governor with a warning that Bowen's managers would double-cross Orr and that the only way to insure Orr's nomination was to throw Vanderburgh's votes to Gutman. Folz replied dryly: "I deal in facts, not rumors," and abruptly turned away.[7]

The first ballot tally on June 23 gave Bowen the nomination with 1,243 votes. Sharp compiled 364, Gutman 354, and Hill 108.

Actually, Bulen was not so far off the mark on the lieutenant governor's race. A number of Bowen backers had strong personal commitments to John Hart and urged the speaker to put out the word that he favored the state representative as his running mate. Bowen refused to do so, although it appeared that some of his supporters spread that message anyway. Orr posted 819 on the initial ballot in the lieutenant governor contest, well ahead of the field but substantially short of the margin needed to win. Hart gathered 447 delegates, while Hamilton County Chairman (and former Public Service Commission Chairman) Robert Webb collected 378 votes and former State Senator William Frazier of Muncie accumulated 370. On the next ballot Orr edged to 926, still short of the necessary majority, while Hart improved slightly to 505. The third ballot gave Orr a decisive 1,277-436 victory, and wounded Hart supporters adjourned to the Indianapolis Press Club to console themselves.

Whitcomb then backed away from his earlier onslaughts with a rather modest endorsement: "I only said I would find it difficult to support Dr. Bowen. I have done many things that were difficult for me to do."[8]

Aside from the bare-knuckle politics involved, the convention campaign also was tailored to convince party regulars that an exciting campaign could be built around Bowen. Although his personal qualities were appreciated, many feared that the physician's low-key style and lack of dynamism might render him unelectable. One of the most effective convention-period devices was a large-format brochure that assumed almost magazine proportions. It portrayed the human qualities of the candidate, related his generalized observations about issues, and began to set forth the theme that would dominate the 1972 campaign: "He hears you." This document, considered by some observers to be the most effective single piece of campaign literature in recent memory, was the work of campaign publicist William Colbert, advertising specialist Gerald Steadham, and Bowen assistant Raymond Rizzo.

Bowen's campaign advisers were media-oriented people who saw the electronic media as the most efficient way to achieve name identification and to create a favorable image for their candidate. January polling conducted by Robert Teeter's Market Opinion Research firm had placed Bowen's percentage at 26, substantially behind his opponent, former Governor Matthew Welsh, who posted a 57 percent voter approval rating. In part, this resulted from a reservoir of name identification for Welsh, who had served as governor from 1961 to 1965. It also indicated that Bowen was not widely known, an expected conclusion at this early point in the campaign.[9]

The media approach emphasized television, supplemented by radio, billboards, direct mail, and newspapers. Blending these is important because the experience of campaign professionals indicates that certain media — billboards, for example — are reinforcing devices and work effectively only if used in conjunction with another media promotion — usually radio. By the end of the campaign, the Bowen organization would spend more than $340,000 for television, $93,000 for radio, $90,000 for billboards, $118,000 for newspapers, and $101,000 for direct mail. Television's allocation represented a substantial sum in those days. The direct mail budget was smaller than that reserved in more recent campaigns when the potential of direct mail fund-raising has been more fully appreciated.[10]

The speaker gradually gained on Welsh, at the expense of the Democratic candidate rather than with undecided voters. A July MOR poll showed Welsh declining to 43 percent support, while Bowen advanced 8 points to 34. The speaker's strength still was not adequate among Republicans (in part due to the reluctance of some conservatives to support him) and among ticket-splitters. However, national political trends were on his side. President Richard Nixon clearly was headed for a thumping victory over Senator George McGovern.

The liberalism of the Democratic presidential nominee and the leftward leanings of his party's platform were easy targets for Bowen and other Republicans. Throughout the campaign GOP orators challenged Welsh either to endorse or to repudiate McGovern, who obviously was not taking hold with Indiana voters. At the same time they asserted that Nixon was certain to be elected and that Hoosiers would be better served by Republican Governor Bowen than by Democratic Governor Welsh.

Bowen continued to focus on the tax issue, saying that the 1963 sales tax increase failed to halt the spiraling of property taxes because it was not accompanied by controls intended to put a ceiling on them. Welsh, he argued, had failed once before and was not the man to deal effectively with this escalating problem. As the summer passed, evidence began to accumulate that he was having an effect.

An October Teeter poll described Welsh as "particularly weak" on the issue of taxes with more voters giving him a negative rating on this issue (23 percent) than a positive rating (22 percent). "Taxes are not a strong issue for Bowen, either, but he is not as unfavorably perceived as Welsh," the survey concluded.[12]

Another issue proved to be prominent in the voter's minds — a growing concern about the spread of drug abuse, especially among youth. It played right into the Republicans' hands because the Democratic state platform included language favoring the decriminalization of marijuana. The GOP pounced upon this plank with glee.

The October poll, which revealed that drugs had become the second most commonly chosen issue in importance, concluded that Bowen was in a particularly strong position with the voters and was scoring well on the drug abuse issue. Twenty-seven percent of voters chose drugs as their first consideration and 56 percent mentioned it among their top three concerns. Teeter found that 37 percent of the voters strongly felt jail sentences for marijuana use should be continued, while 23 percent opposed jail terms with equal vigor. A majority still didn't fully identify either candidate with this issue, but Bowen was credited with taking the more popular, hard-line stance.[13]

As the race tightened in September the Bowen campaign edged away from its positive issue-and-personality themes and devoted more effort to attacks on Welsh and McGovern. It seemed to be a result of more strident comments from Democrats which reached their peak in remarks of former Democratic National Committeeman Frank McHale during a fund-raiser at the Indianapolis Athletic Club:

> When you think of a doctor, you think of men who have taken the oath and who have dedicated themselves to saving humanity. . . when they step out from that rank and start to do something else, you start to question them. . . Why should they desert the people to whom they are dedicated and trained to save and to help, and with the great shortage of doctors we have in Indiana today. He has not only deserted and abandoned the medical profession, but he has abandoned the principles for which he ran and was elected to the legislature.

McHale went on to describe the speaker as the "Charlie McCarthy of the Whitcomb administration" and averred that the only difference between Whitcomb and Bowen is that "Whitcomb at least looks like a governor."[14]

Instead of dismissing this attack as the ranting of an elderly partisan delivered in the club that is the bastion of the Hoosier Democratic party, Republicans took it personally and began to reply with gamier press releases of their own. However, by this time the speaker had succeeded in closing the gap on Welsh and the prospects for the GOP national ticket promised nothing less satisfying than a total rout of McGovern.

Teeter's October poll placed Bowen at 44 percent, Welsh at 43, and the undecided at 12. The presidential sample indicated that Nixon had gained nine percentage points, to 65, while McGovern had dropped two points, to 26. The president was taking an "almost incredible" 79 percent of the Indiana ticket-splitter vote. Bowen was leading Welsh for the first time among ticket-splitters and was very close to the winning pattern needed in Indiana (85 percent of Republicans, 15 percent of Democrats, and 60 percent of independents). Bowen's last weeks were buoyed by an overwhelming majority of newspaper endorsements of his candidacy. The Republican ticket galloped to victory on November 7, with Nixon smashing McGovern by nearly 700,000 votes in Indiana and the speaker outpolling the former governor by 303,000.

Teeter was commissioned to conduct a post-election analysis. Its results vindicated the governor-elect's tax restructuring theme and discounted the pre-convention fears of those who considered support for tax increases of any kind to promise only a quick exit to political oblivion.

Those interviewed named only four issues as having a significant impact upon their decision to vote for Dr. Bowen: a new tax structure, 14 percent; property tax relief, 10 percent; concern for people, 8 percent, and sincerity/integrity, 6 percent. No other response totaled more than two percent. More striking was the reaction that these voters accepted the likelihood that Bowen would increase their taxes. Forty-six percent believed that he would raise taxes, while 26 percent responded to the contrary. Of the sample, a hefty 58 percent favored a program of property tax relief that would make up the lost revenue with other taxes. Only 22 percent were opposed. The findings were auspicious for a new administration that was planning to change the tax structure as its first — and highest — order of business.[16]

IV   TRANSITION

The governor-elect moved quickly to shape an administration because he recognized that he faced scores of important decisions within a span of about 60 days. The transition, Bowen sensed, represented a fundamental test because the actions he took and the atmosphere he created would go a long way toward setting the overall tone of the new administration. Transitions are haphazard affairs to begin with. Indiana's governmental system has been inclined to disregard the physical, staffing, and financial needs of the governor-elect. Yet the one-term limitation had guaranteed a transition — often between warring political parties — every four years.

In some respects, the 1972 changeover of power was simplified by the fact that Indiana was not switching political party control; for the most part, second echelon appointees would be retained automatically. This advantage was at least partially offset by the fact that an incoming governor must make enough changes to put his own stamp upon the new administration, to define a breaking point from the past and from his predecessor. This was true of the Whitcomb-to-Bowen torch passing because of their wide breach over tax and finance policy. (It would be an even trickier undertaking for Robert Orr eight years later because of the "son-of-Bowen" aura that surrounded his accession to the governorship). The cleavage that would have resulted from the wholesale ouster of Democrats in a change-of-party transition probably would have enabled these processes to go forward with less consideration for the issues of gubernatorial style.

A few decisions involving the governor's staff had been made in advance of the November balloting. I later learned that the governor had settled upon my appointment three weeks before the election. Unaware of this, I walked into a cramped suite of rooms in the downtown Indianapolis

Quality Inn on the Thursday following the election. J.B. King, Raymond Rizzo, Robert DeBard, and William Lloyd were there with Bowen, who got right to the point. "I guess you know why I've asked you here," he said. "I'd like you to be my press secretary and to handle a few other chores that would justify making you a full-fledged assistant."

"Count me in," was my reply. It was as simple as that. No discussion of pay or other specifics. Our handshake represented a rather speculative bargain between two men who were almost strangers.

The governor also had resolved to appoint Rizzo, who had been his key assistant in the speaker's office; DeBard, a former state police officer, then director of the criminal justice training program for Indiana University, and a campaign aide to the candidate; and Lloyd, a Bloomington attorney who was active in the campaign. Lloyd had been brought into the governor's office during the previous summer through an agreement between the candidate and Governor Whitcomb. These appointments, the first of the new administration, were made public on November 9. The group occupied transition quarters in what had been a conference room at the rear of the governor's suite in the Statehouse. It was a cramped and noisy place, lacking any privacy. If Bowen wanted to conduct a private conference, the others had to leave. Rizzo, DeBard, and Viola Walker, the governor-elect's secretary, operated from this location. I opted to remain in the lieutenant governor's office where I had isolation and working space for what already was a growing accumulation of books and other governmental bric-a-brac.

There are four main themes to a transition. Inevitably commanding the most attention is the selection of personnel. This is the exercise in which political insiders are able to use their clout and wire together connections that can have important implications for whoever truly wields influence. Second is the development of a legislative program that suffers from a built-in handicap. The legislature's formal organization precedes that of the new governor, and interim committees already have filled the lawmaking pipeline with a profusion of recommendations. Third is the organization of the governor's office — apportioning the turf, devising management approaches to handle a copious workload, and selecting subordinate staff members and making them fit into the puzzle. The final task is preparing to grasp the reins with full strength on inauguration day in order that the new administration is prepared to cope with unexpected tests that may confront it in its early weeks. A new governor's response to these challenges often defines the media and public perception of his competence. It might be proper to add a fifth requirement, that of dealing with the "anxiety factor". Those who earn their livelihoods in the Statehouse or its environs are made uncertain by changeovers of power. While there is nothing intrinsically wrong with keeping them off balance, prolonged uncertainty can breed confusion, unnecessary strain, or mischief.

As might be expected the initial focus was on the selection of personnel. Bowen activated a patronage advisory committee for major positions. Republican State Chairman James Neal presided over its gatherings. Other party officials were Betty Rendel, Virgil Scheidt, Lavon Yoho, John Sweezey, Quentin Blachly, Thomas Milligan, and William Gee. Gerald Olson, a Bowen campaign adviser, also was a member. Lloyd, Rizzo, DeBard, and I functioned in an ex-officio capacity.

We sought to remove ourselves from the bleatings of jobseekers and the inquisitions of newsmen by venturing to the Far Horizons Resort on Longboat Key, gulfward of Sarasota, Florida. Here, we could discuss in private these personnel decisions, although the telephone circuits sustained a brisk pace of verbal traffic between the participants and the curious who had been left behind. The legislative leadership joined us briefly: Senators Phillip Gutman and Walter Helmke, and Representatives Kermit Burrous, John Guy, and John Hart. They were on hand for strategy sessions concerning presentation of the administration's tax package to the General Assembly and budget priorities for the coming biennium. Lieutenant Governor-elect Orr and J.B. King were present throughout the deliberations. The jaunt also provided the first opportunity for the candidates and their wives to relax. Through social dinners and bull sessions by the swimming pool, it became a mechanism for solidifying relationships between the governor and party leaders, while exposing lesser-known staff members to GOP officials.

The majority of the first-rank department head appointments were settled upon during business sessions at Sarasota. Bowen did not attempt to dominate the proceedings, but occasionally interjected in quiet sentences his preferences for appointment. Invariably, he prevailed without dispute. It was my first exposure to the Bowen technique of "letting others have his way." The process of deliberating upon appointments was a rather informal one. There were lists of names under consideration for various positions and a smattering of resumes on hand. However, most of the information used in these sessions was carried by word of mouth. Eventually, the committee would examine detailed job descriptions for the various posts up for consideration, but for the moment, the winnowing process was carried forward on the basis of personal knowledge of the positions and the people under study to fill them.

For example, discussions of the Department of Natural Resources focused on its difficulties stemming from frequent changes of directors, and a perception held by many in the group that it was an agency in trouble. A rather superficial examination of its problems contributed little to the selection of a new director — the group had several names before it — but it was of little import, anyway, since the governor had decided to appoint former State Representative Joseph Cloud.

Their unfamiliarity with the functions of certain state agencies occasionally put the political chairmen at a disadvantage. The selection of an adjutant general was one such case. Based upon a southern Indiana lobbying effort, county chairmen proposed the appointment of Major General Kenneth Brewer, the recently retired commanding general of the National Guard's 38th Infantry Division. Few in the room were aware of what the adjutant general post entailed. DeBard and I, the only National Guard officers present, were able to guide the proceedings. When we described Brewer as an adequate appointment, but characterized the incumbent, Major General Alfred Ahner, as by far the superior choice among the five names before us, the others backed off in deference to our insiders' knowledge. Bowen then confirmed that Ahner would be his preference.

One of the complicating factors in a process such as this is the awareness that there are several people for whom positions must be found because of their prominence or their roles in the recent campaign. If job selections move too quickly, opportunities for these individuals may be foreclosed. On the other hand, if decisions are handled as a package, one sticking point can retard the filling of several administrative posts. Securing a niche for Robert Morris, one of the campaign finance managers, produced one such snag. Morris's name surfaced in discussions of the jobs of commissioner of administration and insurance commissioner, but I detected an undercurrent of opposition to his inclusion in a major post — for reasons that remain unclear. The Morris situation received a good deal of behind-the-scenes attention in whispered caucuses for about two days, but the matter finally was disposed of when Orr agreed to take him on as executive director of the Department of Commerce.

Bowen's appointments took on a decided legislative flavor — as was to be expected since he was familiar with the abilities of many of his House colleagues. They represented the only "farm club" at his disposal. One shortcoming of the political system is that it does not seek out talent but instead sifts those resumes which float over the transom. "Executive search" seldom is employed because the mere suggestion would tip off party regulars that a governor intended to deny a position to one of their own. Outsiders filter into the system and help to keep it in balance, but the lack of a calculated recruitment policy leaves state agencies with a number of second-rate managers. Despite this fault, the political system has provided adequate talent to state government, although one could argue that the demands upon government are such that it cannot accept officeholders who are only adequate. Bowen's philosophy toward the selection of personnel was expressed quite simply: "First, they must be competent. Second, they must be loyal. . . Third, we must be compatible."[1]

The Sarasota conference completed the basic makeup of the Bowen administration. In addition to those already mentioned, the governor chose former State Representative Raymond Sanders as commissioner of administration; Edison Thuma, director of the Legislative Council, budget director; House Majority Leader Richard Boehning, chairman of the State Highway Commission; former Shelbyville Mayor Ralph Van Natta, commissioner of the Bureau of Motor Vehicles; Dr. William Murray, to be retained as commissioner of the Department of Mental Health; Robert Konkle, to remain as superintendent of the State Police; DeKalb County Sheriff James Sims, to become chairman of the Alcoholic Beverage Commission; former State Representative John Coppes, employment security director; Carleton Phillippi, to remain as chairman of the State Tax Board; Oscar Ritz, to stay on as insurance commissioner; James Faris, to hold his job as director of financial institutions, and Donald Newman, a Mishawaka pharmacist and unsuccessful congressional candidate, to be director of the Indiana Washington Office.

The position of welfare director was narrowed to two candidates — Marion County Welfare Director Wayne Stanton and former State Budget Director Philip Conklin. Stanton was the preferred choice if he checked out with the Marion County Republican organization. Pending approval by labor leaders friendly to the GOP, William Lanam was tabbed as labor commissioner. Decisions on health commissioner, corrections commissioner, veterans' affairs director, civil rights director, and Administrative Building Council director were deferred. Kenneth Beesley was to remain as head of the State Board of Accounts until the committee had time to consider the matter further.

Upon the return to Indianapolis, appointments were doled out to the media on a schedule that identified key department heads before inauguration day. Several others were decided within a short time: Stanton; Lanam; Robert Heyne, retained as corrections commissioner; Tommie Holland, civil rights commissioner; Earl Heath, veterans' director; and Charles Betts, commissioner of the Administrative Building Council. The appointment of deputy mental health commissioner William Paynter as commissioner of the State Board of Health did not occur until February, 1973.

Only one of the major personnel decisions reached at Sarasota came unglued, and it did so in short order. The committee had agreed to retain James Mathis as commissioner of the Department of Revenue. Mathis was acknowledged as one of the standout department heads in the Whitcomb administration. Many within the Bowen camp believed that this position was crucial to the success of the property tax program, but Mathis was identified with a former governor hostile to it. Doubts began accumulating in Bowen's mind, and they were fed by a few Mathis critics. Several days later the governor-elect all but concluded that Mathis had to go, but he still agonized over the decision. Bowen and I had a lengthy conversation about the subject and he seemed eager to hear confirmation that he was doing the right thing. I responded that the mere fact he was having doubts probably represented sufficient grounds on which to base a negative decision, given the close working relationship required between a governor and his revenue commissioner. Bowen later told Nixon Newspapers Political Editor Al Spiers that it was his most difficult personnel decision during the transition period:

> James Mathis was one of the brightest men carried over from the Whitcomb administration. . . a fine, excellent administrator who I'm sure could have transferred his loyalty to me. But we differed in philosophy concerning methods of financing local government and public education. We simply weren't compatible, so I had to make a change in spite of his competence — which I recognized. It was kind of tough to do. . .[2]

The dumping of Mathis resulted in a chilling of the transition harmony with the outgoing administration and stirred bad blood between Bowen and the conservative editorial page executives of the *Star* and *News*. Donald Clark, a former state budget director, Indiana University finance officer, and then finance vice-president for Indiana Vocational Technical College, was Bowen's choice as commissioner of the Department of Revenue.

The personnel process also produced another advisory committee, this one chosen to screen secondary positions in state government. It was chaired by William Gee, the Marshall County Republican chairman and a Bowen stalwart. Olson functioned as executive secretary and Sue Glick provided staff support. Like those of the major patronage committee its members were organization Republican officials: Marjorie O'Laughlin, Seth Denbo, Orvas Beers, William Means, Harriet Arland, Margaret Hill, John Price, Robert Skinner, Bruce Haller, and Donald Cox. The governor's staff generally was not involved in its discussions — more from the pressure of other responsibilities than from any intent to stand apart from the process. These committees — eventually referred to as Big P and Little P — met regularly during the early months of 1973 and then gradually became inactive.

The organization of the office proceeded without the ill will often associated with nest-building in a new place. The governor's decision that each of his executive assistants was to be co-equal fashioned a staff system that served his personal needs and also contributed to the overall effectiveness of the office. The employment of six executive assistants stimulated diversity of thought while making it difficult for an individual to become either the governor's alter ego or his chief of staff.

The term "executive assistants" was recommended by a team of consultants from the Indiana University School of Public and Environmental Affairs which had been enlisted to help organize the office. Headed by Dr. Roy Jumper, SPEA's director of professional development, it made a number of worthwhile contributions to the process of amalgamating a collection of more than 20 individuals into a working governor's office team. When asked why the office should adopt the new titles, Jumper's people responded that it was in line with current trends and was a more "modern" description of our functions. Anyway, it sounded nice, though we were not so naive as to believe that some of our journalistic friends would substitute it for the habit of describing us as "aides" — a term conjuring images of batmen and gophers.

The selection of office space did not produce disharmony and there was only one disagreement as to the allocation of working areas. SPEA recommended that the news secretary be situated in one of the offices directly accessible to the governor. Lloyd objected, wanting to locate the function in the back office loft because he disapproved of the parade of reporters who regularly traipsed into the governor's main outer office, presumably disrupting its work and gaining a position to see who might be waiting to visit the governor. His was not a persuasive argument and I was installed in the cubicle adjacent to the governor's secretary — a dingy place, soon clogged with books and papers, that became my lair for eight years and also proved to be the best vantage point in the governor's suite. It gave me the opportunity to eyeball everyone who crossed our threshhold.

In addition to the details of office organization, the staff was occupied with learning the tasks essential to taking charge on January 8. Executive orders were examined because they expire upon the end of a governor's term and require immediate renewal if the programs and policies they encompassed were to be sustained without interruption. Assistants learned the procedures for activating the state's security forces in the event of disaster or other emergencies and were a bit in awe of the paperwork and procedures seemingly required to employ the National Guard and State Police. (In time, frequent experiences with emergencies reduced this to an oral exercise in which paperwork was deferred until time permitted). Procedures for handling mail and apportioning responsibilities were devised, again with the help of the SPEA team.

Only then did the staff begin to realize the extent to which appointments to hundreds of state boards and commissions would occupy the time of the governor and his assistants. The requirements of profession, geography, and political balance complicated the burdensome number. It was determined that a full-time secretary would be required to manage the workload. The staff explored a number of ways in which the system might be made more efficient. Despite refinements to the appointive process, errors and obsolete data were encountered even to the end of Bowen's second term.

The division of agencies among executive assistants was carried out in a congenial fashion, although there was a bit of jockeying and informal bartering. Rizzo's portfolio included liaison with the General Assembly and supervision of legislative programs, education agencies, welfare functions, and speechwriting. Lloyd's encompassed most of the administrative boards, judiciary, Republican State Committee, Highway Commission, Public Service Commission, Bureau of Motor Vehicles, and Insurance Department. DeBard supervised public safety and corrections agencies: State Police, National Guard, Corrections Department, criminal justice agencies, traffic safety, and Fire Marshal. In addition to those of media relations, my duties embraced the Department of Natural Resources and several ancillary boards.

Our numbers were completed by the addition of two other executive assistants. Dr. Lee Ellen Ford, who had provided the governor with reams of issue material during the campaign, was given liaison with health and mental health agencies, along with the Civil Rights Commission and a number of smaller boards and commissions. The other assistants were somewhat uncomfortable with her appointment; we did not think that she would fit into the Bowen style of operation. She was intense, with rigidly-held views, and far more liberal than the governor. Rizzo and I endeavored to talk the governor out of hiring her, but he rejected our point of view with marked brusqueness. The final selection was that of William Ray, an Indianapolis businessman and civil rights leader. Bowen wanted a black on his personal staff to underscore his interest in minority involvement in state government, and Ray came with laudatory recommendations from Marion County Republicans. He was given liaison with local governments, the Labor Department, economic development agencies, and a number of other boards and commissions.

Although they were not members of the governor's personal staff, Sanders, Thuma, and Clark were regarded as members of the immediate family. In addition to taking on liaison responsibilities with a limited number of agencies, they became full partners in the policy-making process and remained so throughout their tenures. As the governor's executive secretary and office manager, Vi Walker also was a member of what became an unofficial gubernatorial cabinet.

The legislative program, built upon the tax program, came together without great difficulty, since the agenda was a limited one. Thuma labored to determine the utility of restructuring a budget developed by predecessors in a manner that would reflect Bowen administration priorities.

Relationships with the outgoing administration cooled further in the final days before Bowen's accession to the governorship. Whitcomb described his successor's tax plan as "a lot of nonsense," and predicted that "we will find out the hard way that this system doesn't work."[3] Meanwhile, outgoing gubernatorial assistant Joseph Root worked late into the night to complete scores of lame-duck appointments as a means of protecting the positions of members of the departing regime. It was an indication that the political interests represented by the retiring leadership were not prepared to yield power gracefully. Further clashes with the party's right wing over the tax package threatened to take a divided GOP into a legislative session of transcendent importance to the new governor.

More than 3,000 persons jammed the Statehouse on January 8, 1973, to witness the inaugural ceremony. Included were former governors Ralph Gates, George Craig, Matthew Welsh, and Roger Branigin. Whitcomb also attended, and afterward quietly returned to his office to collect a hat and coat, and hastily departed. Bowen was sworn in by Joseph Kotso, who had headed his Lake County volunteer campaign. The new chief of state received a rousing ovation from partisan Republicans who thronged the hallways and crowded the railings on the third and fourth floors.[4] Beth Bowen stood at the governor's side and was introduced by him as "one whose help has been very instrumental in any achievement that I have ever had."[5] Bowen called for an administration "not callously built upon the opportunistic policies of the quota, but one which is deeply rooted in full, open, and public participation." His administration further had "the responsibility to lead, to be an outspoken advocate of the public, a positive force for the sound administration of public affairs."[6]

It was not a thrilling address; inaugural statements seldom are. It did not set forth a platform — that was to be saved for addresses to the legislature — but it evoked an impression of the Bowen style, the determination of a new leader coupled with the humility of the people's servant.

The atmosphere within the governor's office was quieter. A few of the staff members skipped the ceremony in order to complete pressing work assignments. As celebrants deluged the outer office for the traditional post-inaugural reception, most of the staff quietly filtered to their desks to take on the duties that now had become ours. The attitude was that of anticipation and confidence, but a confidence that fell far short of cockiness. An overpowering sense of tradition is felt quickly by those who occupy this expansive suite of offices, where the eyes of former governors stare from portraits on the walls. Little did we know on this day — surely among the most pleasant of our lives — of coming events that would demand our labors, unexpected emergencies that would challenge our abilities, of the numbing effect of too many years in positions which take more out of you than leisure-time diversions can replenish, or of the aching sadness with which Bowen's administration would come to an end eight years in the distance.

V   THE CRITICAL TEST

The Bowen administration completed its most important piece of business in the early weeks of its first term — a successful and politically popular restructuring of the state's tax system. The evolution and enactment of the tax package was a frustrating ordeal. On several occasions it appeared that the governor's plans would be shattered. The Senate, in particular, was only lukewarm to the program, and help from Democrats was totally lacking except for one crucial test in the upper chamber. The 1973 General Assembly wrestled with a series of landmark public policy issues — abortion, Sunday liquor, broadened rights for eighteen-year-olds, equal rights for women, and no-fault insurance — but it is remembered chiefly for its action on taxes. Since Bowen's subsequent reputation as governor hinged upon that issue more than any other, it is fair to say that the 1973 session "made" the Bowen administration.

Despite top-heavy Republican margins in both houses — 73-27 in the House and 30-20 in the Senate — approval of the governor's programs was less than automatic because of philosophical differences with leaders of his own party. In addition, the relationship between Bowen and Senator Gutman, the president pro tempore, was restrained since Gutman had been the governor's main convention opponent. It was not known whether the administration could expect reprisals from him.

The governor's principal address to the lawmakers occurred on January 24 — a lengthy message setting forth his budget priorities — and proposals for property tax relief and revenue restructuring. The budget included $4.5 million in revenue sharing funds to construct a new women's prison; expansion of work release programs, development of a juvenile diagnostic center, and creation of a medical services division within the corrections system; sufficient state funds to match federal water pollution construction grants expected during the two-year period; $5.5 million in revenue sharing funds for state commitments to reservoir projects; added staff for the environmental division of the State Board of Health; a shift of funding for the State Police away from the motor vehicle highway account to the general fund (which would free $4.5 million to local government highway projects); new money for the Industrial Development Revolving Fund; $21 million to increase state employee salaries (the first broad-scale raise in six years); $15 million in revenue sharing funds for a Vietnam veterans' bonus; $1.5 million to help finance an addition to the Indiana State Library (to match a $2 million challenge grant from the Lilly Endowment), and added personnel in the Labor Department to help administer the new federal Occupational Safety and Health Act.

He warned that the one factor threatening the ability of the state to budget within existing revenue sources was welfare spending, which imposed a staggering obligation upon the state. It was open-ended in nature and involved "an unbelievable jungle of laws, rules, regulations, forms and quotas."[1] Bowen stated that the $257 million recommended as a biennial welfare appropriation was not enough and that the administration would be forced to request an additional $53 million from the general fund, along with a $30 million allocation from revenue sharing. He called upon the General Assembly to join the administration in seeking sweeping reform of the welfare system, arguing that the state would lose the ability to govern if it failed to confine soaring welfare costs to reasonable dimensions.

The property tax relief program was described as meeting the tests of being substantial in size, highly visible to the property taxpayer, lasting in nature, and equitable in the distribution of revenue. It was intended to use all new monies collected for property tax relief and not permit the siphoning of any of it for other state government spending. The tax program at this stage of its evolution called for a 25 percent reduction from 1973 levels for all property tax bills payable in May, 1974; November, 1974; and every May and November thereafter. Direct payment credits would be made from a property tax relief fund, which would receive its money from an increase in the sales tax from two percent to four percent, and a similar increase in the corporate net income tax. It also included a graduated system of sales tax credits intended to provide the greatest benefits to low-income families.

Another — and controversial — feature of the proposal was its granting to local government the opportunity to adopt an individual adjusted gross income tax. This would provide additional property tax relief while giving local officials an alternate non-property tax source of local revenue. Under its provisions, counties had by June 1, 1973, to reject the local option feature. If they let it become law they would levy a one percent individual adjusted gross tax on income earned by their residents. Counties declining the option plan would not be permitted future budget increases beyond their percentage increases in assessed valuation. The one percent collected would not be returned immediately, but would be phased in over a four-year period. This could allow an additional six-to-seven percent reduction in local government property tax bills. In addition, local governments participating in the option program could, after January, 1976, levy an additional one-half percent or one percent individual adjusted gross income tax which would be totally available to fund local government operations previously paid for with property taxes.

A fundamental departure from earlier tax packages was the system of controls. As noted, the non-adopting counties could increase budgets only to the limits of percentage increases in assessed valuation. Adopting counties would have their tax levies frozen at the December, 1972, levels. Furthermore, all school property tax levies would be frozen, with upward and downward levy adjustments permitted only to allow for increasing or decreasing enrollments. Two property tax control boards — one for local government, the other for schools — would deal with emergency funding needs.

The program also called for a "circuit-breaker," or special credit feature, intended to provide a further tax reduction to elderly or disabled renters and homeowners. The governor also proposed that increases in school operating costs be financed at the state level.

The plan sidestepped any major revision of the business tax structure, although the governor stated that he recognized inequities did exist. He said they should not be compounded by further inequities that might result from a restructuring undertaken before the facts were known. The private sector had struggled in the legislature for several years to alleviate problems associated with the state's business inventory tax. Solutions proved elusive and the tax remained a significant revenue producer for the state.

In contrast to his budget address, the governor's State of the State message, presented to the lawmakers on January 30, was far more general in tone. Bowen discussed his support for administration-sponsored bargaining legislation for public employees, but was far less specific on the subject than in later years, when he set forth a series of rigid principles to define legislation that would be acceptable. The section on economic development was orthodox in its tone and very general in its recommendations, as was the segment on natural resources and the environment. The governor proposed a legislative study of the issue of the state's vulnerability to lawsuits. Courts had wiped out the sovereign immunity doctrine. Nearly half a billion dollars in pending lawsuits was the result. Bowen also recommended a review of the state's insurance needs, since few state facilities were protected.

Although not quite ready to endorse a specific scheme for no-fault auto insurance, the governor said that the time for its enactment was nearing and the legislature should give priority to the completion of the research needed to develop a program. He did set forth four criteria for a no-fault program: that it result in a true reduction in premiums, that it provide a speedier settlement of claims, that reasonable access to court settlement be available to resolve complex damage situations, and that it guarantee an increased percentage of premium dollars be returned to the policyholder.

Even before the tax package began its tortuous path through the legislative process, a series of modifications was considered. Doubts began to surface within the administration about the overall program. Legislative Council Fiscal Analyst William Styring, upon whom the administration relied heavily for revenue data, voiced fears that supporting data might be too optimistic. The health of the property tax relief fund could be a relatively short-lived phenomenon. Budget Director Thuma quietly questioned the tone of the program, suggesting that it might represent a departure from what he considered to be the people-oriented atmosphere surrounding the governor and his administration. They were reluctant to confront the governor with these reservations. When Rizzo and I conveyed this information it became clear that Bowen was interested primarily in ensuring that the backup statistics were sound. We did not press the point.

The first major alteration came in the House Ways and Means Committee, which decided to flip the local option provision from a "reverse option" in which the counties had to vote to opt out of the program to a true local option in which they were to exercise the initiative to vote their counties into the plan. Questions about the constitutionality of the former approach were the basis for the change.

The package moved quickly through the House, but it soon became evident that the Senate might consider revisions. The upper chamber's GOP leaders were careful to point out that they could not guarantee sufficient votes for passage. Meanwhile, the administration was considering yet another change, that of replacing a system of "vanishing credits" for sales taxes paid on groceries. This refinement first was suggested by Gerald Olson, the government affairs representative for the J. Irwin Miller-Cummins interests and a Bowen campaign adviser. Olson indicated that Cummins and a few other private sector interests would be willing to support an increased tax load on business in order to permit a grocery exemption, since it would make the overall program more appealing to the Senate. The governor quickly seized upon the plan and announced his support for it on March 2.

However, the Senate leadership responded rather coolly. Finance Chairman Lawrence Borst said the governor's recommendations would "change the whole philosophy of the tax package."[2] This was a bit far-fetched and hinted at extensive obstacles that would have to be overcome. Borst's committee made a number of alterations that had the effect of scaling down the level of property tax relief from 25 to 20 percent, and gave counties the ability to levy option taxes as low as one-fourth of one percent. The committee restored the circuit breaker provisions which had been dropped by Bowen when he recommended the grocery exemption.

The revised program was accepted by the Republican majority on the Finance Committee and by the GOP caucus on March 6. Borst cautioned that the caucus decision merely gave the committee "direction" on how to proceed with its report. "In no size, shape, way or form did it bind them. . . to putting a red or green light up there," he said.[3]

Senate votes on third reading (final passage) provided one of the most dramatic incidents in years when the four bills were handed down on March 14. The first measure was the local option income tax bill. Lieutenant Governor Orr held the voting machine open for several minutes as tallies switched between red and green. At one point there were enough "no" votes to kill the bill. Senator Leslie Duvall of Indianapolis, a respected conservative who said he had been undecided on his vote two days earlier, took the floor to say: "At some point in time we must relieve local government from the chains and the inequity of sole reliance on the property tax."[4] He would vote aye, he said. Then Senators Charles Bosma of Beech Grove and Leo Sullivan of Peru, both Republicans whose vote recording lights were burning red, switched their levers to favor the legislation. Their changes locked the balloting into a 25-25 tie. Orr closed the machine and quickly announced that he was voting in favor. Dissenting from the governor's position were five GOP senators: Joan Gubbins of Indianapolis, Joseph Harrison of Attica, John Shawley of Michigan City, Robert Sheaffer of Shelbyville, and Earl Wilson of Bedford. All Democrats voted against the bill. With the test vote thus disposed of, the three other bills were handed down and Orr broke three more ties. Bosma told reporters that he had been undecided on the merits of the bills but had decided "if I'd be the one who would prevent them from taking a new approach to taxation, I thought I would not restrict them."[5] Sullivan later said that it had been his intention to vote against the measures unless his vote were needed.

However, the program's hairbreadth survival in the Senate provided no basis for optimism, since it became obvious that both the House and the governor had serious reservations about the Senate's revisions. With the package headed for the uncertain future of a conference committee, several observers began to recite obituaries for the tax relief plan. On March 20 the governor said the Senate had weakened the program. Three days later, Bowen clarified his objections by stating that he could not accept the Senate version because it had reduced the amount of relief and had relaxed the controls.[6] Meanwhile, House Republicans voted to dissent, forcing the issue to conference.

The mood within the governor's office was glum, since Gutman's delay in naming Senate conferees was taken as an unfavorable signal. It was apparent that a great deal of distrust existed between the House and Senate Republican leadership. As the days passed, internal gloom deepened while the Senate continued to drag out the onset of serious negotiations. Styring, meanwhile, had developed a pointedly negative philosophical and cash flow analysis of the package — a conclusion that had a marked effect upon House Speaker Burrous. Thuma was increasingly concerned, in part because legislative preoccupation with tax issues had stalled consideration of a number of fundamental questions surrounding the budget. James Young, the governor's liaison with the Senate, also was losing his enthusiasm.

On March 30 the conferees broke up in disagreement. Bowen advisers met the next day in J.B. King's office to discuss the situation. John Hart, who had shepherded the program through the House, concluded that the package probably was dead but that actions should be taken to protect Burrous, who had gotten very far out in front of his caucus during the process. Thuma, at this point, was prepared to drop the tax program in favor of concentrating on the budget, which he deemed in jeopardy. Only King stood firm for pressing the matter. This group met one day later with the governor. Hart had become more positive. He and King urged that Bowen force the conferees to adopt a report and put it to a vote, irrespective of the outcome. The governor said little, but his determination to make one more attempt was visible.

While these murmurings were rebounding within the governor's office the opponents of the tax package were mounting a furious assault — on it, on the governor, and on others who dared to favor it. Former Governor Whitcomb assailed the program on March 30, contending that the GOP legislators had "lost touch with the public" and that tax restructuring was not necessary.[7] A group called the Taxpayers Lobby of Indiana began a strident campaign against the governor. Its chairman was Herman Andre, an arch-conservative who was functioning as a front man for M. Stanton Evans, editor of the Indianapolis *News*. Evans transformed the editorial pages of the newspaper into a playground for Bowen critics. Cartoons, columns, editorials, and letters reviled both the governor and his restructuring plan. Fortunately for the governor the Andre-Evans tactics became so heavy handed and squirrelly that they lost much of their credibility. Andre, for example, vilified the program as "nothing but a contemptible swindle to pay off Republican party political debts at the expense of the Indiana taxpayers." He also attacked King, the principal legal architect of the plan, by saying that the "gilt-edged corporate clients" of Baker & Daniels, King's law firm, would benefit from the program.[8] The normally composed governor reacted angrily to Andre's charges:

"If you want it straight, it was a big fat lie. You can take the high road or the low road. The high road involves the presentation of facts, correct information, rational debate and argument that is constructive. And the low road involves character assassination, misleading through incorrect data or omission of certain facts.[9]

The governor described King as one "who probably knows more about taxes than anyone in the state of Indiana" — one who should and would be paid for the time he worked with the House Ways and Means Committee to write the legislation.[10]

Gutman was 40 minutes late to a meeting of the governor and the conferees on April 2. Bowen handed them a compromise tax package and told them he wanted the conferees to sign the printed version, recess the legislature until Thursday, and put the issue to a vote Thursday or Friday. It amounted to an ultimatum; the governor was digging in at a critical moment. The president pro tempore couldn't get out of the meeting fast enough. At a news conference later that day Gutman said the Senate conferees would sign the report, but added that he considered the Senate leadership absolved of any responsibility to pass the program.

Bowen's compromise accepted the incremental basis of levying a local option tax (but changed the manner in which the Senate had constructed it), increased the supplemental corporate tax, eliminated certain exceptions to the freeze on property tax levies, and struck out several Senate-passed amendments that would have given school corporations a variety of exemptions from the freeze.

The administration's hopes were shattered on Friday, April 6, when the Senate rejected the conference committee report on the sales tax bill by a 22-28 vote, despite the fact that Lieutenant Governor Orr called a recess and kept the voting machine open for more than an hour. Senators Bosma, Duvall, and Sullivan voted against the bill this time and were joined by Senator John Mutz of Indianapolis. Senator Harrison was recorded in favor, having voted the other way on the March 14 roll call. State Police guarded the chamber during the recess but administration forces were unable to persuade any senators to reconsider their positions.

At this point many observers wrote off the whole issue, although a few lobbyists specualted that other attempts might be made. The mood within the governor's office was grim over the weekend; the consensus was that Bowen had been beaten. Suspicions about the Senate leadership were fueled further when Gutman visited Bowen to offer up a fallback program known as "Plan D". It was a Stan Evans concoction based on a myriad of false assumptions and would have advocated sharp cuts in the budget and the allocation of all federal revenue sharing funds to property tax relief. On the following Tuesday King asked me several questions involving Senate parliamentary procedure and was tenacious in getting answers, which indicated that his interest was more than academic. King's inquiries suggested another attempt to enact the bills.

Burrous pledged a last ditch effort to salvage the program,[11] while King and Young began negotiating with senators to change votes. An interesting potential ally then emerged in the person of Democratic State Chairman Gordon St. Angelo, who agreed to pursue Lake County Democrats in hopes of garnering their support. St. Angelo's motives weren't clear, but some surmised that he wanted changes in license branch fee legislation that would bring additional revenue to a badly strapped Democratic State Committee. He also may have wanted to be sure that a program potentially damaging to the GOP was enacted. Administrative lobbying focused on Senators Wayne Townsend, Robert Mahowald, and James Plaskett. On Thursday, April 12, Mahowald met with the governor and pledged his vote. Plaskett followed suit the following morning. Meanwhile, Bowen aides called off dealing with St. Angelo, because he was getting nowhere with Lake County senators and the aides were producing Democrats on their own. Young at this time was holding hands with GOP supporters to insure that there was no fall-off.

The conference report on House Bill 1197, the school formula, was called down that afternoon and prevailed 26-23, with Mahowald and Plaskett joining the Republicans. Duvall, Gubbins, Mutz, Shawley and Sheaffer voted against it. Senator Wilson was absent. H.B. 1133, the control bill, was adopted quickly by an identical vote, as was H.B. 1144, the local option and corporate income tax measure, a few moments later. The final vote was stalled for more than three hours as the leadership worked to keep a reluctant Sullivan in harness and waited anxiously for Wilson's return to assure that Orr would have the opportunity to cast a tie-breaking vote in the event that Sullivan defected. Wilson wandered back into the chamber, saying that he had decided to walk to the Veterans Hospital to see a friend, only to discover that the friend had died. He and Sullivan registered negative ballots, which enabled Orr to cast the deciding vote that made the final count 26-25. The House adopted the conference reports by top-heavy margins — again with only GOP votes. The governor was elated. He told a news conference:

> "At long last, Indiana has a balanced tax structure, a system that restores equity among our taxpayers. We have broken the vicious cycle of property tax increases. We have set the stage for a more rational method of financing education. We have eliminated many of the inequities that have driven jobs out of our state. . . I made a commitment to the people of this state that I would work to achieve visible, substantial, and lasting property tax relief. My administration will live up to this commitment by seeing to it that the system works in the manner it is intended to work.[12]"

Mahowald and Plaskett were soundly abused by the Democratic leadership, and charges of deal-making were hurled with a good deal more abandon than the circumstances justified. Speaking of his meeting with Mahowald, Bowen said that the senator asked him to restore funding for the Northern Indiana Crippled Children's Hospital, a point on which both agreed because it was in line with one of the governor's campaign promises. Bowen also said he assured Mahowald that he would make an effort to insure that the South Bend bypass project moved forward. Mahowald had made no secret of the fact that he might not seek re-election in 1974, which freed him to take the political risks associated with his vote. Plaskett faced reporters soon after the vote with this statement:

> I've been on the Budget Committee for several years. Not seeming to be conceited, but I feel I know the finances of the state about as well as anyone connected with it anymore. I've been there that long. The budget is in bad shape. We've got state obligations and we need the money. We got revenue sharing, which should help out considerably. I'm not satisfied with this tax package, never have been. But the tax package is no more the same now as the first time I voted against it. It is better than what we had. And it's a start to get some tax reform.[13]

Plaskett's eventual appointment to the Public Service Commission was taken as a sign that a bargain had been struck, but I have discovered nothing that would detract from the governor's insistence that he made no promises. Those who believe otherwise overlook several points. Plaskett was concerned about property taxes — as holder of extensive farm acreage he was in a position to recognize the consequences of failing to control them. More importantly, the senator traditionally had functioned as the intermediary between Senate Democrats and Republicans. He often was the mediator of partisan disagreements and frequently was the architect or engineer of political compromises. The vote was not out of character. Finally, Plaskett — one of the shrewdest operatives in the upper chamber — no doubt saw the advantage of forging an alliance with a governor who likely would be occupying that office for the duration of Plaskett's active political career. Under the circumstances, Otis Bowen was the best possible person to owe him a favor.

As it turned out both Plaskett and Mahowald were punished by their party at the polls and denied renomination.

Bowen signed the tax package into law on April 24. The Taxpayers Lobby subsequently filed a court challenge, but was unable to delay its imposition and finally lost the case. Andre quickly faded from the headlines.

Another controversial issue facing the lawmakers in 1973 was that of wiretapping. The governor was uncertain until the final days of the session whether to sign a bill that would have permitted the surveillance by police of any oral communication. It would have required approval by a justice of the Indiana Supreme Court upon application by a county prosecutor. Within the staff, Rizzo and I were the most vocal against it, while Lloyd and DeBard were defenders. On April 25 a contingent of law enforcement representatives joined the staff meeting to argue in its behalf. They included Attorney General Sendak, State Police Superintendent Konkle, and Marion County Prosecutor Noble Pearcy, and his chief trial deputy,

Leroy New. They did not make an effective presentation; after their departure the four staff members again argued the issue. The governor resolved it by asking me to draft a veto message. He rejected the bill that afternoon, pointing out that the proposal was less restrictive than federal procedures, that it would permit electronic eavesdropping in all felony cases, and that disclosure of information obtained as a result of wiretap surveillance could occur in a civil suit. His message read, in part:

> I am as dedicated as anyone to the need for bringing criminals to justice. But serious doubts exist as to the scope of this bill, the potential for infringing upon the rights of innocent citizens and the role of electronic surveillance in obtaining convictions. I believe that a tightly restricted wiretap bill — with severe penalties for abuse — could be applied to the fight against organized crime and narcotics traffic. I believe it was the intent of this bill's advocates to use wiretapping and other forms of electronic surveillance toward these specific objectives. I applaud that intent, but in my opinion the proposal is much broader than that.
>
> Events of the past few years, including leaks from the grand jury investigating the Watergate affair, indicate that the ability to maintain confidentiality of information is very much open to question. Statistics show that four of every ten eavesdropped conversations are entirely innocent in nature.[14]

Although the governor harbored a number of reservations about the idea of Sunday liquor sales, he had indicated that he would enable a tightly restricted proposal to become law, although he might not sign it. The liquor bill proved to be one of the more controversial debates of the 1973 session, and the governor wavered on a number of occasions. Supporters argued that it was needed to stimulate convention business in the state. Bowen finally agreed to let it become law without his signature after closely reviewing its contents with Alcoholic Beverage Commission Chairman James Sims. He became convinced that it was, indeed, restrictive, and that the commission still would retain the power to interpret its provisions in a very conservative manner.[15] Also enabled to become law minus Bowen's signature were measures restoring capital punishment and regulating abortion. Bills dealing with no-fault insurance, the Equal Rights Amendment, and a repeal of the phosphate detergent ban never reached his desk. However, the session was noteworthy in that it adopted a number of social measures, including broadened rights for 18-year-olds, an "irretrievable breakdown" divorce law, and collective bargaining for teachers.

The General Assembly also approved a record $4.37 billion biennial budget which included substantial increases for local schools. It earmarked about $293 million for welfare programs and $770 million for streets and roads. Nearly $45 million was allocated for increased state employees merit wage increases. The Vietnam veteran's bonus also was approved. Construction funds for river ports at Jeffersonville and Mt. Vernon, the state library addition, State Fairgrounds improvements, and a new National Guard armory at Indianapolis also were included.

The final bills were acted upon the morning of April 26. The governor celebrated in a rather low-key manner the winding down of what for him had been a politically crucial session. The Bowens, the Rizzos, and I adjourned to Brown County State Park for an afternoon of mushroom hunting and an evening of quiet conversation at the Aynes House, the gubernatorial retreat within the park.

Although the political consequences of the tax package were yet unknown, the 1973 session was a striking achievement for Otis Bowen. His patience and determination in pursuing his principal policy objective won out. In the process he established himself as the leader of the Republican party. Never again would the party's conservative wing mount a serious challenge to him. Bowen demonstrated that he was tough enough to rule, laying to rest the long-standing doubts of many politicians that he had what it took to be an effective governor. The insinuations of deal-making, made much of by his opponents at the *Star* and *News*, actually helped the governor's reputation with political professionals because they understood the use of political muscle. They at least thought they saw these tactics employed by him during the crucial maneuvering that resulted in the adoption of the tax program. Finally, Bowen bested the Indianapolis newspapers — historical foes of his tax policies — and earned their grudging respect.

Had Bowen failed in the 1973 session, the administration might have taken a far more somber turn. Political mischief had become a way of life in recent years within the GOP and certainly would have continued if the outcome had been adverse. On a day late in the session, on which it appeared that the tax package was dead, his advisers gathered to begin drafting an alternative strategy to salvage the administration. Given the climate, they concluded that, while possible, it would be difficult to rebound from such a setback. Instead of a governor in command, we would have had a governor beleagured.

VI THE WATERGATE YEAR

The crippling of the national Republican administration after recurring revelations of White House wrongdoing in connection with the Watergate scandal provided the dominant political theme for the second year of Bowen's administration. It was a period in which the governor, like the vast majority of Americans, was a perplexed and troubled bystander to an unprecedented national drama.

Always a team player, he wanted to give President Nixon the benefit of the doubt. In the early months the governor was cautiously supportive. As negative evidence accumulated, he began to harbor serious doubts about the President's fitness to remain in office, but was careful to keep these sentiments to himself. During the early stages of the scandal, disdain for what he deemed to be harassment by congressional Democrats overshadowed his reservations about Nixon. To Bowen, the affair had turned into a witch hunt. With characteristic restraint, he responded to ever-more-frequent disclosures of malfeasance.

> Watergate must be laid to rest. All facts must be laid bare. All wrongdoing must be identified and illegal acts must be differentiated from exercises of poor judgment. There is a proper process for this; it is a legal one, but it often moves with exasperating slowness. However, there is nothing so urgent that demands the abandonment of ethics.[1]

In May, 1973, he answered reporters' questions about the besieged national administration by saying that Nixon should not resign. It still would be possible for the President to lead the nation, "providing everyone quits prejudging him before all the facts are known."[2]

Privately, Bowen parted company with the national administration in the autumn of 1973. Vice President Spiro Agnew's resignation after pleading "no contest" to income tax evasion charges, followed closely by the so-called "Saturday night massacre," in which Hoosier Deputy Attorney General William Ruckelshaus was a casualty, produced this hardening of attitude. Although any likelihood that the administration would be vindicated receded almost weekly, Bowen maintained silence and still nurtured hope that the situation might take a more favorable turn.

The governor remained patiently quiet through the spring of 1974 and publicly broke with the President only days before Nixon's nationally-televised resignation speech. When the White House admitted on August 6 that the President had attempted to thwart an FBI inquiry into the scandal, Bowen voiced his first on-the-record expression of concern.

> "What can you say — other than express bitter disappointment. The opportunities now, I think, are narrowed down to resignation; or going ahead with the trial and being declared guilty by the Senate, at least on that one count; or the possibility of being found not guilty of the impeachable offense and continuing as usual; or the possibility that he step aside while all this is going on and let the Vice President take over until the trial is all settled. I personally, besides feeling very disappointed, feel bad inside, feel like I've been wounded."[3]

The governor expressed no preference among these courses of action, although reporters were badgering him to come out in favor of resignation. Bowen said only that he hoped Nixon "takes into account the best interest of the nation and of all Americans."[4] With regard to the outcome of a trial, the governor reasoned, "If this is the final bit of evidence, I would say it would be very difficult, with that admission, for any senator not to agree with the first [impeachment] article."[5]

On the night of August 8, Bowen and Senate candidate Richard Lugar sat in easy chairs near the governor's desk to watch the final act of the resignation drama unfold on national television. Newsmen gathered nearby. The governor fidgeted in his chair, scratching nervously under his chin and clutching a folder holding the statement he would make.[6] After it was over he told reporters, "I'm glad to see the affair ending. . . resignation proved that no man is above the law."[7]

He recommended no further action against the deposed chief of state. Loss of the presidency was enough punishment.

What was to become a political love affair with the new president, Gerald Ford, blossomed rapidly. He told newsmen, "I am very impressed with his down-to-earth, conscientious, deliberate method of doing things."[8] When Ford solicited recommendations for a vice-president, the Hoosier governor responded with a short telegram nominating Ruckelshaus, Defense Secretary Melvin Laird, China Ambassador George Bush, and Governor Robert Ray of Iowa.[9] Ford's choice of Nelson Rockefeller was accepted gracefully, since Bowen had developed an admiration for the New York governor's brilliance during sessions of the National Governors' Conference.

The new president's quick pardon of Nixon caught him by surprise. "My first impression is that it's a little bit early, but I don't want to second guess President Ford," Bowen said. "Could there be a fair trial anyplace? It would be difficult to find jurors who had not made up their mind previously one way or another."[10] Ford should have waited a few weeks, the governor believed. In any case, the President's decision spared the nation and the Republican party the agony of a drawn-out, bitter trial that would have become a televised orgy for Democrats and Nixon's media critics.

Although the trauma of Watergate and the Arab oil embargo obscured most other occurrences, the second year of Bowen's administration was significant in a number of respects. For the second time in its history the General Assembly met in the short, even-year session. An administration now fully settled into office was given its first real opportunity to put an imprint upon a broad-range legislative program. The year also was the testing time for the governor's newly enacted property tax relief program. Finally, a crucial off-year election loomed in the autumn.

Legislators gathering at Indianapolis were given a moderate administration laundry list of programs and projects, but one that had broad appeal and helped cement the new governor's standing with the public. Comforting, too, was the financial outlook; 1973 had been a boom year for the state's economy. Personal income had ballooned at a more rapid rate than in any year since 1951. Unemployment had dropped by more than a full percentage point to 3.7. This favorable economic news also meant that a modest state surplus would be further strengthened.

Only minor adjustments to the operating budget were recommended, amounting to $2.7 million and largely offsetting unanticipated increases in the cost of food and fuel for state institutions. The capital budget, however, was designed to accelerate several agency construction programs and begin momentum in new areas. The largest single item was $16 million for a sweeping modernization of the state's park and recreational system (a subject treated fully in another chapter). More than $4 million was advocated for the mental health system to enable each of the state's hospitals to meet fire, safety, and health codes. Additional sums were earmarked for repair and rehabilitation. More than $1 million was identified for capital improvements to maximum security facilities at prisons and to upgrade the training installation at the Indiana Boys' School. Although the assembly trimmed $3 million from the capital program for natural resources, the administration's budget requests were accepted with little controversy.

One innovative plan involved legislation to accelerate the completion of Indiana's interstate highways. Advanced by State Highway Commission Chairman Richard Boehning, it was a simple but unusual approach. The state's Arterial Road and Street Fund carried balances substantially in excess of current requirements. Meanwhile, certain federal aid funds were obligated to Indiana — but would not be conveyed until later. By making a loan of $15 million from the arterial fund and paying it back over a period of time with federal appropriations, the state could complete most interstate system projects in four years instead of ten. In doing so, the state would save $40 million otherwise consumed by inflation if the original timetable had been adhered to. After a few adjustments to resolve uncertainties among legislators, the accelerated interstate program was signed into law by Bowen on February 17.

Another gubernatorial priority involved emergency medical services. A statewide plan for emergency treatment for accident victims had been prepared in 1969, but little visible progress had taken place since then. Bowen's natural interest in devising a more responsive capability to handle the more than 190,000 persons who suffered accidents each year was given an added boost by the fact that federal highway regulations required an EMS program. Within a short time Indiana might face financial penalties in the form of reduced highway aid allotments.

The administration created regulations and a training program for EMS personnel. After the law's enactment by the 1974 legislature, the Emergency Medical Services Commission began an ambitious program of training and certification of ambulance personnel; integrated communications and response systems of law enforcement, ambulance providers, and hospitals; channeled aid money for local purchases of EMS equipment, and set standards for the type and availability of emergency medical hardware. Occasionally, the undertaking proved controversial because it cut across a number of local "turf" considerations, while operators complained that standards established for ambulances were too inflexible. By the end of Bowen's term, however, the majority of Indiana counties had developed EMS systems under centralized management and more than 9,000 technicians were trained and certified.

The 1974 General Assembly also appropriated $2.2 million for development of the Clark Maritime Centre on the Ohio River; a supplemental funding program for schools, especially those in financial straits; money to pay for the fuel allocation program operated by the State Energy Office during the oil embargo; nearly $3 million for State Police construction projects, and more than $4 million for the construction of new mental retardation and mental health centers.

Few issues divided a legislature heavily dominated by Republicans. The governor prevailed on almost every item on his agenda and the session was the least controversial one during his eight years in office.

When Hoosier property taxpayers received their May, 1974, bills, much of the initial hostility to the governor's tax restructuring program of the previous year began to evaporate. Citizens had been paying higher sales taxes since May, 1973, but now saw tangible results of the Bowen plan. Tax bills were cut by 20 percent statewide. In counties adopting the local option income tax, reductions approached 30 to 35 percent. The health of the state's economy, reflected in larger revenues from the sales tax, permitted advance distributions of property tax relief entitlements to counties on a stepped-up schedule. Nearly $18 million had been disbursed in February to help cities, town, and schools that otherwise would have been forced to borrow money to meet expenses until May property tax collections began to roll in. Units of government which did not require the advance draw to meet cash flow requirements were able to invest these funds.

As spring gave way to summer, Bowen and other Republicans turned to campaigning. Apprehensive about the November outlook because of continuing and damaging fallout from the Watergate affair, they went out of their way to disassociate Indiana Republicans from the national scandal and the deposed president who had become badly tarnished because of it. The governor observed that the only Hoosier involved — Ruckelshaus — had been one of its victims. Watergate, he argued, would be damaging to the party only if its adherents allowed themselves to become numbed and dispirited. Campaign polls were inconclusive with regard to the senate duel between incumbent Birch Bayh and Indianapolis Mayor Lugar.

Lugar had troubles of his own. Beginning in February, front pages of the Indianapolis *Star* trumpeted allegations of widespread corruption in the Indianapolis police department. The series, which later earned the newspaper a Pulitzer prize, was the product of a six-month investigation into bribes and protection for illicit activities. The GOP senate candidate was compelled to whittle his campaign schedule in order to deal with the crisis. Bowen defended the mayor. "He is a man of integrity and I know that if this is going on, he is embarrassed and I think he will be acting vigorously to correct it." the governor stated.[11]

It was to no avail. Nixon's resignation, Ford's hasty pardon, and the taint of corruption in Indianapolis brought disaster to the GOP in the November balloting. Bayh edged Lugar by 71,000 votes as the mayor slumped badly in his home city. A congressional delegation that had numbered seven Republicans and four Democrats flip-flopped as five GOP incumbents were tossed out of office. Diehard Nixon supporter Earl Landgrebe was dumped, as was pro-Nixon House Judiciary Committee member David Dennis. Congressmen William Hudnut and Roger Zion were overwhelmed in the Democratic tide. Most surprising was the ousting of twelve-term Representative William Bray, unseated by the youthful David Evans in his second challenge to the veteran congressman. The 71-year-old Bray, who had hammered Evans by 50,000 votes two years earlier, simply had stayed too long.

Worse for Bowen was the fact that the Indiana House, which had been 73-27 Republican, turned over to the opposition by a 56-44 margin. Republicans barely held the Senate, 27 to 23. Democrats also re-elected four Statehouse officials. Larry Conrad's defeat of William Allen in the secretary of state's race reinvigorated what had been sagging political fortunes, and

Conrad now seemed positioned to take on the governor in 1976. State Treasurer Jack New defeated Michigan City Mayor Randall Miller, while Auditor Mary Aikens Currie disposed of Jean Merritt, all by margins in excess of 100,000 votes.

Political observers then forecast trouble for Bowen's property tax relief program. But their judgments proved to be premature, for tax relief already was locked into voters' consciousness after two installments of reductions. Thoughtful Democrats weren't about to dismantle it. Newly elected House Speaker Phillip Bainbridge was quick to say that Democrats "are not going to do anything that raises property taxes."[12] His party would focus on increasing contributions from business taxpayers and, perhaps, consider adjustments to the local option tax that might give cities more freedom to spend. Despite the GOP electoral disaster, the governor by this time had overcome the principal hurdles standing in the way of his favorite undertaking.

VII

TROUBLED AGENCIES — PART ONE

State government is difficult to manage, if for no reason other than the diversity of services it provides Indiana's citizens. Although there is much it could learn from the private sector, those who advocate "running state government like a business" ignore its purposes, the reality of its organization, and the pressures which are brought to bear upon it. A private corporation would never entertain a 150-member board of directors (the legislature), nor would it institutionalize two warring political parties. Unlike private enterprise, state government has few clearly definable and measurable objectives. There is no profit motive or "bottom line" upon which to gauge its proficiency. Re-election is the only meaningful yardstick of accomplishment. Public officials talk in terms of efficiency, responsiveness to needs, and quality of service — abstractions that are difficult to quantify. A change of political parties can result in an expensive change of priorities.

In spite of these obstacles to quality performance, a number of governmental functions are carried out efficiently and non-controversially. Others seem to be chronically troublesome. Still others whose functions are relatively insignificant in terms of the overall operation can achieve notoriety far in excess of their normal role because of scandal or disagreements with constituent groups — all in the era of television, which dotes upon confrontation politics and picket lines.

While Bowen's administration faced a number of unique and widely-publicized issues, it is fair to say that its administrative challenges were not extraordinary. A number of weak points, notably in mental health and corrections, were identified as the result of controversies or incidents which exposed major deficiencies in their operations.

Surprisingly, the one state department that had been a long-standing troublemaker functioned with relatively little controversy during Bowen's two terms. Observers often had joked that the party losing an election should be compelled to run the Bureau of Motor Vehicles, a running sore of citizen complaints and journalistic wrath. Fortunately for the new governor, his predecessor's administration had undertaken a number of reforms that modernized its operations. Its new commissioner, former Shelbyville Mayor Ralph VanNatta, was adept at working with county chairmen who ran the license branches. Previously, the bureau had been a liability to governors. This was not the case during the 1970s.

It is difficult at times to separate stupidity from malfeasance or bad judgment from more sinister motives. Typically, Bowen dealt with allegations of impropriety that might involve violation of laws by ordering State Police or State Board of Accounts investigations. Infrequently, the governor's personal staff might supervise an inquiry if it seemed that poor management or inadequate judgment might be the culprit. Although his administration had its share of problems, the governor generally came off favorably in the public's eye because he was quick to acknowledge them and to react when others brought tangible accusations to his attention.

The administration's first encounter with internal problems occurred in March, 1973, after disclosures that a deputy insurance commissioner had authorized a $76,000 refund to a Virginia title company for overpayment of taxes. Normal procedures had not been followed. A State Police investigation revealed no basis for bringing action against the official, but the governor fired the deputy. Another deputy offered his resignation. Although no case had been made against Insurance Commissioner Oscar Ritz, gubernatorial assistant William Lloyd, who had joined in the departmental investigation, persuaded Bowen that the commissioner did not seem to be in control of his agency. The governor then asked for Ritz's letter of resignation. It was the first of several often unpleasant critiques of the performance of state agencies.

MENTAL HEALTH

The Bowen administration's first strong indications that things were not well within the state's mental health system were revealed in June, 1973. Front pages of the Indianapolis *News* were splattered with exposes of patient mistreatment, theft, unsanitary conditions, and lack of professional care at Central State Hospital. The stories created a furor. Bowen moved speedily to confront the issue and named a special investigating team to conduct a thorough inquiry. It was directed by gubernatorial assistant William Lloyd and office management consultant James Smith. State Police investigators were attached to the probe.

Their findings were disturbing. Buildings and grounds were cluttered with litter; cottages, restrooms, and maintenance areas were filthy; window ledges were layered with pigeon excrement; security was almost non-existent. Aging buildings were falling apart, and there was little evidence of a maintenance program. Hospital management gave little indication that it even was attempting to operate the institution; no one seemed to be in charge of anything. Although a modern structure that would replace many of the worn-out facilities was near completion, investigators warned that it soon would fall into disrepair unless the quality of supervision changed dramatically. The group also recommended the replacement of physicians who had been on lengthy medical and educational leaves.

By the time Bowen dedicated newly completed patient care units at Central State on September 10, 1973, the institution's most glaring defects had been corrected. The governor outlined his goal of full accreditation for all of Indiana's mental health institutions. To do so would compel an intensive program of capital improvements and an expansion of medical and professional care.

The Central State incident was only one of several that underscored fundamental management deficiencies within a state mental hospital system that was undergoing important changes. Although a number of management and personnel alterations were completed during Bowen's governorship, the administration remained unconvinced that the leadership of its mental health system grasped the fundamentals of what it took to operate a multi-million dollar network of capital facilities.

The system was inherently faulty, but difficult to change. By law its top officials were required to be medical and psychiatric professionals. Few would quarrel that overall departmental policies should be set by people with these backgrounds. Moreover, the development and implementation of patient treatment programs properly were their province. Day-to-day operations of hospitals, kitchens, laundries, and living units were another matter entirely. Little in the training of psychiatry gave one a foundation in the management of facilities, dollars, and people. Yet it was in this category that the Mental Health Department faced its greatest shortcomings.

Attempts to improve the system met with stiff resistance. Suggestions that requirements for certain administrative positions be revised to make room for people trained in management rather than mental health were met with hostility. The mental health lobby was quick to accuse the state of trying to turn the system over to political hacks and to revert to an era of snake-pit mental institutions. Influential with the General Assembly, the mental health association had tunnel vision. It perceived progress primarily in terms of ballooning legislative appropriations, and responded venomously if lawmakers had the temerity to set budgets at levels lower than requested. Unfortunately, its membership failed to comprehend that many of their objectives for improved patient treatment would have been met if existing appropriations had not been diluted by inefficiency.

At times there were clashes over philosophy. Perhaps most irritating to the governor was the matter of security. He had no fundamental disagreement with Mental Health Commissioner William Murray that institutions should maintain an atmosphere of openness; it was far more therapeutic if patients did not consider themselves to be prisoners. The fact that patients were departing by the hundreds annually indicated that conditions had gotten out of hand. The governor's discomfort increased when Murray characterized escapes as "being off-campus" or "elopements". (When Ray Rizzo first heard the latter description he assumed that two inmates had run off to get married.).

Bowen complained that fully open institutions were dangerous. Wandering inmates were easy prey. Hospitals were vulnerable to penetration by thieves — or worse. Some inmates represented real threats to outsiders. The governor insisted upon greater emphasis on institutional security, and the escape rate diminished.

Another source of discontent was the department's attitude toward certain categories of inmates. Of special concern were criminal sexual psychopaths. Under state law a defendant adjudged to be a criminal sexual psychopath — usually as the result of a rape trial — was ordered to the custody of the Department of Mental Health, instead of to confinement at a state penal institution. The law was flawed, as was the attitude of mental health administrators. It did not effectively deal with the consequences of a departmental determination that a convict was untreatable. If psychiatrists reached that conclusion, it was presented to the sentencing judge. Judicial acceptance of this finding meant that the prisoner went free. In one celebrated case in 1976 an inmate who had committed more than a score of rapes was referred back to the judge as untreatable. Although psychiatrists warned that he would commit other rapes if released, it appeared that mental health officials only wanted to be rid of a problem patient and were oblivious to the implications. The governor's office intervened after it learned of this from an Indianapolis *Star* reporter. The staff was furious that the Department of Mental Health had not provided advance notice of their intent to dispose of the patient. Public safety officials could have made arrangements to use another device to hold on to him. The man was an acknowledged psychopath; the public was entitled to protection from him. Two days of frantic maneuverings resulted in a solution that kept the convict within state custody. Eventually, CSP sentencing provisions were altered to address this problem. The incident underscored the air of unreality that pervaded the atmosphere of mental health operations.

The economics of running a mental health system were further warped by an earlier legislative decision to emphasize community mental health centers dispersed around the state in lieu of the traditional handful of state hospitals. This transition was a matter of state policy. Community centers afforded treatment in a hometown environment closer to families. It was generally accepted that they were superior locales for care and rehabilitation in all but the most difficult cases. When Bowen took office there were eight community-based centers which received state support amounting to about $2.5 million annually. When he left the Statehouse the number had grown to 28 and the budget commitment had climbed to more than $33 million.

A corresponding decline in patient populations at state hospitals occurred during this period. A July, 1971, census placed patient numbers at 10,601. By June, 1980, the population had slumped to 4,941 — fewer than half.

The state was maintaining substantial excess capacity. However, proposals to close state hospitals were met with bitter resentment. Patients who could not be absorbed into community institutions faced relocation to state hospitals further removed from their families. Legislators and local officials viewed hospitals as community economic assets — sources of jobs. While state government understood the value of its hospitals to their hometowns, the overriding priority was that of managing a soundly-functioning mental health system. It was a difficult notion to sell. Only Norman Beatty Hospital at Westville was removed from the system during the Bowen Administration. Its maximum security unit was absorbed by the Department of Corrections.

Although the state's commitment to mental health care intensified during the 1970s and the quality and diversity of patient care were improved, management shortcomings were not brought under control. When governor-elect Orr's transition team met with representatives of the outgoing administration in November, 1980, Bowen's advisers were forced to concede that the mental health department still operated far below the attainable standard of proficiency. They also acknowledged that the existing management of the department was unequal to the task required of it.

CORRECTIONS

Leadership problems in the early 1970s magnified the already burdensome responsiblity of managing a prison system that is state government's most unpopular obligation. Although Indiana's Constitution stipulates that rehabilitation is the only purpose of its penal institutions, that dictate had been met only infrequently throughout the state's history. The prison system had little in the way of a built-in constituency; it was far more appealing for legislators to vote dollars for parks, education, or highways. Money for prisons never kept pace with needs.

Many citizens still cling to a belief that prisons are for punishment and that barbed-wire walls should shield the law-abiding from the "criminal element." The constitutional mandate itself seems rather naive, for many of the inmates in maximum security units at the Michigan City state prison reasonably cannot be considered rehabilitatible under a rational societal concept of that term. Corrections institutions are volatile, troubled places. Confinement even under the most favorable conditions is sufficient to engender discontent. Personal attitudes that brought men and women to prison further inflame the atmosphere. Cramped conditions and racial hatred add to the tension. Maximum security cellblocks contain men serving multiple life terms for murder; they have nothing to lose. Further killings and maimings can only result in additional inconvenience. They do not alter the basic fact that these inmates have no hope, and that wardens and guards have little leverage to prevent further outrages.

Prison disorders are the worst challenges faced by a governor. Even the most cool, evenhanded, and responsible attitude cannot insure a favorable outcome. The public wants swift, punitive action. Yet, if hostages are taken — either prisoners or guards — the overriding objective must be that of securing their release. Prison officials can offer few inducements to hardened men. Any compromise that results in the saving of life is liable to be greeted with scorn from second-guessers far removed from the crisis.

Rebellious state prison inmates, numbering in the hundreds, took three prison guards hostage on Labor Day weekend in 1973. They presented 25 demands for improved conditions as a condition of freeing the hostages. Bowen responded that he would not initiate reprisals if inmates released the guards unharmed and did no further damage to the institution. The governor's use of the word "reprisals" was calculated. The rioters sought full amnesty. Bowen and corrections officials wanted to be able to bring action against ringleaders at a future date. However, the governor's subtlety was lost on most reporters, who characterized his stance as one offering amnesty.

The hostage incident became a waiting game. It was difficult to consider storming cellblocks because the doors opened inward and had been barricaded. Prison guards effectively were locked out of cellblocks to which only they had the keys. Negotiations moved slowly because the state was unwilling to make any significant commitments until the guards were freed. As the hours passed, inmates became weary of the disruption. Prison officials received indications that the disorder could end if a way were found to release the guards in a manner that would not be accompanied by bloodshed.

Inmate leaders wanted television reporters present during the exchange to witness any reprisals against rioters. Prison officials were less than enchanted with this suggestion. The presence of newsmen — especially those armed with cameras — might be inflammatory. Furthermore, news reports of activities inside the prison would be known to inmates who possessed radio and television sets. A reporters' pool was created and observed the guards' release on Monday, September 3. The 35-hour incident ended peacefully, although heavy damage had occurred within the three cellblocks involved.

Several groups credited Bowen for his restraint in handling the matter. However, Warden Russell Lash had been at odds with the governor and Corrections Commissioner Robert Heyne on several occasions during the uprising. Lash had friends at the Indianapolis newspapers and conveyed his criticisms to them. The editorial page of the Indianapolis *News* poured heavy criticism upon Bowen and accused him of coddling the inmates. In a subsequent interview with a reporter from that newspaper, the governor commented, "I do find it difficult to comprehend that some editorial writers and cartoonists seem to believe the only way to resolve a prison disorder is to litter the cellblocks with corpses."[1]

Leadership problems within the department surfaced during the riot's aftermath. Lash attempted to bring reprisals against several inmates, forcing the governor to countermand the warden's administrative decisions. Relations between Heyne and the warden were icy. The commissioner was noticeably absent from the controversy after the riot ended, having gone off to "inspect" other corrections facilities while the governor and his staff attempted to sort out a number of problems. Both Heyne and Lash lost stature with Bowen over their handling of the affair. Lingering sniping between the two corrections officials became regular fare for news stories that autumn. Problems involving Lash ultimately were resolved when Oklahoma approached him with an offer to head its corrections department. The governor gave the warden a glowing recommendation in hope that he would depart. Lash took the job.

A number of modernization projects were completed at the Michigan City institution, including the remodeling of cellblocks and the establishment of a medical team to provide better treatment of inmates. A new warden, Leo Jenkins, was able to reduce tensions, although the institution continued to smoulder. Rival gangs quietly battled for control of cellblocks and the widespread traffic in illicit drugs. On one occasion a small group of inmates succeeded in taking the warden and his family hostage for several hours. In September, 1975, two inmates armed with knives held six hostages in the prison hospital, but released them a few hours later.

The practice of using minimum security work details at the state farm and other institutions was discredited on December 26, 1974. State Police surrounded a frame farmhouse in northern Indiana, where an escapee from a minimum security work detail had stolen a handgun from a prison farm supervisor and taken a mother and two daughters hostage. The convict, Riley Moses, also known as Riley Moseley, Jr., killed two of the women after an eight-hour standoff. Coming on top of several other less publicized incidents, the Moseley episode convinced the governor that fundamental problems existed with respect to security at state penal institutions.

A special task force on institutional security, chaired by gubernatorial assistant James Smith, confirmed his concern. One immediate result was a massive cutback in minimum security inmate work details at prisons, the State Capitol, and other locations. Alterations in security policies and correctional officer qualifications and training also resulted from this grim incident.

Lurid descriptions of conditions at the crowded Indiana reformatory were carried by the Indianapolis *Star* in September, 1976, prompting a gubernatorial decision to conduct an investigation into its management. The report concluded that the *Star's* account of conditions was overstated, but that a number of Corrections Department policies were not being carried out at the reformatory. The investigating team built a substantial case for removing superintendent George Phend. Bowen pondered his dismissal. Heyne then told the governor that he would resign if Phend were toppled. Corrections Commission Chairman William Bontrager, who had led the investigating team, said that he would not stand behind the governor if Phend were removed. This left Bowen with no room for maneuver.

An October 7 news conference convened to disclose the investigators' findings was Bowen's most uncomfortable encounter with the media during his eight years as governor. He had been trapped rather neatly by corrections officials into doing little, if anything, about the reformatory situation. His only recourse was to take heat from reporters who questioned him angrily for nearly 30 minutes. As the conference ended, Heyne quietly said to one of his aides, "Well, we survived another one." Jim Smith and I overheard this statement and made certain that the governor was made aware of it. This episode insured Heyne's removal as Bowen reshuffled his administration for the second term.

While many assume that recurring problems within a state corrections system are unavoidable due to the nature of the administrative responsibilities involved, Heyne's replacement by former West Virginia Corrections Commissioner Gordon Faulkner demonstrated that strong leadership could be a powerful influence.

Bowen also shored up his standing with an often-balky corrections commission by naming Daniel Evans, Jr., an Indianapolis attorney and deputy campaign manager, as its chairman. Faulkner and Evans, with backing from gubernatorial assistant Smith, made it plain that they were in charge. Corrections administrators accepted the new situation.

Faulkner moved quickly to carry out a number of personnel transfers. He achieved reorganization without the rancor usually associated with reshufflings that at best were lateral transfers and in some cases amounted to demotions. Capital improvement projects that had proceeded at a snail's pace during the first term accelerated under Faulkner's leadership.

Prison populations mushroomed during the latter 1970s as new provisions of the state criminal code provided automatic and determinate sentencing of felons. Conversion of the maximum security unit at Norman

Beatty hospital to a facility for corrections use was carried out in the face of formidable political obstacles. The administration carefully built its case, battled objections from area legislators, and succeeded in winning approval for the Beatty project.

Few episodes of violence marred the second term, despite a growing prison population. The most abrasive incidents involved disputes with the Justice Department over conditions within the penal system. A federal study, using information that often was years out of date, provided the basis for Justice Department notification that it was prepared to sue the state and force substantial appropriations for modernization. Negotiations proceeded with less than satisfactory results. The federal government seemed determined to proceed against Indiana, irrespective of factual circumstances. Bowen's irritation increased. He accused the Justice Department of negotiating in bad faith. In a letter to Assistant Attorney General Drew Days, the governor described deficiencies catalogued by the Justice Department as "unspecified generalities, and, for the most part, grossly outdated conditions which have been rectified by the Department of Corrections."[2] The governor went on to recount improvements that had been completed, and closed with further criticism.

> I could note many other instances in which there are glaring differences between the department's contentions and reality.
> The issue is rather fundamental. Is the state of Indiana violating the constitutional rights of its corrections system inmates? At this point, the Justice Department has not made its case on that basis but, rather, centers its arguments on conjecture, assumptions, subjective judgments, and just plain bad information.
> I had hoped that the department's attitude would be far more constructive than what has been displayed thus far. Unfortunately, we are fast approaching an impasse which will result in unnecessary court action that, in the end, will be financed by the taxpayers.[3]

Sparring between state and federal officials continued throughout the second term of the administration — but with inconclusive results, other than to require an extensive expenditure of man-hours to duel with the feds. Days threatened at one point to halt the flow of federal funds to Indiana, but didn't carry it out. Attorneys for the Legal Services Organization brought unrelated actions against the state. They were far from resolution when the administration left office.

STATE POLICE

Indiana's State Police are a visible and professional force which enjoys widespread respect — and rightly so. But, the spit-and-polish efficiency of these blue-uniformed troopers masks a department frequently torn by internal factionalism and dissension. Overtime, frequent transfers, unpopular assignments, and only average pay scales are a way of life. While these factors account for some of the department's turmoil, other forces are at work, too. All uniformed organizations — military and para-military — are plagued by at least periodic infighting. Factions can be built around an individual leader or emerge in a geographic region.

Structures such as the State Police seem to be more prone to internal bickering than their civilian counterparts. Furthermore, a trend in the 1970s toward union-like organizations stimulated trooper discontent. Department superiors and many outside observers deemed unionization incompatible with the management style of highly disciplined forces and their formalized chains of command. In addition, law enforcement professionals are inherently distrustful of civilians. This attitude seemed to prevail with peculiar prominence within the Indiana State Police. Intrusions by governors, budget directors, or legislators frequently were met with resentment. Certain types of law enforcement work are more thrilling than others. What was described as a "Starsky-and-Hutch" mindset caused many troopers to prefer drug busts and "sting" operations to the more tedious routine of road patrols and traffic ticket-writing.

One of Bowen's early State Police decisions was to retain Superintendent Robert Konkle. Popular with political conservatives and a sought-after public speaker, Konkle was a visible promoter of the department and its interests. During the early months of the new administration the superintendent confronted several situations whose cumulative effects undermined his standing. Blacks charged that the department was riddled with racism and claimed that no steps were being taken to secure additional minority troopers. Allegations of misuse of a special investigative fund used to buy drugs in evidence-gathering also were made public. A transfer policy adopted by Konkle was assailed. The reassignment of Major Richard Rambo became a focal point of dissatisfaction. Bowen overruled the superintendent and insisted that the State Police Board pass judgment on any involuntary moves. The governor also intervened to block a proposal for a new State Police headquarters building that had been subjected to criticism for reasons of cost. Adding to the potential for disagreement was the presence of former State Police Captain Robert DeBard as the governor's executive assistant for public safety. DeBard's portfolio included liaison with his former agency; he and Konkle occasionally crossed swords.

By July, 1973, these forces combined to produce an uneasy situation within state government. Many Bowen insiders had become convinced that Konkle should go. Several legislators were dissatisfied with his performance. The governor, however, declined to act. He recognized that some of the superintendent's woes were not of his own making. Konkle's standing with the media and conservative politicians also would make it difficult to force a change.

Konkle solved Bowen's problem by announcing his retirement effective

October 1. Pressure may have had something to do with his decision, although the departing chief was careful to say that the action was of his own choosing. "A lot of people may not believe it," the governor said, "but I had nothing to do with it, I am sorry to see him go."[4]

A five-member committee was chosen to make recommendations for a new superintendent. Its screening was limited to active or retired members of the State Police. DeBard chaired the group. After interviewing more than a score of potential applicants, the committee concluded that there were several good candidates, but that none of them appeared able to reverse the department's sagging morale or to confront a series of difficult management decisions. The committee than settled on DeBard.

There were indications that he might have engineered the decision. (For example, three years later another screening committee interviewed many of these officers in a talent hunt for DeBard's successor. Several were found to be well-qualified for the superintendency). Bowen accepted the committee's recommendation. One of its members, James Smith (who succeeded DeBard in the governor's office), later acknowledged to me that the group seemed to be guided by its chairman toward an inevitable conclusion.

The administration then wrestled with the problem of releasing the findings of a search committee that had recommended its own chairman for promotion. Republican State Chairman Tom Milligan proposed that an existing patronage committee of the GOP be used to make the announcement in an effort to divert any heat. I objected to this approach, contending that the public viewed the State Police in a special, non-political context. We would be criticized for seeming to turn the appointment of a State Police superintendent over to the party structure. Bowen agreed with this view, but Milligan became furious. In a brief meeting in Bill Lloyd's office, he shouted criticisms about the meddling of political amateurs and accused me of considering him to be stupid. I said nothing and walked away. This incident spurred a marked deterioration in our relations.

Several reporters questioned the appointive process when the governor announced DeBard's selection on September 27, 1973, but the administration's handling of the affair did not have lasting consequences. The new superintendent took office five days later. A widespread reshuffling of key personnel then occurred, including the reinstatement of Major Rambo as the departmental controller.

DeBard had no better fortune in quieting discontent within the agency. An overhaul of the department's crime information center spurred fresh controversy. Meanwhile, loosely-organized trooper organizations were jockeying to increase their membership within the State Police. One way to stimulate membership was to magnify the impact of existing problems and to identify new ones — real and invented.

A federal court suit over the issue of black recruitment exacerbated morale problems. The acceptance of new trainees was halted while it was in litigation. The ranks of troopers thinned as vacancies caused by retirement went unfilled. Tempers stirred as overtime increased. A preliminary decision by Judge Cale Holder gave the administration flexibility to resolve the matter. The judge found that discrimination existed in hiring and promotion (only three blacks were members of the 945-man force). He ordered corrective action without specifying its direction.

Bowen urged the superintendent to move rapidly to schedule a new trainee class and secure a significant number of black applicants. DeBard countered that this process would be delayed for months because the intelligence tests (which had been a point of dispute in the lawsuit) would require many weeks to validate. He was urged to forget the tests and use an alternate gauge. The governor's office was concerned that the administration might lose an opportunity to resolve the issue on terms acceptable to the state. If it failed, a federal judge might assume practical working control of its police agency. DeBard gave little indication that he understood the significance of these circumstances. Bowen and Smith prodded him to take action.

The final settlement called for 40 percent of each recruit class to be set aside for black applicants until their numbers amounted to seven percent of the department. Existing intelligence tests were scrapped and the department was required to assign black troopers to all areas of the state to give them the expertise necessary to qualify for promotion.

DeBard was unable to pull the department out of its slump. Bowen reluctantly decided that he must be relieved when the second term of his governorship commenced. The superintendent was reassigned as a State Police lieutenant colonel. The governor installed Major John Shettle as his successor. Shettle had been passed over in the screening three years earlier.

The new department leader gained the confidence of the governor and his staff by his method of handling a number of law enforcement problems during the second installment of Bowen's governorship. An August, 1977, package of pay increases and other incentives briefly stilled dissension in the ranks, but a series of personnel problems later reinflamed the situation. Acknowledged as a superior administrator, Shettle suffered from a tendency to come off as rather aloof in dealings with troopers. That trait was seized upon by troublemakers who began a campaign against him. Most vocal in criticism was the State Police Alliance, the most strident of the trooper organizations and one that got off to a terrible start with the superintendent and the governor's office. Even when the organization made reasonable points, it was not well-received because of its reputation for acidity. As Bowen's era ended, his successor faced a rising clamor for Shettle's dismissal.

Governor-elect Orr retained his police chief, in part because of his competence, but also because of a belief that changing personnel by itself would do little to ease the situation. Dissidents soon would turn their fire on anyone who held the superintendent's job.

Despite what appears to be a record of little more than internal friction, the department discharged its responsibilities in a capable fashion during the Bowen years. State Police managed strikes and other disorders with cool efficiency, assimilated blacks and women, renovated police posts, and inaugurated more sophisticated law enforcement techniques. However, the agency's recurring internal troubles lowered its standing with many of the people in power at the Statehouse.

MEDICAL REGISTRATION BOARD

The most bizarre incident of Bowen's first term centered on the strange case of Dr. Robert Hales. It was a potentially explosive and embarrassing affair for the administration and one that forced the physician-governor to take a tough stand against representatives of his own profession.

It was the custom of Indianapolis *News* Statehouse reporter Jack Averitt to drop by the governor's office each morning for coffee and to check for newsworthy items. "Anybody hired or fired?", was his standard opening line. On the morning of July 11, 1975, I was ready with this unusual reaction: "What if I told you that a doctor committed to the mental health system after a sodomy trial later escaped and has succeeded in getting his license back and now has a $26,000-a-year job as a physician at the state prison." Averitt went white.

The governor's office had learned of the situation on the previous afternoon and immediately perceived its implications. Aside from being the type of monumental screwup that delights reporters and is the source of page one material for days on end, the revelation stained what had been one of the governor's initial objectives for the Indiana corrections system. Creation of a medical division within the Department of Corrections had been an often stated priority and Bowen received legislative assent to proceed.

Furthermore, the Hales affair touched upon his own profession. A board of physicians had cleared Hales; a corrections system doctor had hired him. The potential for trouble intensified when, incredibly, the Board of Medical Registration's first reaction was to defend its decision to re-license him. Fortunately, the administration entered the controversy with a distinct advantage insofar as the news media were concerned. We had owned up to the scandal. Bowen immediately ordered executive assistants Rizzo and Smith to conduct an investigation.

Hales had been convicted in 1970 as a criminal psychopath and was committed to Norman Beatty Hospital for treatment. He escaped in 1971, but was recaptured several months later. Another escape occurred in 1973.

While Hales was absent, living in Rhode Island, he petitioned for reinstatement of his Indiana license. The medical board apparently was aware of his conviction, but not his escape. Board members recommended relicensure. One letter of recommendation provided by the applicant, however, had made reference to Hales' walking away from the hospital in 1973, but the board's staff neglected to pursue that clue.

Meanwhile, Dr. Ed Brown, medical director for the Department of Corrections, was looking for doctors for his fledgling program. It was tough going. Work within prison walls is neither appealing nor financially remunerative in terms of physicians' salary norms. Somehow, Brown was made aware that a physician might be available to him — Hales. Following a series of evaluations the board granted a conditional one-year permit with the proviso that Hales practice only within the Indiana State Prison. He went on the payroll on July 1. The Beatty Hospital administrator read a news clipping in the LaPorte *Herald-Argus* announcing the hiring, recalled that Hales was an escapee, and telephoned Mental Health Commissioner William Murray. He then notified the governor's office. State Police removed the errant doctor to Beatty Hospital.

The July 16 report by the governor's assistants recommended severe disciplinary measures against the Medical Registration Board staff for its slipshod handling of the matter. Other recommendations were designed to prevent similar occurrences in the future. Bowen forwarded the report to the board president, Fred Smith, and requested that it act upon the recommendations.

The board then tried to consider the matter in secret session, infuriating reporters. It relented only after I insisted that the meeting be open. Members then voted to take no action against the staff; comments by several doctors indicated a belief that nothing improper had occurred. The governor's staff was flabbergasted and Bowen became irate.

The governor demanded action or resignations. Next day the board reaffirmed its earlier decision to do nothing. Fred Smith, a close personal friend, then offered his resignation. Bowen accepted it. Other members followed suit within two days, as did the Podiatry Board. The governor began to prepare a list of new members, and refilled most vacancies by month's end.

The administration was not scarred by this episode. It had disclosed a problem and had taken proper action. The governor imposed his will upon members of his own profession, which added to his credibility as a leader.

ENVIRONMENT

Burdened with unpopular regulatory responsibilities in a state government traditionally hostile to environmental controls, the anti-pollution divisions of the Indiana State Board of Health struggled through a difficult decade in the 1970s. At times it appeared to be little more than the reluctant agent of a federal government whose sweeping environmental laws and regulations dictated most health department functions. Assailed on the other flank by antagonists in the private sector, who collected supporters within the General Assembly, the agency often found itself starved for funds and without allies at a time when the federal Environmental Protection Agency was spewing forth fresh mandates on wide-ranging fronts.

Infrequently, Indiana had adopted far-seeing environmental management legislation. Its 1967 surface mining reclamation act and subsequent restriction of the phosphate content of laundry detergents were notable examples. Overall, the record was quite conservative, even though a densely populated industrial state of relatively small size was no less prone to pollution woes than its counterparts nationwide. Indiana tried to maintain a traditional approach to pollution management for several years after Congress, embracing the social goals of Lyndon Johnson's Great Society, framed an activist federal regulatory role in air and water quality maintenance.

Continuing control of Congress by advocates of an expansive government involvement in pollution abatement ensured a steady flow of new laws and regulations in the years that followed. A comprehensive Indiana environmental statute was enacted in 1971. Like many new state programs it was subjected to the legislative tradition of initally funding a concept on a limited scale, then allowing the infant to grow to adulthood only if lawmakers were satisfied with its progress.

Throughout Bowen's terms as governor the health agency operated under significant handicaps. Perhaps most serious was that which was implicit in its guidance from the Indiana General Assembly. Lawmakers seemed to be saying, "Do as little as you have to do — just enough to keep the feds off our backs." To insist upon mediocrity is to ensure that it will come to pass. This historic legislative attitude so weakened the administration of environmental programs that Indiana was ill-prepared to cope with the requirements of the 1970s, even on occasions when efficient supervision would have been beneficial to state interests.

The environmental divisions of the Board of Health also lacked a supporting constituency. The Highway Department had the "road gang" — contractors, trucking industry, and motor clubs. The Department of Natural Resources was supported by sportsmen, outdoor writers, and legislators who took pride in projects in their districts. Pollution boards, on the other hand, only attracted critics.

Environmentalists should have been natural allies, but Hoosier conservation groups have not been particularly effective in legislative advocacy. The Natural Conservancy enjoyed the best relationship with the state administration, but its agenda is a limited one — preservation of environmentally significant tracts of land. Largest among the groups is the Isaac Walton League. Its influence was dissipated by the sometimes contradictory goals of its sportsmen members and its environmentalist participants. Moreover, the league's leaders had a reputation for abrasiveness that made state officials reluctant to associate with them. The Audubon Society and Indiana Conservation Council were organizations of stature but their primary concerns were not in the mainstream of issues that dominated the political system in Indiana during the 1970s. Only the League of Women Voters gave evidence of serious interest in some of the financing, structural, and regulatory problems that were at the heart of environmental management disputes during the Bowen administration. This organization's priorities touched several issues and it was unable to marshal sufficient momentum in environmental affairs.

An early administrative hassle brought into sharp focus several federal, state, and local problems associated with environmental improvement. New and upgraded municipal sewage treatment facilities were eligible for federal funding for three-fourths of a project's cost. State and local government shared the remainder. The Environmental Protection Agency regulated these grants and the agency required the states to set priorities for funding. Extensive regulations guided the projects — which required years to complete — through three stages of planning, design, and construction. City governments usually employed engineering firms to write the plans. State government reviewed them and forwarded them to EPA, based upon the priority system established by the Stream Pollution Control Board. EPA then conducted further reviews. Revisions frequently were required, since local governments and their consultants often erred in preparation. A plan might lob back and forth between the consultant and the state, or the state and EPA, several times before it was in approvable form.

There were other complicating factors. Engineering firms designed facilities larger than communities needed, for profits would be increased in subsequent phases. City officials might go along — even if they were aware of the padding — because the completion of a more ambitious improvement program could mean that additional facilities would not be required for many years. Besides, funds might not be available in the future. Although this approach inflated the local cost, the city's share represented only 15 percent of the overall price tag. However, EPA officials were sticky on the point of over-building and were quick to reject questionable proposals.

State health officials were hard pressed to accommodate the volume of business. Tight budgets limited the number of professionals who could sustain the flow of paperwork and projects. The environmental movement had created an economic boom for consultants and engineers. It was a seller's market for professionals as billions of dollars in anti-pollution money flowed through the economy. The onset of the environmental impact statement produced mountains of profitable written reports.

State government's pay scales gradually became uncompetitive. Recruitable engineers and sanitarians were fresh off the campus and required on-the-job training before they became proficient. Many good ones were pirated by consulting firms after state government had financed their apprenticeships. Less experienced state engineers found themselves evaluating the work of more experienced private sector counterparts. Vacancy rates increased for certain critical skills. To resolve the problem would have required state government to pay its pollution staff substantially more money than counterparts in engineering agencies such as the Highway Department. Controversial to begin with, that proposition would have required the endorsement of a legislature reluctant to have the state become more deeply involved in environmental management.

EPA complicated the matter further late in 1973 by requiring the states to adopt new schemes for priority-setting midway in a fiscal year. It was tardy in publishing new regulations to guide the national construction grants program. These factors combined to choke the system. As the June 30, 1974, fiscal deadline approached it became apparent that as many as $15 million in projects might die in the pipeline. The money would have reverted. The state, through Lieutenant Governor Orr, with help from its congressional delegation secured the agency's agreement to enable lower-priority projects that were ready for funding to leapfrog others still in difficulty. The money was obligated in time.

The system continued to clog. In March, 1975, about $84 million in projects were in jeopardy due to delays on the part of consultants, local governments, state government, or EPA. After a crash program to resolve shortcomings at the local and consultant levels, the pace quickened and funds were approved.

This pattern of last minute action continued in succeeding years as federal pollution control allotments grew rapidly. Communities threatened by bans on new sewer hookups hastened to modernize aging systems. However, tighter local budgets in the later 1970s reduced the flow of new projects into the approval process. For the first time the state faced the possibility that some of the entitlement would revert because of the lack of local interest.

A widely publicized air pollution dispute erupted in 1974 when the Justice Department threatened to close down a unit of United States Steel's Gary works because the company repeatedly had not met deadlines for installing modern pollution control equipment. Air quality conditions in the industrialized northwest Indiana region were among the worst in the midwest and federal officials prepared for the first test of the enforcement provisions of the Clean Air Act.

Nine years earlier the company had agreed with the city of Gary to phase in pollution abatement equipment or to retire polluting units. Several deadlines were missed. City and federal officials lost patience. A fourth deadline for bringing into compliance an older hearth — Unit Number Four — was scheduled for December 31, 1974, and the company again said it could not meet it. U.S. Steel had agreed to do so under a federal court consent decree.

Federal officials were stiffening against further delay. If there was to be an extension, the company should be required to pay a fine, they contended. Bowen was dragged into the controversy because the closedown would have left 150 employees without jobs.

The governor stated that Indiana would not stand in the way of an extension if the city of Gary would remove its objections and the corporation and EPA were able to resolve upon a timetable acceptable to the judge. The dispute generated widespread publicity and heavily involved the governor and his staff during the closing days of 1974.

The company was as formidable an obstacle as the Justice Department. Its chairman, Edgar Spear, demanded an extension without a financial penalty. A fine, he argued, amounted to "tribute" to the federal government. As a matter of principle the company would not pay it. The governor's office considered Spear's principle to be a phony one and his attitude unreasonable and arrogant.

On New Years Eve, I became the contact point for a series of telephone calls involving the governor, Spear, Senator Vance Hartke, EPA General Counsel Alan Kirk, and EPA Regional Administrator Francis Mayo. Hartke wanted Bowen to support the company's position. The governor might have done so, were it not for Spear's intransigence. EPA's representatives pointed out correctly that this last-minute exercise was meaningless unless the company petitioned the court for a rehearing. EPA hinted that it was willing to accept compromise as long as the outcome did not represent a complete caving in by the federal government. That would be a bad precedent for future attempts to enforce the law.

The company refused to budge. Despite requests that it take necessary legal steps to reopen the matter for consideration, U.S. Steel's lawyers remained silent. On January 2, Hearth Number Four went cold. Its workers were idled. The abruptness of the corporation's action gave indication to Statehouse observers that its motives might extend beyond those of standing up to federal agencies. Demand for steel had weakened in recent weeks. The dispute gave U.S. Steel a convenient excuse to close an obsolete facility while blaming environmental regulators for the impact. Bowen and his advisers had the uncomfortable feeling that they had been used.

An emotional election-year controversy erupted in 1976 after the disclosure of abnormal concentrations of chemicals known as PCB's in milk and fish in south-central Indiana. Polychlorinated biphenyls had wide applications because they were very stable under a variety of temperature and chemical conditions. These properties made them especially suitable for use in inks, hydraulic fluids, plastic compounds, electrical capacitors and transformers.

Their attributes also were the source of their greatest shortcoming. The compounds would not break down naturally and would remain present in the environment for years. Temperatures in excess of 2000 degrees fahrenheit were required to destroy them. PCB's collected in the fatty tissue of animals and fish and also entered the food chain through soil contamination. When researchers learned that the chemicals could produce a variety of adverse health effects upon humans, their production was halted.

Vast quantities of polychlorinated biphenyls remained in industrial processes and in dumps and landfills, where they could leach into water supplies. In Michigan, hundreds of heavily-contaminated cattle were slaughtered and tons of grain were burned as a result of poisoning by a sister compound, polybrominated biphenyls. Indiana's confrontation with the problem focused on possible discharges by the Westinghouse Corporation at Bloomington and on contamination of grain stored in silos with PCB-treated linings. Milk, fish, and animal samplings showed concentrations of the compound that exceeded federal standards for toxicity.

Nothing arouses the populace more than a food scare. The prospect of milk-dumping and cattle slaughtering gave the PCB issue automatic visibility. The extent of its contamination was worrisome. Would PCB-poisoned farm land be unuseable for decades? Health officials weren't certain.

State and federal officials stepped up testing in order to assess the dimension of the problem. Several herds of cattle were killed. While some milk tanks were dumped, other supplies were converted to skimmed milk, which contained less fat and therefore less contaminant.

A variety of actions commenced against Westinghouse. In general, the concentrations of PCB's in Indiana were far less serious than in the more highly-dramatized incidents in Michigan. After the initial crisis mentality wore off and politicians became weary of berating the subject, a more thoughtful approach to state and national control measures was undertaken. PCB's were destined to acquire enduring status as an environmental issue.

The Board of Health was the target of criticism because it had only limited capability to test and monitor a pollutant about which little was known. The state also was in a quandary because its regulatory authority over stream pollution centered on the individual or corporation that actually discharged the compounds into waterways. A state lawsuit would have been directed against the city of Bloomington, from whose sewer system the PCB's were being channeled to nearby waterways. Democratic gubernatorial candidate Larry Conrad tried to make a political issue out of the problem, contending that the governor's administration had not responded adequately. Conrad was unable to sustain more than brief media or public interest in this point of view.

Another unpopular duty of the environmental divisions of the State Board of Health was that of preparing a new plan for stepped-up regulation of air pollution. It was an outgrowth of the Clean Air Act; the law's provisions were made more stringent in 1977. Unending disputes with industry and local government ensued, because the stakes were substantial. Urban areas faced possible prohibitions against the development of new industry if they failed to meet federal standards. Costly pollution control equipment might be required for power plants and other existing facilities.

Indiana cities and businessmen generally were less than knowledgeable about the sweeping mandate that Congress had enacted. Their first brush with the issue came in encounters with state air quality officials who were caught in the middle. Unfortunately, the state people associated with this planning were technicians who at times appeared to be insensitive and unbending. They were in a no-win situation, in terms of politics or public opinion, and proceeded on a technical basis to carry out their required role.

The intent of the clean air legislation was rather easy to understand; the regulatory apparatus and schemes for implementation were bewildering. Testing was a sore point. EPA would accept only certain approaches to monitoring and modeling. State and private interests countered that other methods of equal validity showed results hinting at less severe problems. It was easy to flunk an air quality test. Windborne pollutants from miles away would adversely affect the monitors at even the cleanest city. The natural emission of hydrocarbons from the swampy borderlands of the Kankakee River would have placed northwestern Indiana out of compliance for this pollutant even if no people lived there.

Businessmen assailed federal insistence that they install expensive equipment of unproven value; EPA officials countered that the private sector was foot-dragging. In the Bowen adminstration's view federal officials often were unreasonable and failed to appreciate the broad-ranging consequences of their attempts to enforce narrow mandates. Business historically had been only a reluctant supporter of pollution control and had little credibility with federal officials and many citizens. Its leaders also seemed blind to the fact that the majority of Americans (in excess of 60 percent in polls taken throughout the 1970s) strongly supported a better environment.

Most of the significant air quality hassles arising from the revised act were resolved — or at least accepted — by the later 1970s. The full effect of the Clean Air Act was not scheduled to be felt until 1982. A change of administrations in Washington further clouded the outlook as to what actually might take place. While the more controversial programs remained in hot dispute, cities and businesses began to implement pollution abatement strategies that would have only a moderate financial and social impact.

WELFARE

Few undertakings of state government produce as much controversy as welfare. The dollar amounts are vast. The delivery system is fragmented among federal, state, county, and township officials. A variety of federal and state agencies is responsible for different pieces of the assistance network. The system seems almost to defy supervision because of its scale, complexity, the required value judgments concerning eligibility, and difficulty in monitoring performance, results, or honesty. Welfare has many critics. Despite a long-standing pattern of governmental commitment to assist the needy, many citizens continue to regard welfare recipients as loafers, bums, and cheaters.

At the outset of his term the governor worried about welfare in terms of finance. Welfare rolls and state-borne shares of their funding were growing at prediction-defying rates. Local welfare shares, generated by property taxes, were becoming increasingly burdensome. Indiana was in danger of losing the bulk of its federal welfare dollars because the state had failed to address numerous "compliance issues" identified by the Department of Health, Education, and Welfare. The state was months overdue in implementing an approved program of screening for welfare applicants and had yet to make an effort to comply with federal welfare control standards. The new chief executive warned the 1973 legislature that the staggering obligations of welfare — which were open-ended in nature — threatened the state's ability to budget within existing revenue sources.

Bowen's decision to appoint Marion County Welfare Director Wayne Stanton to head the state's welfare agency placed a hard-nosed and frequently controversial executive in charge of Indiana's activities. Stanton's intricate knowledge of the complex system was equalled by few officials throughout the country. However, his tough stances on a number of specific issues brought clashes with federal officials, recipients, and the news media. Only the governor's patience with an unbending welfare director enabled Stanton to survive several confrontations that would have tempted other governors to dismiss a subordinate so unwilling to accept direction. Gubernatorial assistants Raymond Rizzo and Brian Bosworth were less fortunate during their respective tenures in discharging their duties of maintaining liaison with the agency. Stanton considered them to be intruders. When disagreements arose, the welfare director occasionally generated letter-writing campaigns from welfare administrators around the state in an effort to diminish their influence with the governor. Considerable tough-mindedness was required, however, to keep welfare programs from bankrupting the treasury. Stanton hung on throughout Bowen's governorship because of his recognized ability to keep costs and programs within reasonable limits.

One early administration initiative brought together the legislature in joint session with the state's congressional delegation, Stanton, and HEW policymakers from Washington. Its purpose was two-fold. One was to acquaint lawmakers with the dimensions of the welfare problem. The other involved the explanation of ways in which Indiana could deal with both the short term considerations of coming into compliance with federal mandates and of devising a long range welfare strategy consistent with the state's revenues. Federal and state legislators gained fresh insight into the problems and the state succeeded in identifying potential solutions to several of the immediate compliance issues.

Results were quick in coming. A statute was enacted enabling the department to adopt a formula to adjust downward the standards used to determine eligibility. Ironically, while Indiana's level of welfare support had been among the nation's lowest, it used among the loosest standards to determine need. The state qualified a great many people for welfare assistance of a relatively low dollar quality — but each recipient received a medicaid card, with its staggering state-borne cost. The formula adjustment, termed "rateable reduction", produced furious debate between Stanton and welfare lobbyists. After prolonged debate and revision, a new formula embracing this concept was adopted.

The state also made significant headway in reducing the error rate in welfare payments. Determining error rates was a rather imprecise art based upon a number of arbitrary judgments. Nevertheless, federal officials stood by this standard of measurement. Prior to the Bowen administration federal estimates of error rates in welfare payments had surpassed 30 percent. In 1973 Indiana submitted a plan to reduce that disparity to eight percent. A number of ineligible recipients were trimmed from welfare rolls and an extensive backlog of welfare appeals was eliminated at a savings of $750,000 in 1973 alone. Regulation of medicaid underwent drastic changes. The state's prompt action removed the threat of federal sanctions.

From time to time the welfare administrator became embroiled in disputes with federal officials who regulated the food stamp program. Critics claimed that Stanton was not making a sufficient effort to advise Hoosiers of the availability of food stamps to the needy. Stanton and the governor failed to see why the state should go out of its way to advertise an expensive program; the truly needy would seek out this assistance, and ambitious informational campaigns would only add to the number of marginal recipients. In time a federal judge ordered the Welfare

Department to develop a program to more fully inform its citizens about the availability of food stamps. Sniping between federal and state officials over the food stamp issue continued throughout his administration.

The most ambitious new welfare program adopted during Bowen's administration was an outgrowth of amendments to federal social security legislation. Known as "Title 20", after a section of the law, its name represented one of those stupid designations used by bureaucrats who never seem to be able to give any program a title that conveys its meaning. Its aim was to enable needy elderly, handicapped, and children address basic living requirements without institutionalization. Such simple issues as the inability to maintain a household, cook, or provide other personal care often impelled elderly and handicapped citizens to resort to institutional care. Title 20 sought to bring these services to them. The scope of the undertaking, begun in 1975, was evidenced by the $70 million price tag for federal and state assistance in its first year. In general, the program functioned smoothly, although Attorney General Sendak was a frequent critic of contracts let with the private sector for in-home social services.

Although welfare costs continued to increase throughout the 1970s, they did so at a more manageable rate. The state's improved handling of its administrative responsibilities corraled what otherwise might have been an uncontrollable function of government.

VIII   ENERGY CRISIS

The energy issue was one of the foremost preoccupations of Bowen's administration. Fuel shortages plagued the state in seven of his eight years chief executive. Four major energy emergencies and dozens of minor episodes commanded his attention. Though energy represented a problem that was far removed from the traditional range of state government activity, its significance insured that Bowen would be one of those held accountable if things went seriously wrong.

Scattered fuel shortages during the winter of 1972 presaged the emergence of the energy crisis as the pre-eminent domestic issue of the 1970s. Cheap and plentiful energy had fueled a prosperous economy and had promoted what seemed to be an ever-improving, uplifting lifestyle for the American household. Shortages — or the threat of shortages — joined with dramatic increases in price to disrupt this economic and social framework to an extent that challenged fundamental beliefs about the way Americans live. The political structure proved ill-equipped to cope with an issue that cut across every facet of American life. Even though energy professionals by the mid 1970s had reached a consensus on solutions, it proved difficult to move them through the political pipeline. Resolution of the energy crisis involved too many controversial, perhaps painful decisions on the part of Congressmen who became ensnared in their own press releases — hasty pronouncements intended to diffuse the heat of the moment and difficult to retreat from, even when the logic of the longer view was overpowering. In time, the majority of politicians assented to policies they earlier had repudiated. The eventual policies represented only a partial fulfillment of the required agenda. The country paid a heavy price for political indecision in wasted years and national treasure. Many who might have put forth the man-hours and dollars to implement solutions instead sat on the sidelines as frustrated observers of the federal government's fumbling confusion.

The energy crisis disclosed how little most politicians and journalists understood the realities of economics. At the same time it exposed economists' ignorance of the political system and of the fact that consumers respond to circumstances other than price and supply. The psychology of the energy crisis for the most part seemed lost on all three groups. The nation frequently ran the risk of some fairly ominous consequences of their failure to appreciate just how badly they were wrenching people's perceptions of lifestyles, hopes for the future, and attitudes toward neighbors down the street. This was the decade in which irate motorists pulled guns on service station operators. Sunbelt cynics coined the slogan "Let the bastards freeze in the dark" in response to the energy woes of their New England brethren. While the Federal Energy Office puttered with fuel allocation rules during December, 1973, Ohio state policemen tear-gassed rioting truck drivers. The omnipresent eye of television magnified modest gasoline shortages into panic situations in which long lines of motorists choked pump lanes at gas stations.

It was simple to cloak oneself in simplistic approaches — nuclear power is the answer; coal is our salvation; run our cars on gasohol; rid ourselves of environmental controls; put solar generators on every urban rooftop in America. Yet an economic element as pervasive as energy and a society as diverse as the United States could not be glued together that simply. But it proved easier for journalists to write about the slaverings of demagogues than the plodding intricacies of economists — the quotes are livelier and it is more fun to take pokes at the system than to ponder constructive solutions lacking in glamor. A number of Indiana Statehouse reporters became quite proficient in their coverage of the energy issue, but their diligence was offset by the gullibility of others in the newsrooms who accepted the glop fed by national sources.

A few politicians believed that they could build reputations on the energy crisis, which accounted for some of the phony bluster. Smart ones sensed that the issue was a loser and adopted defensive positions. Others' energy posturing amounted to little more than taking routine potshots at a vulnerable federal establishment, a strategy hardly calculated to do more than further sour an already bitter climate. In the short run it might be profitable to stir up the mob, but politicians who decide to rile the masses also should be certain that they possess the means to calm the furor.

The Bowen administration became involved in the energy crisis on the day it took office. Its early moves were rather tentative ones; the issue was of unknown dimensions. As evidence accumulated that shortages might not be a short-lived phenomenon and that the federal government stood relatively impotent in its organization and will to deal with the problem, state officials took on a more aggressive stance. The Statehouse would become a lightning rod for public resentment if shortages proved to be severe.

It was a tricky strategy, inasmuch as the overwhelming share of legal authority rested with Congress and the federal executive branch. Carving an appropriate state role turned out to be difficult. At the administration's end, doubt remained about a practical style of state involvement. Could a state truly have an effect when the issue was of global proportions? In time, state priorities centered on the promotion of conservation and the management of emergencies, short term goals representing areas in which state government could make meaningful contributions to its own citizens.

Although the energy shortages of the 1970s had their roots in federal fuel pricing policies of the 1950s, a number of forces collaborated in the winter of 1972-73 to tilt the supply situation from surplus to shortage. The government's earlier decision to price natural gas below its true value had removed incentives for exploration and depressed the price of competing petroleum and coal. Several Indiana utilities advised industrial customers in 1971 that, while current levels of supply could be sustained, they should not count on additional gas in the future. The post-war natural gas boom was going bust, with immediate consequences for Hoosiers. Natural gas and propane are widely used for grain drying at Hoosier farms and elevators, with the latter fuel enjoying popularity in rural areas because it is portable. However, 70 percent of propane is produced in association with natural gas. Propane supplies began to tighten as the stream of natural gas ebbed.

Weather then conspired to magnify the shortage. The autumn harvest season of 1972 was an unusually wet one. Corn and beans stood in muddy fields as farmers, impatient to harvest, had to await drying conditions favorable for machinery operation. A wet fall brought abnormally high use of propane-fired agricultural grain dryers, which borrowed heavily from supplies that had been set aside for home heating and industrial production for the remainder of the winter season. When Bowen took office on January 8, spot shortages already were occurring.

A second aspect of the natural gas problems related to the types of contracts used to market the fuel. Although contracts are not titillating subject matter, a brief description is necessary to grasp the overall situation. Natural gas contracts were of two types. So-called "firm" contracts conveyed what the name implies. Customers would get an agreed-upon volume. The second category was that of "interrruptible" contracts which essentially were a hedge against cold weather. Heating fuel consumption parallels temperature. Periods of bitter and prolonged cold weather place more demands upon a gas utility's system than it can accommodate. Interruptible contracts were a device to limit consumption during lengthy cold spells and avoid either the risk of system failure or the expense associated with building storage and distribution facilities to handle peak loads. One provision of these agreements required customers to maintain back-up fuel systems, but some interruptible customers never had experienced utility cutoffs. Complacency and contract cheating were the results. Where backup systems were installed, usually oil or propane, tanks often remained empty. Occasionally, alternate systems never were put in place. Owners gambled on the unlikelihood of curtailment against the immediate costs of installation. By January, 1973, interruptible customers were being cut off, often for weeks at a time. This, in turn, created a scramble for alternate fuels and further constricted the propane market.

Another contributor to the first winter energy shortages went unrecognized in subsequent assessments. Throughout the lower Midwest, an extensive reshuffling in the oil marketing business took place in 1972. Gulf and Phillips, major marketers in central and southern Indiana, all but abandoned the Hoosier state. Phillips, in particular, had served numerous fuel oil distributors and mom-and-pop gasoline stations in small towns and rural hamlets downstate. The companies' retreat from Indiana tipped the scale toward a tighter market.

Indiana escaped serious oil cutbacks during the winter of 1972-73, but states such as Iowa were forced to go into the fuel oil business. Dozens of rural towns in the Hawkeye state ran out of oil and that state purchased two million gallons for hardship distribution.

The potential for trouble in Indiana became apparent only at the time the new administration was coming to power. While Bowen was delivering his inaugural address the federal Office of Emergency Preparedness telephoned to seek a contact point in the governor's office.

They wanted to alert us to possible shortages. I took the call and agreed to meet with OEP representatives the following day. Their line of reasoning was persuasive; I advised the governor that we should become active in the energy issue. "At this point, you know more about it than anyone else on the staff, so you take charge of it," was his simple response, one that sent my career careening in a far different direction from what I ever would have imagined.

The Governor's Energy Conservation Committee was formed that day. It included representation from state agencies with interests in energy and emergency management, joined by representatives of the fuels industry and business associations. Robert Morris, executive director of the Indiana Department of Commerce, was named chairman. He agreed to provide staff support from his department.

The selection of Morris and his agency was both a calculated strategy and a shot in the dark. The administration didn't want to create a new energy agency; it yet had no strong grasp of what the state's role might be. No other existing department seemed a logical place in which to house the function. Commerce made sense because Bowen viewed energy shortages in terms of their impact upon the state's economy. Its designation avoided the expense of administrative support that would have to be earmarked for a new entity. Morris's aggressive personality and take-charge attitude also weighed in consideration. In retrospect, it was a reasonable decision, especially in light of the reluctance of the General Assembly to appropriate money to support energy programs. Commerce proved to be a good place through which to funnel the copious federal financial assistance which poured forth in subsequent years. At times the department's energy responsibilities almost overwhelmed its other functions.

The committee's first meeting occurred on January 10, a day on which a new round of natural gas curtailments was announced by the industry. Although amateurs in energy policymaking, its members quickly grasped the idea that the promotion of conservation represented the best hope for a short-term easing of fuel problems. Conservation was the basis of a brief report written for the General Assembly.[1] An informal arrangement for resolving hardships then evolved, with Morris as the contact point. A number of propane customers received allotments from distributors who had more ample supplies. A relatively mild winter was the state's primary ally in forestalling deeper natural gas curtailments or oil shortages.

As 1973 unfolded, pipeline companies projected deeper curtailments for the following winter. Utilities advised interruptible customers that periods of interruption might begin in September and last through the heating season. The first murmurs of production cutoffs threatened by the Organization of Petroleum Exporting Countries did nothing to allay state government's fears.

Bowen and his energy advisers quickly found themselves at odds with the Nixon administration's approach to dealing with energy shortages. The underlying philosophy was that of letting the marketplace deal with the problem. William Simon, then a Treasury Department official, gained the White House's ear with this point of view. For all his acknowledged brilliance in economic affairs, Simon failed to understand that social, political, and psychological factors also played a role in the problem. People don't always function in tune with the calculations of an economist's pocket computer, particularly in a modern political era in which vocal interest groups can wire around the economic system to obtain preferential treatment through Congress or the regulatory apparatus. With energy as the issue, the nation faced a considerable shakeout of traditional practices and conventional values. It was a social question as well as one of economics. Simon and the administration were insensitive to this fact. They were on soggy ground, too, with regard to economics.

Energy had not functioned in the free market since the mid-50s, when Federal Power Commission regulation of the wellhead price of natural gas warped the pricing structure of all fuels. It also seemed that retail costs would have to change drastically in order to stimulate a basic shift in consumer attitudes. After all, one doesn't leave a $6,000 car parked in the driveway because gasoline prices are hiked a dime a gallon. Consumers' fear about fuel availability — not price — drove them to higher-mileage autos in the mid-70s. It wasn't until gas prices nearly tripled by the decade's end that a sustained reduction in demand for the fuel occurred. Fear was fanned by embargo-period lines at service stations. Television cameras panned idle rigs at truck stops. Hoarding began, not to take advantage of today's lower prices but to insure that fuel would be available next week to get to work or to the grocery store.

Although the Treasury Department had set the overall philosophical tone for energy policy, the Interior Department had regulatory authority to guide the government's actions. Interior began to draft policies for allocating fuel based upon priorities of use, a policy at odds with Treasury.

Bowen, Morris, and I were perplexed by these developments. We recognized the role of the marketplace in framing long-range solutions to the problem. However, we had learned enough about petroleum production and the potential for newer sources to know that the changeover from an oil-based economy could not occur overnight. It had taken 30 years to tie America to a petroleum economy. The billions of dollars invested in the nation's capital structure — buildings, manufacturing equipment, and transportation vehicles — could not be retooled immediately. Moreover, petroleum fuels were in a declining production trend. There was no guarantee that higher prices would do more than stabilize the supply of conventional fuels. The bonanzas that some perceived in deep shale, the outer continental shelf, tar sands, or the wastelands of the Artic north slope represented extraction challenges that even higher prices might not overcome. What was called for was a government policy that recognized a historic transition was taking place. Government should endeavor to make this changeover a manageable one, carried out with less pain than that inflicted by the rough forces of the marketplace.

Allocation policies concocted by Interior could have been one such device, but Bowen and his advisers were in frequent disagreement because they were so poorly contrived and ineptly administered. By the time the Carter administration took office, these ever-more-complicated allocation programs had replaced any serious attempt to deal with the fundamental nature of the problem. I termed it an "equity in misery" approach in which Congress was more preoccupied with insuring that all shared shortages equally than in finding answers.

Government was only bandaging the wounded. Despite unending frustrations with regulatory policies, Indiana continued to defend the concept of allocation. It was a vehicle that could help reassure politicians and consumers that more radical measures — rationing, for example — were not required. If allocation could deal with the most pressing hardships, it might assuage the populace and forestall more frenzied schemes.

The "fairness" idea built within Congress a strong constituency for gasoline rationing. The nation came close to rationing in 1974 and 1979. Bowen consistently and stoutly opposed its imposition because any coupon rationing program has inherent flaws. It is an administrative undertaking of nightmarish dimensions, fraught with the likelihood of bungling and fraud. World War II rationing was irrelevant to the 1970s. Wartime rationing was intended to conserve rubber and the useful life of automobiles, not gasoline. The nation needed Rosie the Riveter on the assembly line, not joyriding. Its administration was inept and corrupt; only the overriding need to win the war prevented rationing from becoming a massive national scandal. Furthermore, America of the 1970s bore little resemblance to the nation of the 1940s. In the earlier years, cities remained homogenized from a geographic standpoint, webbed with trolleys and buses, linked by scores of trains. Suburbia didn't exist.

Coupon rationing ignored the fact that there are no "typical" energy consumers. How do you rationally design a system that meets the needs of the inner-city resident of Indianapolis and the rancher in North Dakota? Complex formulae involving accessibility to public transportation and other schemes devised by Washington planners during the 1970s only underscored the number of exceptions. Rationing, in the view of the Bowen administration, was nothing more than a prescription for economic depression and public disorder. Yet bureaucrats persisted, in part because there were discretionary uses of the automobile that were tempting to corral. Transportation consumes one-quarter of the nation's petroleum deliveries. Another factor was the strong environmentalist leanings of key members of the Carter administration. Environmentalists don't like the automobile; they consider it to be immoral, ethically and esthetically. It was doubly easy for them to take aim at this consumer of fuel.

The Nixon administration's first flirtation with fuel allocation came in the form of a propane allocation program in the early autumn of 1973. The plan was a dismal failure. It took effect on October 2, but the regulations were not in the hands of the states or the industry for weeks. The rules established virtually everyone as a priority user, which did nothing to encourage conservation. The program only brought hoarding on a massive scale. Strings of tank cars were shunted to Indiana rail sidings and sat idle for months. Empty anhydrous ammonia tanks were filled with LP gas, but hoarders didn't know that residue from agricultural fertilizer could react with liquid gas to corrode faucet fittings, with potentially disastrous results. Federal regulations removed vast quantities of propane from the market, which more than doubled its price during the subsequent heating season. Propane hoards only slowly filtered back into the system. Fortunately, the Indiana harvest period was warm and dry; nature was more compassionate than the federal government.

The energy crisis broke into the headlines with full fury in November after OPEC imposed an embargo and President Nixon addressed the nation in somber tones. Bowen already had announced an intensive fuel conservation program for state government agencies and later coupled it with a 50-miles-per-hour speed limit for all state vehicles, except those used in emergency runs.[2] It became standard policy during the next seven years to announce fuel curtailments for state government prior to making similar requests of the private sector and general public. These actions drew attention to the situation and were essential if government were to expect the public to cooperate.

Interior's comprehensive fuel allocation regulations were unveiled on December 1, 1973. Their philosophy provided clues to what was wrong with the approach. Certain users, agriculture for example, were entitled to all the middle distillate fuel (heating oil, diesel, and gasoline) they said they needed. A second echelon of priorities provided an entitlement of the same amount of fuel consumed in the previous year. Still others were entitled to 90 percent of their previous year's consumption. Non-priority users had to be content to share in the remainder. The state was given ten percent of the available supply of middle distillates to utilize as a hardship reserve.

Several things were wrong with this plan. Highest priority users had no incentive to conserve; the system practically encouraged them to inflate their demands. The categories didn't take into account the interdependence of the American economy. One couldn't carry through the concept of giving farmers a priority without granting the same status to fertilizer and agricultural chemical makers. Priority for bread makers is easy to understand, but what about Hershey bars and red-pop? Where do you draw the line? The management of the system ignored the way in which oil and gasoline are marketed. Fuel oil distributors were expected to make calculations to determine which of their customers were entitled to various amounts of fuel, a task wholly beyond the capability of all but the largest distributors. It was further compounded by sharp differences in the supply capabilities of major oil firms. Those obtaining crude oil from domestic sources were healthier than competitors who were heavily reliant upon imports. By spring, some of the latter would be able to provide only 30-40 percent of normal volumes to non-priority users.

The most glaring defect was the fact that not enough fuel stood behind the priorities. It did little good to promise a farmer all the fuel he required when his local co-op could not fulfill his needs. The fumbling start-up of the regional operations of the new Federal Energy Office didn't help either. Regional authorities had the central role in supervising the program and in making ultimate judgments about hardship relief. The Chicago office, manned by fugitives from the Internal Revenue Service, fell weeks, then months behind in its paperwork. The allocation system soon became clogged with unfinished business. Morris and I shuttled back and forth to Chicago and Washington in attempts to straighten out dozens of problems.

The allocation program was held together only by the reserve available to the states. Using this authority, Indiana juggled shipments of fuel and resolved the most pressing hardships. The cooperation of the oil industry was invaluable because state officials often pushed their authority to the legal limit. Although oil men received heated criticism during the energy crisis, their cooperation was important to the state's success in weathering the embargo. The Indiana Petroleum Council and its director, David Davis, were responsive to the state's frequent requests for aid. Some of its demands bordered upon the unreasonable and went beyond the provisions of the allocation program.

From the outset it was apparent that the energy crisis might set off region against region in a scramble for fuel. The loudest yelps came from the Northeast, historically dependent upon cheap foreign oil to churn its utility turbines. Federal officials prepared plans to wheel electric power from the coal-fired generators of mid-America to the oil-starved utilities of the northeastern seacoast. Simon, then director of FEO, advised that Indiana might be called upon to contribute 20-30 percent of its electric generating output to the northeastern grid system.

Bowen reacted negatively. "I don't think there is a selfish bone in anybody's body here in Indiana," he said. "If we truly have energy to spare, then fine. But if we don't and it is going to reduce our industrial capacity and it's going to make some homes cold in Indiana, then I think we have to fight to retain our supply of energy here."[3] The federal plan further inflamed already raw nerve ends when New England utilities insisted upon a price structure that would not have fully compensated Indiana utilities for the power they provided. The additional coal burned to meet northeastern needs would have to be replaced at a higher price. Indiana argued that New England should pay these costs. Under their proposal Hoosier ratepayers would have subsidized homeowners and businessmen in the Northeast. The matter went into inconclusive litigation. Luckily, the transmission lines of the grid system would not accommodate anything near the 20-30 percent envisioned by Simon. Only a trickle of power edged eastward. This was the first of a series of regional disputes that all but ruined relationships between the Midwest and Northeast. Although Hoosier officials never adopted the "let-the-bastards-freeze-in-the-dark" mentality of southerners, the Bowen administration was highly irritated at these rip-off attempts.

As dwindling fuel supplies put the nation on the brink of gasoline rationing, Indiana's energy program was jolted by the death of Robert Morris. He was killed on January 10, 1974, in a private airplane crash, along with three other Indianapolis businessmen. The next morning was one of the gloomiest I can recall, for Morris had become a close friend as well as a colleague with whom I had worked for hours each day. Few words were said; secretaries fought back tears as Eldon Campbell and I sat atop desks just outside the door of Morris's now-empty office. Campbell, who had been the department's economic development leader, was named by Lieutenant Governor Orr to succeed the late director. Although bewildered by the prospect of taking on a totally unfamiliar responsibility, Campbell agreed to manage the fuel allocation program if I would supervise overall energy policy. Later that day the governor designated me chairman of the energy committee. Despite his initial reluctance, Campbell proved to be a highly effective fuel administrator during the embargo period. It was an achievement for which he deserved greater credit than he received.

During the unsettled weeks of winter, mail arrived in bundles, delivering outpourings of advice and prejudice. The energy crisis became a false cloak for other schemes. The temperance-minded demanded that the state close taverns and liquor stores because they were non-essential wasters of fuel. A variety of recreational functions — bowling alleys seemed to get frequent mention — came in for special criticism. People who didn't care for basketball thought the state should cancel games. Roundball buffs argued that people would use more energy in individual homes than collectively in a high school gym. Although coal-produced electricity was not in short supply, brightly-lit shopping centers became targets. Opposition to the forced busing of school children focused on fuel use, even though the social issues that had produced busing orders went far beyond the volumes of fuel consumed by these fleets of yellow vehicles. The mobile home industry gratuitously suggested that the state remove the legal requirement for a trailing vehicle to warn following motorists of wide loads. The suggestion paraded as conservation but was rooted in a desire to cut labor and transportation costs. They weren't alone in seeking advantage from emergency. Much of the governor's office mail was ill-informed but well meant. Far too many of the communications, however, were expressions of selfishness, prejudice, and hatred. Those who read these letters developed deep forebodings about the coming years of shortage. How would these people react to a truly serious emergency? At what point would the calm voices of the Otis Bowens at some point be drowned in the outcry of lobbyists for special interests, the wayward press, and political demagogues? These tense, confusing months left permanent marks upon those who had the responsibility to help hold the fuel system together. The experience bred deep resentment against anyone who, for whatever motive, made a game of arousing the public's discontent. We would confront the energy emergencies of future years with gnawing doubts about our prospects for success.

Indiana's patchwork emergency response program prevailed during the rest of the embargo. By late February, available fuel oil and diesel amounted to only 85 percent of normal levels, but the system held together as officials plundered the state fuel reserve to keep distributors in business. The style of the Bowen administration proved helpful. Northeastern politicians frothed in sky-is-falling outcries as long lines developed at gas pumps. They hollered crisis language, abused the oil industry, and clamored for additional federal intervention. In Indiana the almost daily pronouncements of the governor and his energy advisers took an entirely different tone. The situation was manageable, they said, if people would remain calm and make an effort to conserve. They conveyed to the public a degree of reassurance that they did not feel, but they were aware that the only result of joining the screamers might be to shift the psychology of Indiana's citizens in a negative fashion that would turn a difficult problem into an impossible one. The strategy worked. Indiana endured the embargo without episodes of long lines at gas stations, except for one four-day period in which many central Indiana service station operators closed down to protest federal policies. A near-miss occurred in Lake County, captive to a Chicago media market in which politicians and newsmen were running amok. Their crisis mentality set off a binge of frantic buying. Fuel inventories in Lake County plummeted as gasoline was displaced from storage tanks to automobiles at an abnormal rate. In reality, the shortage was not severe, but the inclination of motorists to top off their tanks more frequently than normal distorted the distribution system to the point that state government was forced to allocate hundreds of thousands of gallons of gasoline to stave off an imminent panic.

Overall, Indiana motorists were conserving gasoline at a ten percent rate. Conservation combined with the hardship reserve to keep the shortage at manageable proportions throughout the emergency. Hoosiers were helped by the fact that the embargo proved to be a leaky one. Instead of a 30 percent shortage that might have resulted from a total cutoff, the nation experienced only an eight percent decline in imports, although few recognized this until well after the fact. An embargo that proved to be a modest one still had been a near-run thing in terms of its social and political implications. It was an ominous portent for a nation that soon resumed its appetite for Arab oil in burgeoning percentages.

However, many thermostats remained dialed down for years and the 55-miles-per-hour speed limit adopted as an emergency measure by the 1974 session of the General Assembly remained on the books throughout Bowen's governorship. The new law saved both fuel and lives. Indiana undertook pioneering research in the use of grain-derived fuels, but the payout was slow in coming because the economics of gasohol did not catch up with those of gasoline until the latter 1970s and only then as a result of government subsidy. The Hoosier state began to consider revised building codes. Its legislature adopted landmark legislation providing tax incentives for the installation of solar devices. Conservation promotion continued throughout the first Bowen term as natural gas supplies remained thin enough to attract public attention to the issue.

By this time, too, state officials had come to a loose consensus about federal allocation programs that had faltered so badly during the embargo. During future emergencies, they believed, the state should be given a small percentage of each fuel to dole out to alleviate hardships. Federal officials should eliminate the various categories of customers, establish one category of priority users who would be entitled to historical fuel deliveries, and put all non-priority users in a second category which would incur the impact of shortages that could not be made up through conservation or the hardship reserve.

Wiping out specific categories or priorities would enable energy officials to avoid the nasty business of making judgments about the worth of human beings to society. It is easy for critics to argue that a tavern owner is not performing an essential service, but his employees require their paychecks no less than a steel worker. The simplified approach also would dodge the fine distinctions between the relative merits of bread as opposed to Hershey bars that only could be drawn in cumbersome regulations. While the elitists — environmentalists and some university professors most prominent among them — wanted to impress their social values upon the public, Indiana hoped to avoid these choices. They inevitably would be degrading to large numbers of people. Moreover, fuel classifications did not fit into tidy packages. It was impossible to write a rule that escaped unintentional discrimination. An economy of America's complexity contains fewer typical cases than many might suppose. While federal policies never dealt with allocation in quite this forthright manner, eventual emergency strategies moved toward the state philosophy.

The states hoped to avoid repetitions of the embargo woes by insuring that management capabilities of the federal government were improved but, more important, by pushing for federal energy policies that would produce fuel and institutionalize energy efficiency. The National Governors' Association began to address the energy issue but was hampered by some of the regional cleavages that already had emerged. The Bowen administration put its main effort in conjunction with fourteen neighboring midwestern states which had common interests in other subject areas. The Midwest avoided the provincialism of New England and the Pacific Slope. Its member states included major energy producers such as Oklahoma, Kansas, and Kentucky, but also counted among their numbers the states of Minnesota and Wisconsin, which had no native fossil fuels, only wood and water. The agricultural economies of the plains were joined with the industrial economies of the Great Lakes region as these states grappled for workable solutions. In spite of outsiders' misconceptions about the midwestern region, it was diverse enough to provide a good basis for framing recommendations. What made sense for the midcontinent might offer sound policy for the nation as a whole. The governors, Bowen among them, took an active role and energy was on their conference agendas almost to the point of tediousness. The principal outlet for regional policy was the Midwestern Governors' Conference Task Force on Energy and Natural Resources, activated in the autumn of 1972 at the initiative of Governor Robert Ray of Iowa. It was the first regional organization to take a broad view of energy problems. From the start, the task force was influential in securing modifications to federal allocation regulations. In 1975 it developed a recommendation calling for deregulation of new natural gas prices that was adopted almost verbatim by the National Governors' Association one year later. This consensus of governors on one of the most controversial issues of energy policy helped move Congress toward fuel decontrol in the later 1970s. Indiana was among the task force's most active members because its energy officials profited by an excellent educational forum. It is easier to learn from people than from books, and a good deal of the expertise gained by the Bowen administration was borrowed from this organization.

The task force also was a convenient old-boy network which provided advance warning of trouble. The high plains states lacked adequate pipeline distribution of finished petroleum products. If gasoline shortages were in the offing they first were felt at the fingertips of the truck distribution system in this region. Heating oil shortages and problems of independent refiners would first emerge in the northern tier: North Dakota, Minnesota, and Upper Michigan, where the heating season extends for nine months in states far removed from sources of supply. Wisconsin proved to be a bellwether for kerosene problems. Indiana was more fortunate, sitting astride the main line of oil and gas pipelines, but trouble signals from these fringe states alerted state officials to move into high gear. By the time of 1979's gasoline and diesel fuel crunch this network had become sophisticated enough that Hoosier energy planners could make reasonably precise forecasts of when to expect difficulty. In turn, the states collaborated to resolve one another's problems and to present a unified position to Washington.

Campbell was succeeded as energy director late in April 1974 by Thomas Kibler, an Indianapolis businessman who held the post until May, 1977, when he was ousted in a clash with other Commerce Department officials over management philosophy. William Sorrells replaced Kibler.

Later in 1974 state attention focused upon coal, which accounted for virtually all of the state's electric power generating capacity, fueled the hearths of many steel mills along the Lake Michigan shoreline, and heated 50,000 homes. The United Mine Workers had a tradition of "no contract, no work" and walked out of the pits in November. Representatives of the states gathered in Washington to discuss ways in which they might alleviate hardships arising from a prolonged strike. In one session with Frank Zarb, then deputy administrator of the Federal Energy Administration, state representatives were joined by a two-member delegation from the UMW. One carried an arm limply, with several fingers missing from his left hand. The other was marred by facial scar tissue. They were the union's lawyers. The ensuing conversations were lively to say the least, and the UMW attorneys made frequent references to "our socialist brothers in England." It was clear that the states were dealing with a somewhat different breed of special interest representatives. Fortunately, the strike lasted only five weeks and the state was not called upon to intervene. During the walkout's closing days, inventories plunged rapidly at coal yards serving the residential and small commercial markets. Bowen advisers pondered what might have occurred if the strike had dragged on for months. They would find out three years later.

Harsh winters continued to keep the natural gas issue in the forefront of state concerns. The heating season of 1976-77 was a near disaster. Temperatures dropped below the freezing level in late December and didn't top out above 32 degrees until February. The state was locked in bitter cold, often at subzero levels. With temperatures ranging as much as 50 percent below readings of the previous January, natural gas suppliers labored to meet requirements that reached record levels. Gas was being drawn out of the system faster than it could be replaced. Wellheads in storage fields froze as temperatures remained below zero for four days and their efficiency in replacing the rapidly declining stockpiles was further impaired. The Ohio River froze for only the second time this century and river transport of fuel was halted. The Great Lakes navigation system and other inland waterways were choked with ice. Heavy snows in the upper Midwest and Mississippi valley played havoc with the distribution of fuel by surface transport.

On the morning of January 17, with the temperature 20 below zero at Indianapolis, it became apparent that the natural gas system was faltering. Prompt action was needed to protect against system failure in utilities such as Citizens Gas & Coke of Indianapolis. A gas utility's network of distribution pipelines will fail if fuel is drawn from it at an extraordinary rate that causes a loss of pressure. Once this happens, the results are catastrophic. Service can be restored to only one customer at a time. In the case of Citizens, with its 130,000 customers, the procedure would have required several weeks during which homes would have been evacuated and buildings would have been exposed to damage by the frigid weather. Indianapolis schools closed that day. The utility's larger industrial and commercial customers were ordered to cut their use of gas to a level that would protect machinery and inventories from damage. Scores of businesses shut down. Indiana Gas Company, which served much of the mid-state region, faced similar problems.

Bowen, Indianapolis Mayor William Hudnut, and utility officials called upon gas users to cut their consumption drastically. The clamor for conservation was coupled with efforts to obtain gas from other regions of the country. The state administration worked with the utilities in an attempt to secure surplus Canadian gas. Bowen and I intervened with Federal Power Commission Chairman Richard Dunham in hopes of getting a portion diverted to Indiana. We lost the initial round but were successful in helping the utility secure additional amounts from the Rocky Mountain states that enabled Citizens to hold the line.

Meanwhile, Indiana faced a near exhaustion of kerosene, which is used in rural homes because it remains liquid in cold weather. However, the trucking industry places a heavy wintertime demand upon the fuel. Diesel fuel begins to clot at 17 degrees and is cut in equal measure with kerosene in order to keep trucks running. These usage requirements all but wiped out inventories. The state energy office worked with the industry to identify kerosene stocks that could be reserved for home heating use. The governor's office urged Washington to reallocate fuel away from aviation and called for quick action to increase refinery output of kerosene. Columbus and Richmond faced shortages so severe that contingency plans were made to open National Guard armories to families whose homes might go cold. Although state officials were able to avoid that extremity, the kerosene situation remained critical for weeks as federal, state, and industry officials shifted already thin stockpiles to areas of greatest need.

Many schools and industries remained closed despite a brief easing of cold weather later in the month. It proved to be only temporary. In the dawn hours of January 28 a vicious cold front blasted through central Indiana, dropping temperatures 20 degrees in one hour as winds gusting to 50 miles per hour lashed a weary state. It was a tense day of wildly ringing telephones and hurried, sometimes agitated conferences as Indiana again confronted the threat of pressure failures in natural gas systems. One forecast projected minus-25 readings for the following morning. The governor met with representatives of the major commercial trade associations and urged them to cut operating hours substantially, beginning that day. They agreed, although the governor's office then endured a barrage of telephone calls from retailers who didn't want their competition to get an edge and proposed intricate — and unworkable — schemes for managing operating hours. The renewed call for conservation paid off. The strain on the gas utilities gradually ebbed. The following Saturday morning's temperatures bottomed out; not at 25 below but at what was considered to be a near tropical minus-ten. The reduction in factory and commercial demand over the weekend period helped to stabilize the situation. (Throughout the January-February fuel crisis the coldest days came on weekends, when gas consumption is lower than on weekdays, a very fortunate combination of circumstances). State government's attention during the weekend period turned to battling the blizzard, which had closed road networks in 35 counties and all but halted home deliveries throughout the state.

The worst jolt came on Monday, January 31, the 33rd consecutive day in which temperatures had not gone above freezing. The giant Northern Indiana Public Service Company, which previously had withstood the emergency without curtailments, abruptly cut off its industrial and large commercial customers. Its pipeline suppliers had reneged on delivery commitments due to the severity of weather nationwide. More than 2,600 businesses were ordered to take only enough gas to prevent weather damage to their installations. Northwest Indiana's huge steel mills began to close down.

That afternoon Bowen asked the White House to declare an energy emergency in Indiana. He estimated that fuel curtailments had produced job layoffs in the 50,000-60,000 range and would worsen as the days passed. More than 3,100 industrial and large commercial customers now were reduced to "plant protection" levels of usage. Bowen asked the federal government to help unsnarl the blizzard-ravaged transportation systems in order that fuel could move.[4]

Caught short by the unexpected nature of the NIPSCO curtailments, the utility's customers were irate and deluged the governor's office with shrill cries for relief. The state could do little but hold their hands. Their complaints turned to outrage when word got around that the utility was continuing to connect new small commercial users who were not covered by the restrictions. NIPSCO justified the practice because the amounts of fuel involved were negligible and normal conditions likely would be restored within a matter of days. It was another example of the insensitivity of utility managers to public and media reactions to decisions which undermined their own credibility and made it more difficult for government officials to deal with emergencies.

On February 3, Bowen's staff sifted evidence that the crisis period had reached bottom and slowly would begin to improve. Public Service Commission Chairman Larry Wallace advised that NIPSCO's deliveries from pipeline suppliers gradually would be restored. Barring another onslaught of cold weather the state had seen the worst of it. Bowen's advisers agreed to make no public statements about the easing of the situation. The administration did not want to sap the momentum of conservation, which still would be required for many days.

Another brief period of subzero cold blanketed the state, but again on a weekend when the distribution networks were under less pressure from commerce and industry. On Monday, February 7, Indiana Gas Company announced a modest easing of curtailments. Thermometers finally registered readings in the 40s by midweek. Curtailments persisted for several weeks but on a moderate scale that did not force plant shutdowns. The crisis had passed.

While Indiana combated the deviltry of winter, a new administration was taking charge in Washington, one pledged to developing a comprehensive national energy program. For the next two years, Bowen and his energy advisers devoted a substantial amount of time to consultations in Washington and elsewhere as the nation finally came to grips with the need to write a blueprint for its energy future. President Jimmy Carter's initial plan, unveiled with a flourish on April 20, 1977, was a hopeless muddle. It had commendable features: tax credits for home energy investments, efficiency standards for appliances, and gradual decontrol of oil to the world market price. The positive aspects were counterweighed by a series of punitive taxes on cars and gasoline, and continued control of natural gas prices (although a small increase would be permitted) that would only extend the decades of political perversion of the energy pricing structure. Since Carter wanted to shove the plan through Congress as a package it seemed probable that its good features would be burdened by confusion over his unpopular penalty tax proposals. The whole proposal was likely to sink under its own weight. Although it preached the benefits of a coal economy and required industrial conversions to coal, the plan offered little more than rhetoric in this regard. People were not burning coal for very good reasons — environmental rules, transportation problems, and its marginal profitability. A sensible coal program had to contain more than sloganeering.

With Carter's program in trouble from the very beginning, much of the money that might have been allocated to energy efficiency by the private sector went into a holding pattern. Businessmen who often had switched fuels several times in hopes of finding a reliable supply again were frustrated in planning for long-term capital investment. It made all the difference in the world whether the final energy plan was to be based upon production or built around mandatory conservation.

Bowen was advocating an energy policy balanced between production and conservation; it followed the thinking of energy professional whose attitude had jelled during the mid-1970s. Conservation and alternative sources such as solar power were considered important, but it was equally clear that new oil wells and refineries were needed too. A combination of production of conventional fuels, new sources, conservation, and the designing of energy efficiency into the American economy and lifestyle were the components of this consensus. Bowen embraced it. His views were heard more frequently as he gained stature among the governors during his final term.

More than two years elapsed before a revised Carter program was fashioned, this time with more emphasis on production and a marketplace approach to oil pricing (although Bowen had serious reservations about the use of money from the windfall profits tax). The plan left many issues unanswered, but Bowen and most other governors endorsed its general principles. A modified version finally was adopted during the following winter — seven years after the nation had had its first encounter with fuel shortages. Much of the impetus came from troublesome fuel shortages in 1979 which, following an eastern coal strike of record duration, put enough pressure upon Congress to take action.

The 1979 gasoline and diesel fuel shortages were the final energy emergency confronted by the Bowen administration. It turned out to be as frustrating as previous episodes. Three successive colder-than-normal winters had drawn down petroleum inventories to thin margins. The problem was compounded when Americans went on a colossal driving binge in the autumn of 1978 and burned record volumes of gasoline. The domestic supply situation began to tighten during the winter of 1978-79. Then, the Iranian government was overthrown and an embargo upon deliveries to the United States was imposed by fanatics who now controlled what had been one of America's primary suppliers. The Saudis upped production in an attempt to compensate for the Iranian cutoff, but the world oil market was thrown into a psychological tizzy anyway.

By February 1 the statistics showed that the nation was in a very marginal supply situation, holding a one or two percentage point cushion that could be evaporated by any unforeseen event. The turmoil in Iran was affecting the world oil market to a greater extent than the facts warranted, but it had a strong psychological effect on Rotterdam fuel brokers and American motorists. Contradictory statements by Energy Secretary James Schlesinger were of no help either.

The first restrictions on gasoline availability occurred in Colorado on February 6. This development brought back memories of the 1973 embargo, when Colorado had been first to feel the negative impact. The state had become one of my barometers for use in forecasting fuel problems. A few telephone calls to energy officials there and in Minnesota persuaded me to begin planning for trouble in the Hoosier state which might strike as early as mid-April. On February 18, the governor's office warned the state that gasoline consumption anywhere near the previous autumn's rate would trigger shortages in April or May. Planning for conservation programs should get under way. Again, it was the low-key Bowen approach — no scare talk, but an admonition that prudent planning now and a common-sense approach to conservation might forestall serious difficulty later.

Supplies deteriorated as spring approached. State officials were particularly watchful of end-of-month situations in which service stations might pump out their monthly allocations and close for two or three days until subsequent allotments arrived. The state's early efforts were directed toward minimizing this threat. Widespread service station closings of even a few days' duration might generate the panics Indiana had always avoided but now were emerging on the nations' seacoasts. Moderate shortages coupled with the unnerving shrieks of politicians like Governor Jerry Brown of California already were causing lines to form at west coast gas pumps.

Each state's principal tool was the "set-aside", the hardship reserve of three percent of gasoline stocks available to the state for distribution. Gasoline from this reserve not utilized for immediate problems was returned to the system on a monthly basis. Indiana held off its return until month's end in March and April. The three percent would amount to a one day supply added to the ensuing month. For a time, this plan was offset by the oil industry's willingness to let service station dealers borrow against next month's allotments. State government viewed this as highly irresponsible; it only promised a worsened situation at a future time. When the governor's office demanded that the industry stop advance draws, most marketers went along with its point of view.

Spot shortages emerged in late April but failed to produce a significant impact. Meanwhile, chaos prevailed at gas stations in California and was spreading through the urbanized areas of the mid-Atlantic states. So-called "odd-even" plans were launched with political fanfare as solutions. The odd-even system used the last digit of a license plate to determine daily eligibility for gas. On alternate days drivers would have the opportunity to fill up. Indiana energy officials rejected this approach, which had been discredited during the 1973-74 embargo. It did not deal with the problem of motorists' topping off of tanks. Unnecessary fills displaced fuel from storage tanks to the automobile and only worsened the apparent shortage. Bowen agreed to a proposal by his advisers that Indiana utilize a "minimum purchase" plan instead. Buyers would be required to make minimum purchases of $6 or $8, depending upon the size of the auto. This would help manage queues at gas stations while limiting panic fill-ups.

The support of service station operators was essential to the success of any scheme. While the state received an encouraging reaction from dealers closely affiliated with the major oil marketers, the attitude of the Indiana Service Station Dealers Association, which on paper had about 30 percent of the operators, was unknown. Fortunately, this group was focusing its attention on Energy Department regulations which limited their revenues per gallon. After a meeting in the governor's office, Energy Director Clarence Broadus and I agreed that their complaint had merit. The state would support their point of view. We had misgivings about the validity of their contentions but decided that support of a questionable position was a cheap price to pay for a good working relationship. State officials also were trying to avoid a threatened mid-May, four-day shutdown of gas stations urged by some in this group. The leadership endorsed the minimum purchase approach and the scheduled shutdown turned out to be a failure.

By the end of May, Indiana was experiencing widespread shortages — in terms of reduced allotments to dealers. Gasoline deliveries dropped to 90 percent of normal. Stations restricted operating hours, many closing at nightfall. However, diesel fuel shortages west of the Mississippi were interfering with an already delayed planting season and wheat harvest. Trucking operations were interrupted. Independent operators began shouting for government to do something about diesel prices and supplies.

Whipped into a fury by their leaders, the independent operators began to cause trouble in June. They attempted to strangle the nation's highway system by blocking interstate service plazas and picketing fuel distribution terminals. While Bowen had sympathy for their economic difficulties, he took a tough line as repeated violence began to occur. As had been the case during the coal strike, the administration resolved to take what action was needed to keep commerce moving. Attempts to blockade fuel terminals failed when State Police intervened. Despite tire-slashings, rifle shots, and demonstrations, trucks kept moving on the highways of Indiana.

Bowen was bombarded with requests that Indiana increase its legal weight limits, one of the key trucker demands. Many of these telegrams came from other governors, who were caving in to threats and who seemed willing to end the dispute at any price. Aside from his historical opposition to weight increases on maintenance grounds, Bowen stubbornly refused to give way because he wasn't about to reward lawlessness. A stormy confrontation with strike leaders at the governor's office ended when he pounded a fist upon his desk and abruptly dismissed them. It was the only time that most reporters ever saw Otis Bowen show anger in public. As departing truckers wailed at this presumably rude treatment, most observers relished the toughness of their chief executive.

Energy Department regulations designed to re-allocate diesel and gasoline proved to be as ineffective as some of the earlier embargo-era rules. The states became involved in frequent discussions with federal bureaucrats in hopes of making them work. However, conservation by motorists had more impact than federal dictates. Afraid that gasoline would not be available, many Americans cancelled driving vacation plans. The shortage remained manageable and the truckers' strike dissipated. By summer's end the conservation rate was near ten percent. It held up throughout the fall, when a gathering recession joined with motorists to dampen energy demand. Indiana was not required to implement the minimum purchase arrangement.

The final year of the Bowen administration was the only period during its tenure that Indiana did not confront energy difficulty. It was a welcome relief to a tired administration. A state energy development board, first proposed in 1977 by Lieutenant Governor Orr but killed by the utility lobby in the General Assembly, finally was created and began to seek ways in which the state could play a greater role in promoting the use of new technologies and native resources such as coal.

Indiana and many other states confronted the energy emergencies of the 1970s with greater effectiveness than observers of the federal system might have reckoned. During periods of shortage the states were more effective in promoting conservation and in deriving usefulness from flawed federal fuel allocation regulations. The states also were laboratories for innovation in grain alcohol research, solar incentives, modern building codes, agricultural conservation, and homebuilding technology — all in advance of federal activity. Their greatest disappointments resulted from the pressure of recurring emergencies and the constant need to do battle with Washington. State energy officials lacked time to support adequately the production projects and new technologies that might have brought more immediate benefits than more recent federal energy programs. The new synthetic fuels programs do not have payoffs until the mid-1980s. It is unfortunate that the legislature had not been more receptive to budgeting funds for energy development at a much earlier date. Certain projects, such as the marketing of solar power, could have gained added impetus if Indiana state government possessed the time and manpower to pursue them more vigorously.

Despite these shortcomings, Bowen achieved his priority goal in energy — that of holding the economic and social system together during troubled, highly uncertain times in which the nation had close brushes with disaster. The governor's style, calm and restrained, was conveyed to his people. Energy emergencies might reach panic proportions in other states; in Indiana they never got out of hand.

IX THE LEGISLATURE, 1975

The early days of the 1975 General Assembly were clouded by concern for the governor's health. After experiencing prolonged throat discomfort Bowen underwent a tonsillectomy in mid-November, 1974. He continued to be bothered. Further diagnosis raised the possibility of a throat tumor. That would have meant — at the very best — radical, face-marring surgery. If the tumor were malignant, his life expectancy might be counted in months. This knowledge had a shocking effect upon the governor, who was fully aware of what might be in store for him.

Surgery was scheduled for January 15. It was agreed beforehand that Bowen should disclose the facts to newsmen; otherwise, rumors would spread uncontrolled. Before making a public statement, he wanted to advise legislative leaders; he did so on the afternoon of January 10. Normally quiet and composed, the governor endured the meeting only with great difficulty. The encounter was so emotional that some legislators immediately thereafter conferred with gubernatorial staff members about plans for transition in the event of his incapacity or death. Several participants expressed the fear he would not be able to retain his composure at the news conference, set to occur a few minutes later.

I confronted him at the copying machine in Vi Walker's office, where he was duplicating a financial disclosure form. We chatted briefly about how to report free football tickets and state fair passes. Then he acknowledged, "I didn't do very well in there." Was he up to a news conference? I asked. "Oh, I guess so," the governor replied. "I've had some practice now". The media session was a restrained affair and Bowen evaded questions as to whether he would resign if the tumor proved to be malignant.

Three people waited in his suite in Krannert Pavilion of University Hospital on the morning of January 15. Beth Bowen concentrated on needlepoint; Rick Bowen prepared a school exam; I fidgeted. Two hours elapsed. Dr. Raleigh Lingeman then entered the room to advise us that no tumor had been located during an extensive exploratory operation. Apparently, the governor's problem was a "neuro-muscular dysfunction", which I translated to mean a "trick" throat. Lingeman and I then went downstairs to meet with a crowd of reporters. A few headed for telephones as soon as they saw our smiles.

Six days earlier a hoarse governor had submitted his laundry list of proposals to the General Assembly. He called for a legislative consensus regarding the proper direction of state transportation policy. Should Indiana broaden and diversify it? How should new projects be financed? What were the appropriate roles for state and local governments? Having reached these general determinations, the legislature then should adopt an administrative reorganization plan.

The governor was unprepared to endorse a particular scheme; a fresh definition of policies should precede it. The administration's transportation specialists still pondered whether to approach a transportation department modeled by function or by mode of transport. Interested legislators were toying with these concepts as well. Bowen's speech also recapitulated recent developments in energy and warned the assembly not to be lulled into complacency by the resumption of petroleum deliveries by OPEC.

The governor disclosed his plan for a commission to evaluate issues of individual privacy and make recommendations: "While immediate attention is needed on the protection of privacy issue," he said, "a balance must be maintained to guard against hastily drafted laws which might create a new set of serious problems impairing the ability of law enforcement officials to carry out their responsibilities properly, hamstringing the efforts of organizations to protect against fraud and abuse, or conflicting with the right of the free press and a free public to know and to communicate."[1]

Bowen listed three areas of concern: safeguarding the right of personal privacy, requiring recordkeeping to maintain standards of accuracy and security, and ensuring that citizens could read these files and correct erroneous information. Former Deputy Attorney General and FBI Director William Ruckelshaus had agreed to chair the privacy commission. A preliminary report of its findings was scheduled for submission to the 1976 legislature, and a final record of conclusions would be delivered to the following session.

Attempts by Democrats to alter the budget process from its traditional two-year basis to an annual one met with gubernatorial hostility. It would further shorten an already brief span for state agency planning (meaningful planning cannot extend beyond the range of predictable budgeting), the ten-month budget-making cycle would be repeated twice as often, additional staff would be required, and the single-year budget would feed momentum for a year-around General Assembly. The governor made note that no one had articulated justification for changing the existing system. However, he did not voice his most basic concern — annual budgets would result in cumulative spending totals exceeding the dollars allocated through a biennial process.

Bowen's budget recommendations included additional funding for education of $341 million, a record increase. The proposal would enable the state to bear a larger share of school transportation costs and would alter higher education funding to enable universities to pay for construction from their general funds, rather than from bond issues to be repaid by increases in student fees. An additional $42 million was suggested for state and local highway projects. This would defer the need to increase motor fuel taxes. Six million dollars was sought for development of Ohio River ports at Jeffersonville and Mount Vernon.

Recent revenue forecasts had projected that a budget surplus of $153 million would stand at the end of the two-year cycle if the proposed budget was adopted. A $100 million cushion was desirable, Bowen said, and $80 million was the absolute minimum. Leftover money should not be spent for state programs. It should be returned to citizens through a reduction in the individual income tax, expansion of tax relief to elderly Hoosiers, an extension of the renters' credit, and exemption of certain medical-related items from the sales tax.

This was a theme that the governor would argue with greater frequency during his second term. If surpluses accumulated, government should not yield to the temptation to spend them. That would only set a higher base from which to calculate future appropriations. The public was better served by having this excess money returned.

Bowen also urged lawmakers to enact a reclassification of state government personnel. The early phase of this process had been a controversial one, carried out by an administration task force. Employees had been skeptical that its motives might go beyond the stated purpose. Numerous state employee groupings didn't fit neatly into the scheme. Compromises to resolve these discrepancies resulted in spillovers among categories.

The administration viewed reclassification as an essential forerunner to the creation of a modern system of personnel management. It was a capability sadly lacking in a state government divided between political patronage and a merit system that only marginally lived up to its name. Merit often had meant little more than the tenuring of patronage employees prior to changes in the political make-up of state administrations. Reclassification was needed, the governor contended, to enable personnel administrators to employ the proper person in the right job slot and to ensure a visible career ladder so that both the employee and the taxpayer might benefit.

Bowen then turned to a pet concern — resolving the growing unavailability and near-runaway cost of medical malpractice insurance. Several national carriers had quit writing policies of this type. Doctors were refusing certain operations and medical specialties due to the legal risks involved. Other physicians practiced defensive medicine "with one eye on the patient and one eye on the courts."[2] Health care costs were rising as doctors ordered additional tests and procedures that might buttress their defenses in malpractice litigation. "Ironically, we have come to a situation which would afford greater legal protection to the average motorist rendering roadside assistance to an accident victim than to the best trained surgical team in the nation, practicing their specialty under optimum conditions," the governor pointed out.[3]

A remedy had not been devised by the time that the governor addressed the assembly; several possibilities were under study. Bowen sought an indication that the legislature was interested in a solution during the current session.

An early legislative tussle centered on the legalization of parimutuel wagering on horse racing in the Hoosier state. Enabling legislation would establish a county option framework for authorizing parimutuel through a referendum. A state racing commission would regulate the industry. The measure rolled through the House 61-38, then survived a narrow 26-24 ballot in the Senate. Bowen made no secret of his intention to veto the proposal. Attorney General Sendak termed it an unconstitutional lottery. When the governor penned a brief veto message on April 11, citing the bill as "contrary to the best interests of the majority of the people of Indiana,"[4] supporters mounted a vigorous campaign to secure enough votes to override his decision. By a 57-34 majority the House did so on April 30, but the issue stumbled in the Senate with only 24 affirmative votes. GOP Senators James Gardner and Clarence Kelly, parimutuel backers on the earlier ballot, now supported the veto.

Another controversial proposal, collective bargaining for police and firemen, collided with the governor's veto. Mayors urged Bowen to reject the plan. Provisions for binding arbitration were potentially costly. The governor, who deeply believed that public employee strikes were unethical, described the bill's prohibition against walkouts as ineffective. He also thought it enabled the bargaining process to intrude into policy decisions that traditionally had been a right of local elected officials. In addition, the bill failed to restrict wage settlements to affordable levels and was not coupled with proposals to reform existing pension system policies and funding sources.

Liquor legislation also hit the wall, but not in the governor's office. A much-criticized practice of the Alcoholic Beverage Commission, setting minimum percentage markups for wholesale and retail liquor and wine prices, had been referred to the assembly for determination after the ABC agreed to do so as part of a settlement in a federal lawsuit. A bill to confirm its policy was adopted by both houses, but became ensnarled in conference committee. The report was adopted by the Senate. It failed twice in the lower chamber on the next-to-last session day.

The governor's urging for a resolution of the malpractice crisis virtually fell upon deaf ears. A proposal advanced by the Indiana State Medical Association languished in a House committee. Bowen pressed Speaker Phillip Bainbridge and representatives of both parties to allow the bill to receive a hearing. They gave way. The hearing attracted widespread participation and publicity; it generated momentum sufficient to thrust the proposal through the House by a top-heavy majority. A cautiously constructed compromise evolved in the Senate, where a lawyer-dominated Judiciary Committee originally was cool to the idea. Intense bargaining ensued.

An acceptable version was reported to the floor and subsequently enacted. Senator Adam Benjamin had been the principal architect of the refinements, devoting more than 150 hours of work to drafting the final document. Signed by the physician-governor on April 17, the new law limited malpractice awards to $500,000 per incident, and financed awards in excess of $100,000 from a compensation fund financed by surcharges on malpractice premiums. The state was to provide insurance to physicians unable to secure coverage from private sources. A review panel was created to winnow out nuisance claims; its findings were admissible in court. The new law survived judicial tests, lowered the cost of insurance, and broadened its availability. Indiana's legislation was acclaimed as a model for other states. The law's enactment was one of the most satisfying achievements of the governor's tenure.

Other significant laws were adopted by the 1975 session. A "rape shield" measure limited the introduction in court of evidence pertaining to a rape victim's past sexual behavior. The 55 miles per hour speed limit was made permanent. An administration-sponsored railroad preservation act provided funding to preserve operations on branch lines that otherwise would have been shut down by the federal government. An employment tax to finance local mass transit projects also became law. Although the latter measure never was used, both bills represented a significant departure from historic legislative indifference to non-highway transportation problems. County courts replaced justices of the peace. However, the Equal Rights Amendment faltered again, collapsing in a Senate committee after passing the House.

The offices of governor, United States senator, and lieutenant governor were placed on a primary election ballot and removed from the convention nomination system under terms of legislation that overcame the opposition of GOP State Chairman Milligan and party chieftains. The new method was adopted by substantial majorities. Under pressure from selected party leaders to veto the electoral revision, Bowen never seriously considered that action. Memories of the 1968 state convention still lingered. The primary seemed to offer hope that public involvement in the political process would be extended. A solid majority of legislators in both houses had voted in its favor.

Hoosier lawmakers muddied up what otherwise might have been a creditable reputation for achievement in the 1975 session by their near miss with disaster over budget disputes. There were fundamental points of disagreement. One was the annual-vs.-biennial budget flap which pitted Democrats against Republicans. Another was the definition of an "adequate" surplus; money not deemed essential as a cash cushion could fuel legislative spending desires.

The two parties battled over revenue forecasts after a late-March revision by the budget agency abruptly reduced anticipated revenues by more than $50 million from an earlier estimate. Coming only three days after the House had adopted a budget, the revelation was seen by Democrats as little more than blackmail to force Senate deletions in spending. Ways and Means Chairman Spencer Schnaitter sputtered that it was "phoney baloney"[5] and the "most blatant attempt at politics I've seen this session."[6] It was released, he said, only to put the Democrats in the position of being free-wheeling spenders during a period of economic constraint.

Bowen foresaw difficulty in achieving all of the GOP objectives. Badly wanting to preserve a two-year budget, he confided to associates that the issue represented insufficient justification to force a special session. Spending levels were another matter. He told Republican legislative leaders on April 4 "it would be cheaper to keep you here all summer" than to accept spending levels approved by the House and drafted by a Senate committee.[7] He stood firmly behind his insistence upon a minimum $80 million working balance.

Budget-making proceeded slowly in a strained atmosphere, made even more difficult because House Democrats were reluctant to share data with budget agency officials. This increased the probability of last-minute technical disagreements. Shadow-boxing proceeded through April with little perceptible movement. Observers worried that compromise would come too late to be translated into a formal budget bill. Only on April 28 — two days before the final gavel — were there murmurs of inclination to settle the dispute. By then the administration was nearly resigned to a special session — if for no reason other than the fact that the budget consisted of "a million notes on a million slips of paper," to use Ed Thuma's description.[8] The governor was prepared to accept a special session dealing with budget controversies, knowing that the initiative remained in his hands until June 30, when the expiration of current authorizations would begin shutting down state government operations.

Finally, on April 29 agreements were reached on the school formula and university funding, two categories that almost always seemed to divide legislators until the last minutes. Republicans gave way on the annual budget issue. But technicalities then threatened to undo the sentiment for compromise. Two versions of budget bills were being prepared by the printer — one to Democratic specifications, the other to Republican guidelines. Only a comparison of their contents, after party caucuses approved them, would indicate whether the two sides actually were close together.

Given the difficulty of completing a final printed version, several lawyers questioned whether a bill delivered to the governor after midnight on the final session day would be regarded as lawful. Bainbridge suggested that authors sign cover sheets which contained no texts. This would maintain a legal fiction of timely presentation to Bowen. Printed bills could be inserted in these jackets later. Bowen emphatically rejected the idea. The budget cleared both houses only minutes before the session expired, and a $3 billion annual appropriations package was delivered to the governor's office. The staff was careful to make receipt for it at 11:59 p.m. Given the confusion attending its passage, Thuma wanted several days to check the budget line by line. Meanwhile, Bowen briskly flourished his veto, accumulating a total of 26 for the session.

The budget director was critical of the legislative result. "It's a mess," he told newsmen.[9] Ambiguous language and confusing line items which gave several agencies annual budgets equal to what had been biennial appropriations in the original bill, prompted his outburst. Higher education was "heroically overfunded" and employees were added to mental institutions at a time when patient populations were declining sharply.[10]

The measure, however, protected an $80 million working balance, provided supplemental highway funding, and did not encroach upon the tax relief fund. Gross errors could be corrected in the subsequent session. Bowen signed it, although he waited the full seven-day consideration period to do so.

X   THE STATE'S NATURAL RESOURCES

The achievements of the Department of Natural Resources in revitalizing the state's recreational system were mentioned frequently by Bowen in end-of-term media interviews as among the leading accomplishments of his administration. The modernization program for state parks, memorials, forests, and reservoirs proved to be highly popular with the public. It also counted as a political asset for the governor.

Parks are inherently appealing. Advocating their improvement was consistent with the public perception of a health professional who served as their governor. Recreational development was a valuable complement to other administration goals. Unlike programs such as property tax relief, which can appear to be rather impersonal manipulations of complicated laws that few understand, parks are highly visible, tangible government services with automatic allure.

What emerged as a priority during Bowen's tenure was not on his initial agenda. He was sold on the notion by his advisers, eagerly grasped staff proposals to further the concept, and became an enthusiastic and consistent supporter of the department's objectives.

A fortunate combination of individuals gave the program a good head of steam. Perhaps most important was the governor's choice of former State Representative Joseph Cloud as the department's director. Cloud more than offset his unfamiliarity with natural resources issues with a level of political savvy and negotiating charm that beguiled legislators out of tens of millions of dollars for capital improvements. His nearly legendary reputation with legislators, lobbyists, and reporters stemmed from his ability to get what he wanted in the appropriations process. However, Cloud was equally proficient at finding middle ground between the colliding forces that daily brought pressure upon his department:

environmentalists or preservationists versus developers, a DNR whose personnel were divided between merit and patronage employees, an agency whose management objectives often conflicted with the desires of county chairmen and others of political influence, and an aggressive and intrusive federal establishment determined to supercede the state in important matters of enviromental policy.

His teammate in leadership was John Hillenbrand II of the Batesville industrial family and chairman of the Natural Resources Commission since the department was reorganized in 1965. In addition to broad expertise in natural resources issues and an infectious enthusiasm that helped promote the department's goals, Hillenbrand brought a political dimension to the situation. A prominent Democrat who had served in administrations of both parties, his presence insured that the Bowen administration's natural resources policies would enjoy bipartisan support. Some of the political sniping normally associated with the operations of the state's second-largest agency would be avoided.

Few Republicans were ready to challenge the chairman's retention by Bowen. He was a holdover from the predecessor GOP administration and the Hillenbrand family was one of the state's most prominent. Only when it became apparent that he might pursue the Democratic nomination for governor did scattered criticism begin to sprout. Even then, Bowen was in no hurry to secure Hillenbrand's resignation. The governor held the chairman in high regard — knowing that he would not embarrass the administration and would take the initiative to step aside whenever his political interests had jelled to a point that would make it unwise for him to continue. Hillenbrand resigned in May, 1979, a full year before the Democratic primary. He was succeeded by James Lahey, a South Bend businessman and also a Democrat with substantial credentials as a conservationist.

The governor's decision to give me the staff liaison function with the department and other resources agencies also proved helpful, since I had developed a familiarity with DNR operations as a journalist and as an ex officio member of its governing commission in 1971 and 1972. In time, the promotion of the department's objectives became a personal hobby as well as a government obligation. I was in a position to protect the agency's interests and press its case within the executive suite of the State Capitol.

The fourth component of the blend of personalities was the quality of the department's executives housed on the sixth floor of the State Office Building. Most of them were career professionals, enthusiastic about their work, but very wary of politicians after a series of unfortunate situations during the previous administration. Insofar as Cloud, Hillenbrand, and I were concerned, they were a joy to work with.

When the Natural Resources Commission met in February, 1973, for one of its occasional retreats at *Jawacdah*, the Hillenbrand family hunting lodge complex near Batesville, the chairman, the director and I began to explore the potential for making DNR a showcase for the Bowen administration. We reasoned that an administration identified with issues of taxation and finance needed a major project of more tangible appeal. Furthermore, much of the unglamorous preliminary work — modernization of sewage systems and a growing web of utility services installed to meet an expanded camping program — had been completed during the Whitcomb administration. This would enable the state to proceed with above-ground improvements that could be completed on a short timetable. They would have high visibility as recreational installations. The governor's advisers also agreed to pursue a more diversified outdoor recreational system to respond to a growing demand for bicycling, long-distance hiking, canoeing, and winter sports. These activities were gaining in public interest.

Bowen quickly approved the concept, in part because Cloud was able to describe objectives in terms of realistic timetables for completion. More important at the time was Hillenbrand's energetic evangelism. The governor was charmed by his eagerness and intrigued that a prominent Democrat was willing to support the administration, yet harbored no ulterior motives in doing so. Hillenbrand's affection for the department and his enthusiasm for its programs helped close the sale.

The group then encountered its first problem — the reticence of department professionals when first asked to frame specific proposals. They were suspicious of a political system that had produced confusion and concern within the department under the previous administration. Staff members were reluctant to be creative because prior attempts at creativity had brought them little more than grief. Within a few weeks, though, Cloud persuaded them that our motives were honest. The ambitious plan sketched for them was achievable if they only would fill in the details.

When the governor's immediate staff adjourned to Brown County State Park on July 24 and 25, 1973, to chart the overall direction of the administration, I was prepared to advance a number of DNR proposals. The gathering accepted the principle that the department was to be one of the administration's showcases.

The program was reduced to written form in a white paper delivered to the governor. It proposed a $10 million capital improvement plan to be presented to the 1974 General Assembly. Funds would be used to rehabilitate run-down facilities, flesh out the existing system to broaden recreational opportunities, and begin improvements at state memorials. Pilot projects involving abandoned railroad rights of way and utility corridors for use as bikeways and hiking trails were included. It encompassed proposals to move forward with surface mine reclamation projects, acquire and expand the state museum, acquire additional nature preserves, and create a division of historic preservation within the department. Each of these projects was feasible within the first term.

By the time the legislature convened the "showcase program" had taken on added appeal as a result of Cloud's inspiration to create what amounted to new state parks — Potato Creek, near recreation-starved South Bend, and Wyandotte Woods, to be carved out of the rugged scenery of the state forest that lapped over Harrison and Crawford counties.

The timing was favorable. The first warnings of fuel shortages presaged a trend toward vacations closer to home. By the time of Bowen's State of the State message the $10 million capital program had grown to $16 million. The governor put forth the case for the DNR capital program in his annual presentation to the lawmakers:

> For many years Indiana's system of state parks, forests, and recreation areas was a showcase to the nation. The scenic beauty and land feature diversity of Indiana was enhanced by a system of parks, forests, and recreation areas that took a back seat to few in the nation. But then, as our population began to grow, and as interest in family vacationing increased, our methods of support of capital improvement of these facilities proved to be less capable of supporting their continued development and refurbishment.
>
> Capital monies went into new projects — mostly reservoirs — as well as into necessary sewage and water treatment facilities within our existing properties. Today, Indiana is ready for the implementation of the capital program which will bring our parks, forests and recreation areas up to levels of operation that will make them better able to support themselves, and better able to serve the needs of more Hoosiers.[1]

Cloud had organized the laundry list of projects in a way that would achieve the objectives of the professionals within his department and have the broadest geographic appeal to legislators. The governor's advocacy of swimming pools was intended to counteract criticism by some legislators and environmentalists of the whole idea of placing pools in the parks. Conservative lawmakers objected to the cost; environmentalists foresaw intrusions into the park system of conveniences that might better be placed elsewhere. But the public wanted pools and state officials recognized that they represented part of the diversity needed within the park system. In time, the newly-remodeled state park inns would include mini-pools for hotel guests; they proved to be popular diversions for patrons of all ages (and welcome baby-sitting devices for weary parents who had come to the parks in search of peace and quiet).

The legislators bought most of the package — $12.7 million of it. Cloud then proceeded at a furious pace to spend the appropriations. A former legislator, he knew the advantages of moving quickly and effectively to spend capital money granted by the General Assembly. Throughout the Bowen years Cloud's regular requests for funding would prove to be pleasant contrasts to those of some departments. While others became tangled in red tape and local controversies over siting that often delayed capital projects for years, Cloud built them. He then returned to the assembly to ask for more. Usually, he got it. Where possible, state projects were augmented by federal funds. In the process of rehabilitating the park system, Cloud also constructed a direct pipeline to the state treasury whose contents flowed with regularity for six more years. Physical improvements to the parks were bolstered by the presence of naturalists, cultural programs, and entertainment at inns and large campgrounds.

One device that might have given further thrust to this ambitious program failed to achieve its potential. Recreational Bonding Commission legislation adopted in 1973 at first was viewed with skepticism by Cloud and Hillenbrand because they feared that it might not contain sufficient safeguards to protect the natural attributes of the parks from the desires of entrepreneurs to carry out extensive commercial development. Therefore, the administration proceeded cautiously — too cautiously, it seems in retrospect. In time, the bonding commission became inactive after its chairman, Ray Dunn, had a falling out with Cloud. The two quit communicating and the bonding concept remained on the shelf. It is, however, a potentially useful recreational development tool — especially in the more stringent financial climate of the 1980s.

Although the administration would have preferred to focus its attention upon restoring the grandeur of the state's recreational system, there were a number of policy issues that commanded its attention. One of them involved reservoirs, historically promoted by the Army Corps of Engineers to control flooding on the nation's river system. Reservoir projects were endorsed by state legislatures because of their recreational benefits and the perceived economic growth brought to surrounding areas in the form of enterprises to serve tourists and the increased value of residential land. Reservoirs had become among the single biggest items of state capital expenditure by the time the Bowen administration settled in office.

In cooperation with the federal government Indiana had completed several major reservoir projects — notably lakes Monroe and Mansfield, and the triad of Upper Wabash impoundments — Huntington, Mississinewa, and Salamonie. Brookville Lake was near completion and Patoka Lake was far advanced in planning and funding. Several others were on the drawing boards: Highland, Big Pine, Lafayette, Big Walnut, Clifty, and — on the longer term — Big Blue.

Reservoir projects — both in Indiana and elsewhere — now were coming under fire. The reasons were diverse. Environmentalism played a substantial role. What was believed to be a mania for structural development on the part of the Army Engineers caused many environmentalists automatically to oppose all Corps projects. Two Indiana projects — Big Pine and Big Walnut — would have inundated what some considered to be environmentally significant and scenic tracts. A tenuous compromise involving alterations kept the Big Walnut project alive. Big Pine soon felt the fury of environmentalists' objections. Landowner opposition dominated in the cases of Highland and Lafayette, which guaranteed that politics would play a role in their futures. Highland — from a water supply standpoint probably the most desirable impoundment in the state — degenerated into a political war between the Indianapolis Water Company, which had few votes, and Senator Birch Bayh, who was courting environmentalists and affected landowners. Later scrutiny of Bayh's objections disclosed that they were based largely upon questionable assumptions about alternative groundwater sources. Nevertheless, his opposition was sufficient to stall the project long enough to derail it.

Economics was another touchy point. Cost-benefit ratios developed by the Corps were hotly debated. The numbers were vulnerable because of the extensive lead time — usually a decade — from a commitment to proceed with a project until the time that water actually began gathering behind the dam. Interest rates used in making economic calculations during study phases often were made obsolete by inflation by the time Congress was asked to vote construction funds. Yet Congress withstood pressure to recompute on the basis of current interest rates because this would have the effect of making the economics of a reservoir a moving target. If Congressmen could by legislative fiat freeze the interest rates used in cost-benefit calculations, they were unable to do the same with respect to construction costs. Construction outlays tended to outpace the inflation rate by a point or two.

Another obstacle was a technicality that resulted from congressional distrust of the states. Several states had reneged on prior commitments, leaving Congress holding the bag. Washington responded by insisting that contracts written at the time of project approval commit the state to fund their full shares. This ran afoul of a constitutional provision in Indiana. It prohibited the binding of future legislatures to follow through on such obligations. This dispute, known as the Section 221 controversy (at issue was Section 221 of the Water Resources Planning Act), meant that Indiana could not sign a contract unless it put the full state share up front in the form of a one-time legislative appropriation. That probably wasn't possible. The appropriation — $10-$20 million in present terms — was a good deal to ask, given the competition for dollars in a legislative session. Other states faced similar legal constraints.

Another problem of reservoirs was defined by their very nature. Their combination of purposes — flood control, recreation, and water supply — often clashed. Flood control is best served by keeping the reservoir as empty as possible for as long as possible, in order that it maintains the maximum capacity to corral flood flows. This emphasis results in a reservoir full of muddy water in the spring but a wide expanse of mudflats during the remainder of the year. Water supply, on the other hand, called for keeping the lake as full as possible to guarantee a reliable source of supply. Recreational interests required a relatively stable lake; otherwise, boat docks would be underwater when lakes were full and separated by hundreds of feet of mud from their users during summer and fall. These conflicts were manageable in the hilly reaches of southern Indiana, but less so in flatter country where a few feet of elevation radically altered the size of a lake.

The governor's natural resources advisers became convinced that reservoir controversies would become more inflamed. It was necessary to devise workable philosophies to assess the value of individual projects. They faced an additional consideration in the person of U.S. Representative John Myers, an influential Republican member of the House Appropriations Committee, popular in his district, and an ardent supporter of reservoir projects.

Initially, state attention focused on Big Pine. Certain environmentalists' objections appeared to have merit. More important, DNR's staff had concluded that the project had been oversold in terms of its recreational values. The normal pool of Big Pine would be in the 1,200-acre range — one tenth the size of Monroe — and only about 600 acres actually would be available for boating. DNR Deputy Director William Andrews reckoned that the lake's confines would preclude the use of motorboats. The citizenry would be hopping mad when it found this out.

After additional research Cloud, Hillenbrand, and I decided that Big Pine should be scuttled. We urged the governor in 1974 to withdraw state support. He declined to do so. The timing was not yet right. He was reluctant to trigger what surely would be a nasty confrontation with Myers over a project in the congressman's home district.

Opposition to Big Pine continued to gather momentum in 1975. The district office of the Corps of Engineers, having just evaluated the results of a restudy that produced gloomy cost-benefit numbers, withdrew its support in January, 1976. Myers labored on Capitol Hill to reverse the decision, but the Corps' action had the effect of killing the project.

The Army's announcement resulted in another discussion with the governor that month. Previously silent on the other projects, Bowen then voiced reservations about Big Walnut and Lafayette. Opponents of these projects recently had visited with him. If he was backing away from these projects, it represented a substantial departure in administrative policy, especially since the legislature had mandated state participation in Lafayette Lake as far back as 1967. When pressed for amplification the governor acknowledged — to use his own wording — that he had been wishy-washy. We agreed that Cloud and I would draft a new reservoir policy.

Our recommendations were returned four days later. Water supply represented the overwhelming justification for reservoirs insofar as state government's interests were concerned. Flood control should rank second, although benefits could be difficult to quantify. Standing alone, flood control was not sufficient to justify a project. Recreational benefits should rate third.

In our scheme Highland was by far the most desirable project, with Big Walnut second. Lafayette Lake, lacking water storage, would not be entitled to state support. Planning on the remaining projects had not advanced to a point that would permit a firm recommendation. We were careful to point out that the new policy would be interpreted as such a radical shift that it might jeopardize other projects.[2]

Bowen readily accepted this advice. After several episodes of shadow-boxing with Myers and Representative Floyd Fithian, in whose district Lafayette Lake would be situated, the governor made public his revised position. In an April 22, 1976, letter to the Corps of Engineers, he urged the Army not to proceed with plans or funding for Lafayette Lake. He cited unrelenting opposition from area citizens and legislators, escalating project costs, reduced cost-benefit ratios, and legal barriers to state participation. "It is my philosophy that the priorities for reservoir construction should place water supply first, flood control second, and recreation third," he stated. "Since Lafayette Lake does not include provision for water supply, it is not a priority."[3]

Lafayette Lake collapsed quickly, although Congress resisted formal deauthorization for several years. For the first time, legislators had been given a reasonable standard with which to gauge the value of water impoundments. They pounced upon it — perhaps too eagerly — as a basis for deauthorizing several marginal projects at the state level. The election of Jimmy Carter to the presidency, coupled with Bayh's continued opposition to Highland, doomed the two desirable projects. By Bowen's second term further impoundments of the traditional Corps of Engineers style had no chance of completion. Carter's hostility proved to be more than the already-retarded projects could withstand. This was unfortunate, we believed, because Indiana would have cause to regret that Highland was not built.

Two reservoirs were opened during Bowen's years as governor. Brookville Lake, dedicated in 1975, became immensely popular and was the largest single public works project completed during the Bowen administration. Patoka Lake, completed near the end of the second term, had been subjected to rigorous advance planning for appropriate commercial and recreational development. Utility lines and access roads were designed and completed before impounding began.

The DNR and the Army rightfully took great pride in their work at Patoka, which promises to become the most significant reservoir project in the state. Located in a region with severe limitations on water supply because of the geology of the southern hill country, Patoka has an important role in meeting the water needs of its hinterlands. Its location in a chronically depressed region also offered hope for badly-needed economic development. Unlike any other reservoir in the state, Patoka might be the catalyst for a local economic revival on a scale experienced around Tennessee Valley Authority projects of the 1930s and 1940s.

The administration also was drawn into the long-smoldering controversy surrounding proposals to expand the Indiana Dunes Lakeshore National Park, created by Congress in 1966. The lakeshore issue was a classic land use battle. Preservationists, park managers, units of government, the private sector, and homeowners frequently disagreed about a proper expansion program, if any was to be considered. As was the case in many other controversies in the environmental arena, false motives insinuated themselves into the lakeshore fight. Conservation organizations attempted to include tracts of land, not for their intrinsic value to the park, but rather because their purchase could prevent construction of the Bailly nuclear generating plant. Expansion could forestall further growth by Northern Indiana Public Service Company on land it already owned. Illinois interests, wishing to cripple the Port of Indiana, wrapped themselves in the false cloak of conservationism in their advocacy of land purchases.

The governor's office and Department of Natural Resources identified several key state concerns with respect to the lakeshore. Fully prepared to cooperate with federal officials in land management, Indiana was unwilling to yield sovereignty over the Indiana Dunes State Park or the lakebed adjacent to the shoreline. This also was state property. Furthermore, state government insisted that the Port of Indiana be protected, both in its present land configuration and in future access to the Burns Harbor facility. If the Bailly generator or other NIPSCO installations were to be written off, they should be dropped on their supposed demerits rather than as the consequence of back-door ruses by environmentalists.

Serious discussion of dunes land acquisition began on Capitol Hill in 1974. Representative J. Edward Roush had introduced legislation calling for an addition of 5,288 acres. The Interior Department responded with a limited design adding 944 acres. Interior officials were only lukewarm toward the lakeshore. They were chary about the idea of managing an urban-area national park under any circumstances. Interior was not accustomed to dealing with mayors and legislators. It had a tradition of operating national parks in fairly remote areas. Coyotes and prairie dogs don't raise hell at public hearings.

The state of Indiana previously had not taken a position on the acquisition of further holdings; the governor concluded that the time was ripe to do so. Cloud, Hillenbrand, Andrews, John Costello (the deputy director for land resources), and I formulated a compromise plan. It called for the inclusion of 2,447 acres, and opposed the purchase of riparian lands along the Little Calumet River or other segments that effectively would have isolated the port. The governor also rejected the addition of the Town of Beverly Shores, primarily because of the expense. The community was then divided over the question of whether to opt into or out of the park.

Hillenbrand and Cloud presented the governor's position in testimony before the House Interior Committee in June, 1974. Among its most important arguments was the need for a final determination of the status of the acreage at issue:

> During the period of years in which this issue has been the subject of intense and often bitter discussion, several unfortunate situations have occured. The natural splendor of environmentally significant areas has been jeopardized. Both community entities and individual homeowners have faced constant uncertainty about their futures. This uncertainty has resulted in the deferral of necessary and worthwhile projects, while making others costly gambles. The potential for sound regional planning has been disrupted.
>
> . . . the time has come to reach a settlement that will preserve this environmentally significant area before it is forever lost. We believe the settlement must recognize the legitimate and diverse interests of the area. We believe the settlement should be a final one — with results occurring rapidly after federal legislative action is completed.[4]

The testimony also proposed the inclusion of Hoosier Prairie, which at the time was believed to be the only remaining vestige of virgin prairie land in Indiana. Federal officials were less than enthusiastic. The 300-acre parcel was miles away from the lakeshore. (Hoosier Prairie eventually was preserved as a result of joint funding by the Indiana legislature and monies from the Interior secretary's discretionary account).

Bowen's position was welcomed. It represented middle ground between environmentalists and the federal agency and removed the most visible points of controversy. Organizations advocating expansion applauded Bowen because it marked the first occasion on which state government had taken a positive attitude.

Two years later a compromise version, taking 3,600 acres, was approved by Congress. The governor was forced to intervene with Representative Ray Madden, chairman of the House Rules Committee, to keep the measure from dying in the last-minute logjam of congressional business. The Interior Department was reluctant to accept the legislation, but Bowen prevailed upon President Ford to approve it.[5] Except for lingering jousting by environmentalists this action settled the lakeshore flap.

Meanwhile, the governor and the department engaged in a running disagreement with the Army Engineers over a federal proposal to extend the Corps' regulatory jurisdiction over much of the nation's river system. In fairness to the Corps, it was under pressure by the courts and Congress to assert more control over waterways. The state's concerns were best summed up by the governor when he urged the Army to call a halt to the proposed regulations, which had their basis in the Corps' historic jurisdiction over navigable waterways. (The engineers proposed to deal with the problem by declaring more streams to be navigable). He termed the guidelines for determining navigability as "so broad, general, and ambiguous that it appears obvious that a determination of navigability may be made with respect to virtually every river, stream or rivulet in the United States at the sole discretion of the Chief of Engineers."[6]

This fracas was more than just another disagreement between state and federal officials over bureaucratic turf. It touched on something more fundamental. The federal government was moving aggressively to gain more authority over the nation's water in the belief that only the federal government was in a position to manage the use of the resource. The government had won a number of cases involving its authority over water originating on federal lands in the west, but had been unable to find similar leverage in the more water-rich eastern regions. The Interior Department had drafted, but had not yet mustered the courage to disclose, legislation that would expand federal authority. The importance of water to life and the economy needs no explanation, but the critical issue at the time centered on the nation's growing concern about energy. Energy development and conversion facilities — whether conventional power plants or exotic synthetic fuels refineries — consume vast quantities of water for process use or cooling purposes. Control over water rights would give the federal government control over the geography of energy development. Indiana was unwilling to yield what traditionally had been a matter of state law and regulation.

Bowen placed the state's concerns before the other governors and gained a number of allies. However, environmental officials in several states refused to join Indiana because they believed that the federal government would be able to provide better protection for their water resources than their own weak water laws would enable them to guarantee. This was a poor commentary on the decline of state sovereignty and responsibility.

Indiana officials were not surprised, however; the states never had stood together on an environmental issue. The political constituency varied too much from state to state. This difficulty carried over into later disputes over federal surface mining regulations. Coal-producing states were responsive to both production and environmental issues. Others invariably took the environmentalist point of view. There were no local miners' votes involved. Furthermore, officials often lacked the sophistication to realize that the ability of coal states to mine the resource might have an impact upon their own ability to secure energy needed for economic development. Issues such as these posed the greatest frustrations in dealings with Indiana's sister states.

However, the flak barrage raised by several states was sufficient to dampen the Army's ardor. The Corps proceeded to designate streams on a more limited basis than its earlier actions had indicated. Indiana continued to pursue the matter with Congress, hoping for a clear prohibition against plans of this type. The state's efforts were not rewarded.

The administration also found itself in opposition to another project — the canalization of the Wabash River that had been favored by the Corps of Engineers and the Wabash Valley Association. Few state officials had taken the plan seriously when it was in a more ambitious form intended to channelize the Wabash and a series of smaller rivers to bridge it to the Illinois Waterway and, thereby connect it to the Great Lakes. Failing to convince the public of the merits of this grandiose plan, the Corps compiled a more modest version. The canal would be limited to the lower 42 miles of Wabash waterway between Mt. Carmel, Illinois, and the river's confluence with the Ohio. Critics of the earlier plan remained suspicious, figuring that the new project would only be the first installment of the repudiated cross-Wabash scheme. The proposal was dropped in 1976 after most Indiana political leaders, including the governor, objected, and the release of an Army study which disclosed that costs would exceed benefits.

In the meantime, several changes were made in DNR's internal operations. A Division of Reclamation was activated in 1973 to manage the agency's growing number of surface mine reclamation projects. Many were conducted with the financial support of the federal government. A Division of Historic Preservation was activated to manage the State Museum and memorials and to carry out new administrative duties associated with the national movement to protect structures of historic significance. It was important to discharge this responsibility competently because the addition of a structure to the National Register of Historic Places carried with it extensive restrictions on alterations as well as beneficial tax incentives. The designation of a site as historic could have significance beyond its boundaries. It could become an obstacle to a nearby public works project. Certainly, the intent of the concept was to protect these treasures from development projects that might have more immediate economic and political clout, but it imposed an obligation upon the department to cull the marginal projects in order to avoid muddying up the map.

After months of negotiations with the city of Indianapolis, the department obtained title to the old city hall building that now housed the state museum. This was required to obtain accreditation for the facility. It set in motion a development plan that placed Indiana's state museum in the forefront of its counterparts around the nation.

Sweeping changes in the department's Enforcement Division also were made. Results were mixed. Although there was nothing particularly negative about the "game warden" image of Indiana conservation officers,

Otis R. Bowen, M.D., pauses in prayer during inaugural ceremony moments before being sworn in to become one of Indiana's most popular governors.
(Photo by Bob Jordan)

Convention-floor banter with former Senator William E. Jenner on the day Bowen won the nomination in 1972.
(Photo by Frank Fisse)

The snow notwithstanding, Bremen's people turn out to boost their favorite son for governor — November, 1972.

Lake County political leader and Bowen friend Joe Kotso conducts Bowen swearing-in with Beth; departing governor Edgar D. Whitcomb and wife Pat observe at right.

A new governor — and his first lady — on inauguration day in 1973.
(Photo by William A. Oates)

The new governor, who campaigned on the slogan "He Hears You" waves to an in- auguration spectator in the Statehouse bal- cony. Wife Beth and Gov. Whitcomb are in the background.

Gala celebration at Inaugural Ball starts with first dance by Governor and Mrs. Bowen.

With President Nixon at the White House in 1972 — a campaign photograph that took months to arrange.

On a familiar rostrum for his first state of the state message — January, 1973.
(Photo by Frank Fisse)

Bowen speaks at his first governors' conference in Rapid City, South Dakota.

*A few of the regulars on the weekly "Report from the Statehouse" show —
(L to R) Rich Green, Gov. Bowen, Bob Bloem, Bob Dunphy and Hortense
Myers.*

*With Beth and bundles of mail from well-wishers after throat surgery in
1975.* (Photo by Frank Fisse)

A somewhat more-than-casual tourist and his wife pose in front of Capitol Building, Washington, D.C.

News reporters and photographers crowd into the governor's office as Bowen vetoes the pari-mutuel betting bill, April, 1975.
(Photo by Jerry Clark)

Bowen initiates Calumet Bike Trail at Indiana Dunes State Park in June, 1976; Joe Cloud and other Dept. of Natural Resources officials follow.
(Photo by D. Bogden)

Teamed up for the second time, Bowen and Lt. Gov. Robert Orr at the 1976 State GOP convention.
(Photo by Frank Fisse)

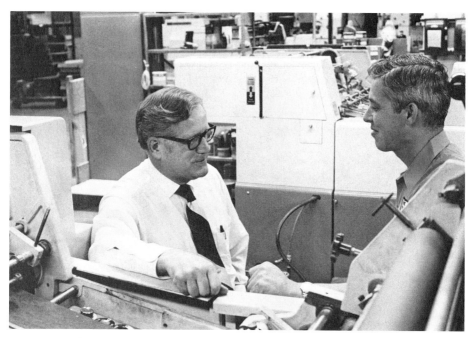

Campaigning for a second term, the first time allowed in Indiana, Bowen talks with Indianapolis factory worker.

Sports fan Bowen and Indianapolis' athletic Mayor William Hudnut get ready to open the 1977 season for the Indianapolis Indians.
(Photo by B & L Photographers)

Three of the GOP's most prominent — Bowen, President Ford and Agriculture Secretary Earl Butz.
(Photo by Kay Totten Spivey)

Charles Griffin, Cub Scout, and other scouts meet with Bowen at Statehouse get-together.

An impromptu chat with leaders of academia, John Ryan of Indiana University and Father Theodore Hesburgh of Notre Dame.
(Photo by Ernie Borror)

I.U.'s most prominent sports fan takes time out for a hot dog.
(Photo by Frank Fisse)

Bowen and Governor-to-be Bob Orr open Optimist Club Christmas program in State-house rotunda.

Indiana Senator Richard Lugar joins Bowen for 1979 finals of Indiana
high school boys basketball championship.
(Photo by Joe Young)

Bowen and Governor Julian Carroll of Kentucky flank President Carter at
a meeting in the White House Cabinet Room.

Bowen meets with Ronald Reagan and Bruce Melchert during 1978 fund raising visit to Indianapolis by Reagan.
(Photo by Charles A. Berry)

An almost lighthearted news conference — May, 1979 — in which the governor reveals that he won't enter the U.S. Senate race. Beth Bowen, Betty Rendel, Bruce Melchert and Rob Bowen join in.   (Photo by William A. Oates)

Bowen bites his lip at emotion-fraught "Tribute to the Bowen Years" in December, 1980. Tribute also is a farewell to·Beth Bowen who mustered the strength in her final days to attend; shown here still providing sympathetic support for her husband.

(Photo by Jeff Atteberry)

Bobby Knight, nation's number-one basketball coach, presents a commemorative basketball to the sport's number-one fan and most popular of Indiana governors.

the level of professionalism left a bit to be desired. Many officers were forced to use private vehicles because of a lack of autos. Cloud frequently joked about their chasing violators while driving pink Chevrolets. Many had come to the force through the political system and possessed only limited law enforcement training. This was disadvantageous in a era of more complicated natural resources regulations and a period during which drug activity and other offenses were becoming more common on property under the department's jurisdiction.

In time the "possum cops," as Cloud and I characterized them, operated out of bright green, marked patrol cars with adequate communications gear. Law enforcement professionals were recruited.

Vestiges of the earlier era remained. Although conservation officers were quick to claim the status of professionals, many went running to their county Republican chairmen if they were unhappy with an assignment or desirous of promotion.

Most disconcerting was the unending internal bickering which seemed to be the lot of all law enforcement agencies. Wearing a uniform incites a preoccupation with internal politics. Law enforcement agencies are ridden with factionalism and an inclination to play games within the system. For people who are so macho-minded, it seemed strange that their operations and attitudes toward superiors were invested with so much pettiness. Some of it results from the geographical spread of these agencies and the limited supervision that results from the nature of field work. It is easy for a few troublemakers to exploit an uneasy atmosphere, made worse by legitimate concerns that are endemic to the breed. The organizational spread also gives rise to "courthouse gangs" within certain divisions or districts. Unlike the State Police, the situation within the Enforcement Division was further irritated by the fact that it was still half-in, half-out of politics, with all the potential for mischief that this status entails.

Cloud's first important policy decision affecting the Enforcement Division was his insistence on promoting a superintendent from within the ranks, a career enforcement officer. On a number of earlier occasions, politically-connected police chiefs or sheriff's officers had provided the recruiting pool for this position. The governor approved his selection of Lieutenant Charles Murphy, a 20-year veteran of the force, as its leader. Murphy proved to be a capable superintendent, although he was the target of periodic sniping. It usually came in the form of anonymous, gossipy letters from officers or their wives. These missives disclosed more immaturity on the part of the writers than wrongdoing by their leader.

Throughout the administration, the department leadership engaged in sporadic skirmishes with dissidents, none of which came to any conclusive result. By the onset of the second term, however, Cloud's attitude had stiffened. Flareups within the division represented the only blemishes on an otherwise popular agency. Serious consideration was given to revoking conservation officers' general police powers and limiting their authority to the enforcement of fish and game regulations. Another plan which received serious consideration in the governor's office would have merged enforcement officers, excise police of the Alcoholic Beverage Commission, and prison guards of the Department of Corrections into a State Police auxiliary force.

Except for Patoka Reservoir, the high-dollar, visible capital programs were brought on line during the first term. Diversification of outdoor recreation continued to gain momentum. So did the less dramatic refurbishment of memorials and other properties, such as state forests which have become substantial recreational locales in their own right. The development of a statewide trails system advanced steadily. DNR acquired a Northern Indiana Public Service Company utility corridor near Dunes State Park, took over abandoned railroad rights of way around the state, and developed Knobstone Trail, a 75-mile route along the scenic ridgelines of southern Indiana between Clark State Forest and Jackson-Washington State Forest.

Obtaining railroad land proved to be especially frustrating. The disarray of railroad land titles was a thorny obstacle, as was the difficulty of dealing with bankrupt corporations whose priorities were elsewhere. Adjacent landowner opposition also proved troublesome and required cautious diplomacy. In some cases farmers were more interested in punching through the railroad grade in order to get easier access to croplands on the other side. Certain rural landowners would have had state officials believe that the typical user of one of these corridors would be a pot-crazed hippie astride an out-of-control and unmuffled Harley-Davidson, hell-bent on rape, arson, vandalism, pillage — and litter.

There remains a reservoir of resentment in some areas of rural Indiana about providing recreational opportunities for their city brethren, unless one happens to own a business which serves tourists. Unfortunately, some of the hostility has racial overtones. The most developable recreational corridors proved to be those having an origin or terminus within an existing state park, forest, or other recreational holding. The department was able to anchor the project to land it already held; personnel employed at the existing facility could monitor and maintain the quality of the new corridors.

Despite this intensification of interest in new properties, the department could have done without one project. Veterans' organizations called for the creation of a state memorial honoring Hoosier war correspondent Ernie Pyle. The Indianapolis *Star* quickly took up the drumbeat. The department was reluctant. The Pyle house which was to be the basis for this memorial had little historic value and would represent a questionable operating burden for a project of little utility. Unfortunately, when one of these journalistic steamrollers gets going it is difficult to halt, even with the soundest logic in one's favor. In situations like this politicians adopt the avoidance-of-pain solution and quiet the clamor by throwing money at it. The governor and legislature meekly accepted the proposal.

The Pyle memorial at Dana has lived down to expectations. It is visited only in dribbles (fewer than 300 people in one recent year); there is nothing unique in the house. Only a collection of Pyle memorabilia tucked away in a basement room has true appeal. Ernie Pyle would have been better memorialized if these artifacts had been placed at the State Museum, or the War Memorial complex, or at the department of journalism at Indiana University whose building bears his name.

The department also began to promote a program of scenic and recreational rivers as an outgrowth of federal legislation designed to foster them. Rigid land-use controls required by federal authorities attracted opposition from other government agencies and utilities, which foresaw the designation of lengthy river reaches as serious constraints upon future highway, pipeline, or utility projects. An excellent water access program was completed on picturesque Blue River, a tributary to the Ohio, but attempts to establish a river corridor on Sugar Creek between Crawfordsville and Turkey Run State Park were stalled by local interests. In the latter 1970s the department advanced the concept of urban river parks. Pilot projects commenced.

Preservation of natural areas threatened with extinction in an urbanizing state received attention during the eight-year period. More than 30 tracts of environmentally significant land were brought into the state's nature preserves system. Protected holdings in excess of 7,000 acres now provide testimony to the state's interest in maintaining in perpetuity its outstanding natural features — unusual geologic formations; rare plant and animal species; and unique forests, caves, bogs, prairielands, lakes, and cliffs. Occasionally, it was difficult to muster legislative support. Lawmakers are inclined to be development-oriented in their outlook on lands acquired by the state. Citizens' organizations, principally the Nature Conservancy, gave valuable encouragement, either in the form of outright donations or by purchasing lands which came on the market. They held them for the department until it was able to make reimbursement from a subsequent legislative appropriation.

The preservation of wildlife, whether for the esthetic enjoyment of observers or the sport of hunters, also gained prominence. It had become apparent that developmental pressures were steadily eroding the habitat for wildlife species. The department concluded that it would be impossible to achieve a full reversal of this decline, but devised a small game program in hopes of slowing it. The 1979 legislature adopted a wildlife habitat law on the pattern of a forest preservation act adopted years earlier. The measure provided substantial tax benefits for preserving lands suitable for wildlife cover. The perceived value of the "Save our Small Game" program was stimulated by the bitter winters of 1977 and 1978, which ravaged upland small game populations with extraordinary rates of winter kill. Pheasant populations that once had flourished in rural northwestern Indiana in one of the nation's prime hunting regions were slaughtered by harsh weather.

However, the department resisted hunters' clamor for authorizing a hunting season on doves. "Dove bills" had become hardy perennials — and the source of occasional hilarity — during legislative sessions. Lawmakers ultimately kicked the ball to the department, granting the director the authority to open this species to the skill of Hoosier hunters. Cloud refused to do so. He reasoned that doves represented less bountiful fare than other game species taken home to mother to clean. Their limited value would be more than offset by anti-hunter sentiment that would be stirred by environmentalists who frothed in opposition. A case could be made for a dove season, from a game management standpoint, and many within the department favored this policy. Nonetheless, the director prevailed in his opposition for eight years.

Preservation programs also spilled over into wetlands, the marshy regions at the fringes of lakes and small streams which provide nourishment vital to aquatic life. Widespread intrusions into Indiana's wetland had spurred the National Resources Commission to adopt a policy in the late 1960s that it would oppose encroachment into "significant" wetlands had spurred the Natural Resources Commission to adopt a policy the courts. It is difficult to preserve a wetland on a basis that leaves the landowner with any economic use of his property. The state's policy came close to a taking of property without compensation — which put it at odds with the Constitution. The commission used the regulatory process as best it could. The department also secured legislative appropriations for the outright acquisition of large wetlands in recognition that this was the only way to guarantee their preservation.

Outdoor enthusiasts benefited from the department's ambitious fish-stocking programs. Realizing that Brookville Lake was deep enough to support cold-water species and that the potential for restocking the tributaries of Lake Michigan offered new opportunities for anglers, the department constructed a coldwater fish hatchery in northern Indiana and distributed its fry and fingerlings to numerous points around the state.

The management of urban area parks was seen as a special challenge. Controversies surrounding the Dunes Lakeshore were not lost on state officials. When a joint federal, state, and local flood control and recreational development project was authorized for the Little Calumet River in Lake and Porter counties, Cloud and his advisers determined that traditional management by either the department or local boards was insufficient to cope with the issues surrounding regional parks. "Little Cal" represented one of the most flood-prone areas of the state, yet the mitigation of floods which threatened literally thousands of homes also provided a method to bring additional recreational opportunities to a region badly lacking them. Cloud proposed a regional commission to manage the project. He was rebuffed by local interests which saw greater potential for obtaining state financing if the matter were left on the doorstep of the Department of Natural Resources. Unfortunately, a local advisory commission floundered in indecision, spats of disagreement, and a revolving-door turnover of members. Most legislators and the State Budget Agency were only lukewarm to the project, which had an overall price tag in excess of $100 million. Initially, State Senator Adam Benjamin was able to secure state appropriations, but his departure to the Congress deprived the project of its only effective ally in the legislature. His successors were only lackluster in their advocacy and could not match his ability to grasp the appropriations process at the short end of the funnel.

In Indianapolis, meanwhile, enthusiasm was developing for a grand-scale urban area state park along the edges of White River in Marion County. Indianapolis interests promoted it with an intensity absent in the northwest Indiana project and secured a $10 million appropriation in 1979. The pot had been sweetened by a $5 million challenge grant from Lilly Endowment. The state administration applied to the White River project the management approach originally designed for Little Calumet. The Indianapolis project was off and running. While northwestern interests were dawdling, capital city legislators made an effective assault on the state treasury. The White River project gained enemies because the $10 million appropriation was siphoned off from other capital projects dear to out-state lawmakers. Its most vocal critics characterized it as a boondoggle for inner city dwellers. Again, one cannot escape an uneasy sense that some of the carping had negative implications involving race. Still others were suspicious that the project was little more than a stalking horse for a domed stadium for the capital city. In retrospect, this last concern was justified. It later became clear that this was exactly what some in the Indianapolis power structure had in mind. However, the governor and White River Park Commission effectively closed the door to its use as an instrument for building a stadium. Even though this policy strained relationships with a few members of the Indianapolis establishment, it was the only proper course of action if the goal actually was that of building an exceptional park. Advancing the White River Park was barely possible; its connection to a professional sports project would have guaranteed legislative repeal.

Legal controversies in two key areas were the focus of attention during the second term. The state challenged federal surface mining legislation. Officials deemed Indiana's existing program to be effective and environmentalists conceded this point. Stringent new federal rules would retard future mining in Indiana and would bankrupt small miners who could not economically cope with its bewildering provisions. The federal program posed ominous implications for bureaucratic mischief. The manning table for the federal operation indicated that as many as four times the number of federal bureaucrats would enforce the new law as had been used by Indiana to maintain its workable program during the 1970s. The Interior Department's approach also ran afoul of the realities of geology. The governor, DNR, and the coal industry sued the Interior Department, citing a number of issues which included questions of state sovereignty. Although the Office of Surface Mining pooh-poohed its objections, Indiana was close to winning the issue in court as the Bowen administration closed out. (In June, 1981, however, the U.S. Supreme Court reversed a lower-court decision favorable to the state).

The other feud involved the historical boundary dispute between Indiana and Kentucky. When all of the legal and environmental rhetoric was stripped away, it was clear that the basis for Kentucky's objections was a desire to kill Indiana's port project in Clark County and to forestall a number of energy conversion projects on the Indiana side of the river. Foremost among them was Public Service Indiana's Marble Hill nuclear facility. Kentucky coal interests opposed nuclear development. The Louisville *Courier-Journal* mounted vigorous attacks for these reasons and, state officials believed, because its publisher lived in a sumptuous homestead on the Kentucky side of the river opposite to Indiana's proposed port. Mr. Bingham emphatically denied a personal interest in the matter, but Bowen once recalled a visit to the publisher's home in which Bingham pointed to the easy chair in which he sipped juleps while enjoying the magnificent view of the river and its borderlands.

The United States Supreme Court affirmed Ohio's contention that the low water mark of 1792 was the proper boundary. This left the northern states with a modest, but important hold on the river's edge. Indiana quickly associated itself with this decision. The two states moved quickly in 1980 to implement the court's intent that litigants determine the precise boundary. This could be a difficult task since the area was only thinly settled in 1792, but was possible in view of the extensive land records compiled by the Corps of Engineers when it transformed the Ohio River from a free flowing stream into a series of lakes maintained at stable levels to accommodate navigation. At this writing, the outcome remained unclear. It was apparent that Kentucky, which had nothing to gain by a settlement, would have to be dragged along kicking and screaming.

Other water-related issues became the source of the department's attention during the second Bowen term. Deputy Director Andrews had for years contended that the state's legal and regulatory framework for managing its water resource and for resolving disputes about water rights was hopelessly out of date. It was a throwback to a rude frontier, agricultural era that bore no resemblance to an urbanized state. Cloud, Hillenbrand, and I decided that a study of water resources issues should be the "think-tank" priority for the department during the final Bowen term. The governor embraced our proposal. He offered it to the 1977 legislature in terms describing an historic transition in state policy away from a preoccupation with flood control and now giving prominence to ever-conflicting demands for consumption of a finite water resource. The governor called for a comprehensive evaluation of water rights law and formulation of management programs to resolve disputes and assure that Indiana's water needs would be met through the year 2000.[7]

The legislature failed to act on the plan. The governor then implemented it administratively. The Governor's Water Resources Study Commission was activated in July, 1977, with Hillenbrand as its chairman.[8] The group, comprising nearly 30 citizens representing a broad spectrum of interests, carried out the most thorough assessment of water issues in the state's history. Early in 1980 it published a thick volume which described in detail the current status of water supply, environmental issues, and legal constraints. The report included forecasts of economic and social trends that would have impact upon the resource.[9] In the closing days of the administration the commission came forth with a comprehensive list of recommendations, including the adoption of a permit system for large users.[10] The commission was not so naive as to believe that its proposals would be eagerly snapped up by the political system, but it accomplished its purpose of developing a rational water scheme for Indiana. At some point in the 1980s, many of its recommendations will gain attention. Growing competition for the resource is steadily gnawing away at the value of the obsolescent system of laws and regulations which now guide state water policy.

The Department of Natural Resources completed capital projects and innovative programs during the Bowen administration that were unprecedented in their scope. They have been treated extensively in this volume because of their importance to the success of the administration. Bowen came to the governorship as a single-issue candidate. His property tax package provided enduring and tangible financial benefits to the people of the state. The department's programs provided a visible, people-pleasing asset of both tangible and esthetic dimensions. Polls taken for the 1976 re-election campaign identified Bowen with tax questions, but little else in terms of specific policies and programs — except for DNR's recreational development achievements. The public, according to the pollsters, did not rate recreation as an important accomplishment, but it was one that was almost universally known about and applauded. It underscored the Bowen style and provided an appealing balance to the mechanics of tax policy. The department's recreational revitalization program, therefore, was one of the foundation blocks upon which the administration's reputation had its most solid base.

XI INSIDE THE GOVERNOR'S OFFICE

The quiet dignity of the ornate and expansive private office of the governor existed in sharp contrast to the boiler room atmosphere of cluttered cubicles nearby where a staff of more than 20 people labored to keep abreast of the oppressive volume of business which commanded Bowen's attention. An office such as his is a turbulent environment. Staff advisers to influential public officials are by their very nature highly-motivated and assertive. Personality is an overvalued currency within the political process and tends to emphasize individuals to the exclusion of institutions. The volume and variety of work contributes to this turmoil, as does the diversity of visitors — who range from the powerful leaders of business and government to transients from a nearby bus station and walkaways from mental hospitals.

What could have been a fragile apparatus of conflicting ideas and personalities instead was a fairly solid management arrangement because of the style employed by the governor. Outspoken disagreements seemed out of place with the soft-spoken chief executive's consensus orientation. Bowen's decision to confer equality upon his executive assistants was a deterrent to jockeying for primacy. Overall, the business of state government was conducted with less disharmony than outsiders might have expected.

The division of functional responsibilities among the six executive assistants has been described elsewhere. This single decision established the basic communications network within the office and between Bowen and his agencies. Although boundary lines occasionally were blurry, the governor and his staff usually were able to guide the flow of routine and policymaking without foulups. At his first meeting with department heads on January 9, 1973, Bowen described the six aides as assistants, helpers, ombudsmen, and troubleshooters — but not cabinet members nor bosses of agency directors. As the administration evolved, many department heads were able to establish comfortable working relationships with these six people of uncertain authority.

In a few cases, executive assistants became departmental superiors in a practical sense, either because the governor's office had concluded that an agency's leadership was inadequate or a gubernatorial staff member was recognized as having a degree of expertise which caused the processes of decisionmaking to flow in his direction. At times the assistants became over-involved in agency functions because department heads sought protection against the fallout from what could turn out to be unpopular or unfortunate decisions. If a gubernatorial assistant were made party to the process, he might also be the receptacle for blame if things went awry.

Conscious effort was required to keep from becoming enmeshed in departmental routine, but the assistants sometimes succumbed to this perversion of what had been intended to be a liaison function. A few department heads possessed an inadequate sense of the broader implications of their actions and required regular monitoring or nudging. Less frequently, the governor's office had a negative view of agency director's capabilities or motives.

Assistants to Bowen were far more visible than their counterparts in earlier administrations, in which the governor had functioned as the single visible source of decisionmaking and communication with the public. Bowen's style, and the sheer volume of issues and agencies, argued against his functioning as the sole chokepoint. The traditional approach also reflected a policy to focus all publicity upon the chief executive and thereby enhance his stature. However, a governor automatically is the source of daily publicity and requires little artificial pumping up if the public's perception of his administration is, on the whole, favorable.

For the most part the assistants worked well together, with little of the backstabbing or confrontations common to the top ranks of government and corporations. Intrigues and manipulations were risky because the governor was quick to take offense at disunity within the office. Although assistants occasionally wandered onto others' turf, permanent divisions did not occur.

Maldistribution of functional responsibilities was one contributor to this situation. The Public Service Commission, for example, was included on William Lloyd's roster of regulatory agencies. Its identification with energy and transportation issues required parallel liaison with me. In time my informal liaison eclipsed his formally-defined relationship with the agency.

What several assistants believed to be an attempt by Lloyd to assert himself as the principal executive assistant caused problems in the early months. Raymond Rizzo and Viola Walker were especially troubled by these moves; if one assistant was to be pre-eminent, Rizzo probably deserved the designation because of his seniority with Bowen. Rizzo, however, did not push the matter, but in concert with Walker and me, moved to thwart Lloyd's ambitions. For a time it seemed that the staff might divide into two factions — one built around Lloyd, Robert DeBard, and management consultant James Smith, and the other around Rizzo, Walker, and Watt. This trend didn't take hold because neither group could afford to clash in the open without risking gubernatorial reprimand. When DeBard departed for the State Police superintendency, Smith replaced him and then evidenced little interest in prolonging the jousting. The new assistant quietly moved to a neutral position, then edged closer to the other group, gradually isolating Lloyd. Factionalism rapidly lost its definition and the staff settled into a state of congenial confusion insofar as determining any pecking order was concerned.

Identifying and getting close to whomever is presumed to be the key insider is a popular game among those who make their living at the Statehouse. Most lobbyists and other operatives had become accustomed to wiring a connection to the one person deemed most influential — usually the "political" assistant. This was a perplexing guessing game during Bowen's administration because any one of three or four people might qualify. Unable to single out one person, lobbyists had to check signals with several Bowen aides. This produced mildly frustrating levels of duplication and unnecessary discussions. However, it had the effect of dispersing information among key assistants, while making it difficult for any one of them to carve a political deal without the others getting wind of it.

In addition to the executive assistants and executive secretary, Lieutenant Governor Orr, Budget Director Ed Thuma (later John Huie), Revenue Commissioner Donald Clark, and Administration Commissioner Raymond Sanders also counted among the inner circle of daily gubernatorial advisers. Their common meeting ground was the thrice-weekly staff meeting during the first term (two times a week in the final four years). These informal gatherings were of about 90 minutes' duration. Bowen would lead off with two or three problems or issues about which he sought information or advice. In turn, the others offered brief reports about developments or raised issues which required gubernatorial action. Bowen liked the staff meeting because it served as an updating device under circumstances which enabled him to solicit opinion on a basis that did not foreclose looking to other sources before making a final decision.

Staff meetings had their shortcomings, though. Thuma, in particular, was frustrated by the occasional superficiality of discussions. More formal agendas, supported by additional facts or position papers, would have provided a better framework in which to debate issues, he believed. The budget director's point of view had merit, but the governor didn't want to give up the informal atmosphere of these sessions. The process also failed to insure that an assistant would volunteer information about an agency decision or administration program that others on the staff were entitled to share in.

Personnel turnover in a governor's office can move at a rapid pace, but Bowen enjoyed continuity throughout his administration. Assistants W.T. Ray and I were on board for the duration, and Smith for all but the first nine months. (To give some idea of turnover, a comparison of rosters of staff assistants to governors throughout the eight-year period disclosed that, nationwide, only four others had been in place for eight years or longer.) Lee Ellen Ford, an outsider almost from the start and involved in frequent disputes with the governor, departed in 1976. Judith Palmer, a budget agency analyst, succeeded her in January, 1977. Lloyd resigned in May, 1978, to return to law practice and was replaced by Assistant Attorney General Susan Davis. Rizzo departed in October, 1978. Brian Bosworth, who had directed "Title 20" programs in the Department of Welfare, took over his portfolio. A seventh executive assistant position was created in January, 1977, for William DuBois, who had functioned as campaign press secretary. Walker, the governor's executive secretary, remained until September, 1980. Sue Senff carried out those responsibilities during the closing months of Bowen's administration.

In addition to the functions of agency liaison and advice to the governor, assistants also reviewed contracts, regulations, and other documents before they were presented to Bowen for signature. Mail was handled in much the same fashion. Incoming correspondence was allocated by functions. Unless it represented a significant question of administrative policy, Bowen first saw mail when it was presented to him accompanied by a proposed response. In all but a few cases — most of them involving form replies to organized letter-writing campaigns — he made a point to review each document.

A number of ancillary functions were attached to the governor's immediate office, including interagency study commissions which didn't fit conveniently elsewhere, and special projects (such as the Governor's Voluntary Action Commission). Most important, however, was the state's Washington liaison office.

Bowen staffed the Washington office more extensively than his predecessors, who usually had employed one person. A four-person staff during the eight-year period enabled the state to be far more effective in gathering information about pending federal legislation and agency policies. The governor and his staff welcomed the contributions of this office, headed by Donald Newman, because it provided information not easily obtained elsewhere. It also offered a convenient conduit to the state's congressional delegation to convey the governor's position on legislation, and to deal with constituent inquiries received by congressmen but more properly directed toward state government.

The Washington staff was less successful in helping the state bargain with federal agencies when disagreements arose. It was not their fault, because federal bureaucrats paid only lip service to the states. Keeping the states at arms length by using only low-ranking federal representatives in negotiations was a frequent technique. Several layers of superiors always seemed to stand in the way of a final decision. Easily ensnarled in the rigid caste system of doing business in the nation's capital, the Washington office occasionally was not able to marshal senior government officials for these discussions. As the governor's assistants and department heads developed their own links to the federal bureaucracy, they often were able to wire higher-level connections than the Washington office could develop on its own. On balance, Bowen's staff rated Newman's operation as a very useful tool, nonetheless.

The governor only infrequently delegated decision-making regarding the hundreds of appointments made annually, although he usually conferred with the appropriate assistant. A secretary, whose full-time job was that of processing appointments, kept track of vacancies. A packet of information, including names of incumbents, statutory qualifications, and letters of recommendation, was provided to him 30 to 60 days in advance of the expiration of terms. From that point Bowen usually handled the process personally. It was a time-consuming chore to which he devoted several hours each day.

An equivalent level of personal concern was applied to clemency and parole issues. If a governor approves recommendations of the state clemency commission, parole is almost automatic. Inmate records first were evaluated by the assistant who worked with the corrections system (DeBard, later Smith), then reviewed by Bowen. The governor frequently rejected clemency recommendations if the crimes had been violent and the time served relatively short. If drugs or alcohol had been a factor, he wanted assurance that rehabilitation programs were a condition of parole.

At times the piles of paperwork seemed overwhelming. The daily volume of letters might run in the hundreds. Thick regulations also required perusal. A mountain of contracts needed signatures in several places. Travel requests, commissions for railroad police, appointments of notaries, and other documents of this type were especially burdensome. During a period in which the private sector had begun to plan for the "paperless" office and relied heavily on computerized communication, state government remained enmired in forms, seals, ribbons, and stamping devices.

In addition to letters, the most frequently generated written documents were gubernatorial speeches. Rizzo, the principal speechwriter, churned out as many as 200 addresses per year during the first term, when the governor maintained an exceptionally heavy load of public appearances.

Although a number of speeches could be recycled — to use the office term for adapting the same address to a number of forums — the writing chores placed a heavy burden on Rizzo, who had a number of equally demanding departmental chores in the education, mental health, and welfare sectors. I backed him up, especially when the subject matter involved energy, transportation, or environmental issues. The governor was comfortable with Rizzo's writing style, with its moderate pace and conversational tone — although, perhaps, overloaded with adverbs and a tendency to sneak up on the subject with a couple of pages of introductory patter. My style was less suitable, carrying the abruptness derived from a wire service editor's training. After Rizzo's departure, speechwriting duties fell upon DuBois, a competent craftsman whose style struck a compromise between the tautness of journalism and the informality with which the governor was suited. When he left to join the Orr campaign in early 1980, these chores were assumed by Terri Johnson, brought over from the State Highway Department, and me, although the frequency of gubernatorial speeches dwindled markedly in the closing months of the administration.

The workload also required that the staff absorb most citizen inquiries and complaints. Office secretaries and receptionists became quite adept at sorting out legitimate complaints from crank calls (of which there were a disturbing number), referring people to proper agencies when that seemed to be the most expedient solution. Usually, though, people wanted to talk directly to the governor, but settled for the voice of an assistant. Keeping one's perspective was difficult, for experience had established that few complainants offered more than a distorted piece of a controversy. Some, however, were legitimate and had to be checked out. It was tempting, too, to assume that criticism against a highly-regarded agency automatically was unjustified. Pressures of time required that many inquiries be referred to the agency involved for final determination. Their conclusions were difficult to challenge.

From time to time the governor faced requests that his office investigate an agency or individual. It was his policy to refer formal allegations of impropriety or criminal conduct to the State Police or State Board of Accounts. However, outsiders occasionally demanded a governor's office investigation. Journalists were frequent sources of these requests. They presumed that the governor would find it difficult to reject their demands for investigations. His agreement to do so also would provide at least a superficial vindication of stories they already had written, while setting in motion a further series of page one episodes that would be easy to write. Occasionally, Bowen staff members joined with the State Police or individual departments to conduct internal investigations, but the governor normally brushed aside demands for gubernatorial inquiries. His staff was untrained in the craft of gumshoeing; giving way also would invite frivolous requests from political foes or special interest groups dissatisfied with an agency or program.

A State Police detail of three or four members was attached to the office to provide personal security for the governor. Bowen was uncomfortable with the arrangement, which to him was more symbolic of pomp than of necessity. However, he accepted the convenience their presence afforded. During the course of the administration, there were only a handful of threats against the governor. Only two of them were taken seriously enough to prompt preventative measures. State Police routinely sifted through letters placed in what Walker termed the "strange file" in hopes of segregating the sinister from the senile.

The governor maintained a more rigorous schedule than his staff. Unless other engagements disrupted his schedule, he arrived about 8:20 a.m. and endeavored to work undisturbed until 10 a.m., unless staff meetings intervened. His desire for solitude frequently was frustrated by a series of quick early-morning interviews with newsmen or brief consultations with staff members. Avoiding business-type luncheons, he preferred the company of Beth for lunch in the surroundings of the governor's residence. Frequently working until 7 or 7:30 p.m., the governor normally carried home another couple hours of work. Bowen's inability to carve out sufficient time for work in private caused him to install a small working desk and chair in the executive restroom, his only true refuge from subordinates. When meeting with interest groups or individuals, he normally invited only the assistant whose responsibilities were associated with the subject matter, seldom surrounding himself with a phalanx of aides.

Bowen's style was infectious and the staff usually found it easy to accommodate his method of operation. Almost daily contact with executive assistants was the pattern. Smith and I probably made the most intrusions, because our involvement with crisis management and the media required that he be given frequent updates.

However, even the quiet informality which pervaded the office was insufficient to prevent what is now termed "executive burnout" — the numbing and wearing down of too many years of daily difficulties. The exuberance of the early years had been replaced by fatigue during the final two years of the administration. The governor's weariness was exacerbated by the personal consequences of Mrs. Bowen's illness. Fortunately, the influx of new assistants — notably Davis and Bosworth — brought fresh thinking and new vigor to an administration growing tired.

XII   RAILROAD CRISIS

The impending collapse of the giant Penn-Central Transportation Company and six other bankrupt eastern rail carriers presented the Bowen administration with the thorniest transportation problem of its first term. It was a challenge for which state government was poorly prepared. Indiana's twentieth century involvement in transportation issues was a near-exclusive preoccupation with highway building. Yet the eastern rail bankruptcies had ominous implications for Indiana and the other states of the industrialized east. Railroad bankruptcies had been common throughout the industry's history. The deterioration of the region's rail network reflected a trend underway since the 1920s. However, the situation in 1973 represented the first occasion on which the outright collapse of a large portion of the region's rail service might occur.

The failure of the Penn-Central merger and the decades-long decline of its predecessor companies was the result of circumstances which do not require restatement here.[1] By 1973 Penn-Central's system was a shambles. Losses edged upward to near $1 million a day. Creditors screamed for a liquidation that would preserve at least a fraction of its rapidly eroding assets. Delays, derailments, and defective equipment were producing shippers' nightmares. Penn-Central represented the backbone of the Indiana rail system, accounting for 47 percent of the route mileage and providing exclusive service to a number of medium-sized industrial cities. Ten of the state's eleven General Motors installations were captives of its service. Trucks would not have been able to replace the heavy volumes of raw materials and finished goods that were shunted in to and out of these factories at a pace which rolled over inventories every 72 hours.

The other bankrupt line in the Hoosier state was Erie-Lackawanna, which operated an important dual-track main line route across northern

Indiana. After teetering on the brink of insolvency for years, the Erie was unable to rebound from the ravages of Hurricane Agnes on its water-level routes in Appalachia.

The railroad bankruptcies presented a vexing political problem as well. Railroading has a unique, almost mystical niche in American history because of its close association with the nation's expansion and industrialization. Until the growth of the highway system, rails had been the common denominator for transportation of both people and commerce, closely tied to local prosperity. Therefore, to community leaders the end of service seemed akin to losing manhood, even though trucking had replaced the rails as the primary transporter of goods to and from small-town America. The very visibility of railroads insured that mayors and local legislators would clamor for the preservation of service. Their reactions often were blind to the fact that railroads had ceased to be used in many communities. Abandonment petitions were little more than symbolic confirmations of half-century old economic trends that had doomed their towns to relative unimportance. Journalists also harbor a special affection for railroads. Every newsroom seems to be inhabited by at least one rail buff. Editorial diatribes often were no more than outpourings of agitated nostalgia for a rail passenger system that had ebbed to a fraction of its former dominance, while they ignored the implications of the deterioration of freight service. This combination of factors guaranteed that much journalistic ink and political rhetoric would flow as government and the industry wrestled with a problem that had smoldered for far too long.

Indiana's approach to the eventual reorganization of the eastern railroads brought a degree of national prominence to Bowen. On at least two occasions his intervention helped to insure that the reorganization was carried forward. A few other governors — Milton Shapp of Pennsylvania, for one — became identified with political demagoguery as they waged futile political fights to protect every branch line in their states. Bowen emerged as a leader among state officials who sought a constructive resolution of the issue, recognizing fully that there were routes whose retention simply could not be justified. Since Indiana was among the states most affected by the reorganization, Bowen's opinions carried weight with a Republican administration in Washington.

Indiana's first taste of the Penn-Central issue took place in February, 1973, when the United Transportation Union threatened a strike. In the hours before it commenced, state officials worked with State Police to isolate and secure shipments of hazardous materials that might be stranded on its system when employees walked off the job. On February 8 the strike commenced, halting rail service to Columbus, Anderson, and Elkhart, while substantially affecting traffic at Indianapolis, South Bend, and Terre Haute. Congress worked overtime that night and sent to President Nixon a joint resolution that halted the walkout for 60 days.

As the months passed Penn-Central trustees began to put the finishing touches on liquidation proposals. The railroad was running out of cash. By early autumn it appeared that the exhausted system might go belly-up within a matter of weeks unless action was taken by the federal government.[2] A fresh blow was dealt on October 15 by safety inspectors of the Federal Railroad Administration, who ordered 500 miles of its 2,800-mile Indiana system shut down because of widespread safety violations. The routes were out of service for only a single day, because state officials and shippers voiced loud objections. The federal agency relented and granted a 30-day compliance period. FRA restricted operating speeds on the questioned lines to eight miles an hour and barred passenger trains from them.[3] Bowen argued that the waiver should be extended:

> The Penn-Central is dying. If the Federal Railroad Administration fails to provide for an extension of this waiver, its action will only hasten the system's death and the subsequent severe economic dislocation that will result. There are some who see this safety compliance procedure as just another device to force a shutdown of the entire system. I earnestly hope that such a course of action is not the agency's intent.
>
> Because of the vital economic interests of Indiana, it is unreasonable not to extend the interim limited waiver until such time as the Penn-Central bankruptcy is resolved and successor corporations or organizations are identified and have time to bring the roadbeds into compliance.
>
> For months, I have been urging Congress and the federal executive branch to bring about a resolution of the Penn-Central problem. Little action is evident. As each day passes, our options become narrower and more costly.[4]

Congress had begun to address the matter. Weeks of feverish and intricate legislative maneuvering culminated in the Regional Rail Reorganization Act of 1973, signed by the President on January 2, 1974.[5] It established the United States Railway Association (USRA) to plan and finance the restructuring of the eastern bankrupts, directed the creation of the Consolidated Rail Corporation (eventually to become known as Conrail), permitted the abandonment of unnecessary routes, and authorized an interim joint federal-state subsidy program to preserve local rail service on routes not identified for inclusion in the final system to be operated by Conrail. The act set forth a series of procedures for the development of the new system. The Department of Transportation was to submit its recommendations within 30 days. The Interstate Commerce Commission's Rail Services Planning Office would conduct public hearings on the report. USRA would prepare a detailed preliminary system plan, followed by another round of ICC hearings. A final system plan then would be completed and forwarded to Congress, which could reject it by adopting a resolution to that effect. Failure by Congress to act negatively automatically would enable the reorganization to proceed. These events were to take place within a two-year period.

The DOT report was well advanced by the time of enactment of the reorganization law. Early indications of its content were disturbing. State officials learned that as much as 40 percent of the state's rail system might be earmarked for potential abandonment. These forebodings were confirmed when the report was released on February 1.[6] It described 2,350 miles of Indiana's 6,405-mile rail system as "potentially excess," a phrase guaranteed to make state officials and shippers nervous inasmuch as the report included in detailed maps the routes of both bankrupt and profitable carriers. The potentially excess segments were colored in orange and soon became notorious as the "orange lines".

DOT was seeking an optimum eastern rail system. Its planners recognized that the planning process could not be carried out in ignorance of the existence of profitable railroads whose routes often paralleled those of the bankrupts. However, the inclusion of profitable segments astounded and confused politicians and shippers alike. None had been led to believe that the restructuring would encompass non-bankrupt systems. Congress had not intended to include them. The effect of the DOT report was that of intensifying the confusion and outrage. Unfortunately, the department made the reorganization process more difficult by the way in which it handled these recommendations. It was another illustration of the failure of planners to recognize that their efforts can be self-defeating because of the manner in which their proposals are framed.

In anticipation of these developments Bowen agreed on January 8, 1974, to activate a task force of state officials to guide Indiana's interests. Its formation was announced a week later. Members included state officials with interests in the transportation and economic development areas. They were augmented by transportation specialists from state universities.[7] I was designated chairman. Initially, it was a rather fumbling undertaking, since the state was without a transportation planning capability to deal with emergencies of this type. In the absence of a coherent arrangement we were fortunate that one of the task force members was Dr. William Black of Indiana University, who volunteered to supervise the technical work associated with the state's response. Public officials in Indiana traditionally have been reluctant to exploit the capabilities of academia because these endeavors too often fail to produce useable results. Black, however, displayed exceptional technical competence. His recommendations provided a solid basis upon which the Bowen administration could press the state's point of view. He also earned the respect of federal planners involved in the reorganization, so much so that he eventually was recruited by Conrail to supervise its state subsidy negotiations during the transition in 1976. In retrospect, the Indiana University contribution to the rail planning effort probably represented the most effective government-university relationship during the Bowen administration. When the General Assembly authorized the creation of a state Department of Transportation in 1980, Black was my automatic recommendation as its first director.

The state's negotiations with a newly-formed USRA commenced later that month when Lieutenant Governor Orr and I met with James Hagen, its vice-president for facilities planning. The session was rather icy. We were aware that Hagen was a principal architect of the DOT recommendations. Although cautious in his commitments, Hagen volunteered to work with Indiana on a regular basis. As the process unfolded, Black represented the state in negotiations involving technical issues (as did his successor, Bruce Pigozzi, in the final months of the reorganization), while I took the lead in overall policy matters. In time we developed a close working relationship with several key USRA officials, among them Arthur Lewis, its chairman and a former president of American Airlines, and Hagen, who went on to become USRA president and later a senior vice-president of Conrail. Another was James McClellan, the assistant vice president for strategic planning and the primary developer of the restructured system. He had been with New York Central and Amtrak, and eventually became director of corporate planning for Southern Railway. Richard Sullivan, USRA's vice-president for public affairs and later secretary of Conrail, was another regular point of contact. The relationship flourished because Indiana was responsibly negotiating the future of rail lines at a time when the other 16 states were taking political potshots at the association.

In testimony before the ICC the governor voiced the state's objections to the DOT plan. He challenged economic data and criticized the implied intent to discontinue lines of solvent carriers, but acknowledged that the state did not intend to burden the reorganized system with routes "that offer no hope of profitability and that would be a continuing drain upon financial and operating resources."[8]

The act required the states to write plans to implement provisions of the subsidy program. It called for the retention of service on lines not incorporated into the new system, provided the states defray 30 percent of the operating losses. Indiana's planning took a different direction. The rail task force was not overly enchanted with the subsidy program — uncertain that the legislature would fund it and preferring a strategy that attempted to retain worthwhile lines within the restructured system while jettisoning the obvious "dogs." Black's technical work developed this theme.

Meanwhile, the reorganization was in a state of confusion. USRA could not meet a late October deadline for completing its preliminary system plan. Penn-Central's creditors challenged the reorganization on the "erosion" issue, claiming that the corporation's assets were being diminished during the planning period on a scale that amounted to the unconstitutional taking of property without compensation. They won the initial round in court, but the government prevailed on appeal.

The ultimate form of the restructuring was by this time generating heated debate. Easterners were wary of a Conrail monopoly. They failed to realize that the system of bankrupts east of Pittsburgh and Buffalo offered only dismal prospects for profitable railroad operations, given a tradition of high fixed costs to serve a declining industrial market. Conservatives argued for a restructuring that would emphasize the profitable railroads. This would have been the ideal solution but was an impractical one because few solvent carriers had the financial resources to make the necessary investments and because no one wanted to operate in the chaotic railroad environment of the Middle Atlantic states. Several Eastern planners wanted to create two government-sponsored railroads to avoid the monopoly problem: a slimmed-down Conrail and a competitor carved out of Erie-Lackawanna and smaller bankrupts in the terminal districts of the Middle Atlantic region (in which the rail map looked like spilled spaghetti). Others promoted the Chessie System as the proper inheritor of the Erie. New Englanders advanced the concept of government ownership of the roadbeds. Many within the national administration preferred what was termed "controlled liquidation", the auctioning off of the system to solvent carriers on a phased-in basis. The sweeping variety of proposals — ranging from outright nationalization to a traditional liquidation — were bewildering to rail planning officials already wrestling with more than enough contradictory strategies for carrying out the intent of the federal law.[9]

The despairing state of operating conditions again was underscored when FRA shut down the Penn-Central main line between Chicago, Indianapolis, and Louisville. The agency cited hundreds of safety infractions. This action forced the rerouting of Amtrak's *Floridian* and *James Whitcomb Riley* and hastened the demise of passenger service to Indiana's capitol city.[10] Freight service later was restored over this route, after patchwork repairs were made, but north-south passenger runs continued to avoid Indianapolis.

USRA's initial round of study identified 1,143 miles of light density Penn-Central lines as potential candidates for exclusion from the Conrail System. The Governor's Rail Task Force focused its attention on these segments and completed a preliminary report on the disputed 1,143 miles of track. It concluded that 199 were for all practical purposes already abandoned and useless to the new system. Another 273 miles were described as little used, unprofitable, and requiring unwarranted levels of expenditure to keep in operation.[11] The governor publicly endorsed these findings in August, 1974, and forwarded them to the federal government.[12] Bowen also warned against further delay in the reorganization process, noting the precarious financial position of the ailing carriers. Indiana's recommendations were the first to be submitted from among the 17 states. Because of their thoroughness and the task force's acknowledgement that extensive abandonments were justified, the federal reaction was favorable. However, this represented only the initial round of extensive negotiations regarding more than 600 miles which remained at issue.[13]

In February, 1975, Congress was forced to allocate funds to continue operations after Penn-Central's trustees notified the federal government that it would begin embargoes of new shipments in February and would cease operations in March. In February, 1975, the state recommended that two additional branch lines, totaling 51 miles, also be dropped from consideration for inclusion in Conrail.[14]

The preliminary system plan released later that month revealed that state-federal differences had narrowed. There existed a serious division of opinion over the manner in which the costs of operating branch lines should be allocated. This was the heart of the branch line problem. USRA's methodology assigned a level of off-branch costs that made most light density lines appear to be unprofitable. State people thought that federal planners were cooking the books.

The governor's reaction was critical of these cost allocation formulas and of the rehabilitation projections used in the preliminary plan. His testimony also questioned whether or not the long-term financial health of the Conrail system could be achieved. However, Bowen described the reorganization concept expressed in the preliminary plan as preferable to other courses of action, such as a controlled liquidation or government ownership of roadbeds.[15]

Meanwhile, the governor was pressing the Indiana General Assembly to enact authorizing legislation that would enable the state to subsidize essential lines that might not be included in Conrail. The proposal, based on model legislation drafted for the Council of State Governments by Black, represented an abrupt departure from traditional state policy. The Public Service Commission was granted a $2 million appropriation and sweeping authority to assist in the preservation of these routes. Influential sponsors, such as Representatives Spencer Schnaitter of Madison, and Robert O'Maley of Richmond, the chairman and ranking minority members of the House Ways and Means Committee (and two legislators whose hometowns faced serious impacts if the bill failed), carried the measure through the House. Senators Phillip Gutman, the president pro tempore; Frank O'Bannon, the minority leader, and Keith McCormick, shepherded the bill through the upper chamber. Legislators were reluctant to assign responsibility to a Public Service Commission mired in controversies over utility rate increases. Lawmakers accepted the fact that the program could function as an appendage to the commission, avoiding the necessity of creating a separate agency. The Indiana Rail Preservation Act was adopted with surprisingly little difficulty as potential opponents (such as the trucking industry) maintained neutrality.

Black and I at this time frequently traveled to Washington to bargain for the inclusion of lines omitted from the preliminary plan. About 250 miles left in limbo in the February plan eventually were restored by the USRA board, either through inclusion in the proposed Conrail system or in offers to solvent carriers.[16]

The Erie-Lackawanna link proved especially troublesome. Its trustees had opted for a reorganization under conventional rail bankruptcy proceedings; only in February, 1975, did they conclude that they could not succeed. Congress quickly adopted legislation authorizing Erie's inclusion in USRA's plans, but the system design was far enough along by then that the newcomer never was given the consideration it merited. This high-speed corridor was left out of the final blueprint. Finally included within the state subsidy program under the control of a short-line entrepreneur who lacked the financial resources to sustain it, the Erie's route later collapsed except for a short segment maintained by agricultural shippers.

Events during early summer demonstrated that few states were yet willing to accept the reality of a fundamental revision of the eastern rail network. Eleven affected governors met in June with President Ford and Transportation Secretary William Coleman. All but Bowen urged a moratorium on the whole procedure. The Indiana governor was blunt in his statement to the gathering:

It is time that we faced reality with respect to the problems of bankrupt railroads. I have some disagreements with the plan of the U.S. Railway Association. It proposes abandonments of some lines that I believe should be retained. I believe there is a need for modification of the system design. I believe there may be a need for modification of the financing, to give greater assurance of the ability of the new system. I believe that transitional programs — such as subsidies — need to be made more flexible.

But I am opposed to delay and I am opposed to the notion that we are supposed to retain large numbers of lines that are heavy money losers.

Every day that we delay the reorganization compounds our problems. Our shippers have been in "limbo" since the DOT report 18 months ago. They cannot plan for the future. Expansion plans are being deferred. Jobs are being lost.

Delay will increase the cost of repairing the system. Delay will further dilute the economics of branch line operations. Delay will cost the taxpayer more than a million dollars a day because Congress pre-empted the normal processes and now must guarantee service in the interim.

Several alternatives are being offered. Each has major flaws. I am not bound to the general planning approach of USRA but I haven't yet seen anything I like better.

The eastern railroad system will not improve until we get the reorganization off dead center. I do not consider the USRA plan to be set in cement. As the years pass, change will be needed.

We must get on with it. We must stop the accelerating deterioration of the systems. We must direct our money toward rebuilding, not continue to squander it to cover operating losses.[17]

Bowen's position put him directly at odds with Pennsylvania Governor Shapp, who had won election upon a platform of vicious criticism of Penn-

Central and who styled himself the states' expert on rail matters. Fortunately, Shapp's whining abrasiveness did not endear him to the Ford Administration. Bowen's practical approach helped influence the President not to delay the reorganization. The governor's position was applauded in Indiana as several newspapers favorably contrasted his position against the fight-for-every-mile mentality of the others. One editorial writer observed that his seemed to be the only level head among the group.[18]

Although the association's final plan, released in August, 1975, left Indiana and federal officials about 325 miles apart in their dispute over what the map should look like, Bowen endorsed the proposal. He listed the reasons cited in the statement to the White House meeting, but also because he was convinced that it was unlikely that a better plan would emerge in time to rescue the faltering situation on the bankrupt railroads. A moratorium would further undermine operating conditions on the branch lines in question, insuring their ultimate failure and increasing the eventual cost to shippers who would be forced to find alternative sources.[19]

Within a few weeks New York and New Jersey joined Indiana in concluding that the plan was acceptable. With three of the five states most affected by the bankruptcy supporting the federal plan — Pennsylvania maintaining its vigorous opposition, but Ohio strangely silent — the probability that a cabal of states could thwart the effort now was less likely. The Public Service Commission then began the process of identifying lines eligible for state assistance through a series of hearings in October.[20]

The final system plan took effect on November 9, 1975, as the deadline for congressional repudiation expired without the adoption of a negative resolution. However, the reorganization process nearly became unhinged because of a number of corollary issues requiring legislation that proved difficult to enact. The most important consideration was that of some form of protection for solvent carriers who acquired segments of the bankrupts against deficiency judgments that might result from the settlement of the complex valuation case that would be litigated before the Court of Claims. Congress had directed USRA to compensate railroad estates for assets to be transferred to Conrail at the minimum dollar value that would stand the constitutional test of not taking property without compensation. Naturally, creditors wailed loudly when USRA set a price tag of roughly $700 million for the track, facilities, and rolling stock to be conveyed. Certain creditors, Citibank of New York, for example, were holding out for preposterous levels of creditor compensation and suggested figures as high as $10 billion. Timing was critical, too, since the solvent railroads had only until December 9 to decide upon the acquisition of routes offered them by USRA. At the heart of the matter were 2,000 miles of Erie-Lackawanna and Reading track intended for transfer to Chessie System. Chessie logically balked at an acquisition whose cost might not be known for several years until the valuation case was resolved. Its purchase of the Erie lines was crucial to the restructuring. The acquisition would establish Chessie as a strong competitor to Conrail in the Mid-Atlantic region. If Chessie backed out, these lines would be incorporated into Conrail's network, leaving it a virtual monopoly east of Buffalo and Harrisburg. This would be unacceptable to eastern interests who then would attempt to delay the startup of the new rail system.

Supplemental legislation intended to deal with this and other unsettled questions was mired down in Congress, in part because Transportation Secretary Coleman opposed a number of its features and was waging a bitter fight to remove them. Coleman's critics believed that he was willing to junk the restructuring in favor of a controlled liquidation and transfer to solvent carriers outside the region.

Amid trouble signs that the reorganization was about to fall apart, Bowen took advantage of a White House-sponsored regional issues forum at Indianapolis to put pressure on the administration. I had prepared a two-page memorandum setting forth the obstacles and the state's point of view. The governor shared the document with Commerce Secretary Rogers Morton and Presidential adviser James Cannon during a private meeting on the eve of the November 25 forum. He urged them to put the heat on Coleman to reach a compromise. Cannon transmitted the memorandum to the White House that night. Morton promised to pursue our concerns. Apparently, it had an effect. Arthur Lewis advised me a week later that the White House had moved off dead center and now was pressing Coleman to get a bill enacted. At the same time the governor communicated these concerns in letters to Coleman, President Ford, and Senator Vance Hartke of Indiana. Hartke had played an influential role in enacting reorganization legislation and had cooperated with the state administration throughout the process. Although the first attempt at an indemnification bill faltered, a second version was signed into law on February 6.

This arrangement was sabotaged at the last minute when Chessie withdrew from the agreement. On February 27 Coleman, who had been up all night negotiating, told state officials gathered in his office that the entire transaction fell through because the Brotherhood of Railway and Airline Clerks would not accept an attrition provision to deal with the jobs of 50 surplus clerks in the Delmarva Peninsula lines of Penn-Central. Southern was to have acquired these segments but refused to do so after BRAC insisted that the clerk positions be protected perpetually. With this as an ominous precedent for the price of labor agreements, Chessie withdrew from the Erie-Reading acquisitions.

We were left with "Big Conrail" after all. With the start-up date for Conrail now only five weeks away, it was too late to develop another strategy. In addition to the unpopularity of the fallback position, Conrail would begin operations on a system 2,000 miles larger than planned or budgeted for. It represented a burdensome barnacle on a system that was marginal to begin with.

PSC Chairman Wallace, Pigozzi, and I wrestled with a deluge of technical issues during the final weeks. We attempted to prevent service interruptions or other impairments. One of them involved the Central Indiana Railroad, which had been omitted from Conrail because USRA contended that it was not part of the Penn-Central System (although it was operated as such and was owned by the same parent holding company). McClellan finally agreed to convey it to Conrail, if only for the reason that he was forced to acknowledge that Indiana had been denied due process in considering its future.

As conveyance date approached, strings of boxcars and gondolas, most of them rusting, rotting hulks, moved slowly off rickety branch lines that were not to be retained. It was a disturbing confirmation of the view held by many of us that track and equipment to be transferred to the new railroad were in far worse shape than federal planners had recognized.

Conrail commenced operation on April 1, generally without incident, although Indiana was forced to go to the ICC to reverse an arbitrary decision to close container loading ramps at Huntington and Fort Wayne. An Amtrak passenger train pulled to a halt near Griffith, where a seven-mile stretch of Erie-Lackawanna line, inadvertently omitted from the federal transfer scheme, technically was abandoned and the crew refused to operate over it.

Conrail at least temporarily reversed the decline of its bankrupt predecessors and undertook extensive rehabilitation programs in its first two years of operation. It remained a troubled giant, whose 17,000-mile system was too large for a region whose industrial base was on the decline. Traffic growth projections from USRA's plans proved overly optimistic. A combination of unforeseen events — two disastrous winters, the nation's longest coal strike, and the harsh economic recession of 1980 — burdened it with staggering operating costs and sharply curtailed its revenues.[21]

Without these events Conrail might have succeeded, although some further slimming of its system clearly was needed. By 1980 it was apparent that another reorganization would be compelled within a few years. Given that forecast, some would argue that the reorganization was a failure. To the contrary, the mammoth undertaking of two years' time preserved the essential elements of a system perilously close to collapse and poured hundreds of millions of dollars into maintenance programs that would enhance the system's value. Although all indications point to the fact that it will not meet its goal of becoming profitable under its present structure, Conrail proved to be an important transition arrangement, especially during a period in which extensive consolidations were occurring throughout the nation's railroads.

Indiana's subsidy program proved to have transitional value as well, although state officials were somewhat dismayed at abrupt traffic declines on certain branch lines. It seemed that, despite their outcries at Public Service Commission hearings, many shippers weren't truly interested in maintaining rail service but only wanted the existence of a branch line to dampen rates for truck service they planned to use anyway. In certain cases, continued operation under subsidies provided shippers time to sort out alternatives. A few subsidy lines were absorbed into other railroads. By 1980 the 13 original subsidized lines had dwindled to seven.

The Penn-Central collapse accelerated the downturn of rail passenger service in Indiana because the National Railroad Passenger Corporation (Amtrak) operated exclusively on its routes. Operating conditions on Penn-Central roadbeds were patently undesirable, but Amtrak was culpable for utilizing some of the worst equipment in its fleet on runs such as the *Floridian* and for maintaining schedules that drove customers away. When the corporation proposed in 1973 to discontinue the *National Limited*, a New York-Kansas City run that served Richmond, Indianapolis, and Terre Haute, and the *Floridian*, a Chicago-Florida train that made stops in Logansport, Indianapolis, and Louisville, the governor and other officials protested vehemently. Amtrak withdrew the petition.[22]

However, deteriorating route conditions forced Amtrak's north-south trains to abandon Penn-Central mainlines from Chicago to Indianapolis. Deprived of their most promising Indiana market, the inevitable decline in service continued. The *Floridian* was dropped in 1978, although Governor Bowen urged a two-year suspension during which the state and federal governments could work out an arrangement that might enable the train to operate efficiently. Transportation Secretary Brock Adams ignored his suggestion.[23]

The *National Limited* also was sacrificed as Congress, weary of growing deficits, decided to trim Amtrak's system. Unfortunately, Amtrak had been running the *Limited* on a basis that guaranteed that its financial performance would look terrible, a point raised vigorously by the governor, the United Transportation Union, and city governments along the route. Protestors called attention to equipment shortages and a ludicrous on-time performance record.

Although state officials were dismayed at these developments, the Bowen administration took the position that a major resurgence of passenger service could not materialize without a reversal of the declining fortunes of the freight lines on whose routes Amtrak's schedules would operate. To restore a line to passenger standards for one or two Amtrak runs a day was prohibitively expensive. It could be justified only if the route were used for freight as well. Rail passenger buffs wanted the state to become more deeply involved, but the administration held to its priority of fixing the more essential freight system first.

In 1980 a combination of upgrading by the Louisville & Nashville Railroad and a special $12 million appropriation secured by Senator Birch Bayh enabled Amtrak to inaugurate a Chicago-Indianapolis run that restored passenger service to the capital city. As the administration ended, officials were studying ways in which the state might promote greater frequency of service along this route. They hoped it might emerge as a major regional corridor that could be extended to Cincinnati and Louisville.

XIII   THE LEGISLATURE, 1976

Few Statehouse observers expected much from the abbreviated 1976 session of the Indiana General Assembly. It was an election year; the legislature remained divided in political control. Candidates nervously awaited the coming campaign. The governor eyed a diminishing general fund surplus and set his sights accordingly. Analysts' expectations were met. Perhaps it was a self-fulfilling prophecy. Departing lawmakers read and heard descriptions of their deliberations as a do-nothing session preoccupied with betting and booze.

Disturbed that even the limited spending program recommended by the State Budget Committee would drain what had been a $252 million surplus on June 30, 1975, to $43 million two years later, Bowen urged austerity. His annual message described the financial proposal as a "basic 'no frills' budget that goes about as far down the road of responsible state operation as we can without cutting back on property tax relief, stripping our operating balances to a dangerously low level, or raising taxes — three possibilities which I will not entertain."[1]

It envisioned a moratorium on new state programs and limited the hiring of new state employees only to fulfill requirements of federally mandated programs. A flat-rate inflation factor was built into the budget. Salary increases were proposed in the 4.5 percent range. Requests for capital spending appropriations were absent.

The governor pointed to turmoil in surrounding states which now faced slumps in revenue only months after they had committed themselves to bloated spending programs. Indiana had avoided these straits by combining the impact of the 1973 property tax restructuring with restraint in the budget-making process. "Therefore, it seems to me that the question before all of us. . . is whether or not we can maintain the prudent self-discipline that it is going to take to spend only a little, when there will be many voices around us whose wants and needs exceed our capabilities," he said.[2] "In case any may have missed the point, I cannot accept more total spending than is projected by this budget."[3]

The administration's roster of priorities was a modest one. Moderate increases in jobless pay benefits were recommended. Lawmakers were asked to re-examine a decision made during the previous session to loosen restrictions on benefits paid to many welfare recipients. Bowen proposed creation of a state transportation agency and suggested that the valuation formula used to gauge the worth of utility properties be altered. Highway maintenance programs, falling behind schedule because of federal policies, should receive an infusion of $30 million from the general fund. Enactment of a new penal code, stalled in the 1975 session, was given gubernatorial priority for action in 1976.

Democrats quickly began to define the political dimensions of a session in which their party held a 56-44 margin in the House of Representatives. (The GOP prevailed in the Senate, 27-23.) Speaker Bainbridge responded: "The governor did not give the legislature any guidance. It was an election year speech designed not to offend anybody."[2] House Ways and Means Committee Chairman Spencer Schnaitter contended that Bowen and his budget advisers habitually understated the revenue picture. Their poor-mouthing only was an attempt to intimidate legislators, he said.

Other Democrats objected to the governor's omission of local government financing, police and fire pension funds, and the Equal Rights Amendment. On the eve of Bowen's State of the State message, House Democrats had unveiled a revised property tax relief plan. It would increase business taxes and step up the draw-down from the property tax relief fund which had provided annual reductions since 1974. Homeowners would have received a smaller annual reduction in property tax bills, but the plan intended to increase the overall savings through income tax rebates. GOP reaction to this scheme was little more than a blank stare. It passed the House and was given quiet burial across the hall.

A deluge of utility legislation poured into both chambers as public outcries over electricity bills were translated into more than two dozen proposals to alter utility regulation. Many dealt with the structure of the Public Service Commission and included bills to elect PSC members, expand the commission's size, or alter requirements for membership. Reduced rates for low income customers, abolishment of the fuel adjustment clause, and a consumers' "bill of rights" also were introduced. Less controversial were measures to beef up the office of public counselor.

Bowen had endorsed the "original cost" approach to determining the value of utility property and a Democratic bill to that effect was submitted. The governor acknowledged that the shift in calculation formulas would not reduce electric bills, but the original cost concept — which determined value upon original cost minus depreciation — was easier for people to understand.

These piles of paper brought forth sharp debate within both houses but produced insignificant results. Even relatively noncontroversial bills were thwarted in the partisan confusion. Effective lobbying by the utility companies bottled them up.

The parimutuel wagering issue — which again seemed to attract an abnormal level of interest on the part of reporters — resurfaced as one of 1976's prominent legislative issues. Attempts to make it more palatable — allocating a percentage of betting revenues to finance public schools, for one — were inserted in an attempt to drum up public enthusiasm. Parimutuel again cleared the House and Senate by slim tallies, but it was speedily vetoed by the governor for a second time. His terse message said only, "This act is, in my opinion, contrary to the best interests of the majority of the people of the state of Indiana."[5]

Two liquor bills emerged as the most controversial aspects of the legislative session. One would have restricted the transport of beer to thwart the activities of a few distributors who were marketing the beverage statewide in truckload lots. The other measure authorized the imposition by the Alcoholic Beverage Commission of minimum retail selling prices for liquor. The commission previously had done so by regulation, but a steamy controversy had caused it to back away from a regulatory approach unless it was reinforced by law.

When House Speaker Bainbridge cast the deciding vote to adopt the latter bill, journalistic blame was fixed upon his party. Bowen was given an opportunity to veto both proposals on "free enterprise" grounds. Editorial writers praised the governor.

Lawmakers' concentration on liquor and betting issues infuriated many outsiders, along with representatives of other causes who watched helplessly as their pet projects died. The two issues may not have been responsible for the extraordinary bill-killing ratio of the 1976 session, but special-interest frustration mounted as the legislature wound down. Of 927 bills introduced, only 159 became law, about 17 percent. It was believed to be a record mortality rate.

At certain times prospects seemed dim even for enactment of a budget. Conference committee members wrangled for days to sort out differences between the House and Senate versions. Only minutes before its scheduled adjournment the assembly ratified a $3.4 billion compromise, although Democrats were extremely reluctant to consent to it. The final spending figure approximated the total compiled by the State Budget Committee at the sessions's beginning. Bowen approved the budget with little enthusiasm. It appeared, however, to sustain a working general fund balance in the range he previously had indicated a willingness to accept.

The penal code signed by the governor on February 25 was thought by many observers to be the only landmark accomplishment of the 1976 session. Its sweeping overhaul of penal statutes consolidated about 2,000 into 200 and struck down scores of outmoded crimes. Sentencing provisions represented an abrupt departure from the former system. Specified terms of imprisonment were instituted. Crimes were grouped according to the severity of the offense. Trial judges would be allowed to fix a determinate sentence between minimums and maximums established for each classification. Judges, not juries, would mete out penalties. Courts could not suspend sentences for felons convicted of prior unrelated felonies or of felonies which involved aggravating circumstances (such as the use of a deadly weapon or rape). The package of new laws replaced a collection that had been in place since 1905.

Most lawyers endorsed the program. A notable exception was Attorney General Sendak, who was critical of some of its features, including the dropping of several crimes. Bowen signed the code anyway. With Sendak present at the news conference the governor observed:

> There has been criticism that necessary portions of the old penal laws have been omitted. The attorney general has drawn attention to a few of these — lynch mob, ghost employees, welfare fraud, dueling, promoting armed rebellion, carrying concealed weapons, and many others. In each instance the omissions cited by the attorney general in his letter to me have been researched and found to be covered in other sections of the bill.[6]

Bowen had taken the precaution of appointing a criminal law study commission to proceed with a final-round examination of the new code in order that flaws could be corrected by the subsequent General Assembly in time for the July 1, 1977, startup of the new arrangement. He was careful to interject, "I don't want anyone accusing me and the attorney general of feuding over this bill."[7]

Responding to reporter's questions, Sendak said that differences existed among lawyers as to whether the omitted sections were needed. "I spent eight years as an Army chief of staff," he observed, "I would have been remiss in my duty if I failed to inform the commanding general of the intelligence I had as to land mines and boobytraps... the governor here has to make the final decision as to whether or not to take the risk and go through that mine field because the greater good will be accomplished for the objective at hand."[8]

Lawmakers adjourned in the closing minutes of February 20 and hastened home, fully aware that criticism would greet them. Journalists placed a "do-nothing" stamp on the assembly. Legislators of both parties put on a good face and tried to persuade constituents that the weeks in Indianapolis had been productive ones. Democrats were unsuccessful in condemnations of Bowen and the GOP for presumed stinginess in funding education, welfare, and local government. If there was blame, the public was inclined to attach it to both houses of a divided legislature. Bowen, who received an acceptable budget and was coasting through an unopposed primary, somehow seemed to be above the clamor, his popularity secure.

XIV   THE SECOND CAMPAIGN

Buoyed by polls showing widespread public acceptance of the governor's performance, and comforted by the nomination of a challenger burdened with political barnacles, the Bowen re-election organization was able to wage the campaign on its own terms. The outcome was predictable. Although Indiana precedents were lacking, since no predecessor had been eligible for re-election in modern times, few of the nation's governors had undertaken the quest for a second term under such favorable circumstances. Yet, the campaign was dogged by concern that the Republican national ticket, still crippled by the fallout from Watergate and apparently unable to heal the wounds from a divisive national convention, would prove too great a handicap to overcome. Furthermore, an incumbent is made nervous by the potential for the unpredictable — scandal, prison riot, the need to take an unpopular action on short notice. Episodes such as these are difficult enough to face in the normal course of events but are magnified with peculiar harshness during the turbulence of a political campaign. By the time Hoosiers trooped to the polls on November 2 these uncertainties had ceased to be of consequence.

Planning for the re-election effort began in the spring of 1973, after the administration had settled in at the Statehouse and won the crucial political battle of property tax restructuring. The early and sometimes faltering attempts to define a political strategy that would lead to a campaign for 1976 grew out of conversations involving Gerald Olson, Clarence Long, James Young, Raymond Rizzo, and me. The committee first wrestled with issues involving the relationship between the governor's campaign and the Republican State Committee, whose majority remained rooted in the Whitcomb era and could not be counted on as Bowen loyalists. At this stage the 1976 committee's discussions were abstract in tenor. Its real usefulness was that of an informal coordinating board during the months preceding the formal fleshing out of a re-election organization which occurred during the summer of 1975.

The prospect of a Senate primary duel between Indianapolis Mayor Lugar and former Governor Whitcomb aroused interest because its outcome was by no means certain, and the result could have an impact upon Bowen's campaign. Lugar was perceived as a source of strength for the ticket. The analysis of Whitcomb's candidacy centered upon the potential incompatibility between the former governor and his successor. Whitcomb's vocal hostility toward the tax program still rankled many Bowen supporters. They also feared that past differences would be used as a wedge by political reporters to create an atmosphere of dissension between the GOP ticket leaders if Whitcomb were the Senate nominee.

Lugar was the preference of everyone surrounding the governor. Milligan publicly disparaged a Whitcomb candidacy, saying the state party organization would not be "enthused" by it since the structure now was dominated by "Bowen people." This generated a minor flap. Indianapolis *Star* Political Editor Robert Mooney, who was sympathetic to Whitcomb's candidacy, endeavored to get the governor to repudiate Milligan's statements. The governor responded only that he had not discussed the matter with the state chairman and that he didn't "lay claim to any one group of people."[1] A month later Mooney reported that Bowen had promised Whitcomb that he would not interfere if Whitcomb decided to enter the race.[2]

The governor was insistent that as much distance as possible be placed between the campaign staff and the governor's personal staff, because he did not want a campaign organization intruding into policy-setting for his administration. A similar cleavage was determined for public relations. This could have been a tricky arrangement, because reporters' questions often do not respect a governor's definitions of turf to be occupied by his press secretary and campaign press aide. However, this element of the campaign ran smoothly because of the choice of William DuBois as campaign press secretary. We were able to discharge our respective obligations without animosity or jealousy. I cannot recall an incident in which there was any jostling between us. King, as campaign manager; DuBois; and Daniel Evans, Jr., deputy campaign manager, were the central political operatives for the re-election. Each of them enjoyed the confidence of the governor and good rapport with the governor's staff.

A series of meetings in September, 1975, gave the campaign its basic definition. In anticipation of a free ride through the primary, campaign strategists planned to use that period to set forth the governor's accomplishments. The autumn campaign would be localized in television media markets. The campaign group would not be drawn into fights with its opponents on details. The public's favorable perception of the governor as a political personality would be buttressed by a campaign intended to acquaint them with his achievements.

These conclusions were based on comprehensive polling conducted by Robert Teeter's Market Opinion Research firm. Teeter had earned the respect of a Bowen campaign staff that placed great weight upon the use of detailed polling as a basis for campaign planning. A July, 1975, survey provided the benchmark for the pre-primary campaign.

In trial heats against Secretary of State Larry Conrad and State Treasurer Jack New the governor posted wide leads, 63-20 and 59-13, largely due to the lack of public awareness of either potential Democratic opponent. Teeter's analysis concluded that most Indiana voters generally were satisfied with the governor's performance and found it easy to vote for him over two men they knew little about. The pollster also observed that a larger percentage would have remained undecided if they harbored serious reservations about the governor. "What must be taken with a grain of salt is the immensity of the leads — not the leads, themselves," he reported.[3]

The most encouraging news in this canvass was the affirmation that property tax restructuring had changed from a source of negative voter reaction to a source of credit, while gradually ceasing to be an issue at all. In July, 1973, two-thirds of those who disapproved of the governor's performance had cited the tax program as their principal reason for dissatisfaction. A year later, that percentage had been cut in half. By the time of the poll in July, 1975, only six per cent mentioned it. What had begun as a substantial political liability for Bowen had been transformed in two years to an asset. MOR's sampling also related that voters considered the state's tax structure to be generally fair to the average citizen; the margin was 53 percent to 36 percent. Even though tax restructuring had been the keystone of the first term, we were somewhat surprised to learn how quickly people forget issues that seem so predominant to those who walk the marble under the gold dome. As MOR reported:

> When queried on the 1973 tax law in particular the voters display a very low recall on what it did, together with a mixed set of perceptions among the voters who did recall something.
>
> Almost 70 percent of the Indiana voters said they didn't recall what changes the 1973 law had made. From the remaining 30 percent, the chief memory of 10 percent was that the sales tax had been increased. Fifteen percent of all the voters remembered some form of tax relief with the most frequent being references to a property tax cut or rebate. Unexpectedly, the responses did not significantly vary by home-ownership or age.[4]

Teeter's findings noted that, despite this mixed picture, a dramatic change had taken place in the number of voters who placed high taxes as among the state's most important problems. "From rates of mention often reaching close to 40 percent during the four-year period prior to Bowen's administration, less than 10 percent of the voters now perceive taxes as a major state problem," the report said. "They may not directly attribute their lower concern with taxes to the governor's program, but their concern has definitely decreased; and the governor has no doubt benefited by that round-about effect."[5]

There were seeming paradoxes in the findings. Although Bowen received a hefty 65-13 approval of his job performance, the voters tended to be in a gloomy mood about the outlook for the state's and their own well-being. Fully one-third believed that conditions in the state were worse than those of three or four years earlier. Unemployment had re-emerged as the single greatest concern. These uncertainties did not translate into specific criticisms of the governor and his administration. Furthermore, those interviewed offered few indications of the direction they wanted the state to take. The poll demonstrated that Hoosier voters were basing their opinions of Bowen on his personal traits, rather than on his actions as governor.

One sidelight related to an issue over which much journalistic ink had been spilled and legislative rhetoric spewed — parimutuel wagering. MOR concluded that the governor was on the wrong side of public opinion on parimutuel, which was favored by a strong 56-31 margin. Moreover, the governor's opposition was widely known. However, other aspects of the poll confirmed that few parimutuel supporters were actively critical of him. Bowen's position on the issue was unlikely to be a triggering point for them to pull the lever against him in November.

In retrospect the July, 1975, poll was not illuminating in terms of its conclusions about the presidential race, because President Ford was paired off in trial heats against Senator Henry Jackson of Washington and former Governor George Wallace of Alabama. Jimmy Carter had not yet become a national phenomenon. Ford led handily with 49 percent, while Wallace polled 20, and Jackson 16. However, the survey gave the President a thumping 60-28 lead over former California Governor Ronald Reagan in the Republican primary race. The most somber findings for the Democrats related to Senator Vance Hartke. He posted a meager 29 percent approval rate, coupled with a 39 percent disapproval tally. MOR pointed out that disapprovals of Hartke's performance had outnumbered his approval ratings for three years. "Locked-in" negative opinions would be difficult for him to overcome in his re-election bid during 1976.[6]

When Bowen had announced his candidacy in 1971 during a snow squall on the front porch of his home in Bremen, the prospect that he ever would occupy the governor's chair was uncertain at best. Four years later the re-election campaign was launched in an atmosphere of good-humored confidence. The governor took the rostrum at Bremen High School to deliver a convocation address to pupils who were overwhelmed in number by his friends, officeholders, and newsmen. The sun was shining this time. Bowen assessed the national mood, expressing worry about the doubt and confusion that now seemed to dominate the country. He observed that the time had come to depart from a failing pattern of governmental operations and regulatory encumbrances. They should be replaced by an attitude that would expect less of the federal establishment. Public officials should insist upon the streamlining of a system gone wild — painful and controversial though that process might be. His re-election announcement, almost an afterthought in the way in which it was delivered, was of about 90 seconds' duration:

> It has been my honor and my pleasure to have been a part — now for nearly a quarter-century of public service — of this effort to make Indiana a better place. I want to maintain this involvement, because I believe that my experience is a foundation for further contributions in the future. My position is unique — the first governor in more than a century eligible to carry forward his efforts to a second term.
>
> Today, I have returned to my home community, to share with students and townspeople alike my thoughts and hopes for Indiana and America. I want you, my friends and neighbors of long standing, to be the first to know of my continued desire to serve this state and its people, for whom I hold a lifetime of affection. I will seek a second term as governor, to preserve and nourish the accomplishments of the first four years, to complete the work now underway, to struggle with issues still calling for resolution, and to face new challenges as we strive to make this great state an even better one in which to live.[7]

Larry Conrad announced for governor on December 14. He conceded that the governor would be hard to beat.[8] Conrad's victory in the Democratic primary virtually was assured by the entrance of two opponents almost certain to split the votes of conservative Democrats. The secretary of state could garner a solid plurality based upon strong backing from the party's labor wing. Conrad was the preferred November opponent because his matchup against the governor represented a classic confrontation between a moderately conservative Republican and a liberal Democrat. The governor would enjoy the advantages of incumbency and the opportunity to attract voters from the more conservative element of the Democratic party.

Of equal importance was the fact that Conrad began the campaign with significant disadvantages. They involved the use of state telephone credit cards for political activity and a so-called master plan for his political campaign. This prospectus was leaked to the media. The campaign document was hardly headline fodder. Inclusion of a section analyzing Statehouse and political reporters, written in snide and sometimes insulting terms, prompted the press to react in a manner of aggrieved self-righteousness. The plan was not sinister, merely stupid for having been written down in the first place. Although Conrad is an engaging and likeable individual (many in the Bowen camp held this view), these two episodes badly scarred his image before the campaign had time to get off the ground.

The polls confirmed it, identifying a strong anti-Conrad reaction within the small percentage of voters who were familiar with him. Teeter pointed out, "Negative perceptions are the most enduring of all; moreover, the unusually high frequency with which they exist about Conrad creates the strong expectation that they will become significantly large as Conrad's awareness increases."[9]

The Bowen campaign staff harbored concerns about several people who would be key operatives in a Conrad campaign, notably campaign manager Robert Wagner and United Auto Workers' District President Dallas Sells. Their volcanic personalities and past patterns of inflammatory partisanship indicated that the campaign might degenerate into a mudslinging affair.

Jack New, meanwhile, attempted to create a base of conservative voters in both parties. He characterized the governor as the biggest spender in state history. Like the secretary of state, New enjoyed the friendship of many Bowen partisans because of his reputation as an amiable political professional. He had acted responsibly (in tandem with State Auditor Mary Aikens Currie) as a member of the State Board of Finance, on which the two Democrats were in a position to outvote the governor.

The other Democratic contender, Senate Majority Leader Robert Fair, was highly regarded as a legislator. Wide philosophical distance separated him from Bowen's people. On the campaign trail Fair described the governor as "vulnerable on the issues" while arguing that he was the best candidate to confront Bowen because of his experience in the General Assembly.[10]

In January, the campaign staff decided to run the governor's television advertising after the primary. It would have more impact because the other candidates would be off the airwaves. These advertisements could separate the governor from the partisanship of a primary campaign, portraying him as one who remained at work tending to the people's business while others battled on the hustings. Campaign advertising would develop two strategies: build upon the public's favorable perception of Bowen as an individual and point out the accomplishments of his administration, using examples tailored to each television market.

Conrad had voiced the intent to make spiraling utility rates the dominant theme of his campaign. He hoped to attach to Bowen the blame for rounds of price increases that had infuriated many voters, especially in the Indiana & Michigan Electric Company service territory. Although there were valid reasons for these increases, it was clear that the utility issue was far too complex for the GOP to feel comfortable that it could mount a credible defense. The results of a February, 1976, MOR poll solved the problem. When asked who they thought was to blame for recent increases in utility rates, voters attached responsibility to the utility companies and to the federal government. Only four percent blamed state government. A miniscule one percent attached the onus to Bowen. Queried about who could do something to keep the rates from increasing further, only five percent named the governor. These findings indicated the Conrad faced tough sledding on the utility issue and that Republicans were best advised to ignore it.

Campaign strategists also grappled with an issue over which the campaign organization had little control, but which had the potential for presenting a volatile situation. Legal obstacles to capital punishment might be removed by the courts before November, placing the governor in a position to decide on the fate of as many as seven death row inmates. On one hand, the public favored the death penalty by a substantial margin. This could make it difficult for the governor to deny executions, especially since he had stated that he would not stand in the way of an execution if all other remedies were exhausted. On the other hand, Teeter and I were concerned that his acquiescence to death penalties would diminish the public's regard for a political leader whose allure derived in part from his standing as a physician — a healer. I likened it to asking Marcus Welby to throw the switch. We could do little but hope that the courts would procrastinate until after the balloting. They did.

Bowen's campaigners became increasingly troubled over the quality of the Ford organizational effort. The February poll showed him losing ground against Reagan and the Ford operation in Indiana seemed rather half-hearted. The gubernatorial campaign could not afford to become involved in a separate race, but a Ford defeat was considered to be harmful to the ticket. The February survey showed the President with a substantial lead, 56-32, but it was eroding. Among voters in the 25-44 age group the President had dropped 16 percent since the summer poll. His overall approval ratings also were in a modest slump.

The sample showed the governor holding a commanding 59-24 lead over the secretary of state and a 59-15 lead over the treasurer. Neither opponent was making significant gains in voter identification. The negative perceptions of Conrad had declined somewhat, but their durability provided some assurance that this would continue to be a factor throughout the campaign. Concerning negative reactions to the governor, MOR had this to say: "Only 3 percent of all voters base their vote on negative perceptions of Bowen — a very low and stable figure for a governor who is completing four years in office. This anti-Bowen vote has remained constant over the last seven months."[12] The new survey showed Bowen running away with the ticket-splitter and independent vote. It vindicated earlier decisions about the approach to the 1976 campaign.

Meanwhile, Lugar's ballot strength appeared to be stagnating at the 50 percent level and Hartke was recording modest increases in voter approval. A Whitcomb-Hartke race was regarded as a dead heat. The pollster made two observations. Whitcomb and Hartke were outcampaigning Lugar and, "it is perhaps time for the Lugar campaign to get started before a real momentum builds behind either or both of Lugar's opponents." About Hartke, Teeter said that the Democrat was running out of time to re-establish the necessary job approval to be re-elected, because a 41-34 percent plurality still disapproved of the way he had performed as senator.[13]

Although New shortened the gap in the final weeks of the primary, Conrad registered a solid victory. Ford lost to Reagan here, 51-49, and 45 of Indiana's 54 convention delegates were awarded to the former California governor. Lugar prevailed over Whitcomb.

Early summer national surveys showed the President down by nearly 30 percentage points. While it was possible that he never trailed Governor Carter in Indiana, the wide national gap was cause for alarm. The guessing game centered on how much of a Carter margin the governor could withstand. In an interview with the Indianapolis News Bowen said that Carter's strength "sure does worry me." He hoped he could withstand a Democratic national margin of 150,000 in Indiana: "I think if the election were held today, I would be in pretty good shape. I would hope our record in our administration is satisfactory and the people would stick with us in spite of what they might do in the national picture."[14]

Although the governor was a Ford supporter, he maintained careful neutrality as a non-voting alternate to avoid offending either side as the GOP gathered in Kansas City for the national convention. His support of the President largely was based upon personal, rather than issue-oriented reactions. Bowen told a reporter: ". . . he's been very attentive to Indiana. I have no problem getting into his office or getting him on the telephone. He's called me two or three times and said, 'this is Jerry'. You don't forget those things."[15]

As it became evident that the President would prevail against the Reagan challenge, much of the speculation centered upon a running mate. Reagan was the governor's obvious first choice for reasons of party harmony. Should Reagan prove unwilling, Bowen suggested John Connally, Iowa Governor Robert Ray, or Washington Governor Daniel Evans as "very well suited" for vice-president.[16]

As convention politicking proceeded, Hoosiers began to hold out hope that William Ruckelshaus, the former state representative who later held key posts in the Nixon administration before his firing in the so-called "Saturday night massacre," might be the nominee. Convention floor gossip placed his name in a small group of contenders. The governor perceived the obvious advantages of having an Indiana-connected vice-presidential nominee. At the same time a Ruckelshaus nomination would be deemed testimony that the party finally had put the messy Watergate affair behind it. Bowen was approached by the President's managers with an invitation to make a seconding speech, should Ruckelshaus be chosen. Rizzo and I drafted the document; it was transmitted by facsimile to Kansas City. On the eve of the decision Ruckelshaus was believed to be among the final three or four possible choices.

Bowen advisers understandably were astounded when the announcement was made that Senator Robert Dole would share the ticket with the President. This, apparently, was Reagan's choice. It added no strength or electoral votes to the ticket. Bowen staffers muttered over a colossal lost opportunity to achieve the party-strengthening that would have resulted from a Ruckelshaus nomination.

The autumn state campaign was a lackluster affair. Conrad's campaign showed signs of disarray, including his abandonment at a crucial time by an advertising agency. The September poll was comforting, indeed. Alarms about the President's standing in Indiana were diminishing. The sample showed him leading Governor Carter 47-38. Lugar was gaining ground again, now leading 53-34. Heavy negative reactions to Hartke (32 percent approval, 46 percent disapproval) still proved the theme for their duel. The governor maintained a wide lead over his opponent, 56-27. There were continued indications that Conrad was proving unable to gain sufficient name identification with the electorate and was retaining a significant negative reaction from those sampled.

The governor was running away from his opponent in the South Bend area, traditionally a Democratic stronghold but also a region of traditional loyalty to the nearby Bremen physician. Bowen trailed only in northwestern Indiana. Among voting segments the poll showed that he failed to achieve his statewide margin over Conrad only among blacks, union members, and Catholics. While identifying a greater public awareness of the Public Service Commission's role in utility rates, the canvass continued to demonstrate that only a single percentage point of voters tagged the governor with the responsibility for high utility bills. In short, except for Ford's rebounding, little had changed since the spring.

The campaign strategy was reaffirmed, although the governor became increasingly edgy about some of the hostile questioning he was getting from reporters, who by this time were bored with the whole business. A mid-October survey by IU-PUI found the governor to be edging upward, with Conrad on the downturn, a trend out of sorts with normal patterns which have challengers closing the gap on incumbents as election day nears. Outbursts by Conrad forces and personal attacks on the governor and J.B. King were having little impact. We brushed them aside without comment.

In retrospect, the outcome seems never to have been in doubt. Lugar stunned Hartke by a record 397,000-vote landslide and the governor racked up a 309,000 majority over Conrad while carrying all but 18 counties. Although Indiana was the first industrial state to appear in the Ford column, the President's loss to Carter took some of the glitter off the victory. Later, some would characterize the 1976 returns as symbolic of an Indiana GOP that had put Watergate behind it and was on the road to long-term revitalization. Bowen was less certain, noting that the state Senate had passed to Democratic control and the only bright spot in congressional balloting was Dan Quayle's upset of the heavily-favored Fourth District incumbent, J. Edward Roush. Roush's tenure had represented an interlude in what had been a tradition of Republican supremacy in the Fort Wayne-based district, anyway. In post-election speeches the governor dampened some of the party's ebullience by pointing out that the balloting disclosed little real evidence that GOP bedrock strength was on the rise. It had been a duel of personalities whose outcome was determined by the reputations of a popular governor and a tarnished Senate incumbent.

XV THE SECOND TIME AROUND

Bowen's landslide victory did not produce the jubilation one might expect. After the intensity and excitement of a statewide campaign a letdown sets in, even for the victors. It's less thrilling, too, the second time around. The challenge of building an administration, of taking on something new, is no longer there.

These factors alone did not fully account for the post-election "blahs" that infected the governor's inner circle. It was not their intent merely to continue the pattern of the first term. Each had goals that represented at least modest changes of direction. But these advisers saw constraints upon their hoped-for agendas. The loss of the presidency cut a political tie to Washington that could have brought even greater prominence to the governor. Instead of cooperating with the White House, Indiana probably would be fighting the national administration. In addition, a fifth legislative session was a gloomy prospect. The administration needed to bring spending under control and make modest adjustments to the 1973 property tax relief program, difficult enough chores in a normal political climate. A divided General Assembly, with Democrats in control of the Senate, all but guaranteed a tougher road. Already-strained relations with Attorney General Sendak seemed headed for a further slump. He had trailed the ticket badly — winning by only 30,000 votes — and Bowen braced for a vindictive attitude on his part.

Finally, several key department heads were less than adequate and had to be replaced. This would involve painful decisions for a governor who was extremely loyal to his subordinates and reluctant to remove them. Would he do it? Bowen's willingness to carry out a moderate overhaul of the administration would be an important factor in setting the tone for a second term.

Changes were not long in coming. Tommie Holland, director of the Civil Rights Commission, was relieved of her post. Embroiled for months in disputes with the commission, she found her support eroded as a backlog of cases accumulated. John Garvey, the commission's chairman, said her determination to seek out civil rights violators blinded her ability to analyze complaints objectively. She operated on the assumption that a person accused of discrimination was guilty, he said. Relations had soured to the point that she was deprived of her authority to hire and fire employees. The commission unanimously recommended that she not be retained.[1]

The governor's decision to concur prompted an outcry from civil rights groups, who charged that his reasons were political. A January 6 meeting with black leaders was fairly acrimonious. "Let's break it off," he said at one point. "We aren't getting anyplace and I'm not going to change my mind. Some of you are acting like people in the grandstand making a decision on the play while the umpire is only six feet away."[2]

Another casualty was Corrections Director Heyne, who had been living on borrowed time for nearly two years. It seemed to Bowen that Heyne wasn't in control of his agency. When asked by a reporter whether the commissioner was performing up to standards, the governor replied: "I'm unhappy with that whole setup . . ."[3] Several gubernatorial assistants also were displeased with the apparent drift within the corrections system. The defeat of West Virginia Governor Arch Moore produced Indiana's new director. Gordon Faulkner was recruited from a similar position in the outgoing Moore administration and took over for Heyne in mid-March, 1977.

Veteran's Director Earl Heath also was bumped. He had earned the enmity of the influential American Legion. Heath was succeeded by John Knop, a former mayor of Huntington and retired Army Reserve lieutenant colonel.

Bowen's most difficult decision was not to retain State Police Superintendent DeBard. He had not been successful in quelling factionalism within the agency. Frequent complaints were voiced about the quality of central office management. The governor and superintendent agreed that the latter would state that he was not seeking reappointment. Bowen chaired a committee which screened numerous active and retired state police before settling on Major John Shettle, commander of the department's planning and inspection division and a 20-year veteran of the force.

Highway Chairman Boehning stepped aside after four years' service and the governor designated former State Senator James Gardner to succeed him. Other changes occurred within Bowen's personal staff. The executive assistant position left vacant by the resignation of Dr. Ford was filled by Judith Palmer, a lawyer and fiscal analyst for the State Budget Agency.

William DuBois, the campaign news secretary, sought appointment to the office staff and the governor added him as an executive assistant. DuBois' portfolio included state tax and finance agencies, along with supervision of a new state government productivity program. I suggested that DuBois relieve me of the news secretary's duties, since involvement in energy, transportation, and environmental issues had become so time-consuming, but Bowen wasn't interested in making a change. Another relative newcomer to the inner circle was John Huie, a Purdue University agricultural economist and finance consultant who had become budget director in July, 1976, when Edison Thuma stepped down to take an administrative position with the State Board of Health.

Bowen's priority for the second term was to control spending. The two previous sessions of the General Assembly had appropriated more money than the state took in. If this imbalance continued, the governor warned, ". . . we will get ourselves into the straits of a New York City. . . and we do not intend to let anything like that happen."[4] He also began to develop modifications to property tax control laws. These would grant more flexibility to local governments to deal with the impact of an accelerating national inflation rate.

The second inaugural ceremony was less exhuberant than its predecessor. Heavy snow and bitter cold kept people away from the Statehouse. Beth Bowen held a Bible while the governor's 79-year-old father, Vernie Bowen, a retired schoolteacher from Leiters Ford, administered the oath of office to his son. The inaugural address was a brief one, with concise references to the achievements of the first term and a commitment to do more than continue the themes of the previous four years.

> Certainly, we will continue to nourish those successful programs undertaken in the first administration. However, new challenges already are emerging and the state administration will face into them with vigor and determination. I am developing additional goals, many of which will be spelled out in more detail during this legislative session.
> I believe that a seasoned administration will be even better prepared to cope with these challenges and responsibilities. I look forward with renewed enthusiasm to the building of an even stronger record of service and achievement. With the cooperation of others at all levels of government and with the help of our citizens, it can be an exciting time in out state's history.[5]

About 5,000 celebrants were expected at the inaugural ball, but their number was thinned by the inclement weather. The orchestra played *Stardust* as a smiling governor and his first lady danced alone on the vast semi-darkened convention center ballroom floor. It is a tradition to begin inaugural galas in this manner. As the Bowens moved with easy-paced restraint in front of a crowd of friends and supporters, there was yet no hint of the personal tragedy whose revelation was only months away.

The governor's State of the State message was delivered to the General Assembly the following morning. It was intended to convey the idea that the second term would be an active one, more than a mere extension of the trend of the first four years. Therefore, Rizzo, DuBois, and I loaded it with subject matter. We overdid it. Even though I whittled about 15 minutes from the final draft, the finished document required 70 minutes to deliver. Bowen took a five-minute break halfway through his speech. It was an amusing acknowledgement of our excesses.

After the conventional assessment of the state's economic situation, the governor moved into his argument for spending limitations. "During the past biennium legislative appropriations exceeded revenue by more than $200 million," he said. "Thus, the last legislative session built an expenditure base for the state which greatly exceeds the state's revenue base. It resulted in a 1976 appropriation level which exceeded the projected 1977 revenue. This obviously cannot continue. It is time for us to accept our fiscal responsibility to develop a budget which lives within the available revenue. For the next two years, this may mean tightening budgets in order to provide employees with the salary adjustments they so deserve."[6] A slimmer construction budget reflected this philosophy. It gave weight to a corrections renovation program, a response to pressure from the courts and a growing inmate population within penal institutions.

The administration budget was projected to produce a working balance of only $16 million at the end of the two-year cycle. Bowen always was uncomfortable with reserves that fell below the $80-$100 million range. "If we miss our revenue estimate by four-tenths of a percent, we will no longer have a balanced budget," he observed. "Obviously, this budget forecast can only be justified by the existence of the tuition reserve fund which is available should our optimistic revenue projections not, in fact, materialize. The tuition reserve also is absolutely necessary in order for the state to meet its cash flow obligations during the year."[7]

Bowen described a "second-generation" local finance and tax control package designed to make modest adjustments to the 1973 tax relief plan. He proposed placing all local governments under similar tax guidelines by freezing property taxes at the 1973 rates, while ensuring that property and local option income taxes could not increase by more than five percent over the previous year. Under the new plan, the total amount of revenue raised by a local unit of government could be increased under specific conditions by as much as seven percent. In emergency situations, ten percent hikes approved by voters in a referendum also could be authorized. The second-generation refinements would preserve property tax relief, give leeway to local governments, keep individual property tax rates at or below their 1973 levels, and ensure that property tax rates would carry no more than their present share of government finance.

The governor also called for enactment of a state-guaranteed student loan program. It would be built upon private lending institutions. They would make credit decisions based upon prevailing loan standards, instead of having a state agency decide eligibility. State government would stand behind these loans which would be repaid by students out of future earnings.

His message also emphasized a theme that would become dominant during the final Bowen years: adequate funding for highway and bridge maintenance. He was not very specific in this instance, conceding that a consensus did not yet exist as to the size of the required tax increases. The governor cautioned that gallonage taxes were not responsive to inflationary pressures and that fuel efficiency also could dilute long-term revenues. A tax pegged to fuel price would raise more money.

The budget bills moved smoothly through the House of Representatives and were delivered to the Senate in the second week of March. Several obstacles faced it there. Influential Republicans did not want to approve a budget until Democrats who controlled the upper chamber accepted the governor's tax package revisions. Others thought the House version of the budget was too costly.

Democrats, meanwhile, had ideas of their own. They were only lukewarm to the second-generation tax program, contending that it was designed to strong-arm county governments into accepting the local option income tax. They also claimed that the program amounted to an admission that the Bowen plan of 1973 had failed. The governor hotly denied this, arguing that the national inflation rate, not defects in the earlier tax restructuring, were the basis for his proposed alterations. Democrats wanted to increase spending in several major categories, perhaps in the range of $400 million. This would require dipping into the tuition reserve fund. Bowen and most Republicans would oppose this action. The fund provides a supplemental reserve for the state as well as a cash-flow steam valve for school districts. Party leaders on both sides stiffened as the session progressed.

Other developments moved more rapidly. Once again, pro-parimutuel wagering forces engineered track betting legislation through the House and Senate. Bowen vetoed it, the third time he had done so. However, this time its advocates mustered sufficient votes to override him. The bill became law. (Later, it was challenged successfully in the courts. The parimutuel issue languished during the remaining years of Bowen's administration.)

An overhaul of the state's criminal laws was signed by the governor on April 12. Attorney General Sendak had opposed the changes, although he generally stood alone in doing so. Others in the legal profession were strongly supportive. The revised code encompassed new provisions for imposing the death penalty. Recent federal court decisions had rendered most state death penalty laws unconstitutional. Indiana's language was derived from a Florida statute that had withstood a U.S. Supreme Court test a year earlier.

The most publicized dispute of the 1977 legislative session involved laetrile, a derivative of apricot pits which some thought helpful in arresting cancer. It was one of the most emotional controversies confronted by lawmakers in several years. Physician Bowen was put in a difficult position.

While the medical profession almost unanimously opposed it, legalization of laetrile became a cause for political conservatives. They assailed federal bureaucrats (Food and Drug Administration officials) who refused to approve its use and claimed that the issue went beyond health technology. Laetrile bans contradicted a fundamental right of freedom of choice. Nervous about the malpractice implications of prescribing a substance that had no record of effectiveness, the medical profession also was concerned that sufferers might opt for laetrile instead of more conventional treatment for malignancies. Radiation therapy and chemical measures frequently were painful and expensive undertakings, with debilitating side effects. It would be tempting to turn to laetrile, which had none of these shortcomings. The latter point carried greatest weight with the governor, although he was cautious in his public statements about the bill.

Angry legislators shouted at one another while pro-laetrile pickets marched in the Statehouse. At times the issue seemed to represent little more than a venting of frustration against a plodding government bureaucracy and a medical profession that had failed to cure cancer, rather than a referendum on licensing a particular drug. Opponents of laetrile accused its advocates of perpetrating cruel frauds upon desperate cancer victims. Supporters countered that laetrile, while unproven, at least offered some hope to those who had no hope.

Bowen was torn between the two sides, hesitant to go against his profession and his better judgment, but not wanting to be an unreasonable obstacle to the bill. As the controversy unfolded, he told reporters that he would allow a laetrile bill to become law if it contained protection for physicians who would be prescribing it at the insistence of their patients.

The governor's personal attitude gradually became more negative. Conference committee amendments provided him with a basis upon which to take a firm position. Conferees had included language that would remove the authority of state health officials to classify drugs. This was a reaction to statements by health officials that they might not approve laetrile's use even if the General Assembly legalized the substance. Bowen feared that the classification issue might affect other drugs and other situations. On April 11 he hinted that the revised legislation might be unacceptable. "This is not the same bill I said I would let become law," the governor told newsmen. "It's a tremendous change in philosophy."[8]

Although the classification issue provided the formal basis for his opposition, Bowen's true feelings were reflected in a concern about substitution of laetrile for more established treatments. He decided to veto the legislation and personally drafted the message. It summed up his most serious reservations:

> The lulling of cancer patients into a false sense of security will occur and this would be tragic. If we approve the administration of unproven substances under the guise of science and remove its control by the Board of Pharmacy and the State Board of Health, I fear that we have permitted emotion to overrule common sense. It is not only wrong to offer false hope to a patient, it is also cruel.[9]

His veto was overridden late in the session, but the laetrile issue became entangled in court. For an issue which had stirred so much rhetoric and journalistic outpourings laetrile remarkably soon receded from public notice and interest.

The 1977 legislature adopted a landmark proposal to open meetings of state and local agencies to public view. Its passage was attended by controversy. Many legislators harbored resentments against the news media, some of them petty, others fully justified. These attitudes, coupled with concern that the bill might open legislative party caucuses to reporters, jeopardized its chances. After a stiff battle the "Sunshine Bill" was presented to Bowen, who earlier had endorsed it. The new law opened meetings of state and local boards and commissions, limited the use of executive sessions, and required prior notice of meetings and their agendas.

Indiana became the 35th state to ratify the Equal Rights Amendment, ending a five-year struggle. The Senate, which had been its graveyard in several prior sessions, sent the measure to Washington after a 26-24 majority was mustered in its favor on January 22. Earlier, the House had adopted ERA by a 54-45 vote. Ratification of the controversial proposal came after its support among the electorate had begun to soften. ERA had been favored by substantial margins in polls taken during the early 1970s, but election year surveys indicated that voter affection was cooling. Several observers concluded that the drop in popularity may have been based upon public weariness with an issue that had been in the legislative forefront for several years. Bowen favored the constitutional amendment, but did not passionately argue its case, a point that caused some grumbling within the ranks of the proposal's more militant supporters.

Another departure from earlier state policy occurred when the assembly approved a $3.6 million aid package for the ailing Chicago, South Shore & South Bend Railroad. The important commuter line operated a fleet so aged that broken parts had to be hand-tooled. Replacements had long ceased to be produced. A petition by the railroad to abandon passenger service had been stalled by the Interstate Commerce Commission until the state had time to act. The state appropriation was to be combined with local assistance and a federal grant to purchase modern equipment for the route. Lawmakers also appropriated $2.5 million to help subsidize the operations of local public transit companies. It was another signal the near-monopoly traditionally enjoyed by highways in state transportation policy was coming to an end.

Legislators were less successful in addressing the growing needs of their historical transportation priority — the 12,000 miles of state and federal numbered highways. Deferred maintenance was beginning to show. Federal funding emphasized construction, not rehabilitation. Existing tax funds were inadequate. Bowen's views on the subject crystallized during the session. He called for a three-cents-a-gallon increase in the gasoline tax, noting that the state highway system was operating with less revenue than it had a decade earlier. Resurfacing was proceeding at half the necessary annual rate; bridge replacement projects were far behind schedule. Democrats refused to support a tax increase and many Republicans were reluctant to accept one. Several test votes showed little enthusiasm for the proposal. The roads were left to deteriorate.

Meanwhile, budget and control package issues remained in doubt. Progress in budget-writing was achieved; revised revenue estimates indicated that additional spending flexibility might be available. Important differences remained, however, and the two parties drifted even farther apart on the second generation controls. Bowen had raised the specter of a special session if a control program was not enacted. Democrats seemed to want to test him on that point. It became a game of brinkmanship as the clock wound down.

They ran out of time. On April 30, the final session day, the budget committee conference report was still being debated, a page at a time. No agreement on tax controls had been reached. Jockeying went on into the evening. A series of separate meetings involving the governor and legislative leaders failed to produce results. Democrats were unwilling to accept a control package unless the governor made further concessions to permit local spending increases. Senate Democratic Leader Robert Fair used my office for a series of hurried conferences while others visited the governor a few doors away. Fair was as nervous as I ever had seen him. Brinkmanship had gone too far.

The governor was convinced that Democrats only wanted to find out how far he would compromise the budget; they were unwilling to support controls. Several gubernatorial advisers believed that the special session threat did not have the leverage of previous years, as a growing number of lawmakers were quite happy with the prospect of a professional legislature. The 1977 regular session collapsed at midnight without a budget and without a tax program. Bowen then briefed reporters. He would give both sides a few days to cool off, then call in the leadership for the purpose of setting a timetable and agreeing to limits on subject matter for a special session.

The governor was forced to veto legislation to compensate crime victims and to provide free medical treatment for rape victims. While a fee system in criminal cases was intended to provide the funds, Sendak advised that constitutional difficulties with this funding approach might leave the state liable for the entire cost. The attorney general estimated that the payout to crime victims could amount to $1.4 billion annually. The vetoes were difficult ones, because the causes were popular and the governor agreed with them. Bowen expected harsh criticism as a result of his actions, and he was correct.

Legislative leaders returned on May 5. During a meeting with the governor they agreed to convene on May 23 and limit the agenda to budget, revenue, and tax control issues. It was hoped that the special session could be disposed of in one or two days. The half-hour meeting and the news conference which followed were surprisingly amicable, given the ill will that had existed a week earlier.

An acceptable control package was adopted on the night of May 23. Eleven Democrats joined 22 Republicans to pass it in the Senate. A budget nearly identical to the one that had lost in the final hours of the regular session also was enacted. Highway funding was the only major casualty.

It had been the toughest legislative session since 1973. Bowen was subjected to criticism that he failed to exercise sufficient leadership. However, a divided legislature had combined with deep rifts within the respective party caucuses to make compromises extremely difficult. Overall, the governor got what he had to have. The tax package's control features were extended for two years in modified form.

XVI DISASTERS AND DISORDERS

Weather disasters assaulted the state with extraordinary frequency during Bowen's tenure as governor. The latter 1970s were years of exceptionally bitter winters — arctic temperatures and waves of drifting snow. Floods and tornadoes brought death and property destruction on a massive scale. In addition, the state's security forces were required to preserve the peace in several labor disorders.

Domestic emergencies, whether natural disaster or civil disorder, are forthright tests of a governor and his administration. Often striking without notice, they require a comprehensive response on the part of public agencies. How well a governor handles emergencies contributes materially to the public's perception of his competence. Disasters leave stark, visible marks upon the land and people. Death and damage require rapid but capable reactions. Devastation and misery provide vivid detail for the newsman's camera, while the unleashing of nature's awesome fury strikes deep within the human consciousness. Disasters are the most exciting news of all; their aftermath commands the vigorous attention of journalists, who also are quick to turn their lenses upon those entrusted with cleanup and repair.

Bowen's reputation was enhanced by his administration's handling of these emergencies and by the manner in which his reassuring personality set the tone for state involvement. The governor's experiences in these incidents transformed him into an outspoken advocate for the National Guard, State Police, and Department of Civil Defense. His enthusiasm for the Guard had implications going beyond support at budget-writing time, for as chairman of the Public Safety Committee of the National Governors' Conference, and later as head of the conference, he emerged as a national lobbyist for Guard interests.

Although Indiana lies in an alleyway across the nation's midsection in which tornadoes regularly strike, the state was spared a major tornado outbreak for nine years after the Palm Sunday disaster of 1965, in which 141 people were killed.[1] On the gloomy afternoon of April 3, 1974, turbulent storms developed in the Ohio River valley and began their deadly sweep across the Hoosier state. The first of at least 30 twisters was reported at mid-afternoon. For several hours at least four separate storm systems carved routes of destruction from southwest to northeast. The most severe storm first touched down near Attica, ripped through downtown Monticello, then tracked northeast to Rochester and Angola. Another system struck the Ohio River borderlands, chewing up rural homes and forest lands before ranging into more densely populated regions near Clarksville, Hanover, and Madison. A third cluster of tornadoes skipped across south-central Indiana through Lawrence, Jackson, Bartholomew, Jennings, Fayette, and Franklin counties. A fourth storm cut a path through eastern Indiana, causing heavy damage at Fountaintown in Shelby County and demolishing the community of Kennard in Henry County.

The death toll reached 41 and Department of Civil Defense damage estimates totalled more than $70 million. Nearly 800 persons were injured. State Police and Guardsmen were activated that afternoon; some were on duty within minutes to begin the rescue effort. The governor called off a scheduled trip to Japan to supervise the relief operation. The following morning Bowen asked President Nixon to declare 29 Indiana counties disaster areas, saying that damage was many times greater than the amount necessary to qualify them for disaster declarations.[2] Eight other counties ultimately were added to the request for federal assistance.

On April 5 the governor, Major General Ahner, and other officials traveled by helicopter to the hardest-hit regions. At Monticello almost everything within a four-block radius of the downtown center was wiped out. The National Guard armory had become a temporary county courthouse.

The view from aloft was a striking one as our aircraft traced the storm's corridor across northern Indiana. In some areas the swath of destruction was more than a mile wide; in others it narrowed to a few hundred feet. Cavorting twisters had obliterated farmsteads and small rural subdivisions while leaving other dwellings untouched only yards away. Trees in woodlots and in small woodlands along river banks had been twisted savagely, their bark and fiber warped and splintered to a degree that made them unsalvageable. However, storm victims already were hard at work. Tractors pulled down the debris of barns and homeowners were perched on rooftops, hammering away at temporary patching. Our flight over the Ohio River country revealed the destruction of thousands of acres of state and national forest land. Not a tree was standing among the damaged buildings at Hanover College, and the "hill" region of Madison was all but paralyzed by downed utility lines, felled trees, and leaking gas mains.

Stout Field on the Indianapolis westside became the center of relief operations. The Guard, State Police, Civil Defense, and governor's office representatives gathered there to coordinate the program and to await the arrival of federal officials who were to respond to the President's disaster declaration. We operated for nearly two weeks in a large warehouse that soon became clogged with people.

Impatient to begin the relief effort in the hardest hit communities, state officials were frustrated by the slow pace of federal activity. The storms had hit on Wednesday; the feds began trickling in on Saturday, lugging thick procedural manuals and bulging briefcases loaded with files. They seemed to be lacking, however, in many of the application forms needed to process assistance claims by farmers, homeowners, and businessmen. The state had identified several cities in which regional disaster centers should be located — Madison, Monticello, Rochester, Angola, New Castle, New Albany, and Tell City. The first two centers had been activated with state personnel that very day.

Thinking that a federal disaster declaration meant things would begin to happen, state officials were eager to get on with the job. Instead, we sat on desk tops, taking telephone calls and sipping coffee, awaiting word from federal officials. They were in meetings — interminable meetings, it seemed. When one ended, another immediately began. By late afternoon itchiness had become irritation. At one point the federal disaster coordinator ducked into my cubicle to ask a rather trivial procedural question. I gave her a blank stare, tapped out my pipe and said softly, "When are you people going to quit these endless meetings so that we can do something about this goddamned storm?" She replied curtly, "After all, it is important that we have the proper coordination." I muttered something about wanting to put people and application forms into cars and point them in the direction of the disaster areas.

Bowen's staff was becoming convinced that the timeliness and scope of federal disaster relief was substantially over-advertised. Little occurred after 1974 to alter our perception. Although several federal agencies had disaster responsibilities, at the time the lead department was the Federal Disaster Assistance Administration in the Department of Housing and Urban Development. HUD, with the possible exception of the Department of Health, Education, and Welfare, was the most notoriously bureaucratized instrument of the Washington establishment. It was not a likely source of rapid movement during an emergency. Many of its key personnel had only limited training in disaster duty; they had been recruited from the ranks of political advance men from the 1972 presidential campaign.

Most important, the bureaucracy had become so preoccupied with avoiding the taint of criticism from its auditors that it took refuge in detailed procedures and forms, hesitant to take risks because the bureaucratic system doesn't reward achievement. (For that matter, it does not penalize failure, either.) The result is a plodding, methodical approach to functions such as disaster relief which commences with the initial act of making a determination whether or not a state, county, or community qualifies for one of the several echelons and types of federal assistance.

In fairness to the feds, there had been numerous instances in which governors, congressmen, and mayors went overboard in making local declarations of emergencies and requesting massive federal intervention.

Mayors, legislators, and Republican county chairmen regularly demanded that the governor add their localities to the roster of proclaimed counties, even though it was patently obvious from professional surveys that damage was negligible. There are several reasons for this. Disasters are exciting. Local officials, hoping to avoid accusations that they are less than relentless in the pursuit of aid for their constituents, kick to the next level of government requests that are wholly unjustified. A psychological foible is afoot, too. No one wants to be left out of the action, and there is perverse distinction in having one's constituency added to the body count. Politicians, especially of the congressional variety, are not at their best during episodes such as these and are inclined to want to commandeer every National Guard helicopter in the inventory to conduct personal inspection tours. Local officials who make unjustified demands and spew political rhetoric serve their constituents poorly, though, by raising false expectations.

While all this is occurring the storm's victims are enduring the most frustrating wait of all. After the initial shock of losing family treasures and suffering the sadness of years of work wiped out in minutes, the human instinct to rebuild begins to churn. The dispossessed become impatient to get on with the task. But the style of government intervention contributes more to confusion than to restoration. Many families and businessmen are under-insured. It is only natural to look to public assistance to cut financial losses that probably would be significant under the most favorable circumstances.

Will government finance the rebuilding of my home? Should I move the wife and kids into a motel in the expectation that government will reimburse me, or do I impose upon the hospitality of cousin Jake? Do I hire a contractor to remove debris? Will the government do it? Will I lose government assistance if I go ahead on my own and fail to follow proper procedures? If I settle with the insurance company, do I disqualify myself for federal help? A myriad of uncertainties keeps these people in limbo until government arrives at the scene with answers. Fortunately, a strong tradition of charity from neighbors, churches, and civic groups usually provides the essentials during this interim.

Government's mania for documentation compounds the problem. Damaged buildings must be inspected in order to gauge their value and to estimate the level of repair work that can be authorized under government aid. In the wake of 1974's tornadoes the state attempted to speed up this process by equipping officials with instant cameras with which they took detailed photographs of damaged dwellings. Where destruction is total, the problem is more difficult. Government financial aid usually is limited to the difference between private insurance compensation and the actual value of the structure. It is almost impossible to appraise a demolished building using these criteria. Federal authorities look to tax and insurance records to document uninsured improvements. Unfortunately, family documents stored in a steel box on the shelf in the master bedroom often have been buried under tons of mud or scattered for miles by whimsical winds.

Once values are agreed upon and the necessary paperwork is signed the victim still cannot be certain that he is over the hump, for the approval process can require weeks, even months. One businessman whose property was devastated by the 1979 floods in Crawford County waited for more than a year for the Small Business Administration to act upon his claim. This is torture, not compassion.

One of the most troublesome elements of disasters such as 1974's tornado outbreak is that of emergency housing. From the victim's standpoint, it might make a significant difference whether government housing will be available in a matter of days or whether families must wait for weeks before they can move in. The process is more rapid in urban areas where surplus rental housing can be obtained by the government and quickly made available. The 1974 storms generally swept through rural areas which lacked local rental properties. This required the importation of mobile homes mothballed at federal installations scattered around the country.

About 1,000 families were displaced by the April 3 tornadoes; more than 800 requested temporary housing. The first 100 households were placed in mobile homes within three weeks after the disaster, but some families waited for nearly two months because of the time required to provide utility services to rural installations.

Remaining disaster centers opened on the Monday following the storm, most of them in National Guard armories and all under the supervision of Indiana Department of Commerce personnel, who were pressed into service because the State Civil Defense Department lacked sufficient manpower. Thousands of people flocked to them during a two-week period. It reminded me of class registration day at Indiana University before the era of computerization.

Civil Defense Director Milton Mitnick, who was coordinating the state's response, kept after federal agencies to force a faster pace on their part. The governor later awarded him the Indiana Distinguished Service Medal, the state's highest award for achievement short of heroism.

State officials who had been spared disaster duty for nearly a decade learned valuable lessons during the 1974 tornado outbreak. The government's most critical shortcoming was communication. State Police, National Guard, and Civil Defense authorities operated radio equipment that did not have compatible frequencies. Only National Guard helicopters possessed hardware that would capture transmissions from State Police. Several choppers were diverted from emergency operations to function as airborne communications centers. By year's end the problem was resolved through the purchase of new equipment that would give several public safety agencies access to a common communications network.

The governor was well-satisfied with the performance of his security forces. His high estimation of the National Guard was a direct result of frequent contact with its members during the emergency. He soon became its most enthusiastic advocate among the governors. As chairman of the Public Safety Committee of the National Governors' Association, Bowen was instrumental in blocking an attempt by the Department of Defense to reorganize the Guard's entire structure above company-level units. After hearing a Defense Department presentation to that effect during an NGA meeting in Detroit, Bowen leaned across the table and said, "If there is any change in the states' ability to use the Guard to function in state emergencies, 50 governors will rise in arms against you."[3]

Adjutant General Ahner served as the governor's principal adviser on Guard issues and also brought to bear the views of the National Guard Bureau and National Guard Association of the United States. Bowen emerged as their primary civilian spokesman on issues such as the 1977 reorganization, which eventually was stalled at the Pentagon. As Bowen gained stature among the governors, Ahner acquired greater prominence within the Guard nationwide. He eventually became chairman of the Adjutants General Association and a confidant of Guard leaders in the Department of the Army.

The Bowen administration's second major weather disaster struck on Friday, January 28, 1977. A state already shivering from deep cuts in natural gas supplies and a winter of record cold was assailed by a fierce blizzard. Sixteen-inch snowfalls combined with 50 mile-per-hour winds to pile deep drifts across northern and central Indiana, closing most state highways and shutting down almost all of the region's secondary roads. Sixty National Guard armories were opened to receive stranded travelers; nearly 1,200 were housed that night. Rescue helicopters were grounded by high winds. Passengers aboard buses stalled on Interstate 65 in White County were evacuated by snowmobile. Brisk winds continued into the next day, coupled with powdery snow. They limited visibility so severely that helicopters remained on their pads. Despite the impassability of roads, motorists tried to traverse them anyway. Dodging roadblocks erected by State Police and county sheriffs, they became stranded and required rescue by snowmobile. More than 400 vehicles were lodged in drifts in one four-mile segment of Interstate 65 north of Lafayette.

Weather conditions improved slightly on Sunday, enabling a limited road-clearing effort to get under way. Opening major highway arteries was the priority task. Restoration of the transportation system would resolve most of the emergency needs for food, fuel, medical evacuations, and the like.

The snarl on Interstate 65 on the windy prairie north of the Wabash River was too much for Highway Department equipment. National Guard tanks were pressed into action to blast routes through twelve-foot drifts. Stalled semi-trailer trucks were more formidable obstacles than the snow. Rigs were chained to tanks and pulled off the right-of-way. With wind chill readings in the minus-60 range, Guardsmen and Highway Department personnel were able to work in the open for only minutes at a time. Unheated tanks and armored personnel carriers provided only limited refuge. The soldiers' military cold weather gear was inadequate for these extremes, and General Ahner scrounged through civilian warehouses and military inventories for additional protective gear.

Bowen sought federal help to clear the roads. His request to President Carter for an emergency declaration, later expanded to a call for full disaster designation which would qualify the state for additional assistance, forecast that it would take three weeks to reopen rural and secondary roads at a cost of $7 million to state and local governments. The governor wanted more than money. He sought heavy equipment for snow removal and the extraction of stranded vehicles.[4]

Again, the feds were hesitant to move. Mitnick, Highway Department Director Roger Marsh, and I met with a contingent of HUD disaster officials on Sunday night for what turned out to be a frustrating duel over documentation. Before considering a disaster declaration for agriculture they wanted to know how many livestock were dead. We replied that twelve-foot drifts imposed significant limitations upon our ability to count corpses.

The group bogged down in disagreement over financial aid for road-clearing. We suggested that state and local governments write the agreements and then obtain reimbursement from Washington. When HUD proposed that federal teams write individual contracts. I winced, remembering the glacial pace of federal intervention during the 1974 tornadoes. Finally, it was decided that the Army Corps of Engineers would undertake the responsibility, one that it carried out efficiently. The first contracts were signed within two days.

About $400,000 in federal assistance for snow removal was channeled to the Hoosier state, but many local road departments exhausted their entire year's maintenance budgets during the storm-clearing effort. As the state began digging out, it became apparent that the blizzard, combined with January's record sub-zero cold, had caused extensive damage to agriculture, buildings, utilities, and highways. The final cost estimate exceeded $130 million. Bowen's request for a broader disaster declaration was spurned by Washington after weeks of delay in making a determination. In the interim local governments had entered into contracts with private contractors for snow removal, anticipating that they would receive federal reimbursement. They were left holding the bag. In retrospect, the federal disaster relief mechanism seemed geared to physical damage caused by disasters such as floods and tornadoes. The widespread and disruptive economic impact of a snowstorm seemed lost upon the feds.

The 1977 blizzard was only a warmup act. A storm of record intensity swept across the Midwest in late January of 1978, and gathered even more ferocity as it approached the Hoosier state. Fortunately, the Weather Service was alert to its potential and gave several hours' advance warning to the public. Among other consequences this forecast had the effect of causing several state officials to cancel plans for a steak dinner at Booker's Red Dog Saloon in North Salem, where we certainly would have been snowed in. National Guard officers began reporting to the emergency operations center at Stout Field on Wednesday night, January 25. State Police officials, Jim Smith, and I bunked in at the bungalow on the grounds of the governor's residence, in order that we would be able to reach the Statehouse on the following morning. Twenty-four Guard armories were opened to receive snowbound travelers.

The full force of the storm was unleashed late that night. Weather Service barometers dropped to record lows. Temperatures fell 30 degrees and 50-mile-per-hour winds began piling snowdrifts. By dawn the state was paralyzed — its transportation systems closed and thousands of travelers forced to shelter. Winds snapped power lines and the lights went out in many midstate rural cooperative systems, although the rapidity of the temperature drop produced less icing than expected. After hours of struggling with accumulating snow, Amtrak's *Floridian* ground to a halt near Roachdale, where drifts piled higher than the locomotives. Passengers were evacuated by snowmobile.

High winds and snowfall continued Thursday morning. We were digging State Police cars out of drifts when one officer sputtered that, despite urgings to Bowen to wait for a State Police driver, the governor insisted upon piloting his own car, already freed from the snow. The trip downtown was possible only because ours was the only vehicle on the street, speeding to maintain momentum through drifts, veering and sliding when we collided with a large mound. Smith and I arrived at the governor's office to find Bowen behind his desk, wearing a flannel shirt, heavy work trousers, and combat boots. When we told him that he had made the cops nervous, he replied briskly: "Don't they think I know how to drive in this stuff? We get heavy snow in Bremen and I still had to make house calls."

As we analyzed the situation it became apparent that little could be done until the wind and snow ebbed. Helicopters were grounded. All roads in the state were closed except for urban routes in Lake and Vanderburgh counties. Guardsmen, police, and highway officials unable to report to duty stations on the previous evening were stranded at home. Tracked military vehicles were being used to round up essential personnel. Fifteen inches of snow had fallen and more was one the way. Extensive power outages had occurred. Crews from the larger utilities were laboring to restore service with some success, but the rural cooperatives were helpless because they lacked heavy equipment that would buck the drifts. Officials arranged to clear three miles of road in Terre Haute to move oil from a storage dump to Public Service Indiana's Wabash generating station, where the coal conveyor system had frozen. Without fuel for the backup oil-fired system much of the Terre Haute area would have lost electric service. The Guard's armored personnel carriers and six-wheel-drive vehicles were used for emergency runs and to pluck motorists from vehicles snagged on central Indiana interstates. At times the drifts were too much for them.

Life at the Statehouse was erratic. Only a handful of other officials had been able to make it: Vi Walker, Ray Sanders, Robert Roeder, and Maurice McDaniel. Sanders broke the locks on storage bins in the State Office Building cafeteria and rustled up vast quantities of tuna salad. That and the basement vending machines provided our food. Initial efforts were directed toward channeling requests for emergency assistance to public safety agencies and answering reporters' queries.

Twenty inches of snow had fallen by Friday morning. The winds had eased and helicopters began flying emergency missions by mid-morning. Armories housed 2,400 stranded travelers and thousands more were waiting out the storm at truck plazas, airports, restaurants, and private homes. People already were beginning to get cabin fever; it showed in the tenor of their telephone calls. There were numerous complaints about power outages at REMCs. Even with Guard vehicles to help them, the rural utilities were unable to get to downed lines.

Dressed in a heavy military overcoat and a winter hat that made him look like a Soviet field marshal, Bowen took a helicopter trip northward that afternoon. His chopper was diverted to pick up a woman facing premature childbirth. One television network later reported that the governor of Indiana had delivered a baby aboard a helicopter. It wasn't true, but we did not insist upon a retraction. Bowen telephoned from Lafayette to report that conditions were worse than during the previous year's blizzard, with wave upon wave of drifts overtopping I-65 overpasses. Even so, angry truckers couldn't understand why we hadn't opened the highways. By this time the Guard's vehicles were succumbing to the snow.

Road-clearing proceeded more rapidly on Saturday. Army Engineers hastily drafted agreements with private contractors to augment state and local operations. Meanwhile, the blizzard had generated a party atmosphere in downtown Indianapolis clubs and hotels. Legislators put a heavy drain upon lobbyists' entertainment budgets. The *Star* and *News* published slim blizzard editions circulated only in the central city. The manager of the Press Club was able to get to work and telephoned to ask how he might help. I relieved him of several bottles of whisky, the club's entire stock of potato chips, and several rolls of coins, for the assaults on vending machines had depleted our pocket change. The curious were getting in the way of the snow removal effort and Mayor Hudnut ordered a curfew. Snowmobiles frolicked on Monument Circle anyway.

A skeletal netword of federally-numbered roads and city streets reopened Sunday and the worst of the emergency was behind us. Mitnick worked with federal officials to acquire food stocks for rural St. Joseph County, where 30-inch snows had halted the distribution of groceries. On Sunday night the governor ordered the phasing out of National Guard personnel, although the battle to reopen rural roads continued into mid-week. I did not get home until Monday, having worn the same clothes for five days.

The spring thaw which followed the blizzard produced floods on the Kankakee River. Guardsmen were activated by the governor to help evacuate people and repair weakened levees. The Kankakee is the core of a vast swampland that has been partially drained for agricultural purposes but remains vulnerable to regular overflowing of its banks. Guardsmen were on duty for two weeks while local officials argued for a state program to resolve the flooding problem permanently. The legislature created a multi-county commission to explore what might be done, but it remained obvious that people who insist upon living in swampland occasionally will be forced to face the consequences.

The final major weather disaster of the Bowen administration resulted from the remnants of a Gulf hurricane which dumped nearly ten inches of rainfall on southern Indiana's hill country in July, 1979. Crawford County, already one of the state's most impoverished, was especially hard hit. A wall of water and mud caused heavy damage at English. Three hundred homes were evacuated. Two hundred families in nearby Marengo also were forced to leave. More than a dozen counties eventually received some form of federal disaster assistance after state officials identified extensive damage to farms and rural road systems, in addition to residential and business losses in several communities.[5] Disaster centers were activated in the region. The federal government's response seemed to be more effective than in previous emergencies. The federal Small Business Administration, however, was criticized for prolonged delays in approving applications.

During Bowen's tenure public safety agencies were activated for a series of labor disputes. State Police bore the brunt of this, since a 150-member riot squad had received special training and could be activated quickly. Both State Police and Guard forces were mobilized for the February, 1974, strike by independent truck drivers, which produced sporadic episodes of vandalism and violence. Shots were fired at non-striking truckers. Semis moved in State Police-guarded convoys across Hoosier interstates. Guardsmen patrolled overpasses and helicopters provided surveillance. State Police also were heavily involved in a second violence-plagued boycott by truckers in 1979.

Industrial disputes required their presence, notably at the strike-plagued Evans Rail Car foundry at Washington in 1980, and at earlier disorders involving Essex Wire Company in Anderson and Morgan Packing Company at Austin. Local law enforcement agencies shy away from involvement in labor trouble because sheriffs and police chiefs are wary of the political consequences of appearing to be anti-union. The state is not supposed to become involved until an emergency exhausts the capabilities of local officials. It seldom works this way in labor disputes, however, since county and city authorities prefer to toss the unpopular chore to state government. Although State Police view their role as that of preventing violence, company officials want them to break the strike while union leaders want them to stay away. Over the years State Police have demonstrated a capacity to manage strike situations in a manner that preserves peace while avoids oppressive intervention in what essentially is a private argument.

Labor disputes involving public employees were a more recent phenomenon. The legislature grappled unsuccessfully during several sessions with proposed collective bargaining legislation. Except for a brief police strike at Columbus in 1974, in which State Police were used, periodic threats of public employee walkouts failed to materialize in the early 1970s. Meanwhile, in other states Guardsmen ran prisons; buildings burned as striking firemen ignored owners' pleas for help. Public safety officials in Bowen's administration began to develop contingency plans for state involvement if these walkouts spread to Indiana. State Police were viewed as the lead agency in local police strikes. A combination of State Police and county sheriff's personnel probably would be able to handle a strike in a medium-sized city. Based upon available manpower, officials concluded that State Police could deal with two simultaneous strikes. If additional incidents erupted, Guardsmen would be activated. However, this was not true of Indianapolis, the state's largest city, where plans in 1979 called for the activation of both State Police and Guard military police to deal with a possible work stoppage.

Local police and fire organizations are under the impression that they are indispensable. A strike will force city government to come to terms, they believe. That philosophy lost some of its charm in South Bend in 1980. State Police Superintendent John Shettle had maintained a close watch upon the situation and was ready to intervene if called upon to do so. When "blue flu" hit, the state quickly took over law enforcement responsibilities. It proved embarrassing to the strikers, as State Police reacted to calls with greater speed than the citizenry had been accustomed to. When the governor's office told the South Bend *Tribune* that Bowen was prepared to put hundreds of National Guardsmen on the city's streets if the situation required it, the strikers began to realize that their walkout might be a losing proposition. It collapsed within a few days.

The state's strategy for dealing with firemen's strikes relied on volunteer units from nearby communities. If their numbers were inadequate or they were unavailable, the governor would activate Air National Guard firefighting units operating from Hulman Field at Terre Haute and Baer Field at Fort Wayne. A 1980 firemen's walkout in Marion resulted in a callup of the Baer Field unit for three days. No major fires erupted during the period.

His experience with public sector labor disputes, coupled with the frequent employment of the National Guard during disasters, prompted Bowen to lobby federal officials for additional training and equipment for its domestic emergency responsibilities. The Pentagon's overriding concern was that of training citizen-soldiers for war. Bowen argued that the Guard was entitled to access to disaster relief equipment in federal inventories and should receive training in its use. Use of the Guard in disasters, he believed, relieved the Regular Army of a potential responsibility. Moreover, military training was inadequate to prepare a Guardsmen for domestic emergencies. Federal and state authorities should not expose these personnel to the safety risks associated with firefighting or conducting relief operations in tornado-ravaged neighborhoods among leaking gas systems and downed power lines. Public sector strikes imposed requirements alien to Guardsmen's traditional experiences. The Military Department of Indiana began taking steps to train additional personnel in these tasks and identified Guardsmen who possessed civilian-acquired skills that might be useful in emergencies. By the time Bowen's administration ended, federal authorities were studying these requests, but no definitive action had been taken in Washington.[6]

Convinced of the Guard's importance, Bowen also was an energetic supporter of efforts to recruit and retain its personnel during a no-draft era in which the Reserve components' strength had dropped nationwide. He intervened to help recruit physicians, since the Guard was critically short of medical personnel. Incentive programs were presented to the General Assembly. Guard rosters that had declined to 85 percent of authorized levels began filling again as state authorities carried out an extensive recruiting and retention program. In December, 1980, General Ahner was able to report that overall personnel strength levels had reached 100 percent.

XVII   COAL CRISIS

The most difficult crisis of Bowen's second term resulted from a prolonged walkout by the United Mine Workers that brought the state to the brink of serious hardship. The administration's emergency management capabilities were tested for many weeks as utilities' coal stockpiles dwindled and the lights began to dim.

The administration began planning for the eventuality six months in advance. State Energy Director William Sorrells and I concluded that a strike was inevitable and that it had the potential for long duration. A five-week strike in late autumn 1974 had caused state officials to assess the vulnerability of the state's economy to a widespread cessation of coal production. More than 50,000 residences were heated by coal. Numerous schools, nursing homes, and state institutions relied upon the fuel. During the 1974 walkout the state had been compelled to allocate emergency coal (usually diverted from state institutions) on only a handful of occasions. However, during the strike's final week the state's monitoring detected a dramatic erosion of coal supplies, especially in the "spot" market, which served most homes.

The June, 1977, assessment was a pessimistic one. It concluded that a United Mine Workers strike against the eastern operators was a certainty. Sporadic strikes had sapped production in the eastern minefields throughout the year, hindering efforts to stockpile coal. The union was shattered by bitter internal strife among three factions which dueled for control. None commanded a majority. UMW president Arnold Miller seemed unable to sustain a majority on the union's board. Disputed elections and National Labor Relations Board challenges highlighted its divisions, while new balloting appeared only to offer the potential to further inflame the situation. Some within the union harbored dissatisfaction so fundamental that they seemed prepared to wreck the organization if that proved to be the only way to pursue their aims. Certain other unions perceived advantages in the UMW's disarray, believing that they might inherit many of its locals in the event of a collapse.

On the other side, the coal operators seemed unified, had announced intentions to maintain a rigid bargaining stance, and appeared to be ready to accept a lengthy strike, believing that time worked in their favor. Both sides saw the contract's expiration as an opportunity to attract attention to the industry's needs, in light of President Carter's stated emphasis on coal development.

Recalling the previous year's weather-caused natural gas shortages, energy officials were concerned that the winter of 1978 might see the twin perils of natural gas and coal shortages occurring at the same time.

The Energy Office of the Indiana Department of Commerce was given the task of drafting a plan. First, it created an apparatus to identify coal users and monitor their stockpiles. These surveys attempted to denote users who could use alternate fuels. The agency began to coordinate its work with state welfare and civil defense agencies, and with the Public Service Commission. The PSC appeared to be the only state government body with sufficient regulatory muscle to enforce conservation and possible reallocations of supplies. It had sweeping jurisdiction over electric utilities — the state's largest consumers of coal. Sorrells and I began to work with federal officials in order to determine what help might come from that quarter.

The contingency plan was based on several assumptions. First, priority categories for state attention and assistance would be hospitals, nursing homes, and private residences, along with other facilities where cessation of operations would place life in danger or pose the threat of serious property damage. Second, the state would endeavor to keep these priority users in operation by securing hardship allocations of coal or other fuels, rather than evacuating people who were served by them. Finally, the state recognized that its ability to influence the supply positions of the big users — utilities and large industries — was limited. Coal supplies available to state government would be insignificant in terms of utility and industry requirements. The plan called for the state to help these users acquire additional supplies.

In the case of the utilities, assistance would focus on their efforts to import surplus power through the grid system from regions unaffected by the strike. The state would help untangle federal regulations that restricted power swaps and blocked temporary conversions to backup fuel sources. If the situation required, the state would safeguard the transportation of coal with the State Police and National Guard. The governor was advised that the plan would not work in an extreme hardship situation unless he was willing to activate these security forces. He said he was willing to do so.

The initial phase of the contingency plan called for the promotion of voluntary coal and electricity conservation. State agencies and large users would be asked to undertake a vigorous conservation program, and to convert to alternate sources where available.

If evidence pointed to a prolonged emergency the state would seek authority from the federal government to reallocate middle distillate oils (such as heating fuel) in order to insure that users with backup systems could get it. Conservation would be intensified and the state would begin to provide coal to priority users as needed.

Under severe shortages the governor would invoke emergency powers to waive regulations that might impede the burning of alternate fuels and to activate security forces to safeguard the movement of coal. Mandatory conservation measures would be imposed and the state would request that the federal government reallocate electric power from non-coal burning utilities elsewhere. This five-page plan[1] became the basis for the state's response and for detailed implementation provisions subsequently developed by state agencies.

The contract expired on December 6, 1977, and the miners walked out. There was little immediate impact because large users had built stockpiles in anticipation of the strike. However, colder than normal weather eroded reserves at a growing rate and violence (or the threat of violence) in the southwestern Indiana coal-producing regions retarded the movement of coal at the retail level. In January, Warrick County Prosecutor Robert Rideout called on non-union operators to shut down, because their workers had been subjected to intimidation by the UMW. The state rejected that approach, questioning a perverse line of reasoning that would deal with a problem by having the law-abiding give way to the violent. Augmented State Police patrols combed the area after nearly 200 arrests were made at Rockport, where arsonists set fire to a loading dock and trucking equipment. Trucks also were damaged at Boonville. The state arranged a coal shipment from Evansville State Hospital to the Warrick County school system because the regular supplier was afraid to haul it.[2]

On January 17, Governor Bowen ordered 10-to-15 percent cutbacks in the use of coal and electricity by state agencies as the first step toward building momentum for statewide conservation efforts. Three days later he called for a voluntary effort by all citizens to achieve a similar reduction in coal and electricity usage, arguing that voluntary conservation could postpone or avoid mandatory curtailments and that conservation in the 10-to-15 percent range usually could be achieved without much inconvenience.[3]

The early response to the call for voluntary fuel-saving was not encouraging. The bruising late January blizzard reduced coal and electricy use because of widespread business shutdowns, but the coal-saving benefits probably were offset by the nearly week-long interruption of coal transportation caused by the weather. Monitoring indicated a conservation effort only in the five percent range. State officials began to consider mandatory conservation orders. Serious dialogue began with the Department of Energy, because it was becoming apparant that the federal government had no appreciation of the situation.

Public Service Commission Chairman Larry Wallace and I joined representatives of other affected states in a meeting with DOE officials in Washington on February 1. Notes I made after the proceeding sum up its tone:

> The meeting with the Department of Energy staff is incredible. We hear what we already know and are told to do what we already are doing. The feds are preoccupied with intra-grid power swaps (which the utilities have been undertaking for some time) and suggest that non-economic dispatch be implemented (this has been a way of life in the East Central grid for ten days). One official suggests a questionnaire designed to index the impact of various levels of curtailment upon industrial production and layoffs. In subsequent discussion I dismiss this as a casualty-counting exercise. Wallace and I report that the department's stockpile figures for Indiana power stations are dead wrong and that we face mandatory curtailments in about ten days. Indiana, Michigan, and Ohio call for the imposition of a Taft-Hartley injunction; Illinois is more hesitant. Taft-Hartley won't mine any coal but will give us access to non-union mines and coal at the tipples of operations now shut down. We are disgusted because there are no conclusions and no commitment to act by the federal officials. Larry and I begin swapping jokes as their performance becomes more ludicrous.

After we reported the outcome to the governor he quickly fired off a letter to President Carter in which he observed that the federal government had no appreciation for either the imminence or the magnitude of hardship that would arise as a consequence of the strike. The governor wrote:

> Soon, the dimensions of the problem will be sufficient to force cutbacks in industrial production. Our citizens will feel the hardship of layoffs... We will endeavor to minimuze hardships but the harsh reality is this: coal must begin to move and the strike must end. . . The time has come for your personal intervention, either to use your powers of persuasion or to invoke those statutory powers available to you. I am keenly aware of the problems associated with a Taft-Hartley order and recognize that it is a risky step. If the administration is unwilling to invoke Taft-Hartley, it must be prepared to take other measures that would have a meaningful impact upon the coal supply situation. At the present time the posture of federal agencies is inadequate to the scale of the emergency. Time is rapidly slipping away.[4]

At the February 2 staff meeting, the governor advised public safety assistant James Smith and me that he was prepared to activate the National Guard. We encouraged him to hold off for a few days, but notified Adjutant General Ahner of the development. Ahner was reluctant to proceed, because bitter memories still lingered after confrontations between the militia and miners in Indiana's coalfields from the 1870s to the 1930s. That day we also were preoccupied with problems in Logansport where Mayor Eugene Monoghan, whose municipal utility was nearly out of coal, had rejected offers of supply on at least five occasions because he didn't like the price. Facing a shutdown the next day, the mayor charged that a Logansport-bound convoy of trucks was waiting at the state line because the governor wouldn't issue the overweight permits necessary to permit their transit. State Police determined the report to be false. Sorrells secured a shipment from the Chrysler Corporation at Kokomo and it temporarily alleviated the situation, which continued to be touch and go for a matter of days because of the mayor's incredible attitude.

State government deliberations concerning curtailment policies began in earnest and proved troublesome from two standpoints. Generally, both utilities and state officials agreed that curtailments of progressive severity should be imposed when coal inventories in utility systems deteriorated to a certain number of days of supply. Forty days was thought to be a logical boundary for the onset of mandatory measures in the 15-to-25-percent range. Unfortunately, meaningful calculations of the number of days' supply on hand proved to be a rather ephemeral exercise. These forecasts are based on several factors: supply on hand, the anticipated depletion rate (largely a function of temperature), expected shipments, and commitments from other utilities to supply surplus electricity at a given rate. These variables can change dramatically from day to day. A utility's computation on a Monday reasonably could project a 40-day supply. Another calculation using the same formula 24 hours later might conclude that 45 days of supply could be counted on. Aside from making it difficult for state officials to have a firm grip on the severity of problems as the strike progressed, it proved to be quite confusing to the public (and most reporters).

Second, there were wide-ranging differences in the supply situation among utilities. A uniform statewide policy would be advantageous from an administrative viewpoint and also would be more credible to the public — which was the prime target of conservation efforts. However, utilities argued with justification that mandatory cutbacks were unfair to those systems in the strongest supply posture. Most notable was Northern Indiana Public Service Company, where mandatory cutbacks would have had a significant impact upon steelmaking, which represented the majority of its industrial load.

On the other hand, a system-by-system curtailment policy would prove highly confusing to the public, a point validated when a policy of this nature eventually was adopted. The Indianapolis media area proved to be a good illustration. Marion County, served by Indianapolis Power & Light Company, avoided mandatory curtailments at a time when virtually all of central Indiana (served by the same television and radio stations) was under substantial curtailments because its utility, Public Service Indiana, was in a far weaker position. Undoubtedly, the wide variances in utility conditions had the effect of sapping the conservation effort, as did recurring announcements of tentative settlement agreements that ultimately were rejected in the ratification process.

On Friday, February 3, Wallace, Sorrells, and I met with representatives of the investor-owned companies, municipal electric utilities, and rural cooperatives to discuss the phasing in of curtailments. The utilities continued to argue in favor of the East Central Area Reliability Council plan, which triggered progressively more severe curtailments at each utility as stockpiles dropped in increments of ten days. Wallace encouraged them to coordinate the implementation because, he said, we could not have 160 utilities giving their customers 160 different stories. NIPSCO refused to budge, since its supply position was substantially better than the others. The group agreed to recommend a maximum effort to achieve voluntary conservation — in the 25 percent range — and give it a week to work. If voluntary conservation proved inadequate, the group would meet again on the following Friday to determine whether curtailments should be made mandatory.

Wallace, Norman Wagner (the executive vice-president of Southern Indiana Gas & Electric and president of the Indiana Electric Association), and I then met with reporters. We called for a 25 percent reduction of electric power use at all levels of consumption, including the residential sector. If that approach failed, we warned, the state faced mandatory cutbacks within two weeks.

Unfortunately, our promotion of conservation already was being undermined by talk of a settlement. In response to a reporter's question, Wagner said: "We've read quite a bit about the possiblity of a settlement, but even if there were an agreement this afternoon, there still would be a period of about 30 days before coal piles would start to increase again."[5] On Monday, February 6, a tentative agreement was announced, but Indiana UMW District President Larry Reynolds advised the state energy office that the union's bargaining council would reject the pact because of its restrictions on wildcat strikes and because the document was nebulous and poorly drafted. Indeed, the bargaining council announced the next day that it wouldn't even put the contract to a vote of the membership.

Since voluntary programs were producing reductions only in the 10 percent range, Wallace and I became convinced that PSC-ordered mandatory curtailments were inevitable. On February 8 the commission declared a fuel emergency and ordered electricity generating companies to present evidence of conservation efforts, coal supplies, and contingency plans as a method of setting the stage for a mandatory curtailment order.[6] However, we began to attract a good deal of attention from the media and businessmen with descriptions of "rolling blackouts" that might be employed as an extreme fuel-saving measure if coal stockpiles plunged to the 20-day level. This is a drastic measure which involves total and revolving cutoff of power to a large geographic region of a utility's service area for several hours. The implications for emergency services were rather awesome. We described the use of rolling blackouts in some detail in order to get attention. It had an effect.

By a lopsided 30-3 vote, the bargaining council rejected the contract. Governor Bowen dispatched another telegram to the White House, which still seemed to slumber despite the marked deterioration of the situation:

> The coal settlement has collapsed and there is no end in sight to the longest coal strike in our nation's history. Coal supplies in Indiana have deteriorated to margins so slender that we are compelled to begin mandatory electric power cutbacks within three days. These cutbacks will force widespread layoffs in our industries.[7]

The remainder was a bit over-dramatic, and intended to be so, in hopes of getting a message to Washington and of giving headline writers around the country something to play with:

> The lights are dimming throughout Indiana. Economic hardship and human misery will occur as the state recedes into the darkness. Our earlier urgent pleas for federal intervention and federal leadership have been ignored. Time has run out. There can be no further delays. You must order the resumption of coal production and transportation.[8]

Wallace, at the outset, was inclined to use a system of curtailment priorities enforced through heavy financial penalties for excessive consumption — much as California had handled water rationing. This was a politically risky approach, but the utilities and regulators considered it to be the cleanest. It also had the merit of being effective. On Friday, February 10, Wallace conducted a hearing to receive evidence on the matter. Over the weekend, amid a flurry of telephone conferences, a compromise plan ermerged. It provided for immediate statewide restrictions on most categories of outdoor lighting. In utilities whose coal supplies dwindled below the 40-day mark, 25 percent cutbacks would be enforced upon industrial and commercial customers, while residential users would be expected to curb consumption by 15 percent. Schools were to be curtailed 50 percent.

On Monday morning, February 13, Wallace and I obtained the governor's approval and then conducted a news conference (carried live by nearly 60 radio stations) to announce the plan. My opening statement was somber in tone:

> For several days Governor Bowen and this administration have warned that the impact of the nation's longest coal strike soon would reach a level requiring mandatory cutbacks of electric power in this state. We now are at that point. The negotiations between the union and the bituminous operatores are in a shambles. There has been no meaningful response, yet, from the federal government. Voluntary conservation, while gaining momentum at the present time, falls far short of forestalling mandatory measures. Some coal is moving to utilities and to other users, but the volumes are inadequate to halt the chipping away at our coal stockpiles. Several of our utilities now are importing power from other states but are not able to secure volumes sufficient to stabilize the

situation. We continue on a downward path, each day bringing us closer to more perilous circumstances.

We described the approach as one whose basic intent was to keep utilities' stockpiles above the critical 30-day level, while attempting to reduce, or at least postpone, widespread industrial layoffs.

Concurrently, the administration began to develop its plan for supporting and safeguarding transportation of coal. Smith assumed overall direction of this aspect of the strike, working with Adjutant General Ahner and State Police Superintendent Shettle. My role was to advise them of priorities for coal movement. They, in turn, would insure that this coal was delivered. Unfortunately, the planning was conducted in a rather foggy atmosphere, since state officials had no way of knowing in advance how much coal must be moved or what its sources and destination likely would be. It was agreed that the state would provide security forces for the movement of coal by trucks or trains but would not become directly involved in coal delivery since transportation assets were quite limited. General Ahner remained reluctant to commit his Guard forces in such a visible and potentially unpopular role (insofar as miners would be concerned), but became convinced of the necessity for action when mandatory power curtailments were put into effect.

On February 14 Smith and I announced the decision to activate the Guard and State Police:

> The governor's declaration confers rather broad powers upon the State Police and the Guard to assist in the movement of coal. However, it is the governor's position that the State Police and the National Guard wil be used to help safeguard coal movements to priority users... We will not go into detail as to the techniques that will be employed, but we can tell you that, when the State Police and National Guard are involved, their presence wil be formidable. They will be prepared to protect themselves and the shipments they are safeguarding.[9]

Stating the situation in this manner skirted the issue of the extent to which Guardsmen would be armed and the circumstances under which Guard personnel would be authorized to use their weapons.

Meanwhile, Ohio prepared to announce curtailments of up to 50 percent to industrial users (amid reports that lawsuits would result), but Pennsylvania and West Virginia contented themselves with the continuation of rather modest levels of voluntary conservation, even though coal stockpiles in Appalachia were approaching dangerously thin margins.

With the situation deteriorating, President Carter finally convened a White House meeting of governors of states affected by the strike. Also present were Energy Secretary James Schlesinger, Deputy Attorney General Benjamin Civiletti, and Transportation Secretary Brock Adams. As Bowen entered the East Room, the President quietly told him: "You are doing some courageous things out there." In his opening comments Carter described the actions taken by Indiana as "the strongest and most effective thus far."[10] The President stated a reluctance to impose a Taft-Hartley injunction, but it was clear, given his inconsequential presentation, that the administration had no other strategy designed to cope with the coal emergency. The reaction from most governors was disappointing as their comments focused on the potential for violence between miners and peace officers if Taft-Hartley were invoked. West Virginia Governor Jay Rockefeller characterized it in terms of guerrilla warfare in his state. Even the normally feisty governor of Ohio, James Rhodes, accepted the answer of a UMW-dictated resolution of the strike.

Bowen's reaction was that he shared these concerns, but was even more worried about the consequences of failing to act. "We're talking about the well-being of 75 million people in these 12 states," he said. The majority of governors urged Carter to use the influence of the presidency to force the coal operators to accept a contract on the union's terms, which only underscored the impotence of this gathering of top federal and state leaders.

Back in Indiana, the coal convoy operation was underway, under the protection of about 50 state troopers and 350 National Guardsmen. The first project was that of moving surplus coal from Public Service Indiana's generating station at Princeton to another PSI facility at Cayuga, where stockpiles had dwindled to an 18-day level. The opening run was disrupted only by the scattering of nails on the roadway. Subsequent convoys were harassed only by miners shouting obscenities and throwing snowballs.

After a few days of uneventful movement, the Guard and State Police altered the security arrangement from convoy escort to security patrols at overpasses and other critical areas, complemented by helicopter surveillance. This allowed a more rapid movement on a greater variety of routes. Guard units were rotated on a weekly basis, because the duty was demanding in nature. Southwestern Indiana-based units were not involved because Ahner did not want to place citizen-soldiers in potential confrontations with their neighbors. Coal also began moving from the tipples at non-union mines throughout the southwestern region. Slowly, state actions were beginning to reduce the rate of erosion of coal stockpiles.[11]

However, evidence that Washington remained in a muddle was confirmed on February 21 when the congressional leadership told reporters that they would support any actions the President might take but that Congress would not become involved in the strike, since it would not reach crisis level until mid-April. Bowen was furious and fired off another telegram to Carter which recounted the measures undertaken in Indiana and closed with these remarks:

Unfortunately, these efforts by the people of Indiana are being undermined by a continued climate of indecision and inaction in the nation's capital. I was astounded to learn today of the attitude of the congressional leadership, which according to news accounts is one of hesitancy to do anything until disaster actually is upon us.

Moreover, I cannot underscore the urgency of action on your part. If you determine that government seizure of the mines is the best option, do it now. If you consider Taft-Hartley to be workable, do it now. If you favor binding arbitration, send the legislation to Congress today. Each day that lapses without decisive federal action further jeopardizes the jobs, safety and well-being of millions of Americans. We in Indiana have demonstrated the gumption to face into this problem in a realistic way. We would like to see that spirit echoed in the nation's capital.[12]

In reply, Presidential Assistant Jack Watson telphoned me the next day to reassure us that the administration shared Bowen's perception of the seriousness of the strike. It was clear that Watson was aware the governor had found a national audience. The White House wanted to calm him in the hope that he would not take potshots at the President. At this point, according to Watson, the administration expected bargaining to break down, with the emphasis then shifting to attempts to settle the strike on a company-by-company basis, using the Pittsburg & Midway agreement as a basis. Watson's appraisal proved wrong within 48 hours, as another in a series of tentative agreements was proclaimed on Friday, February 24.

The state administration was quick to point out that there would be no changes in state curtailment policies until the settlement was ratified. Announcement of the agreement didn't add a pound of coal to the state's ebbing reserves. We had seen phony settlements before.[13] It was significant that Indiana & Michigan Electric Company had dropped below the 40-day reserve and joined PSI in mandatory power cutbacks to its users.

Another confusing issue was the impact of the strike upon employment in Indiana. Projecting the potentially grim outlook became a popular journalistic game at the end of February. About 3,000 layoffs had been documented, but economists and state officials were hounded for forecasts. Unfortunately, such forecasting is a rather imprecise art. One much-quoted yardstick — the Chase Econometric Model — was based on the assumption that for every percentage point drop in energy availability there would be a percentage point surge in layoffs.

As some utilities edged near reserve levels that could dictate deeper curtailments, formulas such as this posed rather scary prospects. Some in the media were quick to seize upon them. However, we knew from past experience in fuel emergencies that models such as Chase's were wrong. Industry could absorb the first 10-to-15-percent cutback in its basic fuel source without significant interruption of production and employment. Conservation measures short of layoffs could be used to gain more efficiency from the supplies available. Indeed, existing cutbacks in the PSI and Indiana & Michigan systems were not producing equivalent reductions in economic activity.

Our experience with the 1973 oil embargo and 1977 natural gas shortage indicated that beyond the 15 percent range, production and job losses would increase in geometric proportion to fuel reductions. In other words, a 20 percent electricity cut might produce a 30 percent drop in workforce for an individual manufacturer. The state projected that a 50 percent curtailment (which would be forced at the time a utility stockpile dropped below 30 days) would cause most manufacturers to shut down. At the end of the first week in March — with the union still balloting on the proposed settlement — Indiana unemployment attributed to electricity shortages had climbed to 7,500.[12]

The latest contract agreement fizzled out over the weekend of March 4-5 as militant miners in Appalachia rejected it overwhelmingly. Cold weather still plagued the state — eight above zero at Indianapolis on that Saturday morning.

The President finally invoked Taft-Hartley on March 6, but left its enforcement to the states. Watson again telephoned to explain the President's position in more detail, and ended with a statement that responsibility for upholding law and order would rest with governors. Carter's decision in no way eased the limitations on federal participation. The President also had said that the Department of Energy would begin moving energy resources to hardest-hit areas. At my request, the department clarified this to mean that it had only prepared emergency regulations to allocate coal and power on an interstate basis. The department believed — for the time being — that voluntary arrangements were working and that emergency allocations of this type would not come into play unless a governor petitioned for them.

As it turned out, the Taft-Hartley procedure was a muddled, confused, half-hearted measure on the part of the federal government. Although the President announced it on a Monday, the actual injunction was not filed until Thursday — glacial movement at best. In addition, Presidential Adviser Robert Strauss commented that the federal government might seize the mines and operate them if the UMW refused to obey the back-to-work decree. Since the miners would have preferred this course of action anyway, Strauss's comments amounted to an engraved invitation to them to defy the government.

Fortunately, as many as 500 truckloads of coal a day were moving in the Indiana smuggling operation, augmented by frequent railroad operations. Coupled with the success of the conservation effort and the ability of utilities to acquire surplus electricity elsewhere, these shipments had the effect of stabilizing the electricity and coal supply in the state. Indiana now was holding its own.

Officials worried, however, that Indiana's success in maintaining the situation at this level would not protect Hoosier workers from losing their jobs. Coal inventories in western Pennsylvania, Ohio, and West Virginia were declining rapidly — yet serious curtailments still were not in force. Given the interdependence of the neighboring states' industrial economies — especially in the auto industry — sharp power reductions soon to be required in their utility systems would have a domino effect on related industries in Indiana.

It wasn't until Saturday, March 10, that federal marshals got around to delivering Taft-Hartley notices to the miners — an indication that the federal government remained less than serious about the enterprise. One day earlier a PSI official had testified that 10,000 tons of coal from the west were diverted from the Indiana utility to the Tennessee Valley Authority. I dubbed it "the great train robbery," to the delight of reporters. Someone in the Department of Energy had been allocating coal hopper cars and reassigned rolling stock intended for Indiana to TVA. PSI hadn't lost the coal, only the means to move it. Other utilities began to report similar problems.[15]

The miners generally ignored the federal order, but did not interfere with operations at several sites where company officials loaded coal the following week.[16] Another tentative settlement was announced, but state officials remained skeptical that it would lead to immediate relief. They began to work with the Department of Transportation to spot rail hopper cars at locations from which coal could be mined and moved immediately after a settlement. Indiana officials wanted to avoid leaving them bunched at idle deep shaft mines in Appalachia that might require weeks to reopen. Water would have to be pumped out of them and extensive safety inspections completed before the miners could return to work. The ratification vote took place on Good Friday, March 24, and, finally, an agreement was accepted. After a Public Service Commission hearing on Monday, March 27, Wallace judged that it was possible to end the mandatory curtailments. He issued an order to that effect. On that day the governor also deactivated the Guard.

Bowen gained stature as a result of his forthright handling of the emergency. It was in sharp contrast to the President, whose actions seemed to be characterized by clumsiness bordering on cowardice. The state administration also was credited with having the foresight to prepare detailed plans for the strike. However, Wallace and I were extremely relieved that the marathon dispute was concluded without the need to resort to more severe curtailments, because we feared that users might successfully block their implementation through court actions. The PSC chairman later wrote:

> The biggest problem with the curtailment proceedings of this commission was in enforcement. This is the main area that really would need some thorough reexamination should the occasion ever arise again to initiate similar proceedings. Had the strike lasted much longer, had fuel supplies reached the

30-day level, or had we had to continue our mandatory curtailment requirements any longer, I am genuinely fearful that the whole thing may have collapsed. . . Enforcement of mandatory curtailment at the residential level by disconnection during winter time is, for all practical purposes, an empty threat.

Probably the best thing that happened during the entire period of the strike was the Governor's early action in providing security for the movement of coal through State Police and the National Guard. Had that not occurred I sincerely doubt if our curtailment plan could have worked at all, and I know it would not have worked as well as it did. Not only did the security for movement of coal keep the shortage from becoming worse than it did, but it also showed people that all levels of state government were asserting some leadership and trying to help them through the situation, and made the public more willing to do its part.[17]

XVIII   THE BOWEN TEAM, 1978

The sixth year was a watershed period in Bowen's governorship. With the end of his term looming ever nearer, politicians of both parties began jockeying for position. They began to look less to him and more toward whomever might be installed as his successor. The governor's influence with the legislature was ebbing. Media preoccupation with the blizzard and coal strike concealed the disappointing outcome of many key administration proposals in the 1978 General Assembly. Advisers to the governor considered the legislative episode to be an outright disaster. However, the autumn campaign redeemed the personal reputation of a leader whose political fortunes had stagnated in the year's early months. Republicans galloped to victory in the off-year balloting as part of the "Bowen Team." Not to be found beneath a lever on any voting machine in the state, the governor's name, nonetheless, was the GOP rallying cry. He was not a candidate. He was the campaign.

A perked-up economy had brightened the state revenue outlook by the time that lawmakers converged upon Indianapolis for the 1978 legislative session. Personal income had risen. Unemployment was down. Abnormal budget surpluses were in the offing. Bowen's strategy for the legislative session was that of identifying limited goals for new spending, but earmarking most surplus funds for return to the taxpayers.

Several proposals were outlined. Property tax relief for older Hoosiers was to be increased by tripling the old-age exemption and by raising the circuit-breaker exemption income level from $5,000 to $7,500. Older Hoosiers also would qualify for a sales tax exemption on utility bills. Permanent reduction of the state's individual income tax from its existing level of two percent to one and nine-tenths percent was another key feature. A one-time rebate of $15 per allowable exemption, which would reduce the treasury by $75 million, rounded out the individual program. For business, the legislature should enact a broader "freeport" statute exempting from the inventory tax warehoused goods destined for out-of-state shipment. Freeport had been a hardy perennial in legislative sessions since the early 1970s, but habitually foundered as its advocates devised exemptions far too costly to state government. Greed consistently outpaced practicality. Bowen proposed adding one percent to the corporate supplemental net income tax to defray much of the cost of revising inventory levies.

The governor's message to the legislature expressed a number of other objectives. Indiana, he said, should establish a budget stabilization fund by expanding the tuition reserve fund to provide a cash cushion during economic fluctuations. A $20 million fund should be created to reimburse local government for losses due to an adverse court decision on property taxes for finished manufactured goods awaiting interstate shipment. New local school and civil government referendum provisions would facilitate taxation above controlled limits if voters desired it. The motor fuel tax should be hiked by three cents a gallon or "we will have a concrete and asphalt version of the Penn Central Railroad on our hands."[1] For the third time Bowen endorsed creation of a state department of transportation. A new juvenile criminal code also received his backing.

One of the touchier gubernatorial recommendations involved granting him the authority to employ attorneys, either to assist state agencies or to provide counsel to the governor. Increased vulnerability to lawsuits, the need for legal counsel as part of the day-to-day operation of state agencies, and requirements for specialized legal assistance not available from the attorney general were cited as reasons. An unspoken motive was the governor's belief that he, as chief executive officer of state government, should have the right to hire his own legal counsel if he did not believe that the attorney general could or would mount a proper defense in a court action.

Bowen had sought to employ James Young as private counsel in a case involving the Alcoholic Beverage Commission, but Attorney General Sendak objected. The courts ruled that Sendak had the exclusive right to represent state agencies. Given the hostility between the two officials and Bowen's contention that an uncooperative attorney general could prevent a governor from discharging his constitutional obligations, the proposal was a high priority item.

Another tough challenge was that of amending Indiana's Constitution to require a three-fifths or two-thirds majority to override gubernatorial vetoes. Simple majorities called for by the existing Constitution weakened a governor's authority to operate the executive branch on equal footing with the legislature.

Several Bowen proposals received a frigid reception. The gas tax increase hit the floor with a thud. Senate President Pro-Tempore Robert Fair said that the governor was "a dreamer" if he thought that the divided legislature would accept the plan.[2] Republicans were equally cool to the idea, having spurned an increase in the 1977 session. Upping the override majority was received with a yawn. GOP leaders were only lukewarm in their support of giving the governor his own legal counsel. Many of them were lawyers; the attorney general was part of the fraternity. Conservatives were sympathetic to Sendak. Democrats, meanwhile, rejoiced in the feud between two elected Republican state officials and were not inclined to do anything to make it easier for Bowen. Senator Martin "Chip" Edwards, the minority leader, advised the governor on January 25 that he intended to withdraw the bill. "Now I know what it is to be a lame duck," the governor groused to his staff one day later.[3]

Reaction to the tax relief proposals was mixed. Breaks for the elderly were endorsed, but the consensus stopped there. Some argued that tax reductions — in individual terms — were quite modest. It would be easier to respond to the yelps of special interests and perhaps more politically profitable to do so. Conservative editorial page writers of the Indianapolis newspapers ridiculed the governor's plan, and, in doing so, missed his whole point. If this money were spent by the legislature, it would become the floor for next year's spending calculations. Rebating it to the taxpayers did more than put cash back into taxpayer's pockets in 1978. It reduced government's take in every succeeding year by reducing the base of spending levels below what it otherwise would have been. This fundamentally conservative point of view was lost on most conservative journalists and legislators. Besides, spending had more tradition going for it.

Budget and tax plans also got a setback as the coal strike dragged on into February. Mandatory power curtailments raised the specter of increased unemployment and reduced economic activity. Economists and state officials were unable to grasp firmly the financial impact. Part of the lost spending power and production would be made up later — but how much? Belt-tightening might be required. Given the uncertainty, Bowen on February 17 recommended that the legislature "do only what is absolutely necessary and call it quits."[4] One administration forecast placed potential revenue losses in the $100 million range. House Ways and Means Chairman William Long, who pegged the decline at $40-$50 million, also wanted to go home: "We're at the point where we can't play games, and I would be for adjourning *sine die*," he said.[5] House Speaker Burrous was equally succinct. "There are no overriding issues," he said. "We could quit today and not miss anything."[6] Democrats were skeptical and wanted to go forward with plans to enact a supplemental budget.

The souring economy further complicated existing disagreements over the budget. Most prominent among them was a dispute over the formula for allocating state funds to local schools. As the session headed toward its mid-March deadline, conferees remained deadlocked until the closing days. The administration's supplemental budget had been introduced at $52 million. A compromise was reached on a $163 million spending program, which included a special $78 million appropriation to repair streets and highways damaged in the bitter winter blizzard and to reimburse local governments which had exhausted maintenance budgets during the storm. The package included repeal of the controverisal tax-on-tax law which had levied sales taxes on the full pump price of gasoline, including the state and federal taxes thereon. Bowen was less than pleased with the outcome. "We didn't win anything and they spent everything," he grumbled.[7]

Lawmakers adopted many of the tax relief programs for the elderly and accepted administration requests for the funding of community mental retardation centers, prisons, and school transportation. A plan for ten new State Police posts emerged from the process with only two of them intact. The juvenile code was enacted, as were child abuse and strip mine reclamation measures which had been endorsed by the governor.

The list of losers was longer. The income tax rebate and permanent reduction of the individual income tax were casualties. The budget stabilization fund, freeport legislation, referendums for excess spending by local governments, and transportation department also died. Bowen had sought a 30 percent inflation adjustment on property assessments. The legislature did not act on the plan, but postponed reassessment for another year.

By any standard the outcome was disheartening. Journalists generally characterized the session's performance as adequate and the dominance of coal strike news had driven the legislature off front pages, anyway. The governor's wounds didn't show.

Normally, the 1978 campaign for the so-called "minor" state offices of secretary of state, treasurer, and auditor wouldn't have attracted much attention. With Bowen dominating the state party, Lieutenant Governor Orr all but assured of nomination to succeed him, and Senator Lugar solidifying his stature, these races seemed of secondary importance. They took on unusual significance for several reasons. The sun was setting on a governor who had dominated Indiana politics for nearly a decade. Only a Senate race against Birch Bayh would sustain his influence. It was time for issues. Even if Orr were successful, his age could mean a one-term the GOP, would represent its foothold in the executive branch. Their holders would enjoy visibility as titular spokesmen for the party on state issues. Even if Orr were successful his age could mean a one-term governorship. The winnowing process of the 1978 state convention might produce a few of the new leaders for the mid-1980s. Moreover, Bowen had faced a divided General Assembly during four of his six years in office. Recapturing the state Senate represented the major item of unfinished business. It would bolster the party's ability to sustain Bowen-era policies into the 1980s. Republican officials also looked to crucial battles over legislative and congressional reapportionment that might occur in 1981. New senators who displaced Democrats in 1978 would be holdovers throughout that process.

It was not Bowen's style to become noticeably involved in the selection of nominees at this level. As the party edged nearer to its June 30 convention, however, he quietly abandoned his neutrality. His involvement was spurred by the decision of former State Treasurer John Snyder to again campaign for the office which he had abandoned in 1970 to pursue an unsuccessful U.S. Senate bid. Snyder and Bowen never had been close. The former treasurer had led one of the factions embroiled in bitter and divisive struggles during the Whitcomb administration. Would his return to prominence rekindle a style of politics that had led to near-anarchy within the GOP during the period in which Bowen was speaker? The governor thought so.

Several county delegations historically loyal to Bowen were quietly persuaded to throw their support to Julian Ridlen, a Logansport attorney. The governor's involvement was not sufficient to insure Ridlen's nomination, but was one of several factors that enabled the candidate to secure a majority. Snyder backers were irritated in defeat, but avoided direct public criticism of the popular governor.

The convention also picked Edwin Simcox, secretary of the party's state committee, for secretary of state. Former U.S. Marshal Charles Loos was nominated for auditor, and veteran Marion County party leader Marjorie O'Laughlin was slated for clerk of the courts.

Strategists then labored to define the game plan for the autumn campaign. A Market Opinion Research poll conducted in October, 1977, reported that the governor's popularity remained high. Only 17 percent of those sampled disapproved of his performance. A modest shift from "approval" to "no opinion" may have reflected little more than a decline in voter interest during a non-campaign year. Property tax restructuring continued to bolster his acceptance. Voters opposed lifting tax freezes in order to give local governments more money. The electorate was evenly split on the issue of increasing gasoline taxes. Unemployment remained the most significant concern, cited by 28 percent of respondents. Crime issues ranked second and energy problems — mainly the increased cost of utilities — were gaining ground.

Robert Teeter's polling firm again surveyed voters during the weeks after the 1978 Republican convention. President Carter was in a slump. Only 38 percent approved of his performance, a decline of 18 percent from October, 1977. Inflation had replaced unemployment as the principal concern of Hoosiers. Utility prices continued to gain momentum. Fully 40 percent of the voters now considered the cost of electricity as either their first or second most important worry. In contrast to earlier polls which showed that voters did not blame the Bowen administration for swelling utility bills, nearly half now disagreed with the contention that the state could do little about the problem. Sentiment for a motor fuel tax increase was on the rise, 55 percent favorable, 40 opposed. Voters generally sought protection against future tax increases rather than a tax reduction — an important point in light of the national furor over California's Proposition 13.

Teeter's survey identified the main problem: "At the moment there is no trend to vote Republican in spite of the very positive attitude the voters have about the way things are going in the state and their overwhelming approval of Bowen."[8] By this time the governor had attained an approval rate of 71 percent — one of the best for any governor in the nation. Teeter then suggested the theme for the fall campaign.

> Plainly, a trend needs to be created. It is not there now. Furthermore, a trend is more likely to develop if it uses Governor Bowen rather than the Republican party. Given the minority status of the party faithful in the state, the lack of any "Republican trend" at the moment, and Governor Bowen's high water mark in popularity, it makes better sense to persuade voters to vote for the "Bowen team" than to simply "vote Republican" or for the "Republican team." While there is no Republican trend, there is no Democratic trend either, which would offer resistance to the Bowen team campaign theme. This is an obvious but important point. The Bowen theme has a good chance of working for no other reason than that there is no competition to it at the present time. To establish the linkage between supporting Bowen and voting Republican will require repetitive admonishments from the candidates and the backdrop support of a paid media campaign. The voters cannot be expected to make the link themselves. Only three respondents in the total survey reached the conclusion on their own that they should vote Republican because "the Republicans would help Bowen." This is not to say the theme is not credible; it is to say that the Republicans must make the point for the voters.[9]

Party leaders were quick to take up the "Bowen team" approach, although State Chairman Bruce Melchert had one reservation. While accepting the overall theme he was troubled by widespread "Bowen for Senator" and "Bowen for President" talk. The crdibility of the approach might be sapped if people decided that his use in the 1978 campaign was intended to promote further ambitions in 1980. The governor and his advisers accepted the chairman's logic and made a conscientious effort to dampen talk of a Bowen role in the 1980 campaign.[10]

Party leaders also worried about the utility issue. As August drew to a close they began to panic in the face of impending Public Service Commission decisions that would grant sizeable rate hikes to Public Service Indiana and Indiana & Michigan Electric Company. Additionally, a controversial Indiana Bell Telephone Company rate case might be completed before the election. The governor was urged by Melchert and John Hart to declare a moratorium on rate hearings and decisions. Non-involvement in what amounted to judicial processes of the PSC had been the governor's policy. He wasn't about to take this action. It also seemed inconsistent. Waging a campaign that was little more than a referendum on the governor's performance, the party now wanted him to depart from long-standing policies. Upon learning of the suggestion, PSC Chairman Wallace pointedly observed that deliberate stalling on the decisions would deprive utilities of revenues to which the rate increases entitled them. The proposal, to this thinking, would have the effect of compelling an indirect multi-million dollar campaign contribution from utility shareholders to the GOP. The governor's office defended Wallace's point of view.

The situation became more acid when Hart later proposed that the governor fire the three PSC commissioners before the election. This, too, would have placed Bowen in the position of repudiating key appointees and policies, and seemed to the governor's advisers to be another contradiction of the campaign theme. The PSI and I & M orders were handed down in September. Relations between the party organization and governor's office were cool for several weeks.

Further strain resulted from the governor's decision to advocate motor fuel tax increases during his campaign appearances. The party wanted him to let the issue ride until after the balloting, but Bowen felt strongly that increases were overdue. A departure from orthodox campaign practice was justified by the fact that a majority of voters now favored a gasoline increase. The governor's primary objective was to obtain early commitments from legislative candidates that they would support the idea in the 1979 session.

Eventually, the utility controversy died down when an October poll recorded a marked decline in public interest in utility rates. Although a surprising finding in light of recent headline-making rate cases, it was an encouraging one. Eleven percent of respondents blamed the commission; four percent, state government; and three percent, the governor.

By this time Simcox was widening his lead over the Democratic nominee, Rex Carpenter, whose support was stagnating. Ridlen was in a tough race against John Ruby, a deputy state treasurer who was conducting an effective television campaign (and the only statewide candidate in either party whose advertisements dealt with issues related to the office sought). Loos was gaining on Pat Byrd, whose support had remained unchanged since a previous sample. Except for Ruby, the Democratic ticket was failing to attract attention.

Television viewers were barraged in October with the celebrated "whoosh" advertisement. Simple almost to the point of being crude, it propelled the names of "Simcox — Ridlen — Loos — O'Laughlin" to the foreground of the television screen, followed by the tag line: "Vote the Bowen Team." Within a few weeks adults and children alike were mimicking the frequently-run commercial. It worked. In light voting, Simcox defeated Carpenter by more than 100,000 votes and Ridlen surpassed Ruby by 75,000. Equally important, the State Senate went Republican. The Statehouse was occupied entirely by GOP officials for the first time since 1970. The Bowen Team was victorious.

The governor's personal popularity had overwhelmed concerns that the campaign strategy might not be able to transfer the voters' loyalty to lesser-known Republican aspirants. The outcome buoyed his standing with party professionals and for a time reversed what had been a slow decline toward lame-duck status. Affirming his hold on the Hoosier voter, the campaign stimulated even more speculation about a Bowen challenge to Senator Bayh. The one-time outsider was confirmed as his party's principal source of public appeal.

XIX

PEOPLE AND INSTITUTIONS

The Republican Party

Although the governor's relationship with the formal Republican party organization was amicable, it represented something of a departure from the normal gubernatorial style. Hoosier political tradition places sitting governors in a more-than-titular role as chief of party. They are not expected to be dictators, but the fact that governors possess executive authority over a state government apparatus that provides the fuel — jobs and money — for a party organization gives them clout that cannot be matched in practical terms by anyone in the party structure. Bowen seemed almost to go out of his way to avoid taking direct leadership of the GOP — a stance that generally was to his advantage, but occasionally put him in competition with a state committee which many observers thought he should have dominated.

Given the circumstances he faced, the governor in retrospect appears to have struck the proper chord. His attitude was shaped by several influences, chief among them his own definition of the Republican party. The precinct workers, volunteers, and citizens who voted Republican represented its real strength. These people, not the state committee, were the ones among whom he had campaigned in small towns and at party rallies around the state during the lonely years from 1967 to 1972, when he was an outsider not yet taken seriously by professionals. Bowen related to the GOP in terms of people and issues, not structure. He was more comfortable during informal discussions with small groups of people at the tail end of a Lincoln Day dinner than in a smoke-filled room with party chieftains. The pros had beaten him in the 1968 convention. As speaker, he stood virtually alone in championing the cause of property tax reform during a period in which Governor Whitcomb and the state party apparatus were cool, or downright hostile, to the concept.

There were practical reasons for an arms-length relationship with the party organization. Unique in his image as a small-town physician and citizen legislator, Bowen might have been tarnished by overt involvement in political strife during a time in which public reaction to politicians — especially Republicans — was at low ebb. Furthermore, his consensus approach to decision-making would not have fit into the realities of personal leadership of the party, which would have required him to enforce discipline and impose his will with some regularity. Caution also was indicated by the fact that the governor was moderate, while his state committee was staunchly conservative. Furthermore, the vicious political infighting during the years preceding his governorship made him uneasy about the people involved and the impact of the political structure upon his administration.

What evolved was a cordial, correct, and low-key approach to party regulars. Careful to consult with county chairmen on appointments to boards and commissions, he derived political benefit from what was essentially a cosmetic exercise. A county chairman would be hard pressed to veto a proposed Bowen appointment without very strong reasons. In effect, the party did not choose the administration's appointees, but ratified the governor's desires. One had to be flattered by a telephone call from the governor (usually placed in person) and the contact provided an opportunity to discuss other matters. This practice made it difficult for party leaders to claim that they were not being consulted about affairs of state. Effective use was made of two patronage committees during the transition phase of 1973, but the new governor's guiding hand moved softly in their deliberations to ensure that he got what he felt was important to him.

There were infrequent flareups between the governor and his party. Issues of patronage, party finance, state government operations, and the direct primary were the principal points of dispute. Occasionally, the governor intervened in party proceedings, to the displeasure of some members of the state committee but, naturally, to the acclaim of others who shared his point of view.

The resignation of State Chairman James Neal in February of 1973 caught the governor by surprise. He knew that Neal had intended to step aside, but the chairman's announcement came sooner than expected. Bowen weighed several names as Neal's successor. The roster included campaign political adviser Gerald Olson, Wayne County GOP Chairman Thomas Milligan, Marshall County Chairman William Gee, and former State Representative Donald Pratt.

Olson was a slight favorite, but the governor worried that his close ties to Columbus industrialist J. Irwin Miller, a prominent liberal, might produce a negative reaction from a state committee still dominated by conservatives. At this time Bowen was locked in battle with conservatives over his tax package. An ancillary duel over the state chairmanship might further inflame the situation. More important, the governor might not get his way. To lose a political battle of this importance in the second month of his administration would have been a damaging beginning.

Milligan was given the nod. Youthful and articulate, he was considered to represent the type of fresh face that might contribute to party-building and improve the image of the Indiana political professional. The county chairman had been popular with Bowen advisers during the administration-building meetings in Florida and quickly was accepted by Bowen intimates as a sound selection. The governor polled each member of the state committee by telephone and they unanimously endorsed his preference.

The new chairman was frustrated in his first venture, that of trying to reassert the state committee's influence on legislation and state government policy-making. The party long ago had abdicated this role, content to make its views known only on matters involving the political process or reflecting the special interests of certain state committee members. Milligan was rebuffed by legislative leaders already pulled to and fro by competing interests and who did not welcome another intruder. Moreover, the state party had little to contribute in a practical sense to the complicated issues which dominated Bowen's years as governor.

The chairman was swimming upstream against a strong current of tradition in which the Indiana GOP was oriented to election processes and patronage — not issues. Bowen, however, would have welcomed party involvement in a wider range of issues. He believed that Republicans must become more solidly identified with priority concerns of voters if they were to broaden their meager membership of only 23 percent of the citizens.

Cleavages between the governor and his party leadership were most visible in the matter of direct primary elections. The organization preferred the county chairman-dominated convention system of candidate selection. Bowen saw the primary as a vehicle to broaden the party's base and to upgrade the credibility of the nominating process. His attitude no doubt also was influenced by lingering memories of a 1968 convention in which a coalition of political bosses had engineered a deal to nominate a slate headed by then-Secretary of State Whitcomb.

By overwhelming margins, the 1975 session of the General Assembly approved a direct primary law for governor, lieutenant governor, and United States senator. Milligan, who actively had battled the bill's enactment, then attempted to blunt its impact. A statewide slating convention and congressional district slating meetings were proposed to give the formal party structure a greater voice in the candidate selection process.

Bowen disagreed. Such an approach would be inconsistent with the philosophy of a direct primary and represented a procedure "that does not have wide public acceptance and that is of questionable political wisdom."[1] The public might resent this approach and the governor was canny enough to recognize that it might only create underdogs who then could run in the primary against the "bosses". Slating mechanisms were shelved.

The dispute resurfaced in 1977 when Milligan was spearheading an attempt to repeal the direct primary statute. Bowen threatened to veto the repealer. The state chairman then fired off a letter to county GOP leaders urging their support for a return to the convention system. It contained a controversial paragraph.

> In 1975, the Governor advised the State Committee that he was signing the Direct Primary Bill because it was the will of the Legislature. This year, the Governor had told the press that he will veto the repeal of the Direct Primary despite the expressed will of the Legislature. This statement has created difficulties in moving the legislation through the House of Representatives.[2]

Milligan in effect was saying that the governor had flip-flopped. Bowen was furious. Equally unsatisfactory was a subsequent meeting with the state committee in which the governor defended his position. Although public statements afterward were couched in amicability, the governor confided to me that the session did not go well, he changed no opinions, and he feared that much of what he said about broadening the party base went right over their heads. However, the governor's public opposition was sufficient to kill the measure in the General Assembly.

In private, the governor and Milligan clashed bitterly over the determination of at-large delegates to the 1976 national convention. J.B. King reported to me that it culminated in what he described as a "vicious" telephone call from the chairman to Bowen. Milligan nearly resigned when the governor refused to change his mind, according to King.[3]

The chairman previously had announced his intent to step down in June, 1977, and the governor wrestled with the choice of a replacement. Gerald Olson remained his preference, and the governor now gave indication that he was prepared to carry the recommendation forward, the negative attributes of Irwin Miller's liberalism notwithstanding.

Secondary problems associated with Olson's ability to continue a relationship with Miller's interests on a part-time basis, because of financial considerations that might run afoul of election laws, were sufficient to derail what already would have been a controversial selection. Olson took himself out of contention.

Earlier, Bowen had considered the use of a screening committee to make recommendations for Milligan's successor. The chairman had little use for the proposal and in a later public outburst blamed Ray Rizzo and me for devising this strategy in order to wire the election of Olson, whom he viewed as our pawn. Milligan was wrong. The committee idea was Bowen's. He first voiced it to me on April 12 in terms that were unrelated to the Olson issue.

A seventeen-member screening committee was activated, in the governor's words, "as an advisory body only to me, not as an attempt to bypass this (the GOP state) committee."[4]

Its deliberations produced three finalists for consideration: Indianapolis Deputy Mayor Bruce Melchert, professional campaign manager Gordon Durnil, and Fifth District Chairman Paul Green. Melchert was heavily favored by the screening committee and Bowen endorsed his election. The committee accepted it, although several members were surly about the process which had led to the decision.

Milligan stepped down with a parting blast at gubernatorial assistants Rizzo and Watt, whom he accused of giving Bowen poor political advice. His four and one-half year tenure, durable for a GOP chairman in modern times, had been a stormy one in which he early had earned the hostility of Bowen stalwarts such as Lake County Chairman Joseph Kotso. Kotso had broken with Milligan in 1973 after the chairman sharply criticized President Nixon. Others thought that the outspoken GOP chief seemed to be in competition with the governor. In retrospect, many of the disagreements appeared to grow out of the chairman's desire to establish himself as an independent party leader in a state whose political traditions conferred upon the governor the implied leadership of the political organization. Rather than function as an agent of the governor, Milligan perceived his role as a separate one: "I am the chairman of the Republican State Central Committee and I answer to the Republican organization," he once stated.[5] Most professionals, including those surrounding Bowen, might have suggested that reality demanded that he also answer to his governor.

Aware of the strain between the governor's office and the state Republican headquarters, Melchert diplomatically moved to sweeten the atmosphere. He succeeded. Relations, particularly with Bowen's staff, warmed considerably. Melchert's personality was more akin to that of the governor and he succeeded in maintaining a balance between two bosses — the party and the state's chief executive.

GOP leaders also chafed at gubernatorial restrictions upon their ability to influence hiring decisions and conduct fund-raising. The tradition of a job-oriented political party died hard. Public opinion, buttressed by court decisions, made it no longer possible to treat the state government apparatus as a feast for the victors of an election campaign. A rough-and-tumble patronage approach to politics was out of step with the times.

In certain agencies, especially the Bureau of Motor Vehicles, party domination of the process proved workable. An agency providing specific services whose performance is easily measurable has been able to accommodate the patronage system with greater efficiency than its critics are willing to acknowledge. In addition, the management of a local license branch is visible evidence of the party and of a county chairman's ability. If service is poor, the branch is a political liability. In other agencies, like the Department of Natural Resources, the patronage system once had the opportunity to manage effectively, but had botched the job. Proficiency in state park operations, for example, is less quantifiable than in the issuance of auto licenses. Years of generally slipshod management had soured the public toward politics within its parks. The Bowen administration's multi-million dollar renovation of inns and other facilities would have been diluted by the continuation of the old style of operation, which actually had been halted by the General Assembly during the Whitcomb administration, through legislation which required that park administrators be professionals. However, a number of holdover managers from the patronage era were able to qualify themselves under the professional systems and performed quite efficiently. The Highway Department, meanwhile, remained a battleground between engineers and county chairmen.

Bowen was sensitive about fund-raising within state government. He was careful to stipulate that party contributions by state employees were voluntary — to do otherwise was to risk lawsuits and invite journalistic slashing. On one occasion Milligan attempted to remove two state highway employees who had refused to contribute to the party. Bowen was forced to overrule him. In general, those who desired to wield patronage clout were reluctant to challenge an immensely popular governor.

Gubernatorial political speeches during Bowen's tenure developed the theme of broadening the party's base. He reminded Republicans that they had not been successful in convincing the American voter that the GOP offered the best option for a political and governmental voice. A 1975 speech to Republican editors was a good example of this approach.

> We're bombarded with articles and news releases about how we can pick up "x" number of seats in Congress if we can get an additional "x" percentage of the vote nationwide. We're told that, in a "normal" year, a certain office should be retained in Republican hands or restored to Republican hands because the particular consituency "normally" votes Republican by "x" percentage. There are political strategists in both parties, I might add, who presume to move blocs of votes, interest groups, and regions across the playing board as if this were all some colossal game of chess. We are not dealing with pocket computer calculators. These are real, honest-to-God people out there — and we are not getting through to them.
>
> We are kidding ourselves if we adopt any political strategy that does not have as its primary objective the broadening of sustained support for the Republican party.
>
> We should build our party organization in a manner that stimulates a

broadening of our base. It is no longer enough to structure an organization whose primary purpose is to get Republicans to the polls. . . we should open the door as wide as possible. . . we should invite people to pass through that door as individuals, not as members of a voting bloc that thinks we are trying to exploit them. . . we should insist upon superior candidates in every contest. It is not enough to settle for an "acceptable" candidate. . . In every situation in which we "trade down," in which we forego a superior candidate for one who is just "acceptable," we have set in motion the process of election defeat. . . we must recognize that a political party exists to provide a forum and a framework for the constructive conduct of governmental affairs. Government does not exist as a sandbox for us to play in.[6]

In a February, 1977, speech, which Indianapolis *News* political editor Edward Ziegner later described as the most important address given by a Republican in a quarter-century, Bowen offered a very somber analysis of the 1976 election, reflecting that there were few bright spots nationwide.

A close analysis of Indiana election returns shows that we gained no ground in establishing a durable voter preference for Republican candidates. Indeed, the slow but unrelenting erosion of Republican strength and affiliation is continuing. While it's tempting to look upon the Indiana returns as a thrilling victory, we must face the fact that it looked good partly because the remainder of the nation looked so bleak. As far as the long-term vitality of the Indiana Republican party is concerned, our state victory represented — at best — a holding action. I recite all of this dreary news in an effort to strip away any complacency that may linger among Indiana Republicans.[7]

It was stark commentary from a governor who had just been re-elected by more than 300,000 votes. Bowen embellished his theme of party-broadening and boldly suggested that the party secure the voluntary retirement of officeholders who had become vulnerable to changing public moods. "It is better," the governor said, "for an officeholder who had 'stayed too long at the fair' to step aside for a fresher Republican candidate who can help insure that the office in question remains in our hands, rather than have the voters forcibly oust the officeholder and replace him with one of the opposition party." He closed by saying "We are the party of Lincoln. But, in honor of that truly great founder of our party, we must not be considered by the voters as the party with great *past* leaders, who won great *previous* victories, in a cause *formerly* embraced by the majority of Americans. We must truly be the party of *present* ability and *enduring* greatness."[8]

THE MEDIA

Observers of the Bowen administration rated the governor's relationship with the news media as remarkable. In a capital city media market in which press pricking of politicians is a hallowed tradition, Bowen seemed to come off with a much smaller volume of carping and criticism than normal.

What was seen as a rosy, even cozy spirit of cordiality masked the fact that Bowen suffered no less from frustrations and irritations common to public officials who are compelled to deal with reporters on a regular basis.

Overall, the governor and his administration enjoyed a number of advantages and used them effectively. One of the most important was gubernatorial style. Reporters had had the opportunity to observe the governor at close range during his tenure as speaker. They liked what they saw. Bowen's allure with the public lapped over to newsmen — despite their vaunted pride in being cynical about men in public life.

Bowen began his term as governor with another asset, not of his own manufacture, but reflected in the difficulties that had existed between the media and his predecessors. Although Governor Branigin was admired as a political personality and Statehouse reporters had a good working relationship with his staff, Branigin was not a press-conscious governor and was noticeably aloof from the electronic media. Governor Whitcomb's term was characterized by often stormy confrontations. Whitcomb was not comfortable with reporters, seldom conducted news conferences, and was inclined to limit his interaction with the media to a weekly half-hour television interview program aired by WTTV. Moreover, there were few on his staff who could speak authoritatively on behalf of the administration. Four news secretaries served during his four-year term. It appeared that the prospects for a better climate under a Bowen administration were promising indeed, if only by contrast to what had gone before.

While it seemed to many in the Bowen camp that I was the logical choice for news secretary, the manner in which the new governor defined my duties was more important than the selection of an individual to carry them out. Bowen insisted that his news secretary be something more than that — an executive assistant enjoying equal status with the others. To justify conferring senior staff status upon his media assistant, the governor decided that I also would have liaison responsibilities with the Department of Natural Resources and several related environmental agencies, because of my experience as the lieutenant governor's representative on the Natural Resources Commission in 1971 and 1972.

This job description proved to be a tremendous asset. Equal stature with other senior aides would allow the press secretary to escape some of the problems associated with intra-office feuds. It would avoid consequences of subordination to another gubernatorial assistant who might have little or no appreciation for the techniques of working with the media. Only the governor was in a position to intimidate his news secretary. It also demonstrated to reporters covering the Statehouse that the press spokesman was not just another flunky. Hazing of political press secretaries is a popular journalistic sport, especially in the "Behind Closed Doors" column of the Indianapolis *Star*. Much of the normal ridicule associated with the position was avoided because newsmen accepted me as a cut above a "flack" who merely churns out releases and parrots the administration line. This became even more prevalent as duties in the energy and transportation areas positioned me as the administration's specialist in subjects which generated a copious volume of reportage during the 1970s.

The new administration got under way on a very solid footing with the media after a briefing of new department heads in January, 1973, as to its policies for dealing with the press. Department heads received a roster of specific instructions for dealing with the media and allowing public access to government business. It emphasized that they were to be "open and cooperative" with reporters, even when it produced inconvenience. The governor's office wanted to be made aware of damaging news in order that we might reveal it first and blunt criticism with candid revelations. They were reminded of the state's open records statute and of the wisdom of not taking board or commission action on controversial matters in secluded sessions away from Indinapolis.[9]

A few agency directors were nervous about the extent to which they were expected to accommodate reporters as priority visitors, but most of those assembled welcomed a precise delineation of guidelines. Press response was enthusiastic, once they became convinced that the governor was sincere. A flood of laudatory editorials followed. Eventually, the text of the media instructions was published by the National Governors Association as part of a hand book for governor's press secretaries.[10]

The governor and his news secretary were fully aware that the test of this policy would be in its implementation. We encountered few problems in carrying it out. The isolated occurrences and the administration's handling of them provided evidence that the governor was determined to follow his guidelines.

One of the first tests involved a federal agency, the Interstate Commerce Commission. When an administrative law judge presiding over a 1974 Indianapolis hearing on railroad reorganization decided that electronic gear would be excluded, reporters urged the governor's office to get the decision reversed. With newsmen in the room, the governor telephoned Robert Oswald, the commission secretary, who then agreed to instruct the judge to admit recorders and cameras. A year later another ICC official attempted to follow a similarly restrictive policy, but was countermanded after I telephoned ICC Chairman George Stafford. On another occasion the State Corrections Commission attempted to conduct an executive (closed) session to make a number of personnel decisions and only reluctantly relented after pressure from gubernatorial public safety assistant James Smith and me. A similar problem emerged with the Medical Licensing Board in 1974. Its chairman begrudgingly opened a meeting after the governor's office insisted upon it. In 1975 a hearing examiner for the Indiana Education Employment Relations Board attempted to confiscate a reporter's tape during a hearing involving a Warsaw school dispute. The governor's office overruled him.

There were other sources of friction, especially the policies of the State Police and Board of Health regarding the confidentiality of certain categories of records. Frequently, journalists' objections were raised by Richard Cardwell, general counsel for the Hoosier State Press Association, with whom I had maintained a cordial working relationship since our joint efforts to open state Senate committee hearings in 1971. Cardwell always gave the administration a chance to resolve a problem internally before unleashing the fury of his members. Occasionally, there were strong disagreements with his positions, most frequently from law enforcement officials whose objections still linger, but we always were able to resolve crucial differences.

The administration also was an active supporter of the 1977 Open Door Statute, advanced by Cardwell and signed by the governor after considerable legislative turmoil surrounding its enactment. The 1973 guidelines had provided a sufficient basis upon which state agencies easily could accept the new legislative standards, which tended to make official the policies that we had adopted administratively years earlier.

Bowen's accessibility to the media proved to be another point in his favor. This occurred in spite of the fact that he made only limited use of the news conference, which I always considered to be grossly overadvertised as a form of communication. They were convened only when the subject was considered to be of widespread importance or when we believed that press interest was sufficient to make it more convenient to talk to all of the reporters at once, rather than endure a series of individual interviews.

Too frequent news conferences, or ones called for secondary or trivial announcements, tend to breed irritability among the press corps. If they are bored with the topic, they tend to drift into other potentially hostile lines of questioning — questions for which a governor may not be sufficiently prepared. Bowen's policy proved acceptable for two reasons. First, many newspaper reporters still harbor a feeling of superiority over their colleagues in broadcasting. Aside from resenting the manner in which television crews tend to dominate news conferences, these grizzled veterans of the print media don't like to share their questions with the competition. Second, with a few exceptions, largely due to scheduling problems or other pressing business, statehouse regulars generally were able to interview the governor on an individual basis. Indeed, many of them preferred it that way.

This is not to say that the governor always relished encounters with reporters. At times the intrusions were troublesome from the standpoints of both questioning and time consumed. Given setup and takedown time, a television station interview of even a few questions usually slices about 20 minutes out of a governor's schedule. Futhermore, certain reporters had a reputation for testiness. The governor no doubt would have preferred to avoid them, especially if the reporter's newspaper or station tended to be critical of his positions on key issues. It was a tribute to his patience and maturity that he was willing to grant certain interviews, even though he knew that they would be unpleasant.

It wasn't always easy. I would approach him with the reporter's request, conveying the subject matter to be discussed (if I knew it). He might fidget and grumble and pointedly bury his attention in a document on his desk, waiting several minutes before asking: "Do I really have to talk to him?" Normally, I would stand there until he got around to answering his own question with a slightly irritated inflection: "I suppose I do." On a few occasions, I would be greeted with icy silence. We would play a waiting game of some minutes' duration. Usually, he gave way. If not, after a decent interval I would ask in a pained tone: "What time do you want to see him?"

At times, Bowen dodged interviews, generally because he was not ready to disclose answers to questions he knew were forthcoming. I am not so naive to think that newsmen didn't know full well that we were putting them off, but the overall quality of the relationship was sufficiently established that these infrequent impasses did not damage the overall climate of goodwill between the governor and the journalists who reported about him.

A number of observers were surprised at the extent to which the governor's executive assistants freely spoke in his behalf. From a public relations standpoint, it had the effect of providing alternate lightning rods on controversial issues. It also had the practical impact of putting the reporter in a conversation with the member of the administration who might be most knowledgeable, rather than funneling the information through a press secretary who might be inadequately briefed or who might bungle the translation. The price of this visibility on the part of the executive assistants was their characterization by political opponents and certain reporters as a "palace guard" that provided a buffer between the governor and controversy. Given the durability of Bowen's excellent public approval ratings, this seemed a very inexpensive proposition. Most reporters accepted the practice because it provided them with facts they needed faster than otherwise might have been the case.

The governor also was accessible because of his heavy schedule of public appearances. They afforded newsmen the opportunity for casual interviews before or after a speech. Speeches, however, were utilized only infrequently as vehicles for making major public pronouncements. This was not a deliberate policy, although some have observed that the governor's speaking style did not lend itself to media coverage at a level equivalent to brief news conference statements.

Oratory was not one of Bowen's strong points, especially during his years as speaker when the addresses were lengthy and liberally sprinkled with extensive quotations. His tendency to talk in a monotone often made these occasions somewhat tedious. Bowen recognized this shortcoming and, eventually, compensated for it by agreeing to shorter addresses that almost never included quoted matter. (Ray Rizzo and I always maintained that it was appropriate to quote Lincoln and Churchill; beyond that, Otis Bowen should be the authority). The governor frequently poked fun at himself about his speaking style, once commenting that "the best way to stay awake during an Otis Bowen speech is to give it."[11]

With the exception of messages to the General Assembly, the governor's speeches usually lasted twelve to fifteen minutes, time enough to make a point without putting the audience to sleep.

However, the sheer frequency of Bowen's speeches during the eight-year period guaranteed almost daily publicity. It helped account for the fact that few "media events" were staged, since the routine of speeches, interviews, and press releases dealing with administration business placed the governor's name in front of the public several times each day. Other communications devices were explored. A column distributed to weekly newspapers was launched in autumn, 1973, and was used widely. The Indiana Broadcasters Association, later the Indiana News Network, carried a similar program to its member stations beginning that year. Occasionally, Bowen would venture to the studios of the Indiana Higher Education Telecommunications Network at University Hospital to conduct statewide news conferences through telephone and video hookups to state university regional campuses, where reporters gathered to interview him.

As a television personality the governor was somewhat less than glib, occasionally fumbling for words and frequently hesitant as he began a sentence. Although this might have dismayed a media consultant, it was another source of his acceptance by the public. Bowen's stage presence conveyed the image of a low-key, down-to-earth personality that confirmed the people's impression of their governor as one of them, not a slick-talking media artist of the type so often seen in the electronic age of politics.

One of the governor's greatest strengths in media interviews was his command of facts about current issues and the operations of scores of agencies within his administration. Surprisingly little preparation time accompanied Bowen's television appearances, especially the regular sessions on WTTV's *Report from the Statehouse*, because it was apparent that he was self-sufficient in his ability to field questions on a variety of subjects. From time to time the governor would solicit brief summaries of current issues before engaging in one of these appearances, but we rarely conducted prep sessions. A number of people voiced surprise at his grasp of such a diverse body of information, but it was consistent with the training of a medical doctor who was compelled to memorize a copious amount of technical detail on a routine basis.

The weekly WTTV program had been an occasional source of friction during the Whitcomb administration because it amounted to an almost exclusive franchise for gubernatorial interviews. Indeed, representatives of WFBM (now WRTV) and WLWI (now WTHR) approached me early in the Bowen administration to complain about the arrangement and to suggest that other stations be given a shot at a public affairs program of this type. I was reluctant to deprive WTTV of this staple because its management had demonstrated the initiative to air it, and was willing to record and distribute the program statewide. The potential problem was resolved when I challenged the others to develop a new proposal that would be acceptable to all of the Indianapolis stations, and they failed to come forth with a recommendation.

The negative elements of the governor's relationship with the news media arose from a variety of circumstances. He harbored resentment toward the Indianapolis *Star* because he considered the newspaper's bitter attacks upon his tax restructuring program to have been largely responsible for its failure to be enacted in 1971. Coming from a rural area, Bowen also was offended by what he perceived to be an unjustified level of influence on the part of the Indianapolis media and the consequent preoccupation of politicians with what is written in the Indianapolis dailies to the exclusion of the more diversified outpouring from other media markets around the state. This probably was felt most keenly in his objections to the "Behind Closed Doors" column in the *Star*, with its unattributed innuendos directed more toward intimidating politicians than informing the public. There were other minor irritants: the rudeness of certain reporters, the knowledge that others often took sides in political or governmental disputes. From time to time he read deliberate distortions into their reportage — and it was an accurate observation.

Bowen's objections to media practices were strongest in two categories — errors of fact and a philosophy of reporting that permeated some of the younger newsmen, especially those who reported for the *Star* and a few television stations. Journalists' excuses for errors — the pressure of deadlines, the difficulties of meshing often confusing information into coherent accounts, the inexperience of some reporters, and the vagaries of the copy desk or television editing room — didn't wash with him. Bowen was busier than any reporter who covered his administration. He was careful to gather information for decision-making and believed it was only reasonable to expect newsmen to be similarly precise. Aware that journalism is a highly profitable enterprise able to employ competent professionals at salaries that would retain them, the governor knew that the salary issue was the lamest alibi of all.

Most irksome about the process was the fact that a reporter's error often forced Bowen to devote time and effort to correct it — to answer mail that might be generated by misinformation, to set the record straight in public, and to devise new ways to implement policy decisions that had been jeopardized by sloppy or vindictive reporting.

With respect to Bowen's second objection, he was dismayed at the intense cynicism with which some of the younger reporters approached their duties. To him, it was a degree of cynicism wholly unjustified by any real experience or knowledge and often was expressed in a sort of journalistic flippancy that arises from the fact that, unlike government officials, journalists are under no obligation to help insure that the system works. Friendly observers might characterize their attitude as little more than the manifestation of a phony macho image presumed to be part of journalistic tradition — perhaps immature but a trait not to be taken seriously. Bowen, however, was concerned about the consequences of their attitude and the perils it posed for thoughtful debate and resolution of public issues. He sensed also the frustration inherent to a profession of observers forced to putter around the fringes of authority and decision-making. Never having the opportunity fully to grasp the levers of power — be it governmental, political, or business establishment — a few newsmen attempt to exert influence by using forums available only to the media. In terms of the exercise of power, unfortunately, journalism appears to be at its most effective when using this power in a negative way. It was this negativism that most got under his skin, because the governor was an intellectually balanced individual, able to appreciate varying points of view.

Editorial cartoons, of which he was a frequent subject, exemplified his distaste for this ever-critical posture. The pre-eminent local cartoonist, Charles Werner of the Indianapolis *Star*, once wrote me: ". . . there is nothing personal in any of my cartoons, and any invective or satire contained in them is only to the extent that, all cartoons, if they are to be humorous, must by their very nature be critical. No one ever saw a funny cartoon that used approbation as a thesis."[12]

This is a fair description of the philosophy of journalistic pundits who wield both pen and typewriter. Bowen, however, never could accept a theory of professionalism that had its basis in negativism. Few non journalists would fault him.

The governor was careful to keep his critical sentiments to himself, although there were isolated occasions on which he made his anger known to a reporter in private.

A gubernatorial dressing-down was enhanced by its infrequency and by the restrained manner in which it was carried out. However, it is symbolic of Bowen's caution that he usually talked to me before these confrontations, seeking assurance that he was not off base. There were a number of undelivered blasts as well. When infuriated — generally by the Indianapolis papers — he would draft a testy letter to *Star* publisher Eugene Pulliam or managing editor Robert Early, then entrust to me the decision whether to mail it. In almost every case, I read them with enjoyment, then quietly disposed of the missives in a desk drawer. It was a form of therapy for the governor, and he was fully aware of the fact that his prose probably would never flail its intended recipient. Despite these misgivings about the press as an institution, Bowen enjoyed an affinity with most of the reporters who practiced it in relationship to his office. Enduring personal friendships with reporters evolved during his years at the Statehouse. Overall, the gubernatorial attitude seemed to be that expressed in a conversation with me in November, 1980. "Most of them are okay and do a pretty good job, but you sure have to work with them," he said.

On November 20, 1980, he was host to a gathering of reporters who had covered his administration on a day-to-day basis. It was a very low-key affair of quiet talk in the living room and library of a renovated governor's residence in which the governor and Beth had taken so much pride. Briefly, he expressed his appreciation for their friendship and cooperation. During the dinner he talked enthusiastically of the paintings, chandeliers, carpets, and furniture that had been contributed, of the renovation of a carport into an entry room, of a library whose books had been provided by state universities. There were wry comments urging them not to make off with the silver service from the battleship *Indiana*, because he had signed for it. As they filed out of the home that he would soon abandon, I could read in their comments and expressions that they recognized a very special era was coming to an end.

LIEUTENANT GOVERNOR ORR

Hoosier political mythology makes lieutenant governors crown princes, their elective duties perfunctory, their party responsibilities considerable. They are the most visible potential successors to a sitting governor. What is perceived to be a largely ceremonial role as commissioner of agriculture provides ready access to the State Fair, county fair circuit, and agricultural community at large. Until recently, a lieutenant governor's influence centered on his function as presiding officer of the Indiana Senate, although he never held power equal to that of the speaker of the House of Representatives. Since the mid-1960s, the predominant obligation has been promoting industrial development, tourism, and international trade in the ex-officio duty of director of the Department of Commerce. It, too, offered publicity without much controversy, although it reflected the evolution of the lieutenant governorship to a meaningful full-time government position.

During the pre-World War II era lieutenant governors frequently moved downstairs to occupy the governor's chair, but the "crown prince" theory of the office took a drubbing in the post-war years. Harold Handley in 1957 was the last lieutenant governor to assume the governorship until Robert Orr succeeded Bowen in 1981. During the intervening quarter-century the relationship between governors and their lieutenants often was stormy. Handley had been engaged in factional duels with Governor George Craig during one of the most bitter periods of GOP history. The 1960 election placed a Democrat, Matthew Welsh, in the governorship, while Republican Richard Ristine occupied the less capacious office adjacent to the Senate chamber. Despite differences in party affiliation, the two men sustained a correct and constructive working relationship. Their cooperativeness had been described in retrospect as better than that normally existing between top officials of the same political party. It was a pleasing contrast to the state of affairs during the succeeding administration of Roger Branigin. He symbolized the "bourbon" Democrats, the party's conservative wing. Lieutenant Governor Robert Rock represented its labor faction. The relationship was frigid. An initially warm alliance between Governor Whitcomb and Lieutenant Governor Folz broke down rapidly amid the political strife of that period. During a seven-month span in 1971, no personal communication was carried on between the two leaders.

From the beginning, the relationship between Bowen and Orr prospered. Loyal to the top of the ticket, Orr was an active and energetic campaigner, supportive of Bowen's position on issues. The new governor gave Orr a degree of stature in the official family that represented a striking departure from precedent. Frequently present during consultations with legislative leaders, the lieutenant governor also was a regular fixture at Bowen's thrice-weekly staff meetings. Anchored to the seat at the west end of the large oval table in the governor's office, Orr sat directly opposite Bowen and was active in the free-wheeling discussions that took place. In addition to giving Orr the opportunity to participate in administration policy-making, his presence afforded the chance to broaden knowledge of state government operations and issues. It was a practical education for the governorship.

There is ample opportunity for friction between a governor and lieutenant governor; it is even more likely among their subordinates. The latter official is in an independent position insofar as his limited constitutional functions are concerned, but he is less free in his role as director of commerce. Salary levels and other manning table issues are subject to the approval of the State Budget Agency. More important, while a lieutenant governor can promote commerce, the tools available to stimulate economic growth largely are outside his supervision. Transportation, taxation, labor policy and the like are provinces of a governor. In some respects it is a frustrating division of responsibility and one that easily could produce irritation.

The very nature of the Department of Commerce is a contributor to dissension. Unlike most other state agencies, which are service-oriented and whose activities are easily monitored and measured, promotional organizations such as Commerce often deal in abstractions. The cost-benefit ratios of funding for tourism promotion, to use one example, are difficult to identify with precision, though officials have every reason to believe that they are good investments for the state.

Furthermore, legislators of the opposition party and potential rivals within his own are prone to see political inspiration in everything a lieutenant governor does to fulfill his commerce duties. The agency's budget battles often are intense.

Finally, like other able and ambitious men who have held this position, Orr (and his subordinates) occasionally felt confined. As one who has served both a governor and lieutenant governor, I have observed that the latter's staff always seems to be looking for additional work to do and turf to occupy. A governor's assistants, on the other hand, find themselves wanting to be divested of some of their considerable burden.

Much of the potential for disagreement was removed by the mere fact that Orr's public attitude was one of eager and unrelenting support of Bowen and his programs. One doesn't dump on an ally, especially when his services are helpful (and particularly when a less-than-satisfactory relationship could have bred mischief).

Minor disagreements surfaced on occasion. A hard bargainer to begin with, Budget Director Thuma at times blocked Commerce proposals that he questioned. His successor during the second term, John Huie, and Commerce Department Director Donald Moreau, clashed frequently, their relationship occasionally strained. Too often, from budget directors' vantage points, departmental objectives appeared to focus upon matters that were institutional or structural, rather than oriented toward performance.

The most serious breach was opened because of disagreements about the State Planning Agency, which once had operated as an economic planning division within the Department of Commerce but later was established as a separate entity   still under the lieutenant governor's supervision.

At the heart of the matter was the fact that state government never had reached a consensus about what its planning arm should do. Initially a pass-through mechanism for federal grants for community planning, the State Planning Agency acquired additional responsibilities as the federal government placed more burdensome planning requirements upon a variety of federal programs. Meanwhile, the legislature remained distrustful of the function. Conservatives were quick to see sinister motives in the agency's very existence. The practical value of many planning projects escaped the perception of most politicians. Some people, including more than a few journalists, saw the whole idea of governmental planning as nonsense. Planners were convinced that they could make a worthwhile contribution to the conduct of state government if only they were given the opportunity to do so.

Their advocates became convinced that the planning function would produce meaningful results only if it were removed from the jurisdiction of the lieutenant governor and placed directly under the governor. However, Orr was interested in making something of planning, while it is fair to say that Bowen wasn't. The governor confessed that he didn't understand its jargon and that many of the processes were foreign to his experience. Burdened with enough to do, Bowen was easily persuaded to let his lieutenant governor grasp the reins.

When the 1974 legislative session formally moved the State Planning Agency to the governor's jurisdiction, Bowen designated Orr as its ex-officio director, which had the practical effect of returning the responsibility to the lieutenant governor. An executive council, comprising key department heads and a few outside interests, charted policy for state planning. It embarked upon a number of ambitious projects — such as a ten-year capital development plan for state government. Although Orr had working control over the process, the governor retained titular authority over the council. Department heads who were cool to specific Planning Agency projects thereby were given a mechanism for foot-dragging. Bowen was their boss; it was easy to deflect planning intiatives from his lieutenant governor.

Further compounding Orr's dilemma was the unpopularity of his planning director, Theodore Pantazis, who did not enjoy the confidence of the governor's staff, Budget Agency, or department heads. His presence diluted their interest in participating in planning ventures. When Pantazis eventually was replaced by Roland Mross, once the planning director for the Department of Commerce and more recently an analyst for the Budget Agency, the State Planning Agency shifted back to the governor's orbit. Orr then began backing away from leadership. Although resentful toward the governor's staff and several department heads, it was to the lieutenant governor's credit that he did not let the affair become a source of division within the official family.

The administration's handling of energy policy was another potential sore point. The administrative functions of energy programs had been placed in the Department of Commerce, because the governor was reluctant in 1973 to create a new agency when its ultimate purpose remained so foggy, and because Commerce Executive Director Robert Morris was keenly interested in the issue and the challenges it presented. As the years passed Orr's department housed energy programs, while most energy policies — especially the management of fuel shortages — were set in Bowen's office. Orr handled this troublesome division of responsibility rather well, emerging as the administration's advocate of energy development while leaving the initiatives of crisis management to the governor. Politically, it was a sound approach, for it diminished the potential for his becoming a lightning rod for resentment during the recurring episodes of energy shortages during the 1970s. Orr's style was such that he probably would have preferred a more visible role in energy, but he adopted the wisest course — avoiding dissension with the governor's office, maintaining a modest profile on an unpopular issue, and carving out the appropriate role as spokesman for the interplay between energy supply and the state's economic development interests.

The lieutenant governor was especially vigorous in his support of Bowen during the 1976 re-election campaign in which Orr extensively canvassed the state. It further cemented an already strong relationship, ensuring that the governor would have no second thoughts about whom should be nominated to succeed him. By the administration's end, the governor felt deep obligations to Orr. Despite Mrs. Bowen's terminal condition, the governor maintained a heavy schedule of campaign appearances and was used extensively in the candidate's television commercials. There was never any doubt in Bowen's mind that Orr should be elected to succeed him — in part, because the lieutenant governor had earned the right through his unstinting backing of Bowen and his programs.

BOWEN AND THE MAYORS

Big-city leaders wondered whether a governor springing from rural soil would be sensitive to the needs of Indiana's urban regions. Bowen's speeches reflected a grasp of many of the main themes of city problems, in particular the slow collapse of the federal funding relationship that had been a bulwark of city finances and services. Unfortunately, the governor's ability to relate to cities never was tested fully. His association with mayors never warmed as a result of their nearly united opposition to the property tax restructuring programs.

The breach that opened in 1973 proved difficult to close, in part because the mayors judged their new governor in conventional political terms — and erred in doing so. Locked in the most crucial political battle of his career during the 1973 legislative session, Bowen fully expected partisan opposition from Democrats. To his dismay, Republican city leaders joined in opposition to the tax plan. Standing alone, this development would not have permanently scarred the potential for goodwill, although one's position on this issue subsequently remained a gubernatorial litmus test of friendship and alliances. The stridency of opposition, and the fact that several GOP mayors began sniping without giving him an opportunity to discuss their concerns, soured his mood.

Evansville Mayor Russell Lloyd, for example, assailed Bowen's program, claiming that it would bankrupt his city's government within a year. Lloyd's assertion lacked a factual basis and the outburst put considerable distance between two political moderates who should have been allies. The mayor's posture set the tone for a number of his colleagues, who didn't let up even after the tax package became law. Cities also challenged the administration's attempts to cope with the impact of reassessment by filing suit against a state decision to adjust the inflation factor that had been built into the process. From mayors' standpoints, the administration was scaling down a potential revenue windfall. In Bowen's view, failure to incorporate mechanisms such as this into reassessment restarted the cycle of property tax increases that he had labored so mightily to choke off.

Wounds never healed because the cities kept up the drumfire throughout the administration, even though the earlier forecasts of dire consequences were not borne out. As time passed the governor became even more strongly convinced that considerable fat larded city operations. Mayors could manage their finances within the property tax controls if they concentrated on priorities, be believed, rather than attempting to place their problems on the doorstep of the State Capitol.

Midway through his second term, the governor had become persuaded that a modest easing of restrictions on taxation and spending was justified. Inflation was surging at an unforeseen rate; certain city functions were under increased pressure. The revisions proved difficult to accomplish in a way that gave the cities necessary flexibility without opening the 1973 initiatives to wholesale alterations that would destroy their usefulness.

State government and the cities were able to find common ground on a number of important issues, but the cleavage over tax policy — of transcendent importance to the governor — overshadowed these more positive developments. During much of the period, a cluster of Democratic mayors was so overt in their political attacks upon the Republican state administration that it became even more difficult for emissaries of the mayors and the gubernatorial staff to patch up existing differences.

ATTORNEY GENERAL SENDAK

The most unpleasant state of affairs within the executive branch during the eight years of Bowen's administration involved the frigid, often stormy relationship between the governor and State Attorney General Theodore Sendak.

Almost from the beginning, state departments were upset about delays in moving contracts and regulations through the attorney general's office. A number of agency heads were convinced that they were getting inadequate representation in liability suits and other legal actions involving state government. More fundamental obstacles became apparent. The attorney general's review of state contracts, for example, was intended to be an evaluation of their "form and legality," but in a number of cases, however, proponent agencies believes that he was attempting to make judgments based upon his conservative philosophy as well. The governor, meanwhile, recognized the constitutional functions of the attorney general's office, but thought that its staff also should be available as an adviser to the governor and state agencies in order that they might avoid costly administrative errors.

Sendak resented several members of the governor's staff, especially attorneys Lloyd and Palmer, because he thought that they gave Bowen legal advice that was both poor and improper. Their legal conclusions frequently contradicted his. The attorney general also had little use for assistants Rizzo, Smith, and Watt for reasons, I suppose, that were based upon a perception that we insulated the governor from problems and counselled him badly on questions of policy. Attempts by agencies to secure their own legal services, especially the Welfare Department, were met with vigorous opposition from Sendak.

Several well-publicized clashes between Bowen and Sendak took place during the eight-year period. One celebrated 1977 case involved the governor's attempt to secure the legal services of attorney James Young to assist the Alcoholic Beverage Commission in lawsuits filed against it by beer distributors who were challenging one of its rulings. Lloyd and ABC Chairman James Sims had reservations about the quality of defense that would be offered by the attorney general's office. In part it was a reaction to prior experience, but they also took note of the fact that Sendak never had replied to a two-year-old request by the commission for a legal opinion as to the validity of the regulation in question. Bowen insisted that Young, a former United States District Attorney, be retained.

Sendak challenged the decision and lost the initial round in Marion Superior Court, but prevailed before the Indiana Supreme Court. In a three-to-one opinion it ruled that the attorney general had the exclusive authority to represent the state. Outside attorneys could be hired only with his permission.

The governor then turned to the subsequent session of the General Assembly in hopes of securing legal authority to employ attorneys to advise the governor's office or to provide counsel to state agencies. It was not successful. (A more detailed account of the legislative controversy is included in another chapter.)

Sendak reacted to the bill's introduction with a news conference in which he termed the governor's proposal an insult to his staff, attacked Bowen's "palace guard" of assistants as responsible for the rift, singled out Lloyd and Palmer for criticism, and claimed that his telephone had been tapped. Although he was victorious in the legislative dispute over legal counsel, the news conference episode marked a noted deterioration in his relations with the Statehouse press corps, many of whom were bewildered by his prolonged tirade.

Another episode further sapped his credibility with reporters. On February 21, 1979, the attorney general attended a legislative committee meeting, had himself sworn in on a bible, proceeded to tell the group that four FBI investigations of the administration were under way, and stated that the incidents provided added evidence that the state needs an independent attorney general. He refused to elaborate further.

It was news to Bowen, who then tried for several days to get in touch with the attorney general for further details. When he had no immediate success, politicians and newsmen alike began to question the attorney general's motives. House Majority Leader E. Henry Lamkin labeled the remarks as "almost irresponsible."[13] Bowen was miffed that he had not been advised and was further angered by his inability to confront Sendak. "He is my attorney," the governor said. "He is supposed to keep me out of trouble, not get me into it. I regret very much there is a feeling that he can't share information with me that I should know."[14]

The two officials finally met on February 28. The attorney general would only discuss two of the investigations. One of them involved a federal arson inquiry at a northwest Indiana day care center that had received federal funding. The other was a multi-state investigation of highway contracts in which the targets were construction companies, not public employees. Sendak stoutly refused to tell the governor anything else.

Bowen repeated this information at a news conference following an encounter in which he had been restrained but furious. For the most part, the media reacted by saying the governor had a right to be informed on matters such as those Sendak hinted at. Moreover, the two cases cited by Sendak were not directed toward the state administration. Their sympathies turned to Bowen.

The final outbreak took place in August, 1980, after the attorney general read press accounts that Bowen had made payments out of the governor's contingency fund for legal assistance to State Administration Commissioner Raymond Sanders and former architectural designer Fred Lott. Bowen authorized the payments after the two officials had been exonerated by a grand jury but were left in the position of having to pay legal fees in defending work done as state employees.

In a testy letter to the governor, Sendak demanded that he immediately arrange to reimburse the state for any public funds "improperly paid" to private lawyers.[15] Aware that the use of the governor's contingency fund was virtually without limit, Bowen flatly refused to do so. While Sendak had not stated any legal authorization for the payments, he had not cited a specific prohibition against them. The governor responded politely by saying, "The payments were entirely proper and morally right and therefore no repayment is called for."[16] Sendak received no media or political encouragement of his position and quietly dropped the matter.

BOWEN AND THE LEGISLATURE

Fourteen years as a member of the House of Representatives, both backbencher and leader, gave Bowen a special sense of the General Assembly as an institution. It was a forum in which he had obtained his education for the governorship. Colleagues from that era were recruited to occupy a number of key positions in his administration. Legislative experience helped him define his conception of the proper relationship between a governor and the legislative branch.

In his closing State of the State message, delivered only a few days before his departure from the State Capitol, Bowen characterized his administration as "reasonably successful."[17] While that terminology was received by many observers as the restrained expression of a modest man, the phraseology was an appropriate evaluation of his legislative achievements. Keeping in mind the give-and-take that is a normal part of the reconciling of a governor's ambitions with the diverse interests expressed among 150 legislators on the floor above him, Bowen had a fairly good batting average insofar as his priority goals were concerned. When an issue was important to him, he pressed it patiently but with dogged determination. Property tax relief, enacted in 1973 amid great turmoil after a series of unsuccessful attempts, was the paramount example. Enactment of a motor fuel tax increase in 1980 reflected a similar pattern, for he first had begun to pursue this objective seriously in 1977.

His most significant defeats came in three areas. One category involved a few pet projects of peculiar personal interest. The 1979 proposal for a joint state-private substitute for national health insurance was a prime example of an issue important to Bowen but a concept too radical for the legislature to swallow in the face of hardened opposition from the insurance industry. (By contrast, he prevailed on the medical malpractice issue — equally alien to the legislative process but a proposal responding to an immediate public clamor and pursued by a governor whose professional expertise was easily deferred to by a confused General Assembly.)

The second area involved a collection of proposals which failed to impress the 1978 session of the legislature, for reasons that are not fully clear. This session, sixth in the governor's term, was the only one considered by Bowen insiders to have resulted in an overall defeat for the administration, although the majority of outside analysts gave him passing marks.

Lastly, there were the second-term budgets. All four, in the governor's judgment, represented unreasonably high levels of spending — an outflow of dollars that probably would exceed anticipated revenues.

Critics have argued that an immensely popular governor should have been able to enforce his will with greater impact upon the General Assembly. A good record could have been a superb record, they argue. One must keep in mind that at least some of this second-guessing arose from disappointment over failed bills in which the complainers had a personal interest. Others, whose opinions I respect, have made similar assertions. Their views are best dealt with be a recitation of several of the philosophical and practical considerations which guide a governor's relationship with the General Assembly.

Most important, the Indiana legislature changed dramatically during the 1970s. No longer a body that met only during cold-weather weeks in odd-numbered years, it had lost much of its flavor as a citizens' assembly. The onset of annual sessions coincided with the year in which Bowen was elected governor. Proliferating interim study committees and other year-round devices were enhancing its power — and giving its members regular access to an Indianapolis media market which had become the dominant outlet for political expression in the state. What had been citizens' gatherings in which party affiliation was the common bond now had become increasingly fragmented by special interests. Party discipline eroded. In earlier times, a governor united in common purpose with a legislative leadership of his own party was almost certain to get his way. This is no longer the case.

Peculiar to Bowen's situation was the fact that he faced a politically divided legislature during half of his term, 1975 through 1978. One might argue that the timing was particularly bad. Division prevailed during the years in which the governor might have been most influential — after the shakedown cruise of a new administration and before lame duck status set in. With a GOP-dominated legislature during this intermediate period, bolder initiatives might have been pursued with less controversy. On the other hand, if there was to be legislative division, this was better timing than the alternatives. A divided assembly at the outset of his first term easily could have denied him the all-important property tax relief program and the Bowen administration could have taken a different turn. With the tax issue well in hand and already beginning to collect growing public support, the influx of Democrats in 1975 had less meaning. A divided assembly in the final years could have combined with the natural decline of his power to destroy Bowen's effectiveness in 1979 and 1980. Only the 1977 collapse of negotiations for renewing property tax controls, which forced a one-day special session, significantly detracted from what otherwise was a more congenial atmosphere than onlookers normally would have expected. Democrats didn't attempt to make radical adjustments to the tax package. Senator Frank O'Bannon, later his party's floor leader, once told me: "We read the polls; we know it's popular; we'd just like to amend certain features like local option."

Former House Speaker Bowen was sensitive to the prerogatives of the second branch of government. Browbeating the assembly would have been inconsistent with his style to begin with, but Bowen well remembered with resentment the heavy lobbying carried on by his predecessor's aides during debates over property tax legislation. At some point gubernatorial interference infringed upon the rights of legislative leaders, and this governor was careful not to overstep the boundary in any but the most crucial circumstances.

He was mindful, too, of the practical limits upon a governor's ability to force his will upon reluctant lawmakers. The brutality with which earlier governors had used the patronage system to intimidate party leaders and legislators no longer was possible or desirable. While a governor presumably could threatern reprisals to county chairmen unless they persuaded lawmakers to his point of view, the practice had lost much of its effectiveness. Legislators were paying increasingly less attention to county chairmen.

The gubernatorial veto is a less-than-powerful weapon. A veto threat cannot be made lightly — or often. A simple majority can override it. Vetoes are effective on secondary issues in which legislators of the governor's party are inclined to go along with his objections if they have no strong feelings about the subject at hand. It is a risky undertaking on an important issue such as a budget bill. On a few occasions Bowen was tempted to exercise his veto but recognized that he risked a major defeat.

A budget is the one absolutely essential document which must be enacted in the odd-year sessions. State government might collapse without it, to the acute embarrassment of its chief executive. Since special interests have influence upon budget writing equal to or greater than governors, Bowen's veto of a budget bill for being too bloated might have had the reverse effect. Taking the dare, lawmakers could override it, wounding him publicly, then proceed to adopt an even larger one under pressure from interests who thereby would have another attempt to influence the process.

Occasionally, observers reasoned that the governor should have given the General Assembly more explicit instructions and outlined a more extensive agenda in his messages to the legislature and in public statements about its progress. Frank O'Bannon's reaction to Bowen's 1979 State of the State message concisely stated the problem: "When he gives a complete legislative program, he is criticized for being a dictator. When he gives a short speech, he is criticized for a lack of leadership. He can't win."[18]

The mechanics of preparing to deal with a legislative session were quite simple. After consulting with his staff and department heads, the governor established an "administration list" of priority items — usually 15 to 30. A second list of bills deemed desirable but not essential was described as "administration-supported." A third roster, a "hit list" of those bills to be opposed vigorously, usually was not catalogued or distributed, but remained firmly fixed in the minds of the governor and his legislative staff. Meanwhile, the State Budget Committee prepared budget legislation based primarily upon the recommendations of the administration through its state budget director.

One member of Bowen's staff — initially Raymond Rizzo, then James Smith — was given primary responsibility for liaison with the General Assembly. The executive assistant with this responsibility was required to work in harmony with the budget director, whose influence over finances conferred upon him roughly equal status in this process. The executive assistant in charge of legislative matters was backed up by administration lobbyists, usually one for each house and hired for the duration of a General Assembly session. Drawn from the ranks of former lawmakers, they included Larry Wallace, James Young, Walter Helmke, Robert Skinner, Maurice McDaniel, and John Coldren. Additionally, private legal counsel was retained to review all bills submitted to the governor for approval. The attorney general also provided a review, but it was one whose intent was to evaluate issues of constitutionality. Bowen's in-house review embraced issues of policy, fiscal impact, technical flaws and workability.

For the most part the governor had a good working relationship with the legislative leadership. Representative Kermit Burrous presided over the House in the six years in which the GOP commanded a majority. A long-time Bowen ally, Burrous was fully committed to the governor's concerns even when they carried the risk of political damage to the speaker. The elevation of Representative Phillip Bainbridge to the speaker's chair after the 1974 election was received with considerable misgivings. A Lake County Democrat could be a formidable obstacle. Bainbridge, however, respected the governor and remembered numerous acts of consideration during the latter's term as speaker. Aside from the normal political rhetoric associated with a leader of the opposition party, the Democrat did not entertain notions of cutting up the governor and went out of his way to state that property tax relief would not be sabotaged by Bainbridge's majority in the House.

A chilly start between Bowen and Senate Republican Leader Phillip Gutman improved after the tax package became law in 1973. Thereafter, the Fort Wayne senator was more cooperative. While some observers considered him dictatorial, Bowen staffers in time came to appreciate Gutman's clarity and precision in communicating what he could support. Rivalry from the 1972 convention campaign did not prove to have long-term consequences. Gutman's successor, Senator Martin Edwards, never developed a close working connection with Bowen and his staff. Personality was one factor. The senator also seemed to represent a throwback to old-style politics in which personally-dominated organizations prevailed through party convention processes.

Relations between the governor and Senate Democratic Leader Robert Fair never flourished. Mutual respect existed between the two, but little real warmth ever materialized. Two other Democrats in the upper chamber helped bridge what otherwise could have been touchy political impasses. Senator Adam Benjamin, the diligent and effective spokesman for his party on matters of finance, was willing to place problem-solving ahead of partisanship. Benjamin earned the enduring respect of Bowen's staff. This was equally true of Senator O'Bannon, who seldom made demands upon the governor and enjoyed the trust of a governor's staff who knew that information passed to him in confidence would not be misused. Throughout Bowen's administration, these leaders — Republican and Democratic — offered ample evidence that compromise and results could be achieved within an environment that far too many observers dismiss as unabashedly partisan.

XX   TROUBLED AGENCIES — PART TWO

EDUCATION

In dollars and human dimensions, education is unsurpassed as a state government priority. By the end of Bowen's administration the annual price tag for state aid to public schools alone exceeded $1 billion, that for higher education nearing $.5 billion. State officials found education to be an uncomfortable obligation, however. Under no illusion that they truly were in control of its management or operations, they were made particularly uneasy by a growing sense of widening gaps between funding and performance and by gnawing worries that the quality of education was diminishing in spite of the outpouring of hundreds of millions of dollars.

Politicians' discomfort was not alleviated by the attitudes of educators. The two groups did not get along very well. Often condescending toward legislators and government administrators, educators left the impression that their function was sacrosanct; they were not answerable to amateurs in the State Capitol. This posture ignored reality. Issues which touched upon the well-being of every child in the state and a system with which political policymakers had dealt in highly personal terms — as former students and now as parents of students — were not ones that could escape the interest of lawmakers or administrators.

Unfortunately, when legislators clashed with educators, they often did so on a basis that seemed to bear out the profession's worst fears. Disputes over sex education, evolution, and placing the Ten Commandments in public schools hardly were calculated to portray lawmakers in a favorable light. Items such as these were nowhere near the central issues of educational policy, but all too often drew unfriendly boundaries between educators and public officials.

The governor was not ensnared by these secondary issues, but did find it difficult to deal with certain of the interests involved, especially the organizations representing teachers. Frequently at odds with Indiana State Teachers' Association executive director Robert Wyatt during his years as speaker, Bowen hoped for an improved climate under the leadership which succeeded Wyatt. It failed to materialize. Although ISTA executive director Ronald Jensen's abilities were respected, the Michigan expatriate conveyed the impression of militant labor union orientation common to that state. To Bowen it was inconsistent with his view of the teaching profession, a well-established sentiment since his father had been a school teacher. If teachers were to take on the trappings of trade unions, they were certain to lose stature with the governor.

Bowen's style centered on consensus, not confrontation, and the latter approach seemed to be the ISTA theme. Any likelihood of bridging their differences was set back permanently in 1976 when the organization offered a dual endorsement of the governor and his Democratic opponent, Larry Conrad. ISTA's endorsement of a candidate who was unlikely to win also was viewed as a repudiation of the governor's first-term efforts to make collective bargaining work and to increase school funding. After laughing about the association's chicken-hearted attempts to hedge its wager, the governor and his staff settled on the principle that bridge-building paid few dividends. In the future no special steps would be taken to come to terms. ISTA lobbyists generally were unwelcome in Bowen's office during the second term; his assistants remained accessible, although they adopted a more stand-offish posture. If Bowen's relations with the ISTA leadership were icy, they were non-existent with the smaller Indiana Federation of Teachers, a more outspoken organization whose officers were peremptorily dismissed as a group of noisy lightweights. In spite of this unpleasant atmosphere, the governor and his administration recognized that teachers had become the most powerful special interest group in the General Assembly. During the 1970s ISTA aggressively recruited teacher candidates for the legislature and succeeded in expanding the organization's influence. The visibility of its undertakings also had the impact of raising warning signals regarding the consequences of a legislature that might someday be under the domination of government employees. This was particularly true from the standpoints of state policy as well as potential conflicts of interest.

A more pleasant state of affairs prevailed at the university level. Several individual university presidents — John Ryan of Indiana, Arthur Hansen of Purdue, and Isaac Beckes of Vincennes — enjoyed an exceptional level of confidence at the governor's office. As an institution, though, Purdue never succeeded in forging a strong working connection with the governor. Whether his views were based upon facts or only on personal impressions,

Bowen became convinced that the Purdue administration's attitude toward him was that of calculated aloofness. Indiana enjoyed a better reputation, in part because of the IU connections of a number of key administration personnel and the natural affinity between government officials and a liberal arts university. Bowen and several of his assistants were IU graduates.

The university, through its School of Public and Environmental Affairs and other components, was involved in ongoing projects for the administration. Ryan was the only university president regularly to rub elbows with prominent administration officials whose portfolios did not relate directly to education. This generated additional goodwill, although his labors for the most part went unrecognized on his home campus.

The universities' effectiveness occasionally was diluted by what was viewed as intense — and senseless — competition. Bowen and his staff were uninterested in some of the fine distinctions and turf prerogatives so jealously guarded by college administrators. One case in point involved a grant to create a federally-funded mineral resources research institute in each mining state. IU — which housed the state's geological survey along with a nationally recognized department of geology — was a logical home base for such an enterprise. Purdue, which viewed these research objectives in engineering terms, launched its own campaign. Seeking to build its reputation, Indiana State University-Evansville desired to expand a fledgling mining program and argued that its location in Indiana's coal region offered geographical justification.

Bowen endorsed IU. After vigorous lobbying by Senator James Harris, the legislature went on record in favor of ISUE. This division left the matter hanging in Washington without a decision. The governor's office later proposed a compromise — place the institute in Bloomington but identify substantial roles for the other two universities. ISUE and Purdue reacted with yawns and declined to bargain. The result was inevitable. What could have been a functioning research center by the time that Bowen left office instead lay buried at the bottom of a pile of paperwork in some federal bureaucrat's in-basket.

A decision by the 1973 General Assembly to establish collective bargaining for public school teachers brought a new responsibility to Bowen early in his term. Franklin DeWald, a veteran federal and state labor administrator, was hired to construct the apparatus and did so in a manner that brought credit to the new Indiana Educational Employment Relations Board. As time passed it became apparent that the system had been overbuilt, but it was not DeWald's fault for doing so. He had been instructed to set in motion a structure that also could accommodate the broader scope of public employee bargaining, whose enactment most observers believed to be imminent. When repeated attempts to adopt bargaining measures faltered in the legislature, DeWald's successor, Victor Hoehne, was compelled to dismantle parts of the existing agency.

Teachers gradually voiced stronger criticism of the board's performance. Their recitations of the number of uncompleted contracts at the commencement of the school year were offered as evidence that the system was failing. Bowen refused to accept this logic, believing that the infrequency of strikes was a superior gauge of achievement. He assumed also that teacher organizations wanted an education relations board that would press school boards for earlier settlements — a timetable that would be to the advantage of teacher negotiators. Reluctance to exert pressure upon local school boards was an outgrowth of the governor's belief that he ought not meddle prematurely in the affairs of elected officials responsible to their constituents. For this reason, Bowen was hesitant to push for mandatory broadening of the scope of bargaining issues — though he agreed with the concept — because it, too, represented an infringement upon their authority.

Unruffled by occasional criticisms, Hoehne, his board, and its mediators sustained labor peace in the public schools, although the task became more difficult in the later 1970s as inflation forced administrators to be more cautious in budget-writing at the same time economic conditions caused teachers to demand more money.

During the 1973 battles over property tax relief, the governor expressed an opinion that the state should assume a greater share of the funding burden for local school operations as one tradeoff for holding the line on property tax rates. What had been a funding ratio of one-third state money to two-thirds local money during the 1960s already was shifting. By the close of his governorship, the respective shares had reversed. The state's portion totaled about 65 percent. Bowen favored holding the state share at the two-thirds level. Power follows money and to go any higher could jeopardize local control of schools. Furthermore, the decade brought modest increases in the actual purchasing power of school aid and teacher's salaries, in spite of raging inflation. Education's advocates argued that this was not enough, but the governor disagreed. These gains, he said, came during a period in which Indiana's school-age population had declined by more than 135,000. Meanwhile, school systems had added nearly 2,600 staff members to their payrolls. These facts made state administrators increasingly skeptical about the claims of educators and raised questions about the adequacy of public school management.

Higher education was a special case. The state's university system was undergoing an important transition from a pattern of burgeoning enrollments to one of stabilizing or ebbing student populations. Challenged increasingly as to the quality of their preparation for graduates who confronted a labor market that had tightened and was becoming more specialized for entry level positions, university administrators faced formidable management and policy choices. Decisions were not made easier by budget-conscious lawmakers inclined to pare curriculum items deemed of secondary or tertiary importance. Faculty members were becoming more militant.

It was a difficult management equation — preserving the traditional academic values of liberal arts institutions, becoming more sensitive to the realities of the labor marketplace in the face of academicians' hostility toward anything resembling a blue-collar orientation, avoiding the blurring of functions of universities and the occupational educational system, managing facilities for stable enrollments after two decades of reacting to steady growth, and arguing for fresh dollars before legislators grown skeptical about the way in which prior appropriations had been spent. Although universities garnered additional dollars, money did not pour forth at rates equal to the primary and secondary systems. Appropriation increases for higher education during Bowen's administration roughly approximated the inflation rate, but there were indications that universities slowly were losing ground in the latter 1970s, especially in maintaining competitiveness of faculty salaries.

Controversy simmered throughout 1973 as the state wrestled with procedures to implement special education programs required under a 1969 law for physically and mentally handicapped pupils. It underscored some of the philosophical and practical differences which separate parents, educators, and government policymakers. An initial set of special education regulations, known as Rule S-1, was turned down by the governor, who then forwarded a seven-page memorandum of recommended changes to the General Education Commission.

Bowen was concerned about some of the subjective judgments inherent in determinations of the extent to which emotional disturbances might be defined as requiring special education programs. While schools should be required to provide special education, parental consent should be given before students were placed in special schools or classes, he maintained. Special education should not become "a convenient mechanism whereby the mildly troublesome child can be removed from the normal classroom setting just to have an orderly classroom," he wrote.[1] Bowen also stipulated that family physicians, not school medical personnel, should prescribe any drugs used in pupil therapy. Moreover, he ruled out the use of psychiatric testing technicians as judges of the emotionally disturbed. Physicians and clinical psychiatrists were the only personnel qualified to make a proper determination of the extent of emotional impairments.

A number of special education professionals attacked the governor's position, explicitly challenging some of his medical conclusions, but implicitly criticizing the effrontery of a politician who would dare to challenge their expertise. Bowen was unimpressed. Aware of the potentially sweeping implications of these practices and of parents' deeply-felt apprehensions about the whole process, he stood firm. Revised regulations, generally conforming to the governor's requirements, finally were signed on September 13.

Financial aid to college students was expanded during the Bowen years. Appropriations for scholarships were augmented by provisions for student loan programs, with financial institutions eventually involved in administration and guaranteeing the funds. In 1979 a gubernatorial task force recommended creating a secondary financing corporation to roll over capital through prime lenders to finance additional student loans and to offer incentives to expand the availability of loan funds.

The credibility of these initiatives was offset somewhat by mismanagement within the State Student Assistance Commission. The commission had awarded monies on the basis of student qualification formulas which increased its dollar commitments. Had the commission taken time to compare the rate at which it was making scholarships and grants against its remaining balances, prudent judgment would have indicated a more conservative approach. Instead, it continued to write checks. Outsiders became aware of the problem only after it had reached troublesome proportions. The 1980 General Assembly was forced to enact a deficiency appropriation to avoid widespread cancellations of student aid.

Concern about the quality of education was intensifying as Bowen's term came to a close. Publicly praising the achievements of the occupational education system, state officials privately wondered if it measured up to what was being advertised. A few formal studies began to lend weight to criticisms that Indiana's primary and secondary schools were losing ground in terms of educational quality. Parents in growing numbers were placing their children in private schools, and frustration with racial desegregation was only partially responsible for the phenomenon. While contending that Indiana's universities were holding their own, college administrators expressed worry that salaries were lagging to a point that would cause an exodus of their most capable faculty members.

Educators at all levels traced the problem to insufficient funding by the state legislature. Leaders of the General Assembly were less certain. Previous increases in funding had not seemed to add to quality or productivity — expecially in grade schools and high schools. Expanded faculty and staff during a period of sharp enrollment declines was viewed as an indication that public school administrators weren't managing resources already available to them. New money, these lawmakers sensed, offered no assurance of progress.

INDIANA TOLL ROAD COMMISSION

Its offices located at Milepost 87 eastbound — far away from the scrutiny of governors or the Statehouse press corps — and its members jealous of what they considered to be complete independence from state government, the Indiana Toll Road Commission was an occasional source of trouble during the Bowen administration. Its very existence was a legal fiction, an attempt to circumvent the constitutional prohibition against state indebtedness. Neither the agency's finances nor its members were subject to the guidelines under which state agencies and employees were required to function. The scale of its income and contracts conferred political power upon a commission whose only practical limitation seemed to be the gubernatorial power of appointment of its members.

Bowen and his advisers refused to accept the concept that the commission was wholly independent. It was unnecessary, they believed, to sustain a management fiction merely to perpetuate a legal fiction. Commissioners were quick to ignore the governor's staff and only acceded to Bowen's wishes when personal pressure was applied; even the governor was stonewalled on occasion.

A State Board of Accounts audit in 1975 brought already-smoldering disagreements into sharper focus when auditors concluded that more than $5,000 had been paid improperly for personal expenses incurred by commissioners. Two prior audits had reached similar conclusions, and the Toll Road's manager during the earlier period reimbursed the state more than $16,000 in challenged expenditures. Although commissioners claimed that theirs was a private business not subject to state government standards for limitations on expenses, several members agreed to repay the disputed sums. In response to a newsman's question, executive assistant James Smith replied that while he had not yet had the opportunity to discuss the problem with the commission, "I have been told the commission now considers itself a state agency."[2] It was one of his more optimistic conclusions.

The governor's office also battled the agency over the issue of truck weights. Rigidly adhering to the state's 73,280-pound limit during the independent truck drivers' 1979 strike, Bowen was caught up in a feud over the commission's almost limitless issuance of overweight permits, coupled with its attempt by regulation to set a higher weight standard than that allowed by state law. Initially, the commission refused to budge on the matter; but it was forced to correct the situation through a combination of new law and regulation — after a prolonged confrontation with the governor.

Most intriguing, however, were the circumstances surrounding the future of the Toll Road after its bonds were retired. While highway officials sought to determine ways in which it ultimately could be absorbed into the state system without an oppressive maintenance burden, others explored ways to extend the commission in order to use its tolls to provide seed money for projected "mini-toll roads" elsewhere in Indiana. The situation was compounded by the fact that the road was not designed or operated at interstate highway standards; heavy traffic and overweight trucks combined to balloon its maintenance costs far in excess of those encountered on similar highways.

Federal legislation was required to convert the tollway to a freeway, and Indiana congressmen were enlisted to boost special legislation to this effect. The procedure took a bizarre twist from that point. A series of new interchanges was proposed at the insistence of congressmen in whose districts the highway was located. This would require a massive new bond issue for interchanges — although they were not required to conform to any federal mandates for interstate routes.

Bowen delayed an initial attempt to market the new bonds during a period in which inflation had driven interest rates to near 20 percent. At this inflated level, the securing of $250 million for construction would have required a payback of more than $1 billion from future tolls. The governor also insisted upon a special commuter rate to ease the impact of the substantially higher schedule of tolls necessary to redeem the new bonds. Although many observers were bewildered by the turn of events, the 1980 legislature accepted a compromise that allowed most of the construction program to proceed. Facing federal deadlines for completion of the improvements, the commission arranged with several engineering firms to begin design work on a speculative basis and then proceeded to market the bonds when interest rates softened. What had begun as a program to transform the tollway into a freeway when the old bonds had been paid off finally concluded as a proposition that burdened motorists with user charges into the twenty-first century.

The Toll Road Commission was the most vocal opponent of the transportation reorganization pursued by the governor in the 1980 legislative session. Arguments that inclusion would jeopardize the new bond issue were not persuasive, though. Repeated tries to write the commission out of the new law were unsuccessful. Refusing to give up, the toll road's supporters endeavored to amend the 1980 transportation reorganization act when lawmakers again convened in 1981. They failed a second time. Under terms of the reorganization law, the toll road was to be merged into a new Department of Highways with its employees operating under the same pay and benefits provisions as regular state employees. Highway Department planners recognized that this could not be accomplished overnight because there were significant differences in pay schedules for a number of categories of toll road personnel. A combination of attrition and a temporary dual system would be necessary. In what may have been a final expression of disdain for state government, the toll road management, in the spring of 1981, gave certain of its employees pay raises that furthered widened this disparity.

PUBLIC SERVICE COMMISSION

Economic forces combined during the 1970s to undermine a national tradition of cheap energy and substitute for it a pricing system reflecting higher fuel costs, inflation, rising interest rates, and the multi-million dollar consequences of environmental protection hardware. Electric utilities which had functioned for decades, in some cases without rate increases, were forced to go to state regulators to seek revenue relief. The political fallout was considerable, and the Indiana Public Service Commission became the object of consumers' and politicians' fury.

Intricacies of utility finance exceeded the ability of most people to comprehend and of most commentators to explain. It was easy for utilities' critics to characterize them as greedy, grasping institutions insensitive to the public interest and supreme in their ability to outfox and suborn those entrusted with their regulation. Opponents, journalists, and irate consumers saw only the impact of higher monthly statements and rate cases of multi-million dollar implications.

Unlike several other states, demands for rate moratoria or radical changes to the regulatory structure failed to gain acceptance in Indiana. Hesitant to tamper with essential public services, a number of outspoken critics were content to secure the political dividends of their rhetoric.

On other occasions, the political inspiration behind the assaults was sufficiently transparent to blunt their impact. Effective legislative lobbying by utilities was another important element. Of equal measure was the stature of PSC chairman Larry Wallace, who was acknowledged even by his critics to be an official of exceptional ability. Finally, Bowen's determination to avoid tampering with what essentially were the judicial processes of the commission, his persistent defense of Wallace, and his refusal to panic over touchy utility issues were powerful influences for moderation.

Wallace succeeded W.W. Hill as PSC chairman in March, 1974. A former legislator and Marion County criminal courts commission, he had served as a legislative counsel to the governor during the 1973 and 1974 sessions of the General Assembly. Uninformed outsiders might define his PSC role as that of clamping down on rates, but the new chairmen grasped the broader fundamentals of his regulatory responsibilities. Utilities were legally entitled to reasonable rates of return. The rate structure must reflect that entitlement while not allowing the companies to pad their revenues. Of equal statutory importance was reliability. When the customer throws a switch, the lights are supposed to come on. Although opponents would claim that existing generating capacity provided excessive reserve margins, the law required utilities to position themselves to meet any demands placed upon their systems. Finally, the chairman was sensitive to the effect of his regulatory philosophy upon the ability of utilities to raise expansion capital in money markets. The substitution of political decisions for economic ones could produce severe repercussions in the salability and ratings of utilities' securities.

Several celebrated telephone and natural gas disputes gained prominence during Bowen's administration, but most of the turmoil centered on the state's five investor-owned electric utilities. Indiana & Michigan Electric Company was an especially tempting target of criticism.

The first widespread furor involved automatic fuel adjustment provisions adopted in 1973. Under this arrangement utilities were allowed to pass along to consumers on a regular basis their actual fuel cost increases. It was adjudged the most effective way to absorb the rapid fuel price surges of the early 1970s without full-blown rate hearings. Since the cost of fuel was a customary operating expense allocated to the rate base, this practice charged customers nothing that they would not be required to pay for eventually. The size of these increases, especially in the I&M service area, produced a clamor for repeal of the fuel adjustment clause, which had been adopted by the majority of states. Although I&M had special problems — its partial reliance upon oil-fired generators made it vulnerable during a period of massive OPEC price increases — the utility's manner of handling fuel adjustments also precipitated anger and frustration among its customers.

Wallace resisted attempts to abandon the fuel clause and used a 1975 rate case to bring its use by I&M back into line. Inconclusive battles continued for several years. Finally, the 1979 legislature modified the law to allow alterations on a quarterly, rather than monthly basis. Another element of the revision involved computing the fuel charge as part of the overall bill, rather than segregating it as a separate item. Opponents characterized this as deceit while others pointed out that it simply recognized that fuel is an integral component of the cost of power. In any event, the change might eliminate a visible monthly irritant to billpayers. The PSC chairman described the new law as "a step sideways" that did not change costs, only procedure.[3]

Rising clamor over energy prices prompted Bowen in 1975 to activate a citizens' commission on energy and utility policy. The group was directed to analyze a wide range of supply, price, and regulatory issues. Chaired by former Evansville City Controller John Gaither, the advisory group presented a series of recommendations to Bowen in December of that year. The governor rejected a few of its recommendations: expanding of the PSC to five members, confirming their appointments with legislation, allowing utilities to recapture costs of construction work while it was underway, and setting a ten-month limit for consideration of rate cases (since the PSC already was disposing of them in less time).

His endorsement was obtained on several key points: increasing the staff of the public counselor and making the counselor's position full-time, altering the "fair value" doctrine of ratemaking to one using an "original cost" formula, a code of ethics for the PSC patterned after one for judicial officers, and granting the commission the power to call its own witnesses and introduce staff reports into evidence in rate hearings.

Several of these matters were addressed in the administration's legislative program for the 1976 session. A flood of utility legislation also was offered by members of the House and Senate. Utility lobbyists, however, succeeded in blocking almost everything. Bowen and Wallace were upset. The shortsightedness of the electric companies in stopping even modest reforms left the govenor's administration open to renewed criticism, with little political ground to stand on. More drastic measures later might be forced upon them by beleaguered Republicans or by Democrats who succeeded in exploiting the utility issue in subsequent election campaigns.

Wallace was particularly irate over the defeat of legislation that would have enabled him to call his own witnesses and secure expert testimony from the PSC staff. Too often he had been forced to render decisions on the basis of incomplete information, but he could not go beyond the bounds of the proceedings. The 1976 experience prompted the governor's office to become more guarded in its willingness to make common cause with the energy industry. Utility lobbyists had prevailed by grasping the short end of the political funnel, using the hands of a few influential legislators. While expedient, perhaps, in the short run, it generated bad blood with backbenchers during an era in which it was becoming more difficult to bottle up controversial bills. Utility lobbyists' intransigence in 1976 had an effect upon the administration when the issue of construction work in progress resurfaced during that latter years of the governor's second term. Several Republican leaders also turned against the utilities during the 1978 campaign when it appeared that the party's fortunes might be adversely affected by growing public resentment over electricity prices.

A new package of consumer protection rules, drafted by the commission and approved by the governor, took effect in July, 1976. Restrictions on disconnections, requirements for prior notice of rate increases, and new procedures for handling customer complaints were included. Bowen considered the complaint section to be inadequate, but signed the overall regulation with the proviso that the PSC strengthen complaint provisions. In the absence of a legislative decision to expand the public counselor to a full-time position, Bowen did so administratively. The commission, meanwhile, created its own consumer affairs division and required that utilities submit information about alternate rate structures when filing new rate increases.

The frequency and size of utility rate increases abated during the second term, although Indiana Bell Telephone Company was widely criticized for a hefty 1978 rate filing. Bowen refused to intervene in a series of campaign-year utility increases, believing that it was improper for him to do so. He also rejected Democrats' demands for a moratorium on all new rate increases until the 1979 legislature could take a fresh look at the problem. Almost three years earlier, the governor had made a series of recommendations upon which the assembly had failed to act, so he saw no purpose in this gesture. In addition, an arbitrary action of this type amounted to the misuse of gubernatorial power.

Insofar as customer relations were concerned, utilities probably suffered permanent scars as a result of the energy price phenomena of the 1970s. Despite the strident political debates which surrounded the issue, the Republican party appeared to incur only minor damage. Democrats were unable to capture the political benefits of the public's negative feelings toward utilities. However, the insensitivity of utility managers and lobbyists to the fortunes of Bowen's administration prompted Lieutenant Governor Orr to make a special effort to place distance between his position and theirs as he campaigned for the governorship in 1979 and 1980. Utilities should not take Republicans for granted, Orr believed, and he went out of his way to make the point.

OSHA

Almost from its inception, Indiana's state-administered program of occupational safety and health was the subject of running feuds with federal officials. While there may have been some basis in labor leaders' fears that a state law pushed by business interests in 1973 was intended to dilute the regulatory force of federal occupational safety programs in the state, evidence accumulated that federal bureaucratic stonewalling combined with blatant politics to put the Hoosier program in jeopardy.

Workplace regulation under the federal Occupational Safety and Health Act gave states the option of substituting their own programs for federal jurisdiction. After securing approval from the U.S. Labor Department, states would qualify for matching funds to help administer the function, which soon was demeaned by the acronym "OSHA". On March 1, 1974, Indiana's implementation plan was ratified by federal officials and what some bureaucrats dubbed IOSHA was born as an element of the Indiana Labor Division.

From the beginning there were disagreements. State inspectors resented the intrusions of federal inspectors who monitored their performance. Federal officials were reluctant to accept the idea that a state could operate any program better than a federal agency. Labor leaders also were critical, owing to the aforementioned reservation. Besides, assailing a Republican state administration for inadequate protection of workers was inexpensive political rhetoric for those whose sympathies lay with the opposition party. The governor, meanwhile, was insistent that the thrust of inspections should be toward correcting deficiencies rather than levying stiff penalties — which put him in disagreement with both union men and the feds. Certain Indiana businessmen were quick to object to the state's regulatory infringements upon their operations; they had supported the Indiana law because they desired a superficial and half-hearted effort. State officials occasionally wondered whether this constant buffeting was worth the trouble. It was an experience akin to that of managing environmental programs in which the state had been little more than a reluctant agent of the federal bureaucracy.

When the White House reverted to Democratic control in 1977 the sniping intensified. AFL-CIO leaders saw the chance to remove occupational safety and health from local control and began to lobby the new leadership of the Labor Department. The department responded sympathetically and stepped up its second-guessing of the state's performance. As the federal vise tightened, state leaders began negotiations in an attempt to preserve the Indiana plan. Led by Lieutenant Governor Orr and gubernatorial assistant W. T. Ray, the state's representatives vigorously defended its administration of the federal provisions. Frustrated by tedious months of bargaining, they nevertheless were encouraged by prospects of a favorable outcome. Months of talks in 1979 and early 1980 produced what Orr and Ray believed to be a tentative agreement to allow the state to continue.

That optimism was dashed on April 2, 1980, when Assistant Labor Secretary Eula Bingham wrote Labor Commissioner William Lanam that the federal agency was beginning the process of decertifying Indiana's plan. Several deficiencies were cited. The state's ability to maintain a sufficient number of qualified industrial hygienists was questioned, as was its ability to recognize a number of serious hazards in industrial workplaces.

Lanam forwarded a comprehensive response to these allegations several weeks later. After noting that a nationwide shortage of industrial hygienists then was commonplace, he noted that four state hygienists recently had been employed by the federal Labor Department in what amounted to an act of piracy. He flatly rejected the assertion that the state was lax in identifying hazards, pointing to data which showed almost identical conclusions on the part of both state inspectors and federal monitors. He also rejected federal criticism of penalty assessments. "If penalties issued by the state differ from those issued by federal OSHA, it may well be that your agency and not the state errs in penalty determination," he retorted. "Further, while we would agree that penalties play a necessary role under the act, the reason both our agencies exist is to attempt to reduce occupational injury and illness, not to raise money for federal or state treasuries."[4] Finally, he pointed to accident case rates which showed Indiana's record superior to the nation's as a whole. Additionally, Indiana was conducting more inspections covering more employees than federal OSHA was able to undertake in states considerably larger than Indiana — a direct challenge to the idea that federal enforcement is superior.

It was known that this documentation amounted to little more than a public relations broadside. Politics, not information, would guide the final outcome. In the heat of the 1980 election campaign, the Department of Labor withdrew its approval of the Indiana program. Bowen and other state officials publicly described it as a political act.

Politics, however, can cut two ways. When the GOP swept to victory in November, Senator-elect Dan Quayle and Senator Richard Lugar began pressing the federal agency to reconsider. Soon after the Reagan administration was installed in Washington, Quayle was able to report that the earlier decision had been reversed. OSHA would revert to state control.

ALCOHOLIC BEVERAGE COMMISSION

The notion that liquor and politics don't mix survives despite a history of tight regulation of the commodity. It is a responsibility with which most governors and legislators are uncomfortable. While they sense a need to maintain controls on alcohol, they are wary about personal involvement because they see only the potential for scandal or unpopularity. Alcoholic beverage issues were especially troublesome during the Bowen administration. In addition to the routine turmoil arising from regulation of a controversial product, the beverage industry was groping toward rather fundamental changes in the way its business was conducted at the same time outsiders were challenging the whole idea of regulation.

Ambivalence best described the governor's attitude toward this issue. As one who had seen the effects of alcohol abuse upon patients, accident victims, and prison inmates whose parole pleas were regular reading fare, his reaction bordered on the advocacy of temperance. As a government administrator, Bowen's inclination was to deregulate substantially an industry with which he was unfamiliar.

These contradictory sentiments were the basis for confusion in the relationship between the governor and his Alcoholic Beverage Commission. Looking back, it seems fair to say that the most well-meant attempts to carry out a philosophy of regulation probably would have foundered on these contradictions. Meanwhile, it gave those whose motives may have been less than lofty a considerable wedge to warp the commission's processes.

The majority of the governor's assistants would have preferred that the commission be abolished. Let the Revenue Department collect the excise taxes and the State Police enforce violations such as bootlegging and sales to minors. Given the long history of government regulation of alcohol and the intense political pressures attendant to the industry, theirs may have been an unrealistic attitude, but one rooted in a desire to separate the governor from a no-win proposition.

Gubernatorial assistant William Lloyd was assigned liaison with the agency. To other staff members, Lloyd gave the impression of being unduly defensive of its administrative decisions and overly involved in the day-to-day mechanics of its operations. When Susan Davis replaced Lloyd in May, 1978, her approach was one of critical scrutiny of regulatory revisions to an extent that caused chairman James Sims to regard her as hostile to the commission.

Sims had been a DeKalb County sheriff and a worker in Bowen's 1972 campaign, and his law enforcement background was viewed by the governor as representing a desirable qualification for the chairmanship. At the outset, Sims and the governor got along harmoniously. Bowen supported the chairman's restrictive approach to implementation of the 1973 statute which authorized Sunday liquor sales. But a series of controversial ABC decisions and a scandal involving the excise police gradually eroded the confidence of the governor's office.

It had been the practice of the ABC to set minimum retail prices for alcoholic beverages, and the "mandatory markup" concept became a focal point of political dissension during 1974. The commission was inclined to continue the practice, despite a series of lawsuits, but the governor concluded that price-setting should end unless the 1975 General Assembly enacted specific legislation to require it. Bills to that effect passed both houses of the legislature in 1975 but died in conference committee. Proponents of mandatory markups tried again in 1976, but to no effect.

The most visible disagreement arose over the matter of ending restrictions on liquor price advertising. The commission's early hostility toward a permissive regulation led to a series of articles in the Indianapolis *Star* assailing the ABC's intent to further restrict liquor advertisements. Bowen then brought pressure upon the ABC to reverse its position and allow advertisements which were not specifically banned by law or existing regulation. The commission remained reluctant to do so and was supported by Lloyd. In discussions among members of the governor's staff in September, 1975, he talked of constructing "positive" regulations that would preserve certain controls — a point of view at variance with that of Bowen. Lloyd stated a desire to draft a compromise that would be acceptable to the commission. Others thought that compromise was not required; the ABC merely should accede to the governor's desires.

The administration's internal dispute surfaced in November, 1975, when

Sims announced a late-December public hearing to consider alterations to several regulations — including price advertising. That timetable would have delayed a deregulation of price advertisements until after the holiday season, a boom period for liquor sales. The chairman's schedule would invite further blasts from newspapers which stood to gain thousands of dollars of revenue if the controls were eased before Christmas.

In a statement on November 26, I was publicly critical of the commission's timing. This stimulated a theatrical outburst from the chairman in a meeting that afternoon with Lloyd, James Smith, and me. Resenting interference from the governor's office, Sims then attempted to entreat us to issue specific directions (which he could use to solidify the other commissioners against the governor's staff). We declined to be so persuaded. When I made an off-hand comment about the slowness with which the ABC was addressing these reforms, Sims dropped to his knees, began pounding Lloyd's desk, and in a quavering voice asked if we wanted the commission's resignation. Unwilling to be caught in that political snare, the three gubernatorial assistants remained mute and the session ended inconclusively.

After considerable legal maneuvering — because the state was trapped between a federal court consent agreement which conflicted with a Marion Superior Court order — price deregulation finally was adopted.

Criticism of Sims escalated during Bowen's second term. While disagreeing with certain commission policies, the governor refused to act because the anti-Sims campaign was one of innuendo unsupported by tangible evidence of misconduct. Certain state officials — ABC chairmen among them — are regular targets of whisper campaigns spread by the disaffected and mischief-makers. Sims' critics were invited by gubernatorial assistants to provide specific allegations to the State Police, but to my knowledge no such representations were made.

An already uncomfortable relationship with the governor's office was further irritated by a 1978 ABC proposal that would have required liquor vendors to place alcoholic beverages in separate grocery sacks labeled with the words "alcoholic beverage." The intent of the regulation was to help law enforcement officers spot and search persons suspected of making illegal purchases. Juveniles were the primary targets. Bowen's staff reacted that the commission itself would become the principal target — of public ridicule. Indeed, the ABC became the butt of public and political criticism which reduced the issue to laughable proportions. Under intense fire, the commission withdrew the "booze-baggie" plan in January, 1979.

XXI   THE LEGISLATURE, 1979

As House and Senate members came together at the Statehouse in January, 1979, it appeared to many observers that the seventh session in his term represented Bowen's final opportunity to leave any fresh imprints upon state policy. The 1980 legislature would no longer be looking to an outgoing governor for leadership; politicians and newsmen alike would be chasing the campaign to determine his successor. The governor, however, had a few key items of unfinished business. His approach to the 1979 General Assembly gave impetus to them, almost to the exclusion of everything else.

The agenda was concise. The legislature should return surplus revenue to the taxpayers, rather than let it become part of the spending base for future budgets. Revised property tax controls should be enacted in order that Bowen's 1973 program could continue into the 1980s. Rising utility costs suggested the enactment of a financial relief program for the state's most vulnerable citizens, its low-income elderly. Finally, Indiana should become the first state to provide for a joint government-insurance industry alternative to national health insurance.

These items were submitted in the governor's State of the State address, a presentation of only 20 minutes' duration, in contrast to some of his earlier marathon performances. Bowen made no mention of highway funding, although he fervently hoped that the assembly might write a long-term solution. Smarting from past defeats on the issue, the governor decided not to go out front on a fuel tax increase, but to wield his influence if sufficient interest could be drummed up in its behalf.[1]

The legislative package represented a $290 million tax relief program. Its keystone was a 15 percent credit against the bills owed by Indiana individual adjusted gross income taxpayers, a $206 million item over the two-year budget cycle. Another feature envisioned reinstatement of the renter's credit which had been a temporary element of the 1973 tax plan. A $200 credit for heating season utility bills paid by an estimated 50,000 households for elderly, low income Hoosiers also was proposed.

The limited life of control elements of the property tax program, coupled with the implications of a pending statewide reassessment, required revisions of a structure which Bowen described as "the most envied in the nation because of its matchless record of producing hard-dollar property tax reductions year after year."[2] A new set of civil government tax controls was offered to the legislature, as was a new program involving a 20 percent residential homestead deduction. Reassessment would shift a greater share of the property tax burden to residential property owners and away from business property taxpayers. Bowen's plan would restore its balance. Furthermore, he desired an increase of aid from the property tax relief fund from its historic 20 percent level to a new standard of 22 percent. A fourth bill would allow a necessary reduction in property tax rates for school cumulative building funds to bring them in line with traditional state policies when applied to enlarged assessment bases.

Bowen's health insurance plan had its roots in a proposal devised by the National Association of Insurance Commissioners. The Indiana plan would require all insurance companies doing business in the state to offer a comprehensive health insurance package. Consumers would not be required to buy it, but insurers would have to make it available. Furthermore, cost-sharing by covered individuals would be mandatory. Availability would be guaranteed to all Hoosiers. When poor health prevented an individual from obtaining adequate coverage, the gubernatorial plan would supply it from a pool. Incentives to provide health care in the most cost-efficient setting without sacrificing quality also were supported.

It was testimony to the general acceptance of the Bowen property tax relief package that the control features moved smoothly through the legislative process with little heated debate or opposition. The fortunes of the tax relief plan itself took a different turn. At the heart of the issue was the fact that the legislature, increasingly accustomed to yielding to the pressure of interest groups, preferred spending to tax rebates.

Given the assembly's previous history of difficulty in sustaining highway maintenance programs, many lawmakers preferred to finance highway needs from the pool of money that the governor had earmarked for return to Indiana citizens. Bowen vigorously dissented from this point of view. Use of the general fund was bad policy because rising costs of highway maintenance would impose an ever-more-oppressive burden upon the general fund budget if this course were adopted. The predictability of budget support for highways always would be in doubt from year to year. Besides, Indiana's historic policy of user payments appeared to make even more sense as the nation began its first fumbling attempts to define alternative transportation sources.

Quick action on his tax relief program was required, Bowen believed, to remove a large block of money from the spending stream. Given enough weeks to think about a $290 million pile of money, lawmakers would become increasingly tempted to spend it for other purposes as special interest lobbyists increased their pressure upon the process. His assessment was sound; his desires were partially frustrated. The tax and utility relief package didn't clear the House until mid-February, weeks behind the previously determined schedule, and opponents already were whacking away bits and pieces. The House version cut the 15 percent income tax relief to 10 percent.

After substantial debate the $9 billion biennial budget was adopted on March 29 as the House concurred in Senate amendments to the bill. For a time it seemed that the lower chamber might be inclined to throw the issue into a conference committee where certain funds cut by the Senate could be restored. This would have the effect of increasing spending to a level that would jeopardize the income tax relief proposal. Finally, after predictable partisan debate, the budget concurrence prevailed by a narrow 52-47 margin.

Meanwhile, the governor had begun to press for a gasoline tax increase. The continued deterioration of roads after 1978's blizzard stimulated a drive for new funding. Early in the session Bowen had signed a bill turning over $19 million of unspent state highway appropriations to local governments for pothole-patching. Another plan, adopted by the assembly on April 4, would have empowered local governments in Marion County and five southwestern counties with especially troublesome road problems to levy auto and truck "wheel tax" surcharges.

April 5 proved to be the climactic day in the 1979 session. Both Bowen's income tax refund and a three-cents-a-gallon fuel tax remained at issue in the House of Representatives. Already having secured a road funding source from the wheel tax, nine of 13 Marion County Republicans abandoned the administration on the gasoline tax bill. When a few of the defectors offered the excuse that they weren't certain that Bowen favored the bill, the governor snorted, "They must be blind and deaf."[3] His fury intensified a few minutes later when the already scaled-down income tax relief bill died without a constitutional majority. Republican Representatives Dan Burton, William Soards, Jerome Reppa, and Elwood Fifield had voted against it.

Immediately Statehouse corridors were rife with rumors that an irate governor would bring reprisals against Marion County by vetoing both the wheel tax and the White River Park legislation. Belatedly Marion County interests began putting pressure on Burton and Soards in an effort to reverse their votes on a reconsideration motion. Mayor William Hudnut telephoned the governor to apologize for the lack of support from Marion County lawmakers, but Bowen was abrupt with him. Meanwhile, the arm-twisting on Burton and Soards succeeded, and their changed votes gave the income tax bill the 51 votes it needed to become law. The measure, as finally adopted, preserved a 15 percent income tax reduction on a one-time basis, then reduced it to five percent for succeeding years. In the final accounting, a legislature which spurned a gas tax bill provided an additional $169 million in general fund assistance for road repairs.

Bowen vetoed the wheel tax anyway, not out of vindictiveness, but owing to a practical recognition that its enactment would remove any incentive for legislators from Marion County and the five southwestern counties to join with others next session to adopt a long-range funding solution. Bowen's veto would keep their feet to the fire for 1980 by insuring that their roads deteriorated at the same rate as routes in the other 86 counties.

As the governor's staff evaluated the results of the legislative session, analysts became increasingly concerned that a series of bills outside the budget had a fiscal impact of $82 million. Their enactment would reduce the state's working balance to an unacceptable level. At least $30 million worth of "outside" bills would have to be rejected. On April 10 Bowen vetoed five measures. A new distribution formula for the inheritance tax ($13.2 million impact); a corrections center in South Bend ($750,000); a package of improvements to Military Park, transit planning, and a new state office building ($3 million); phaseout of hotel-motel gross income taxes ($1.5 million); and a sales tax exemption on certain pollution control measures ($16 million) were the casualties.

Marion County interests considered Bowen's rejection of the improvements bill affecting Military Park and the capitol complex to be a final reprisal for the loss of the gas tax bill. The governor turned it down because it was of secondary importance to other pending measures, but he was perfectly happy to let Indianapolis think that he was upset with the local power structure.

The administration's health insurance plan had faltered in mid-February after lobbyists for two powerful insurance companies, Blue Cross and Lincoln National Life Insurance Company, succeeded in killing it. Bowen had been seeking a compromise between a private-sector insurance system and what he feared was an otherwise inevitable nationalization of health insurance unless states such as Indiana found middle ground. It proved too controversial a plan for Indiana lawmakers, who consigned the Bowen program to the oblivion of a legislative study committee.

The 1979 session saw another effort to repeal the direct primary for governor and lieutenant governor, with Senate President Pro Tempore

Martin Edwards leading the campaign. The measure passed the Senate, then died in the House, but Edwards made it known that he would stuff the proposal into a conference committee report. Bowen made it clear that he would reject any primary repealer legislation, but the Senate Republican leader continued to try. He did not prevail. Edwards' heavy-handedness on an issue which some of his critics considered to be a self-serving attempt to promote his own political aspirations had the effect of damaging his standing with the media and a number of his colleagues.

Electric utility support for a measure to revise rate structures provided another controversy during the 1979 General Assembly. The concept, known as "construction work in progress," was designed to enable utilities to recover their expenses for capital improvements in stages, rather than wait until a project was completed and in service. It had several economic and practical advantages. Financing of large projects would be simplified and utilities would be able to scale down extensive interest payments during the construction period. Rate increases would be passed along to consumers in smaller doses, rather than in one big lump.

While sympathetic to the economic arguments, several within the administration harbored reservations of another sort. GOP State Chairman Bruce Melchert and I emerged as its principal opponents. The utility issue, we argued, always had been one of political volatility that could blow up given the right set of circumstances and the right candidate to exploit them. "CWIP" was such an issue; Senator Wayne Townsend might be the candidate. If the issue became a focal point of demagoguery in Indiana in the way that utility rate crusades had brought political turmoil elsewhere, Townsend at least might be propelled to the Democratic nomination. What might happen in the autumn was anybody's guess. The final result of enacting CWIP could be to place a hostile governor in the Statehouse who then would fight to secure its repeal. The utilities would have gained nothing at the expense of Lieutenant Governor Orr and the GOP.

Utility lobbyists rejected our line of reasoning, arguing that utility matters were not likely to become a predominant issue and that John Hillenbrand was a shoo-in for the Democratic nomination. Townsend wouldn't be a factor. Melchert and I were equally reluctant to accept their thinking. For one thing, the utility lobbyists leading the campaign — Larry Mohr, Phillip Bainbridge, and Richard Stein — all were Democrats who might not be expected to share equally our concern for the future of the Republican party. Secondly, they were thoroughly comfortable with the prospect of businessman Hillenbrand in the governor's chair, perhaps more so than the lieutenant governor, who occasionally had made public statements critical of utility practices. Interestingly, I discussed this matter with Hillenbrand, who agreed with my point of view and saw the enactment of CWIP as a boon to the Townsend campaign.

The state chairman and I continued our opposition to the CWIP issue, which had become part of a piece of legislation known as the "Christmas tree bill" because it contained a series of issues affecting utilities. When I made an offhand comment to administration legislative counsel John Coldren that the passage of CWIP was an act of suicide for the Republican party, he spread that message among GOP legislators. Coming from the administration's energy specialist, it had an impact. Support began melting away. Mohr later told another gubernatorial assistant that he had obtained enough votes to pass the measure through the House of Representatives "until Watt and Melchert started talking."[4] CWIP died.

The controversial legislative session produced several other significant results. It began a phasing out of the intangibles tax levied upon holders of securities. Public schools received a 26 percent increase in state funding which put the level of state aid over the $2 billion mark. Mental Health funding was bolstered by 21 percent.

Perhaps its most significant political consequence was that of embittering what always had been a rather touchy relationship between Indianapolis legislators and their out-state colleagues. Distrust between Indianapolis and the hinterlands had been a staple of Indiana political tradition. It had worsened in the 1960s as an aggressive and effective Marion County GOP organization led by L. Keith Bulen attempted to expand its influence. While Bulen was acknowledged as a masterful tactician, his dealings with many out-state politicians were less than satisfactory. Perhaps unintentionally, the chairman and his lieutenants often came across as arrogant to outsiders who already were looking for reasons to take offense. Likewise, the Indianapolis business establishment had maintained a peculiarly condescending attitude toward officials of a state government whose presence had been responsible for the city's very existence.

What already was resented as an Indianapolis superiority complex became coupled with a perception of grasping local greed during the 1979 session. Capital city legislators had sabotaged highway funding for the remainder of the state but also pressed for special funding for local projects: planning for a "people mover," improvements to Military Park and the Water Company canal, more red bricks for the Monument Circle project, White River Park (whose appropriation came at the expense of recreation projects in other areas), and state acquisition of the old American United Life Insurance Company building to enable the company to build a new center-city skyscraper home.

Rural legislators would have applauded if the governor had killed the White River Park project, but he did not do so because he thought it had merit. However, the outcome of the 1979 legislature had other implications. Tentative moves to position William Hudnut in a challenge to either Lieutenant Governor Orr or Congressman Dan Quayle in the governor's or senate races were met with icy resistance from rural conservatives. The anti-Indianapolis sentiment later played a role in the defeat of Representative E. Henry Lamkin for the speakership of the House in 1981. By the time Bowen left office, the political chasm between City Hall and Statehouse seemed to have widened.

XXII

THE GOVERNOR IN NATIONAL AFFAIRS

Bowen achieved a level of national prominence denied his predecessors whose limit of one term prevented them from acquiring enough seniority to move to leadership positions in governors' organizations or the national Republican party. However, tenure alone didn't account for his rise. Party leaders became aware of his immense popularity in Indiana; he then was courted by White House aspirants.

The furor over state taxation which gained momentum after the celebrated California "Proposition 13" ballot issue brought national attention to Bowen's achievement in curbing Indiana's property taxes years earlier. He was viewed as a political clairvoyant because of it. His background as a physician, unusual for a governor, gave him credibility when he discussed health issues. Most of all, governors and other national leaders were comfortable with a man who seldom engaged in political posturing and who quietly involved himself in national affairs without the brashness and arrogance that typified far too many politicans who aim for eminence in Washington. Bowen was popular among his political peers for the same reasons he was popular back home.

As a new governor he approached his "national" duties with the quiet restraint that had characterized his entry into the state legislature. Bowen believed that one had to serve an apprenticeship and take time to learn the system before attempting to go out front. He had thinly-disguised contempt for freshman governors who immediately began to measure the desk in the oval office of the White House. Their presumptuousness offended him. The habit of certain governors, notably Jerry Brown of California, to use national gatherings as springboards for media prominence also was an irritant. Bowen admired governors who sat and deliberated issues, unlike Brown, who only remained in the room long enough to make a statement designed for national media consumption. The Hoosier governor also had little use for Washington reporters who covered these conferences. While state executives wrestled with multimillion-dollar issues, journalists cared only about politics.

The governor's first encounter with his colleagues, at the February, 1973, winter meeting of the National Governors' Conference, was uneventful. He listened quietly, did not inject himself into the discussions, and accepted appointment to the conference's Human Resources Committee, one of the less glamorous assignments in its committee structure.

During his first term Bowen became aligned with a cluster of fellow moderates, with whom he developed a rapport that was personal as well as political. Initially and nominally, they were led by Washington's Daniel Evans, perhaps the most liberal-leaning of the group, but a quiet and articulate state chief executive. Evans' personality was echoed in Iowa Governor Robert Ray, who like Bowen became incredibly popular in his home state. Rounding out the group was Michigan's William Milliken, the most charismatic among them and an effective Republican leader from a state frequently dominated by liberal Democrats. Their relationship amounted to informal consultations on issues and political questions — nothing structured, but an inclination to reach consensus among themselves.

Leadership in the governors' association rotated between the two political parties. Republican caucuses selected its chairman in alternate years. Some indication of the stature of these four governors can be derived from the fact that each of them was elected by their colleagues to the organization's chairmanship during the 1970s.

Bowen's first visibility in gubernatorial circles came at the 1974 summer meeting of the National Governors' Conference in Seattle. He led a successful fight to block the association's planned endorsement of the Kennedy-Mills national health insurance plan. It represented the first installment of an ongoing battle to preserve private sector dominance in health care. Bowen emerged as a leader among the governors in the fight against nationalization.

A similar reputation unfolded with respect to medical malpractice after Indiana enacted what many observers believed to be landmark legislation to corral the ballooning costs of malpractice insurance and to insure its availability to practitioners. Malpractice was widely publicized during the early 1970s. Doctors threatened strikes; hospitals warned of cuts in services. A number of states explored possible solutions to a problem many believed to jeopardize the availability of health care. Indiana's 1975 statute was considered a model. Bowen frequently was called upon to explain how his state was able to resolve the complex and intense disagreements among doctors, lawyers, and insurance companies. He did so on a number of occasions, pointing out that states were in a position to become individual laboratories for devising solutions to this and other nationwide problems.[1]

Governors are asked to serve on a variety of national public and semi-public boards and commissions; usually the involvement is ceremonial. They lend their names to worthy causes. Bowen was reluctant to accept these appointments unless they afforded the opportunity for personal involvement. One example was the Education Commission of the States, created in the 1960s as a research and policy development organization whose underlying objective was blunting federal intrusion into education, which had been an historic responsibility of the states. Bowen's active participation quickly resulted in his appointment to the organization's executive committee and his election as chairman in 1976.

His first presidential appointment occurred in 1975 to the Commission on Federal Paperwork, an eight-member group that included congressmen, federal administrative officials, and representatives of the private sector. It was intended to reduce the burden and cost of federal reporting requirements imposed upon citizens, recipients of federal aid, businesses, government contractors, and state and local governments. Initially, the governor welcomed the appointment because he considered the elimination of oppressive and expensive reporting mandates to be a very worthy goal. Bowen's enthusiasm turned to dismay when the commission itself seemed about to founder in bureaucratic exercises which generated pounds of paper. In reaction to his outspoken criticisms the group streamlined its functions, and he was more or less satisfied with its progress. Unfortunately, like too many other study commissions embracing noble purposes, its findings generally were ignored by Washington.

Bowen's national reputation also was enhanced by his leadership during the eastern rail reorganization, in which he often stood alone among the 17 affected governors by pressing for a practical restructuring of the bankrupt lines. The rail industry, Department of Transportation, and United States Railway Association considered Bowen's to be the most constructive posture adopted by any of the states affected by these bankruptcies — which threatened widespread reductions in rail service throughout the region. (Indiana's involvement in the eastern reorganization is treated fully in a separate chapter).

By the end of his first term the governor had developed a deep affection for President Ford. It had its basis in personalities rather than politics. The relationship was further strengthened by Bowen's desire to be a team player and support his party's national leader. He had ready access to the White House though he seldom imposed upon Ford. Presidential assistant James Falk, who maintained liaison with governors, frequently used Bowen as a sounding board.

In spite of a clear preference for Ford's candidacy in 1976, Bowen sat on the sidelines during the primary and convention duel between the President and former California Governor Ronald Reagan. The governor's priority was the success of the Indiana ticket. He did not want to become embroiled in a moderate-versus-conservative party fight that could affect adversely the prospects for state candidates in the autumn.

Aside from the political consequences of Jimmy Carter's narrow victory in November, Bowen was distressed by Ford's loss. The governor understood that this quiet, sometimes stumbling leader had had a soothing effect upon the nation during the post-Watergate trauma. Ford's abrupt rejection by the voters seemed poor repayment. It also meant the end of what had been evolving as a special relationship between the governor of Indiana and the White House.

In February, 1977, James Smith and I urged the governor to consider advancing his personal interests within the governors' associations. A check of records revealed most other prominent Republican governors already had served as chairmen of the national group and that Bowen would be the senior Republican who had not headed the Midwestern Governors' Conference. The governor replied that he had not yet made up his mind about which direction to take but agreed to position himself for one or more chairmanships. The logical next step was to put forth his name for the vice-chairmanship of the 15-state Midwestern Governors' Conference at that year's meeting. Vice-Chairman Arthur Link of North Dakota, a Democrat who was elevated to the chairmanship after the defeat of Republican Christopher Bond of Missouri, probably would hold over for a full year's term, which would not end until the summer of 1978. If named vice-chairman in 1977, Bowen would be an almost automatic successor. Telephone calls to Milliken and Ray iced the arrangement. The Hoosier governor was voted vice-chairman of the MGC at its session in Afton, Oklahoma.

By this time Bowen was chairman of the National Governors' Association's (its name had been changed from conference to association) standing committee on Criminal Justice and Public Safety. His interests focused on problems with the federal Law Enforcement Assistance Administration, the federal agency which funneled millions of dollars in public safety aid to states and localities. LEAA was a controversial and troubled agency; governors frequently disagreed with its policies. Another category of concern was the Justice Department, which was bringing a variety of lawsuits against the states. This committee also framed recommendations with respect to National Guard interests. Bowen, with advice from General Ahner and Major General Francis Greenlief, executive director of the National Guard Association of the United States, became a leading advocate for the Guard. The committee made numerous recommendations calling for modern equipment for its units. It led the fight against Department of Defense reorganization plans that many feared would seriously impair the Guard's effectiveness. In 1978, Bowen yielded the committee chairmanship to take a seat on NGA's executive committee, a prerequisite to qualify for the association chairmanship.

As it turned out, the Indiana governor assumed the chairmanship of the Midwestern governors in 1978 and was elected to lead the 18 Republican governors that year. His elevation to the chairmanship of the national governors' group in July, 1979, overlapped the other appointments. During August, 1979, Bowen led all three organizations.

Health policy and the fallout from Proposition 13 were the governor's main themes at national meetings during the final years of his second term. Bowen continued to oppose attempts by Senator Edward Kennedy to secure the association's endorsement of national health insurance. He prevailed. Less successful was a drive to encourage other governors to develop limited state-sponsored insurance programs that might forestall further federal intervention in health care. In an address to the Boston convention of the NGA in 1978, Bowen criticized the federal preoccupation with health costs, arguing that the public sought quality health care and was unwilling to sacrifice excellence for cost containment. "Never have I heard a patient support any desire for 'quantity' above a fundamental need for 'quality'," he said. "Quite literally, the American public wants more and better health care, not more and poorer care."[2] He went on to assail the federal record in Medicaid and Medicare.

> The public has witnessed both Medicaid and Medicare being adjusted in coverage for cost reasons, raising doubts both as to the quality of the care delivered, and the ultimate stability of coverage. Medicaid has become an additional burden upon middle income taxpayers, as well as a bureaucratic quagmire that threatens to totally pulverize whatever semblance of a traditional federal-state relationship that once might have existed. Finally, if cost is now to become the controlling factor in our nation's health care policy, is there any shred of evidence that a federally dominated program of any type has proven to be better and cheaper than the alternative it replaced?[3]

Bowen called for the enactment of state-level health insurance and cost containment legislation. "Utilization of the private insurance system, under the supervision of the state's insurance regulatory mechanism, would eliminate or reduce many of these costs and at the same time provide an alternative approach to health care needs and do it through private enterprise, with freedom of choice, less red tape, and with the administration of the program closer to the home and locale of the patient, which is bound to make it more responsive and controllable," he contended.[4]

The governor's foresight in pressing for tax reform in 1973 gave him added credibility in the later 1970s. California's referendum spurred talk of nationwide tax revolts. Governors and legislators hastily sought programs that would put them on the right side of the issue. Frequently in demand for information about Indiana's successful undertaking, Bowen was quick to point out that reasoned reductions in property taxes and controls on spending might enable other states to avoid the meat-axe approach of Proposition 13. Fellow Republican governors were warned not to ignore voter sentiment but recognize that there are limits to how the taxing and spending powers of government should be used. As they approached the issue of tax and spending limitations, he offered two guidelines: limit both taxes and spending and do not spend unless it is fully justified. If revenues increase to a level that permits increased overall spending, reduce the tax burden rather than adopt the traditional policy of additional spending.[5]

Bowen's tenure as NGA chairman from July, 1979, to July, 1980, proved disappointing to him because Mrs. Bowen's illness limited his involvement in the final months of his term. He had hoped to use the forum it provided to promote his views about state-federal relations and to argue the point that the federal government had overreached its ability to deliver services and set policies. The states, which in recent years had demonstrated a greater degree of creativity and concern, were competent to reassert responsibilities which had eroded from them since the 1950s. Mrs. Bowen's hospitalization prevented his attendance at the annual meeting in 1980, which he would have chaired.

Indiana's forthright response to the prolonged mine workers' strike in 1978 also brought national attention to the Hoosier chief executive. The Hoosier state became the focal point of national media interest because of actions taken to stave off hardship. Bowen was the subject of network television and national magazine interviews. President Carter's staff, meanwhile, counted him among those to be reckoned with during the emergency because his tough stance had drawn favorable public reaction. Carter didn't want Bowen as a critic. After a meeting with the President, several cabinet members, and the affected governors, a delegation of state executives met with the White House press corps in a crowded room in the executive mansion. The administration had positioned West Virginia Governor Jay Rockefeller to give a report on the session — a version friendly to its interests. Rockefeller's statement was interrupted by shouts of newsmen who wanted to hear from the Hoosier. Finally, Bowen took the microphone, but with characteristic restraint, muted his deeply-felt criticisms of the President's conduct during the strike.

As the 1980 campaign gathered momentum, national candidates sought Bowen's endorsement, for their reading of Indiana polls showed that his support could be significant in the state. However, the governor again exercised restraint. He foresaw another potentially divisive pre-convention campaign and did not want to split the Hoosier GOP in a way that might hurt the chances of Lieutenant Governor Orr to succeed him. Privately Bowen hoped that Ford would come out of retirement, although he viewed this as unlikely. In Ford's absence Reagan was the odds-on favorite to win an Indiana primary, and there seemed to be little value to visible involvement with another candidate. Ford absent, George Bush was Bowen's preference. A moderate with extensive experience in government and a charismatic public image, the former congressman-ambassador-national chairman seemed to him to be qualified and electable in the autumn. Bush had approached the governor late in 1978 to explore the possibility of securing his support.

Reagan, on the other hand, was more conservative than Bowen and their initial acquaintanceship did not lead to a warm relationship. The California governor had the habit of making tardy grand entrances with a phalanx of aides and state troopers at governors' meetings, a type of showmanship at odds with Bowen's perception of the way governors ought to conduct themselves at working sessions.

The situation was compounded by the fact that Bowen's long-standing ally, John Hart, was spearheading the Indiana campaign for former Treasury Secretary John Connally. Given these circumstances, it made sense to remain quiet.

Several Hoosier Republicans began drum-beating for a Bowen vice-presidential candidacy. Deeply flattered by this attention, the governor was fully aware that realities argued against it. Age probably disqualified him from serious consideration as a running mate with Reagan. Moreover, the Indiana governor lacked a national constituency and name recognition. Ticket-balancing also worked against him. While a Californian or a Connecticut-Texan might look to the Midwest for a vice-presidential nominee, Governors Thompson of Illinois and Milliken of Michigan represented "swing" states with electoral votes more crucial to a GOP majority. Indiana's 13 electors probably would be taken for granted. In addition, Senator Lugar also seemed a likely prospect for the number two job. Lugar took priority over Bowen among Indianapolis Republicans, who only wanted the governor's active help in one more state campaign — to be followed by a hasty exit to retirement that would remove him from a politically influential role.

In February, 1980, before the accelerating decline of Beth Bowen's health became fully known, the governor told me that he would accept an invitation to run with Bush but remained uncertain as to how he would respond to an offer from Reagan. The rapid deterioration of her condition during the summer of 1980 almost certainly would have ruled out national campaigning. Named co-chairman of the GOP platform committee with Texas Senator John Tower, Bowen was active in its early deliberations but bypassed the national convention to remain with Beth.

Ever the loyalist, the governor reacted positively to the national ticket; his enthusiasm was fueled by the presence of Bush as Reagan's running mate. Slowly Bowen warmed to the prospect of a Reagan presidency, in part because the candidate was proving to be a far more effective campaigner than he had once thought would be the case. The GOP sweep of the White House and the Senate was received enthusiastically although the governor was most gratified by Orr's landslide victory in the governor's race and Dan Quayle's unseating of Birch Bayh in the Senate contest. Bowen's reputation among the governors was confirmed when the president-elect offered him the post of White House administrative assistant to deal with state and local governments, a position held by James Falk in the Ford administration and Jack Watson under Carter. Speculation also emerged about a Bowen appointment to the important sub-cabinet position of Undersecretary of Health and Human Services, an appointment combined with that of surgeon general. The timing was wrong. The invitation to serve on the presidential staff came within days of Beth's death. Bowen's letter declining the offer included a statement to the effect that he might be more receptive to a Washington assignment several months in the future.

XXIII   THE FINAL MONTHS

The final months of Bowen's administration should have been the happiest of times for the governor and his staff. The pressures of governing a state had eased. Only Chrysler Corporation's drift toward collapse presented a fresh challenge in that closing period. It might have been a pleasant finale, with the governor visiting civic meetings and Republican gatherings for the last time as chief executive to reminisce and to bask in the acclaim for the most popular administration in modern times. Freed of the obligation to plan new programs and to wage another campaign, Bowen would have had the opportunity speak out on public issues in a more effective vein, to go beyond policy questions and present his views on the future of federalism and the duties of state government. It didn't turn out that way.

The final months of Bowen's governorship were a time of profound gloom, marred by personal tragedy. An already-weary governor and his staff lost what little enthusiasm remained; they only wanted the administration to come to an end quickly and quietly.

The governorship had begun to take its toll on a man already past the age of 60. Bowen confided to me in January, 1980, that he wished the term could have ended that month. Seven years was enough. He had reached this conclusion prior to becoming fully aware of Beth Bowen's accelerating decline.

Several members of the governor's inner circle also were ready to leave. After 1978's coal strike I was all but burned out, impatient to soon depart. However, there was no pressing inducement for an early abandonment of the Statehouse. The governor, worried that several other aides might exit to private life before the term ran out, encouraged me to remain. Reluctant to bail out during what almost certainly would be a difficult period for him, I agreed to see it through. Jim Smith also was eager to go and made a firm decision to resign during the summer of 1980. When the deadline came he tried to work up the nerve to inform the governor but couldn't quite bring himself to do it. When Mrs. Bowen was hospitalized late in July, Smith realized that he, too, was committed to stay for the duration.

It had become apparent that something was wrong when Beth Bowen suffered a minor fall in June, 1977, and complained of lingering effects. The public first become aware of her condition on September 18 of that year. During an auto trip from Bremen to Indianapolis she complained of severe pain and was hospitalized briefly at Kokomo. Reporters learned of it by accident through a State Police message. The *Star* and Associated Press telephoned me that night for confirmation. Several hours elapsed before I was able to reach the governor. He called, his voice quavering, to confirm that she had a rare cancer of the bone marrow. "The short-term outlook is fair and the long-term outlook is terrible," he said.

Bowen was reluctant to disclose publicly that his wife had cancer. The office statement issued the next morning limited its description to "a chronic, serious disease of the bone marrow."[1] The governor resisted reporters' urgings to be more specific. Mrs. Bowen's disorder, multiple myeloma, attacked bone marrow in the way that leukemia assails the bloodstream. The governor was grim, believing that she might not live for more than a year. Later, we learned from her physician, Dr. Walter Daly, that the outlook was more optimistic. Although her condition slowly deteriorated, therapy retarded the onslaught of the disease until the late winter of 1979.

Beth's condition made it even more difficult for the governor to plan for the future. Bowen was under intense pressure from Republican leaders to confront Senator Bayh, who would be up for a fourth term in 1980. No one else could win, they argued.

Concern for Beth's health was only one of his reservations, although it was an important one. A frequent critic of the Washington establishment, the governor had little desire to become part of it. His age — 63 at the time he would take office — effectively limited him to one term and would confine him to what then seemed certain to be minority-party status without hope of acquiring seniority sufficient to wield influence. The life-style of the nation's capital city had little appeal to either Bowen or his first lady. Numerous GOP admirers suggested that election to the Senate would be a fitting capstone to an already glittering public career. That logic was lost upon the governor. "Why be one of one hundred when you've already been one of fifty," Bowen grumbled.[2] In his value system the Senate did not represent a promotion. It was, after all, an institution that bore heavy responsibility for so many of the nation's recent failures.

Still others proposed that he take the Senate seat for two years, then resign. The durable Bayh would have been taken out of the picture, and the party would have an opportunity to hold on to the seat under more favorable circumstances. Their proposal misjudged Bowen's concept of ethical behavior. He would have felt an obligation to serve out the full term.

GOP leaders' persistent wooing was rooted in the fact that the governor had become the predominant Indiana political personality of the 1970s. His popularity remained immense. Polls continued to grant him a phenomenal 80 percent approval rating (equalled among Republican governors only by Ray of Iowa). Bowen had led his party to impressive victories twice before. The Hoosier GOP now was too reliant upon a man it once had rejected. Could the party win without him its leaders wondered?

Despite his misgivings, Bowen probably would have taken on Bayh if Beth's health had been normal or if his initial forecast of the time span of her illness had borne out. A grieving governor would have wrapped himself in the all-consuming grind of statewide campaigning and the demands of the Senate in the hope that personal pain might be eased. However, the temporary stabilizing of her condition dissuaded him. In 1978 it became apparent that Beth's illness would be a prolonged one; this fact effectively closed the door to a Senate campaign.

By September, 1978, the governor's closest confidants were convinced that he would not run. He did not explicitly reveal a decision but gave off signals easily read by those who knew him well. Several Bowen advisers began to explore alternatives. Fourth District Congressman Dan Quayle attracted their interest. Ray Rizzo, J. B. King, and I concluded that Quayle was a logical candidate, although he would be drawn into a stiff uphill battle against Bayh. The congressman's landslide victory in November, 1978, stirred his interest in the 1980 statewide campaign. Quayle had been a friend since the Whitcomb administration, and I sent word through an intermediary, David Griffiths, that a Bowen candidacy was all but written off. The congressman unobtrusively should begin positioning himself to go against the incumbent.

A "provisional" Quayle organization was formed in December. It was understood that the candidate would be careful to say that he favored the governor but would explore a Senate candidacy if Bowen took himself out of consideration. The two met in February, 1979. The governor did not reveal his decision but only told Quayle to "be ready."[3]

On March 9, 1979, Bowen told me he wanted to announce his intentions soon after the legislature adjourned. He had compiled a rough draft of the statement to be issued upon that occasion. It was a dismaying document. The tone was sour. Fatigue, weariness of the rantings of special interests and demagogues, and a preference for dealing with patients rather than constituents were cited as reasons. It was inappropriate and far too negative as the rationale for announcing the retirement of the state's most popular public official.

Within moments I learned why. Chemotherapy treatments that had retarded the progress of Mrs. Bowen's cancer had been halted a few days earlier. The white blood cell count had dropped too low. Unless another form of therapy arrested the disease, its progress would accelerate. I took the governor's statement without comment. William DuBois and I made a series of revisions, each designed to give the statement a more positive flavor. Bowen accepted our version.

The governor, with Beth and Lieutenant Governor Orr at his side, brought reporters to his office on May 8, primary election day. "I will not, repeat will not, be a candidate for the U.S. Senate in 1980," he stated. Three reasons were given:

> I am 61 years of age. While my health is excellent and I do not consider myself old, I have reservations about seeking election to an office which I would assume at age 63 and which would commit me to serving until I was 69.
>
> I have been actively involved in politics and public life since 1952. That period has involved major leadership responsibilities as speaker of the House and governor. Those responsibilities, because I work at meeting them, have limited the time available to do more personal things. Now I find myself wanting to give myself greater opportunities to be with Beth and with our family.
>
> I feel a properly conducted campaign for the Senate would require so much time that I would not be able to do justice to my responsibilities as governor. I have the strong conviction that, twice having been elected governor, I owe it to those who voted for me to give the fullest possible attention to that responsibility in my final 20 months in office.[4]

Bowen named more than a score of Republican leaders and influential citizens who would be qualified candidates. It was designed to deflect questions about his preferences and was received in good humor by reporters. The first name on his roster was that of Quayle. "Dan Quayle would make a splendid candidate, but this is not an endorsement," he said.[5] Orr told newsmen that he was disappointed, but had been prepared for the governor's decision. "It sure would have been nice to dust off the old Bowen-Orr buttons," he said.[6]

Bowen's statement produced a warm outpouring of newspaper editorials. Writers applauded his decision to place family above political ambition and reflected upon the striking popularity and substantial accomplishments of his terms as governor. Editorialists also acclaimed his decision to announce his intentions at an early date. Other Republicans would have time to mount credible campaigns.

Bowen never revealed his initial private trial balloon for a GOP Senate candidate: President Arthur Hansen of Purdue University. The governor was rather standoffish toward Quayle. The two men were miles apart in style and personality. The governor was a firm believer that one had to serve a governmental apprenticeship, to pay certain party dues before earning elevation to political prominence. Quayle was a newcomer, generally lacking in experience. Bowen's hesitation also reflected the congressman's family and business ties to the Pulliam newspapers. (Quayle is a nephew of Eugene Pulliam.) Historic feuds with the *Star* and *News* still rankled.

Given a strong head start and opponents whose campaigns failed to generate momentum, Quayle emerged as the odds-on favorite to be Bayh's challenger. Bowen was sympathetic to the campaign of Insurance Commissioner H. P. Hudson. He was flattered that a member of his administration might be the nominee and held the commissioner in high esteem. Intensely involved in the governor's endeavors to forestall national health insurance in favor of state programs, Hudson had earned his respect. To be associated with Bowen on an issue of primary importance almost assured that an enduring relationship would result.

The governor was less taken with the candidacy of Highway Director Roger Marsh. Marsh was another favorite, first appointed to the Alcoholic Beverage Commission, then named highway director, and once under consideration to be state Republican chairman. In light of Marsh's disappointing performance in a 1976 congressional primary and lack of a political base, Bowen failed to see any purpose to his campaign.

Both Hudson and Marsh sought the governor's endorsement. They received encouragement but no commitments (although it was easy to come away from a meeting with the governor actually believing that one was the preferred candidate — especially if securing his endorsement had been the purpose of the visit).

By autumn, 1979, many Bowen political associates and staff members were involved in Quayle's campaign. Hudson's effort sputtered; he withdrew from the race only weeks after entering it. Marsh, convinced that he had lost the congressional primary because he had campaigned against his autumn opponent, Representative Philip Sharp, rather than his primary foe, William Frazier, launched a vicious campaign against Quayle. He was encouraged in this strategy by former GOP state chairman Tom Milligan, a Marsh adviser and a foe of Quayle. In doing so Marsh violated the Eleventh Commandment: "Thou shalt not speak ill of any other Republican." GOP leaders were furious. By January, 1980, the governor regarded the congressman's victory as a certainty. He told me, "I can support Quayle. I wish he had a couple more terms under his belt as congressman, but I can be enthusiastic about him." Quayle overwhelmed Marsh by nearly four to one in the primary. Bowen then actively campaigned for him in the fall.

The governor's own future was the subject of reflection throughout the second term. Unfamiliar with business and uncertain about prospects for re-establishing a medical practice, Bowen was content to talk about retirement and frequent fishing jaunts. He had led too active a life to accept these options, but had little grasp of opportunities that might exist for him. Occasionally, we discussed our futures. During one session the governor conceded that he didn't know what to do. I observed that his principal difficulty would be that of determining which corporate boards to turn down. "You mean they pay people for that?" he queried. If you know the man, it is not a surprising response. I found his naivete rather charming.

Another of our discussions, sometime in the winter of 1978, stimulated this gubernatorial pronouncement: "If that I.U. athletic director's job wasn't coming open until 1981, I know exactly what I'd do." It would have been natural, although outsiders probably would have been amazed. Bowen's associates began to send out feelers. I suggested that Indiana University consider a variety of proposals, owing to the uncertainty about what might appeal to him when the time came for a career decision. In 1980 Rizzo and I proposed him for membership on the board of Hook Drug Company. Its chairman, Norman Reeves, seized upon the idea and secured Bowen's assent two days later. This commitment led to another offer from Indiana National Bank. The governor's eventual decision to become a member of the faculty of the family practice department of the I.U. Medical School was consistent with his interests.

The mood of depression within the governor's office was echoed throughout the state, but for an unrelated reason. The worst economic downturn since the Hoover-Roosevelt era gathered momentum in the autumn of 1979. Inflation raged near 20 percent. The auto industry was in chaos, its new 1980 model year a disaster. Layoffs which had begun the previous summer made deep cuts in the auto-producing workforce. The malaise rapidly spread to steelmakers and suppliers. Homebuilding stagnated as mortgage money evaporated. The state's tax revenues slumped as economic activity abated. Bowen's final legislative session, 1980, offered little more than a gloomy prospect of another attempt to wean the legislature from its addiction to higher spending.

The governor had three priorities for the legislative session: limit spending, protect the property tax relief program, and find a way to pay for highway maintenance. Opening sections of the State of the State message were upbeat in describing achievements of the two branches of government during Bowen's administration, but he quickly turned to the business at hand. Inflation was described as unprecedented and almost catastrophic. The value of the dollar was in decline. Indiana was beleaguered economically. The recession would produce substantial reductions in state revenue in 1981. Each one percent decline in personal income reduced state revenues by $20 million. Even so, the chief of state warned against the temptation to raid the property tax relief fund.

The property tax relief fund must not be considered as surplus funds to be dipped into for any expenditure. It is dedicated to rebates for property owners. To divert money from this fund to any other purpose will, over a very few years, break the fund and destroy the program. I urge you never to force a choice between continuation of property tax relief and any other program, no matter how desirable or necessary that program may seem. Therefore, I will not accept any changes in the uses to which this fund is put.[7]

Highway funding, he stated, was the single most significant unresolved issue of the 1970s. Indiana had fallen far behind in its duty to preserve a modern highway system. "At this moment, our highway funding picture is so bleak that it would take until the year 2005 to complete all the projects in the Highway Commission's ten-year, long-range program," said Bowen. "That statement does not take into account what inflation may do over that quarter century period and what is happening to gasoline gallonage receipts as a result of conservation and dollar-a-gallon or higher gasoline prices."[8]

The governor expressed a willingness to accept any approach which provided a long-range solution, preserved a safe working balance in the general fund, and did not dilute the property tax relief program. "We no longer can look to the general fund for long-term highway maintenance and construction," he argued. "We can no longer look at this problem in terms of temporary patchwork by raiding the general fund in a particular session and then attempting to make the alibi that we have solved the problem. We need a permanent solution, and we cannot defer that decision."[9] Failure to act in the 1980 session would reflect bad political judgment on the part of both parties and irresponsible government as well.

Bowen's annual message also endorsed a plan to reorganize the state's transportation agencies, create a budget stabilization fund to build a revenue reserve for economic downturns, expand the state energy assistance program, and adopt necessary health planning legislation to avoid the loss of federal funds.

The speech omitted reference to an aid program for the tottering Chrysler Corporation, which maintained heavy concentrations of employment at Kokomo, New Castle, and Indianapolis. The Kokomo installation was a modern one, geared to production of transmissions for the new generation of Chrysler subcompacts. New Castle's was an aged facility with little or no hope of retention for the corporation's sole use. The administration was uncertain as to a proper approach. Philosophically, the governor was opposed to bailouts of the type proposed by Chrysler. Its management had been less than impressive in early dealings with state officials. Arrogance and condescension had characterized their presentations. Most important, few expected Chrysler to survive. Why subsidize an operation certain to fail when the money might better be husbanded for the economic after-effects of its eventual collapse?

Bowen decided that state assistance would be proper if its financing were backed by sufficient collateral, including a first mortgage interest in corporate property. He also believed that Indiana should be called upon only after complementing private and federal assistance had been obtained. A program meeting these guidelines was presented to him late in February. Using the Kokomo installation as security it authorized the state to provide up to $39 million in loan guarantees upon approval of a special board empowered to tap a bank reserve fund.

A highway funding bill also reached the governor's desk, but only after considerable turmoil in both houses of the assembly. Marion County legislators had been blamed for the defeat of road-funding proposals in the 1979 session. The capital city lawmakers were prime targets for the lobbying of the administration and legislative leadership. In anticipation of gasoline prices hitting the $1.50 per gallon range by year's end, a graduated tax was resolved upon. It would be pegged to the average price of fuel determined by semiannual calculations. Upon enactment the existing eight cent tax would increase to nine. Irrespective of fuel price increases the tax was limited to 12 cents in 1980, 14 in 1981, and 16 in the following year. Its proponents estimated that nearly $70 million in added revenue would be raised during the initial fiscal year. The measure also appropriated $10 million for mass transit assistance.

Its passage was a last-minute achievement and one carried out with a good deal of arm-twisting to bring Marion County legislators around. A late-night session on Saturday, February 23, (the final day for action without suspension of the rules) produced acceptance of the package with no votes to spare in the House. Minutes earlier the Senate had adopted the measure 27-22, one vote more than the required constitutional majority. No Democrat cast a favorable vote in either chamber. Bowen, Speaker Burrous, and Marion County GOP Chairman John Sweezey pressured reluctant Republicans to go along with the proposal.

Although less than satisfied with the final version because of its distribution formula, Bowen signed the gas tax bill because he thought it would bring to conclusion a four-year struggle to provide adequate road funding. Initially, the new system of taxation produced less revenue than expected. Gallonage prices which had been expected to jump by 50 cents hovered near the one-dollar mark as a recession, motorists' conservation, and a more fuel-efficient vehicle fleet dampened demand.

The transportation reorganization also became law, culminating a six-year effort to modernize the state's capacity to deal with a growing roster of transportation issues. It, too, overcame a fierce struggle despite endorsement by the committee assessing state government reorganization. Highway interests always had been opposed. The Highway Department had been almost sovereign — often, it seemed, not a part of the executive branch. The trucking industry feared diversion of highway revenues to mass transit. Most aviation interests were negative. The Port Commission resisted inclusion, posing the argument that port operations more closely resembled an economic development program than transportation ventures. The Toll Road Commission, sublime in its isolation, for years had fought any meaningful supervision by state government. Only railroad and public transit advocates stood firmly behind the bill. The governor assented to removing the Port Commission, partially as a consequence of his close friendship with its chairman, William Young, who opposed absorption. Other entities, however, remained under the umbrella.

Amid accusations that federal health authorities were blackmailing the state, the legislature reversed a decision of the previous year and accepted a health planning proposal intended to reduce duplication in the health service field. Failure to have done so would have jeopardized $74 million in federal aid money.

Legislative irritation with federal bureaucrats then spilled over to another issue which emerged late in the session with a less successful result. Under requirements of the federal Clean Air Act, Indiana was mandated to meet deadlines for compliance with air quality standards set by the Environmental Protection Agency. Most areas of the state were able to comply with only moderate countermeasures. The larger urban areas were another story. If conventional remedies would not bring a region into compliance, the federal law required a series of tougher restrictions, including annual vehicle emissions testing. Administrative costs would be higher than under an existing vehicle safety inspection program which, ironically, was in the process of being repealed. Most important, bringing a defective auto into compliance could be an expensive proposition. Older autos might not be repairable; newer vehicles could require tuneups. If a state proved unwilling to implement an emissions testing program, the EPA administrator had the authority to penalize it by denying highway funds and federal assistance for municipal sewage treatment projects. The price tag for Indiana would surpass $100 million annually.

EPA officials and their Indiana counterparts were in disagreement over the enforceability of current state regulatory authority. The Board of Health argued that prior legislation and regulations provided sufficient enforcement power to run testing programs where required. EPA regional administrator John McGuire's staff disagreed. He startled the legislative leadership with a letter promising sanctions if the current session of the General Assembly failed to pass new legislation. McGuire threatened statewide penalties, but exceeded his authority in doing so. It was limited to non-complying regions: Lake and Porter counties, Clark and Floyd counties, and the urban areas of Indianapolis, Fort Wayne, and South Bend.

The governor was surprised by EPA's action since it was believed that the Indianapolis, Fort Wayne, and South Bend problems could be addressed through measures short of emissions testing. Moreover, McGuire had given no advance word of this bombshell. Bowen objected to the whole idea of sanctions which transcended federal agency boundaries and was irritated by EPA's threatened action. At the same time he recognized that the agency had authority to impose them. The Carter administration was unlikely to overrule the agency. California already was embroiled in a similar controversy. Sanctions had been threatened against Illinois and Kentucky. A negotiated settlement was needed to protect Indiana's federal assistance in two important public works categories.

The legislature, however, was in no mood to compromise. The atmosphere soon became irrational. To begin with, the Indiana legislature is not known for pro-environmentalist leanings. Lawmakers from the unaffected counties wanted to thumb their noses at the whole idea. Legislators from affected counties feared the political heat of voting for the implementing language prepared by the State Air Pollution Control Board, which they saw as the instrument of unpopular programs resulting from earlier federal dictates. It was a tempting target for their wrath.

Administration urgings for a reasoned approach bore no fruit. Senator Bayh also tried to counsel moderation, but was shouted down in an angry caucus of House Democrats. The legislature refused to act upon the administration's proposed legislation. Bowen then raised the possibility of a special session if an administrative compromise could not be ironed out. The legislature concluded its work in the final week of February after adopting a $74 million supplemental budget. The governor signed it grudgingly; it would further erode the balances of the general fund and represented another occasion on which lawmakers appropriated more money than the state would receive.

The administration immediately moved to seek resolution of the EPA funding issue. An initial meeting with representatives of the four affected counties was touch-and-go. After considerable bluster and political statements designed for consumption back home, they agreed to explore a combination of state administration and local enforcement of the controversial program. Meanwhile, state officials were successful in resolving a series of disagreements which removed the Indianapolis, Fort Wayne, and South Bend urban areas from the mandate. The administration and congressional delegation brought great pressure to bear upon the federal agency in an effort to secure its agreement that Indiana already had sufficient enforcement authority. After a number of superficial provisions were agreed to, McGuire relented on the enforcement obstacle. A reporter observed that the entire controversy had been unnecessary. I agreed with him.

Sanctions later were brought against Kentucky, proof that EPA was not making idle threats. However, the installation of a new administration in Washington gave indication that the emissions mandate might be one casualty of a new approach to environmental regulation.

The transportation reorganization commenced in May with appointment of the Transportation Coordinating Board and the designation of Dr. William Black as the first director of the new Department of Transportation. The board wrestled with the mechanics of merging the agencies but confronted lingering sniping from legislators who had opposed the bill.

Unfortunately, the assembly's approach to reorganization of government agencies produced some of the objections. The "sunset" concept (an unfortunate term since it conveys no decipherable meaning to the average citizen) was intended to modernize state operations. It meant both the removal of obsolete agencies and the remodeling of other functions to make them more efficient. The majority of legislators trumpeted sunset as a device to kill off boards and commissions and to give evidence that the political system was serious about reducing the size of government. Given that climate, the designation of transportation functions as the first category to be considered under the mandatory elimination program may have been questionable. Indiana's performance in transportation was inadequate; it fell far short of contemporary realities. An expanded state role, not a reduced one, clearly was called for. A proper transportation restructuring meant the creation of a new agency, larger and with more functions. The fine points of this seeming contradiction escaped the comprehension of a few legislators who immediately set out to unravel the reorganization. The administration stood firm and pressed ahead with the merger. Later, Orr, as governor-elect, also gave the transportation department his strong backing. Bowen's original idea was to ensure that his successor possessed a mechanism for dealing with transportation issues of the 1980s. The new governor recognized the validity of this reasoning.

The Chrysler legislation also brought new controversy. Company officials were uncommunicative and insensitive to the state's concerns. While asking for money on an earlier timetable than had been agreed upon, Chrysler then disclosed its intent to lay off more workers and to put most of its New Castle operations up for auction. This aroused a storm of protest. Had Chrysler reneged? Bowen and State Treasurer Julian Ridlen (who had patiently supervised the complex processes of loan-making) met with corporate officials to get answers. Chrysler President Paul Bergmoser offered reasonable responses, but the confrontation would have been unnecessary if the company had applied common sense in communicating with one of its primary lenders.

Ridlen also was forced to undertake an extensive reworking of the agreement after the governor voiced fears that collateral pledged by the corporation might be inadequate to protect the state's interest. That, too, was resolved. However, the administration remained generally pessimistic about the outlook for the company's salvation; few saw a role for Chrysler in the world auto market.

As the administration began to draw to a close, the governor's attention was diverted further to his growing concern about Beth. Her illness had reached an advanced stage. He cancelled participation in the Republican National Convention and National Governors' Conference to remain with her at the residence, where she had been bedridden for several weeks. Mrs. Bowen was readmitted to University Hospital on July 26 with serious complications from the medication she had been taking. Dr. Daly advised her husband that she was not expected to survive for more than a few days. The governor moved into an adjacent room and devoted most of his hours to assist in her care. The strain began to show; he was dispirited and dead tired.

Intensive medication by her physician produced what Bowen later described as a near-miraculous recovery. She returned home on August 8, handicapped by a body brace designed to limit the risk of breaking bones threatened by her worsened overall condition. The brace left her nearly immobile.

The governor's role in the fall campaign was limited in terms of personal campaign appearances, but he was used extensively in television advertisements in behalf of other candidates. The "Bowen Team" was off and running again, it seemed, for one last time. Television viewers were overwhelmed by Bowen-Orr, Bowen-Quayle, Bowen-Crane, and Bowen-Hiler messages. For a brief period, the governor showed some of his former spirit. Quayle was within striking distance of Bayh; Hiler might be headed for a stunning upset of House Majority Whip John Brademas. Orr was comfortably ahead of John Hillenbrand. The governor threw himself into electioneering with greater enthusiasm as Republican prospects brightened. The final weeks of the 1980 campaign were a warm and satisfying twilight to his governorship, almost a referendum upon the peoples' affection for Otis Bowen, and a final outpouring of appreciation for an administration that already was acquiring legendary status.

The governor was overjoyed when the GOP romped to a landslide victory. Especially satisfying was Hiler's upset, which Bowen had forecast weeks earlier to the dumbfoundedness of most observers. After joining Quayle for a news conference on the morning after the balloting, we walked back to the Capitol with the governor still in an exuberant mood. He slapped a fist against the other hand exclaiming, "If only we could have beaten Evans and Sharp."

The bright mood was short-lived; Beth Bowen had been readmitted to

University Hospital on October 11. Intravenous chemotherapy produced excruciating side effects, and her pain was becoming more intense than medicine could abate.

It is difficult to convey the aching sadness of these final weeks, and painful to write about them. The governor was heartbroken, for he knew the end was near. Bowen lived at the hospital, sleeping in his clothes when he slept at all, often awake all night to help administer medication and to bring her food and water. His exhaustion was evident; he was unable to complete a conversation with one of his staff members without breaking down in tears. Judith Palmer spent hours each day at the hospital. Susan Davis, Jim Smith, Sue Senff, and I made an effort to maintain the appearance of normality in the governor's office. Each day a state trooper collected a box of paperwork for him to sign at Beth's bedside. We discharged most other gubernatorial responsibilities in his name, seldom troubling him with anything but the most important matters.

The outpouring of journalistic and public expressions of appreciation for 26 years of service by this quiet, respected country physician were of no solace either. Editorial writers lavished praise upon the soon-to-be-departing governor, investing the eight years of his administration with a luster tinged with nostalgia. While they wrote of his decency, honesty, and compassion, he nursed his dying wife of 42 years. His staff numbly carried on the routine.

Beth Bowen's spirit, meanwhile, remained indomnitable. She still communicated with friends by telephone or by notes scrawled upon assorted scraps of paper. In spite of a physical condition that only could be described as alarming, she insisted upon being present in a wheel chair for a "Tribute to the Bowen Years," which attracted 3,000 friends and supporters to the Indianapolis convention center on December 12.

Her last communication with me was a brief note, still legibly scratched upon a fragment of paper. Knowing of my penchant for browsing through second-hand bookstores, she had requested that I look for two out-of-print titles. "There's no hurry, whenever you find the time," it ended, written by a gallant lady who wanted me to believe that she intended to be around for a while. It was accompanied by a framed needlepoint artwork, reflective of her favorite hobby and completed earlier that autumn while she was hospitalized.

As December ended her condition became critical, heavy sedation inadequate to quell the pain. With her children gathered in the hospital room, she lapsed into unconsciousness on the morning of the final day of the year. That afternoon I took reporters aside individually and advised them that obituaries might be needed that night. At 3 a.m. on New Year's morning Palmer called to say that Beth had died a few minutes earlier.

Its dome shining brightly in the darkness, the vast state capitol was deserted early that morning, except for a solitary security guard at the north door. It took longer than usual to walk across the wide expanse of hallway and through the rotunda, where I lingered to observe the impressive architecture of a structure that had been the surrounding for so many memories. It was too early to telephone the media; most offices had not yet opened. The minutes dragged by until 5:30 a.m. when it was time to begin making notification — a terse communique of only three sentences scribbled upon a notepad.

Thousands of Hoosiers mourned Beth's death. She and the governor had captured their affection as few political couples ever had. This modest, gentle, and thoroughly proper first lady had contributed immensely to the people's perception of Bowen's administration. She was sincerely mourned throughout the state. Hundreds filed through the governor's residence to pay their last respects.

The family returned her to Bremen for a tear-filled ceremony in bitter cold and snow on January 4. A Lutheran pastor eulogized her as "a lady of unlimited ability and energy, stamina and strength, kindness and compassion, care and concern, empathy and sympathy, intelligence and common sense, wit and wisdom, courage and consideration, devotion and determination ... a more admired and esteemed first lady of any governor of any state would be difficult to find. Beth Bowen loved Indiana and its people, and we loved her."[10]

The long-known certainty of her terminal illness did not diminish the governor's grief. He was devastated. Weeks earlier, I had drafted a closing State of the State message to be delivered on January 8 but now encouraged the governor not to give it. Unable as he was to carry on a conversation without tears, it seemed that his once again taking the speaker's rostrum — where he had stood so often with Beth quietly observing from the balcony above — might be too shattering. Bowen insisted upon trying and became irritated as his staff pressed him to settle for circulating the text. We may have made him mad enough to stiffen his nerve.

He faltered at the beginning, barely retaining his composure, then devoted his full attention to the script before him. It was a recapitulation of the Bowen years, a reciting of achievements — mental health, highway funding, transportation, welfare, environmental policy, natural resources, criminal justice, energy, education, public safety, and local government. For the last time as governor, he argued the case for the preservation of property tax relief. It had worked. It had been durable. It merited retention. Bowen warned about a trend toward circumvention of its controls:

> "If you believe that further readjustments of the state revenue system are needed to guarantee government the income it needs, I would urge that you keep this history in mind. We will not solve the fiscal problems of the 1980s by undermining a program that worked so well in the 1970s.[11]

Bowen then delivered the valedictory on his administration.

It is only natural that I have mixed emotions as I prepare to depart this Capitol building. I have spent many years of my life here and have participated in countless discussions and deliberations that have touched the lives of almost every citizen in this state.

I leave the office of governor with few or no regrets. I believe that my administration, which was launched on pledges of addressing important state problems, keeping in close touch with the people of Indiana, and endeavoring to increase the openness and humanness of government has been reasonably successful.

. . . it is time to give way to those who must lead the state of Indiana through the 1980s. They have my heartfelt best wishes. I am fully cognizant of the frustrations, problems and controversies that they will endure, just as the outgoing administration was compelled to confront during the past eight turbulent, yet exciting years. I am confident that the new generation of leadership is more than equal to the task, and will build upon the record of its predecessors and will move the state in the directions needed to insure the continued well-being of our citizens.

Again, thank you and goodbye.[12]

"Reasonably successful." A subdued commentary upon his administration, fully characteristic of the man. It was not lost upon reporters. He then returned to his office where Smith and I had been listening to the address on a speaker system and said tartly, "You didn't think I could do it, did you."

We puttered in those final days with packing boxes and suffered the intrusions of state archivists eager to get their hands on all of the official records. There was little else to do and little that we tried to do, for the governor remained trapped in personal sorrow. A final bundle of "Sagamores" was completed before the expiration of his term. Troopers lugged boxes of personal files to the governor's new condominium. Desks were cleared to make way for our successors. Few of the staff would remain in the Orr administration; most of the remainder were only looking forward to the day when we could depart from an office now overburdened with poignant memories.

Otis Bowen's administration ended officially on January 12, 1981 — a day of celebration in a crowded Statehouse as the new regime took power. For those of us not destined to remain, Bowen's governorship had ended days earlier. Flags fluttering at half staff in the chilly winds of January had been constant reminders that this was so.

APPENDIX A

Biographical Sketch of Otis R. Bowen

Otis Ray Bowen was born February 26, 1918, at Richland Center, near Rochester. He attended high schools at Kewanna and Fulton and graduated from Francesville High School. The governor received his medical degree from Indiana University in 1942 after earning an A. B. degree from I. U. in 1939. After completing his internship at South Bend Memorial Hospital he was commissioned a first lieutenant in the Army Medical Corps and advanced to captain during wartime service in the Pacific theater of operations. Dr. Bowen established a medical practice in Bremen in 1946. He was elected Marshall County coroner in 1952 and a member of the Indiana House of Representatives in 1956. After losing by four votes in the 1958 election, he was re-elected to the House in 1960 and served six more terms. Bowen was House minority leader in the 1965 legislative session and served as speaker in 1967, 1969, 1971, and 1972. While a member of the General Assembly, he served as chairman of the Legislative Council.

Elected Indiana's 42nd governor in 1972, he was re-elected in 1976. During his administration he served as chairman of the National Governors' Association, Republican Governors' Association, Midwestern Governors' Conference, Education Commission of the States, and Interstate Mining Compact Commission. Bowen was a member of the executive committee of the Council of State Governments, Advisory Commission on Intergovernmental Relations, President's Commission on Science and Technology, Commission on Federal Paperwork, and Advisory Council to the United Student Aid Fund. He has been a member of the boards of trustees of Valparaiso and Ancilla colleges and on the advisory committee to Vincennes University. While governor he was a clinical professor of family medicine at the Indiana University School of Medicine. He holds honorary doctoral degrees from Anderson College, Ball State University, Bethel College, Butler University, Calumet College, University of Evansville, Manchester College, University of Notre Dame, Purdue University-Calument, Rose-Hulman Institute, St. Mary's College, St. Joseph's College, Tri-State University, Valparaiso University, and Vincennes University. He also was awarded the Benjamin Rush Award of the American Medical Association.

He is or has been a member of county, district, state, and national medical associations: the Bremen Kiwanis and Chamber of Commerce: Alpha Omega Alpha, Phi Beta Pi, and Delta Chi: the American Legion and Veterans of Foreign Wars, and St. Paul's Lutheran Church of Bremen.

After leaving the governorship, Dr. Bowen was appointed to the faculty of the Division of Family Practice of the Indiana University School of Medicine. In 1980 and 1981 he was elected to the boards of directors of Hook

Drug Company, Indiana National Bank, Meridian Mutual Insurance Company, Indiana Blue Shield, and Lilly Endowment. President Reagan appointed him to a newly-created commission of Federalism in 1981.

APPENDIX B
Biographical Sketch of Elizabeth A. Bowen

Elizabeth Ann Steinmann Bowen was born April 8, 1918, in Chicago but was reared in Crown Point where she attended St. Paul's Lutheran School and graduated from Crown Point High School in 1936. While attending Gary Business College she met Otis Bowen, who then was a pre-medical student at Indiana University. They were married February 25, 1939. Mrs. Bowen worked as a federal civil service employee in Gary and Indianapolis while Dr. Bowen completed his studies and internship.

She assisted Dr. Bowen in his medical practice in Bremen after its establishment in 1946. In her community she was active in St. Paul's Lutheran Church and was president of the Marshall County Medical Auxiliary and Bremen Mothers' Club. Active in the Auxiliary to the Indiana State Medical Association, she held a variety of positions including treasurer, first vice-president, and president.

Mrs. Bowen also was a member of the board of governors of the Riley Memorial Hospital Association, honorary chairman of the Indiana task force for the International Year of the Child, and a member of the national advisory committee of the Child Abuse and Neglect Project of the Education Commission of the States.

In 1978, Vincennes University awarded her an honorary Doctor of Humanities degree and she was named Indiana Mother of the Year.

The Bowen children are: Richard H. (wife Sandra), of Lawrenceburg; Judity I. (husband David L. McGrew, Jr.), of Bellevue, Washington; Timothy R. (wife Jacqueline), of Muncie; and Robert O. (wife Patricia), of Indianapolis.

A Note On Sources

The author relied most heavily upon the official documents of the Bowen administration, newspaper clippings, and extensive personal notes and files. Correspondence, memoranda, and other official documents regularly were turned over to the archives division of the Indiana State Library during the administration. Correspondence was filed by topic or state agency name. Bound volumes of news releases, executive orders, proclamations, and the governor's weekly newspaper column were assembled during the closing months of the administration. The archives division has the originals, as well as copies of the governor's speeches. With very few exceptions, he spoke from prepared texts. The Beth Bowen Library, to be built at Bethel College, will have a full set of these volumes. Beginning in February, 1974, the governor's office subscribed to a news clipping service, paid for by the Republican State Committee. These clippings, filed in envelopes by week and year, are in the possession of the Indiana Division of the State Library.

Notes To Chapters

CHAPTER ONE

1. Indianapolis *News*, March 1, 1972.
2. Indianapolis *News*, January 6, 1972.
3. Louisville *Courier-Journal*, January 2, 1977.

CHAPTER THREE

1. Indianapolis *News*, February 18, 1971.
2. *Ibid.*
3. Indianapolis *News*, April 26, 1971.
4. Indianapolis *News*, February 17, 1971.
5. Indianapolis *News*, June 22, 1972.
6. *Ibid.*
7. Observed by the author.
8. Indianapolis *News*, June 23, 1972.
9. Polling data for the campaign is extracted from the October, 1972, Market Opinion Research (MOR) survey for the Republican State Committee.
10. Expenditures were summarized in a January, 1973, report compiled by campaign aide Ann Wantz.
11. MOR October poll, p. 2.
12. *Ibid*, p. 17.
13. *Ibid*, pp. 17, 27.
14. Indianapolis *Star*, September 21, 1972.
15. MOR October poll, pp. 1-2.
16. Market Opinion Research, poll for the Republican State Committee, November, 1972.

CHAPTER FOUR

1. Peru *Tribune*, March 5, 1973.
2. *Ibid.*
3. South Bend *Tribune*, January 5, 1973.
4. Indianapolis *Star*, January 9, 1973.
5. *Ibid.*
6. Bowen inaugural address, January 8, 1973, pp. 3-4.

CHAPTER FIVE

1. Bowen budget message, January 24, 1973, p. 21.
2. Indianapolis *News*, March 2, 1973.
3. Indianapolis *News*, March 6, 1973.
4. Indianapolis *Star*, March 15, 1973.
5. *Ibid.*
6. Indianapolis *News*, March 22, 1973; Indianapolis *Star*, March 23, 1973.
7. Indianapolis *Star*, March 31, 1973.
8. Indianapolis *News*, March 28, 1973.
9. Indianapolis *Star*, April 6, 1973.
10. *Ibid.*
11. Indianapolis *News*, April 9, 1973.
12. Governor's office, news release, April 13, 1973.

13. Indianapolis *Star,* April 14, 1973.
14. Governor's office, news release, April 25, 1973.
15. Governor's office, news release, April 11, 1973.

CHAPTER SIX

1. Indianapolis *News,* May 14, 1973.
2. Indianapolis *News,* May 25, 1973.
3. Transcript released by the governor's office, August 6, 1974.
4. Louisville *Courier-Journal,* August 7, 1974.
5. *Ibid.*
6. Plymouth *Pilot-News,* August 9, 1974.
7. *Ibid.*
8. Louisville *Courier-Journal,* August 9, 1974.
9. Governor's office, news release, August 12, 1974.
10. Governor's office, news release, September 9, 1974.
11. Indianapolis *Star,* March 1, 1974.
12. Bloomington *Herald-Telephone,* November 9, 1974.

CHAPTER SEVEN

1. Indianapolis *News,* September 7, 1973.
2. Governor's office, news release, November 1, 1977.
3. *Ibid.*
4. Indianapolis *Star,* September 7, 1973.

CHAPTER EIGHT

1. Governor's Energy Conservation Committee, report to General Assembly, January 12, 1973.
2. Governor's office, news release, October 25, 1973; Department of Administration memorandum, November 8, 1973.
3. Indianapolis *Star,* December 12, 1973.
4. Bowen to Presidential Assistant Watson, January 31, 1977.

CHAPTER NINE

1. Bowen State of the State message, January 9, 1975, p. 10.
2. *Ibid,* p. 23.
3. *Ibid,* p. 24.
4. Bowen veto message, H.E.A. 1541, April 11, 1975.
5. Louisville *Courier-Journal,* April 2, 1975.
6. Indianapolis *Star,* March 25, 1975.
7. Indianapolis *News,* April 5, 1975.
8. Conversation with the author.
9. Indianapolis *News,* May 7, 1975.
10. *Ibid.*

CHAPTER TEN

1. Bowen State of the State message, January 7, 1974, pp. 7-9.

2.   Watt memorandum to Bowen, January 26, 1975.
3.   Governor's office, news release, April 22, 1976.
4.   Testimony before the House of Representatives Subcommittee on National Parks and Recreation, Washington, June 17, 1974.
5.   Bowen to President Ford, September 30, 1976.
6.   Bowen to Army Secretary Calloway, September 30, 1975.
7.   Bowen State of the State message, January 11, 1977, pp. 28-29.
8.   Governor's office, news release, July 27, 1977.
9.   Governor's Water Resources Study Commission, *The Indiana Water Resource: Availability, Uses and Needs* (Indianapolis: Department of Natural Resources, February, 1980).
10. ----------, *The Indiana Water Resource: Recommendations for the Future* (Indianapolis: Department of Natural Resources, December, 1980).

CHAPTER TWELVE

1.   For good summaries of the eastern railroad problem see: U.S. Department of Transportation, *Rail Service in the Midwest and Northeast Region* (Washington: DOT, February 1, 1974), Volume I, and George W. Hilton, *The Northeast Railroad Problem* (Washington: American Enterprise Institute, 1975).
2.   Indianapolis *Star*, October 4, 1973.
3.   Indianapolis *Star*, October 18, 1973; governor's office, news release, October 23, 1973.
4.   Bowen to FRA, October 22, 1973.
5.   P.L. 93-236.
6.   U.S. Department of Transportation, *Rail Service in the Midwest and Northeast Region* (Washington: DOT, February 1, 1974), two volumes.
7.   Governor's office, news release, January 14, 1974.
8.   Bowen testimony, ICC hearing, Indianapolis, March 11, 1974.
9.   Governor's Rail Task Force, *Rail Reorganization in Indiana*, a report to the General Assembly, October 7, 1974.
10. See Washington *Post*, August 2, 1974.
11. Governor's Rail Task Force, *USRA Segments in Indiana: State Analysis and Recommendations*, August 20, 1974, four volumes.
12. Bowen news conference statement, August 28, 1974.
13. Muncie *Star*, September 1, 1974.
14. Governor's office, news release, February 10, 1975.
15. Bowen testimony, ICC hearing, Indianapolis, March 17, 1975.
16. Governor's office, news release, June 30, 1975.
17. Bowen statement, June 8, 1975.
18. Marion *Chronicle-Tribune*, June 11, 1975; see also Lafayette *Journal & Courier*, and Gary *Post-Tribune*, both of June 13, 1975.
19. Bowen to Rail Services Planning Office, August 26, 1975.
20. Governor's office, news release, October 14, 1975.
21. For post-Conrail appraisals of Indiana's rail system see Indianapolis *Star*, August 1, 1976; Louisville *Courier-Journal*, July 7, 1977; Indianapolis *Star*, November 19, 1978, *et seq.*
22. Governor's office, news releases, July 13 and August 31, 1973.
23. Richmond *Palladium-Item*, May 10, 1978.

CHAPTER THIRTEEN

1.   Bowen State of the State message, January 8, 1976, p. 4.
2.   *Ibid*, p. 5.

3. *Ibid*, p. 6.
4. Indianapolis *Star*, January 10, 1976.
5. Bowen veto message, S.E.A. 170, February 12, 1976.
6. Muncie *Star*, February 26, 1976.
7. South Bend *Tribune*, February 26, 1976.
8. Muncie *Star*, February 26, 1976.

CHAPTER FOURTEEN

1. Indianapolis *Star*, May 18, 1975.
2. Indianapolis *Star*, June 20, 1975.
3. Market Opinion Research, poll for the Republican State Committee, July, 1975, p. 2.
4. *Ibid*, p. 42.
5. *Ibid*, p. 44.
6. *Ibid*, p. 27.
7. Bowen convocation address, Bremen High School, Nov. 17, 1975.
8. Indianapolis *Star*, December 15, 1975.
9. MOR poll, July, 1975, p. 3.
10. Indianapolis *Star*, April 11, 1976.
11. MOR poll, February, 1976, pp. 17-18.
12. *Ibid*, p. 14.
13. *Ibid*, pp. 78-79.
14. Indianapolis *News*, August 16, 1976.
15. *Ibid*.
16. Indianapolis *News*, July 11, 1976.

CHAPTER FIFTEEN

1. Mount Vernon *Democrat*, December 22, 1976.
2. Indianapolis *Star*, January 7, 1977.
3. Indianapolis *Star*, December 12, 1976.
4. Indianapolis *News*, December 31, 1976.
5. Bowen inaugural address, January 10, 1977.
6. Bowen State of the State message, January 11, 1977, p. 2.
7. *Ibid*, p. 4.
8. Indianapolis *News*, April 12, 1977.
9. Bowen veto message, H.E.A. 1405, April 21, 1977.

CHAPTER SIXTEEN

1. For an account of disasters and disorders throughout the state's history see William J. Watt and James R.H. Spears, editors, *Indiana's Citizen-Soldiers* (Indianapolis: State Armory Board, 1980).
2. Bowen to President Nixon, April 4, 1974.
3. Observed by the author.
4. Bowen to President Carter, January 31, 1977.
5. Bowen to President Carter, July 30, 1979.
6. See Bowen speeches to the annual meeting of the National Guard Association of the United States, October 4, 1978, and October 10, 1979.

CHAPTER SEVENTEEN

1. Indiana Department of Commerce, Energy Group, *Coal Strike Contingency Plan,* September, 1977.
2. Indianapolis *Star,* January 14, 1978; Indianapolis *News,* January 14, 1978.
3. Governor's office, news release, January 20, 1978.
4. Bowen to President Carter, February 2, 1978.
5. Indianapolis *Star,* February 4, 1978.
6. Indianapolis *Star,* February 9, 1978; South Bend *Tribune,* February 9, 1978.
7. Bowen to President Carter, February 10, 1978.
8. *Ibid.*
9. Governor's office, news release, February 14, 1978.
10. Both statements were recorded by the author, who was present at the meeting.
11. See Louisville *Courier-Journal,* February 15, 1978; Indianapolis *Star,* February 18, 1978; Elkhart *Truth,* February 18, 1978.
12. Bowen to President Carter, February 21, 1978.
13. Indianapolis *Star,* February 25, 1978.
14. For more detail, see the governor's letter to Senator Floyd Haskell, March 6, 1978. Haskell was chairing a Senate inquiry into the strike's economic impact.
15. Indianapolis *News,* March 11, 1978; Anderson *Bulletin,* March 11, 1978.
16. Linton *Citizen,* March 13, 1978.
17. Wallace memorandum to Watt of April 14, 1978.

CHAPTER EIGHTEEN

1. Bowen State of the State message, January 12, 1978, p. 15.
2. South Bend *Tribune,* January 13, 1978.
3. Conversation with the author.
4. Indianapolis *News,* February 17, 1978.
5. Louisville *Courier-Journal,* February 19, 1978.
6. *Ibid.*
7. Conversation with the author, March 6, 1978.
8. Market Opinion Research, poll for the Republican State Committee, July, 1978, p. 5.
9. *Ibid,* p. 6.
10. Conversation with the author, July 27, 1978.

CHAPTER NINETEEN

1. Anderson *Herald,* May 23, 1975.
2. Milligan to convention delegates, April 7, 1977.
3. Conversation with the author, June 11, 1976.
4. Governor's office, news release, July 20, 1977.
5. Anderson *Herald,* May 23, 1975.
6. Bowen speech, Indiana Republican Editorial Association, April 26, 1975.
7. Kosciusko County Lincoln Day, February 12, 1977.
8. *Ibid.*
9. Watt speech to department heads, January 29, 1973.
10. National Governors' Association, "The Governor's Press Relations," Washington, November, 1976.
11. Indianapolis Press Club inauguration, January, 1977.
12. Werner to Watt, April 23, 1973.
13. Gary *Post-Tribune,* February 23, 1979.
14. *Ibid.*

15. Letter of August 27, 1980.
16. LaPorte *Herald-Argus*, August 28, 1980.
17. Bowen State of the State message, January 8, 1981.
18. Indianapolis *Star*, January 11, 1979.

CHAPTER TWENTY

1. Indianapolis *News*, August 9, 1973.
2. Elkhart *Truth*, May 21, 1975.
3. Indianapolis *Star*, April 15, 1979.
4. Lanam to Bingham, May 15, 1980.

CHAPTER TWENTY-ONE

1. Bowen State of the State message, January 10, 1979.
2. *Ibid*, p. 3.
3. Indianapolis *Star*, April 15, 1979.
4. Later related to me by James Smith.

CHAPTER TWENTY-TWO

1. Bowen speech, American Academy of Family Physicians, Chicago, Illinois, October 6, 1976.
2. Bowen speech, National Governors' Association, Boston, August 28, 1978.
3. *Ibid*.
4. *Ibid*.
5. Bowen speech, Republican Governors' Association, Williamsburg, Virginia, November 27, 1978.

CHAPTER TWENTY-THREE

1. Governor's office, statement, September 19, 1977.
2. Conversation with the author, October, 1978.
3. Quayle gave this account to the author.
4. Governor's office, statement, May 8, 1979.
5. Indianapolis *Star*, May 9, 1979.
6. *Ibid*.
7. Bowen State of the State message, January 9, 1980, pp. 6-7.
8. *Ibid*, p. 8.
9. *Ibid*, p. 8.
10. Indianapolis *News*, January 5, 1981.
11. Bowen State of the State message, January 8, 1981, p. 11.
12. *Ibid*, pp. 12-13.

INDEX

Medical Registration Board, 65-66.
Melchert, Bruce, 206-207, 213, 257-258.
Mental Health, Department of, 55-57.
Mental health issues, 54-57.
Merritt, Jean, 52.
Midwestern Governors' Conference, 88-89, 264-265.
Miller, Arnold, 187.
Miller, J. Irwin, 210, 212.
Miller, Randall, 52.
Milligan, Thomas, 27, 63, 103, 156, 210-214, 273.
Milliken, Governor William, 262, 264, 267.
"minimum purchase" gasoline plan, 95-96.
Mining controversy, 123-124.
Mitnick, Milton, 179, 181, 184.
Mohr, Larry, 257-258.
Monoghan, Eugene, 190, 191.
Mooney, Robert, 156.
Moore, Governor Arch, 166.
Moreau, Donald, 225.
Morgan Packing Company, strike, 185.
Morris, Robert, 28, 80-82, 84-85, 226.
Morton, Interior Secretary Rogers, 144.
Moses, Riley, a/k/a/ Riley Moseley, 59.
Motor Vehicles, Bureau of, 54, 213.
Mross, Roland, 226.
Murphy, Superintendent Charles, 119.
Murray, William, 29, 56, 66.
Mutz, Senator John, 41-42.
Myers, U.S. Rep. John, 113-114.

National Governors' Association, 88-89, 180, 217, 264-266.
National Governors' Conference, 48, 175, 262.
National Guard, 31, 175-186, 188, 195, 198, 264.
National Guard Association of the U.S., 264.
National Limited, 146.
National Railroad Passenger Corporation (Amtrak), 140, 145-147.
Natural gas shortages, 79-81, 90.
Natural Resources Commission, 108, 122.
Natural Resources, Department of, 27, 67, 107-125.
Nature Conservancy, 67, 121.
Neal, James, 27, 210.
New, State Treasurer Jack, 52, 157, 160, 162.
New, Leroy, 44.
Newman, Donald, 29, 130-131.

The text of *BOWEN* is set in a 10 point
Baskerville typeface. Typesetting by Triad
Composition, printing by Central Publishing
Company, binding by Robbins and Sons
Bindery.